Mission Shaped by Promise

American Society of Missiology Monograph Series

Series Editor, Michael A. Rynkiewich

THE ASM MONOGRAPH SERIES provides a forum for publishing quality dissertations and studies in the field of missiology. Collaborating with Pickwick Publications—a division of Wipf and Stock Publishers of Eugene, Oregon—the American Society of Missiology selects high quality dissertations and other monographic studies that offer research materials in mission studies for scholars, mission and church leaders, and the academic community at large. The ASM seeks scholarly work for publication in the Series that throws light on issues confronting Christian world mission in its cultural, social, historical, biblical, and theological dimensions.

Missiology is an academic field that brings together scholars whose professional training ranges from doctoral-level preparation in areas such as scripture, history and sociology of religions, anthropology, theology, international relations, interreligious interchange, mission history, inculturation, and church law. The American Society of Missiology, which sponsors this series, is an ecumenical body drawing members from Independent and Ecumenical Protestant, Catholic, Orthodox, and other traditions. Members of the ASM are united by their commitment to reflect on and do scholarly work relating to both mission history and the present-day mission of the church. The ASM Monograph Series aims to publish works of exceptional merit on specialized topics, with particular attention given to work by younger scholars, the dissemination and publication of which is difficult under the economic pressures of standard publishing models.

Persons seeking information about the ASM or the guidelines for having their dissertations considered for publication in the ASM Monograph Series should consult the Society's website—www.asmweb.org.

Members of the ASM Monograph Committee who approved this book are:

Michael A. Rynkiewich, Asbury Theological Seminary (retired)
Craig Ott, Trinity Evagnelical Divinity School
Roger Schroeder, SVD, Catholic Theological Union

PREVIOUSLY PUBLISHED IN THE ASM MONOGRAPH SERIES

David P. Leong, *Street Signs: Toward a Missional Theology of Urban Cultural Engagement*

Christopher L. Flanders, *About Face: Rethinking Face for 21st Century Missions*

Stephen Pavey, *Theologies of Power and Crisis: Envisioning/Embodying Christianity in Hong Kong*

Mission Shaped by Promise

Lutheran Missiology Confronts the Challenge of Religious Pluralism

Jukka Antero Kääriäinen

American Society of Missiology
Monograph Series

VOL. 14

☙PICKWICK *Publications* • Eugene, Oregon

MISSION SHAPED BY PROMISE
Lutheran Missiology Confronts the Challenge of Religious Pluralism

American Society of Missiology Monograph Series 14

Copyright © 2012 Jukka Antero Kääriäinen. All rights reserved. Except for brief quotations in critical publications or reviews, no part of this book may be reproduced in any manner without prior written permission from the publisher. Write: Permissions, Wipf and Stock Publishers, 199 W. 8th Ave., Suite 3, Eugene, OR 97401.

Pickwick Publications
An Imprint of Wipf and Stock Publishers
199 W. 8th Ave., Suite 3
Eugene, OR 97401

www.wipfandstock.com

ISBN 13: 978-1-61097-833-0

Cataloguing-in-Publication data:

Kääriäinen, Jukka Antero.

    Mission shaped by promise : Lutheran missiology confronts the challenge of religious pluralism / Jukka Antero Kääriäinen, with a foreword by William R Burrows.

    American Society of Missiology Monograph Series 14

    xviii + 276 pp. ; 23 cm. Includes bibliographical references and index.

    ISBN 13: 978-1-61097-833-0

    1. Lutheran Church—Missions. 2. Religious Pluralism—Lutheran Church. I. II. Title. III. Series.

BV2533 K15 2012

Manufactured in the U.S.A.

Books published in the American Society of Missiology Monograph Series are chosen on the basis of their academic quality as responsible contributions to debate and dialogue about issues in mission studies. The opinions expressed in the books are those of the authors and are not represented to be those of the American Society of Missiology or its members.

*I dedicate this book to my best friend,
soulmate, wife, and partner in mission,
Laura Kääriäinen,
without whose ceaseless support and encouragement
this project would never have been completed.
I love you!*

Contents

Foreword · ix
Acknowledgments · xvii
Abbreviations · xviii

Introduction: In Search of a Lutheran Missional Hermeneutic · 1

1   The Gospel as Promise · 29

2   A Paradigm of Grace as Promise of Mercy Fulfilled · 79

3   A Paradigm of Grace as Nature Fulfilled: Karl Rahner · 112

4   A Missional Paradigm of Grace as Nature Fulfilled: Jacques Dupuis · 151

5   *Missio* Shaped by *Promissio*: Confessional Lutheran Engagement with Dupuis · 177

6   Proclamation and Interreligious Dialogue: A Dialectical Relationship · 226

Bibliography · 255

Index · 269

Foreword

by William R Burrows[1]

JUKKA KAARIAINEN'S STUDY OF the missiological implications of Lutheran insights into the teaching of Saint Paul that the Gospel of Jesus is first and foremost a promise is an example of contemporary *ressourcement* finding new things among the old in the treasure house of Christian tradition. His proposal is straightforward. Namely, that we wrestle with the idea that the church's mission (*missio* in Latin) revolves around making known and embodying the promise (*promissio* in Latin) that God forgives sins and offers human beings the power to become a new creation by entering the portal of death with Christ and finding new life in the Spirit. Kaariainen's reading of the Gospel and tradition through the lens of the great sixteenth-century Reformer is important, not simply to remind us of the genius of Martin Luther, but because Luther's late medieval retrieval of Paul—accomplished at the threshold of modernity—enables us, who stand on the threshold between modernity and whatever replaces it, to retrieve the living, beating heart of the gospel. In the process of so doing, he helps us to formulate a *Christian* identity that can be serene in relation to other religious Ways without abandoning our own particularity for the thin pottage of relativist stew. That is no small feat. In the paragraphs that follow, I want to put flesh on the skeleton of what I assert.

Nothing has dominated discussions of Christian identity and mission from the middle of the twentieth into the early twenty-first century as has the challenge of historical and cultural studies that force us to

---

1. William R Burrows is Managing Editor Emeritus, Orbis Books, Research Professor of Missiology, World Christianity Department, New York Theological Seminary

Foreword

realize that Christianity has become a global faith and, at the same time, relegated to the position of being just *one* of the world's religions. Equally important, the Christendom fusion of religion and culture is crumbling just as Western culture is forced to abandon its delusions of superiority. Christians are caught in the dialectic tension between healthy relativity and debilitating relativism as historical consciousness leads us inexorably to acknowledge that any claim to know the meaning of world process is belief not fact. It has been hard for many Christians to accept that much of what they were claiming was the superiority of Christianity was actually belief in the supremacy of Western culture. It is in this context that Kaariainen becomes most helpful, for he retrieves a vision of God and God's relation to the world that is profoundly informed by the kerygma of the New Testament and does not involve any assertions of superiority or inferiority. He accomplishes this by retrieving horizon that recognizes that integral to biblical revelation of who God *is* lies the *Deus absconditus* (the hidden God) whose ways are not our ways. More than that, Kaariainen presses us to realize—in the context of an apparently irreducible, stubborn persistence of religious plurality—that we should not pretend to know more than we know about how God operates to accomplish his purpose of redeeming Creation and humanity from sin when otherwise good people do not embrace Christ.

How does this affect attitudes to "other" religious Ways and Christian mission?

If we look back at the beginnings of the modern missionary movement, when Portuguese merchants and their chaplains sailed down the coast of Africa in the mid-15th century, it was easy to imagine that Christendom's fusion of religion and culture was God's model for the way the whole world was meant to be. Christian missions, accompanying the growth of colonies, trade, and empire—albeit with varying degrees of rejection of and complicity in the enterprise of their royal and merchant benefactors (and sometimes opponents)—were one of two dimensions of a Western advance in which, at least in the popular mind, Christianity provided theological warrants for Westerners pursuing hegemony. Many Indians, Africans, Chinese, Japanese, and Native Americans, of course, had their doubts about the bargains they were often being forced into (Africans bought and sold by Catholic priests, for example), but they had to deal realistically with the power that stood behind the Western incursion into their worlds. Many went along with the cohabitation of Christianity with imperialism and colonialism (they are not the same thing!) and became Christians. Most, especially in Asia, did not. When they did convert, it must be noted, they often found life-giving elements in Christianity that the missionaries were scarcely aware of. Catholics in Peru, for example, found meaning in the "little stories" of the mestizo saint Martin de Porres (1579–1639), that their Spanish masters had no hint were subversive in regard to the colonial project.

As decolonization picked up speed after World War II, there has emerged not just the globalization of the Christian movement, but also a globalization of insights into (1) into the syncretic nature of "world" Christianity and (2) into the riches and pluriformity of world religions and cultures. In the West, even among the Christian faithful, former certitudes about the possibility of "pure," supracultural, orthodox, "biblical" faith and the absolute necessity of explicit faith in Christ as the necessary and universal savior began to dissipate, especially among the educated. Taking its place were the choice between rigorous adherence to biblical literalness; and acceptance of cultural relativism and agnosticism about the truth value of every religious tradition's insights grows. Neither, however, is adequate.

What has all this to do with Jukka Kaariainen's book? Just this. His is a thoughtful approach to helping us re-remember that when we identify the Gospel as a promise but also embrace a revelation of God's hiddenness, we are close to the hermeneutic lens with which the Scriptural canon was assembled. This sounds, of course, like classic Lutheranism, but it is more than that. In wrestling with Roman Catholicism's approach to the salvation of the religious other, Kaariainen recognizes the wisdom of Catholicism's *Nostra Aetate* in teaching we should have confidence that God's mercy reaches people in surprising, inexplicable ways. And he quotes Michael Oleksa's magisterial remark that concretizes that teaching, when he notes, "The Christian, while knowing where Christ is, can never be certain where he is not." Kaariainen's chapters on Karl Rahner's and, especially, Jacques Dupuis's proposals for explaining this mystery within the Catholic nature/grace paradigm, are critical but generous. He convinces me that an approach rooted in the gospel = promise/sin-forgiveness paradigm brings is a more adequate interpretation of Scripture and that, in adopting it, one recognizes that trust in God is the central element of both the Jewish and Christian Scriptures. But promises don't work, as Kaariainen says, "unless they are trusted." Mission, accordingly, is the task of making the promise known, cooperating with the Spirit in helping those who do not know Christ yet to know and trust him.

Foreword

By contrast, Catholicism in the Middle Ages developed a rich theology of grace that inculcated trust in the church as the sole channel of the grace that leads to salvation. The accent goes to educating people to trust the church as the instrument founded by Christ to deliver grace. Yes, the notion of grace includes both the "uncreated" grace of God's gift of self and the "created" grace of things that lead people to turn from sin and develop habits and virtues. But the emphasis went on being an obedient faithful member of the church, an all-encompassing reality in most of Europe by the eleventh century. Mystics went deeper to be sure, but popular catechesis took a shortcut by inculcating a reified concept of grace delivered by sacraments. Alas, in reacting against the sacerdotalizing of the sacramental system, the Reformers put so much emphasis on preaching the Word that over time wordiness crowded out the symbolic performance of sacraments that can reach far deeper into the human heart that words.

While there is much to be said for a system that proceeds from the analogy of grace as *medicina sanans* ("[sacred] medicine healing [nature]," Kaariainen's work shows why the sin/forgiveness paradigm is more profoundly biblical and equally capable of dealing with our contemporary perception of richness and wisdom in other traditions. Am I denying that grace heals human nature, as Catholics analogize grace to medicine? No, but thinking of grace this way can lead to its reification and imagining that other medical delivery systems can heal just as well. Which is all well and good until one realizes that in Scripture what heals is coming to know and trust God's promises and through coming to know the Gospel of Jesus in the power of the Spirit. Thus Kaariainen puts us squarely within the interpersonal categories of Scripture and avoids Catholic sacerdotalist tendencies to monopolize the channels of grace to what is done by validly ordained priests and bishops, as well as to reify grace as something accessible only through approved ecclesial pharmacies. Kaariainen's conversation with Nostra Aetate and its iteration with various nuances in other Vatican II decrees, but especially his in-depth analysis of Jacques Dupuis's contributions to the Christian theology of religions, are extremely fruitful in showing us that Catholics still have something to learn from the Reformation. In Kaariainen's approach, one also sees that the learning goes the other way as well.

Overall, Kaariainen helps Christians thread the tiny eye of the Markan (10:25) needle as he retrieves Lutheran insights into the Pauline Gospel and employs them to clarify contemporary missiological

Foreword

conversations. Although he does not put it this way, I found myself realizing that Kaariainen's approach does not gloss over the ideal that the perfection demanded by Jesus involves selling all and serving the poor, as we are counseled to do in Matthew 5:28. In that verse, insights that coalesced in the sixth century BCE in the Deuteronomic reform movement were refined in Second Temple Judaism by the Pharisaic movement that Jesus himself was part of. In the rigorous ethical teaching of Jesus, the command to love God and neighbor as one loves oneself led to the realization that the sort of self-sacrifice Jesus proposes in the Sermon on the Mount is necessary if one is to follow the law perfectly and become what a human being is meant to become. Jesus embraces that rigorism, but he did so in a paradoxical way that showed there is a different kind of righteousness available to those who humbly seek pardon for not being able to reach that mark. I oversimplify Kaariainen's nuanced argument, but the Way of Jesus leads to knowledge that salvation is possible, not by lowering the standards, but by God's offer of mercy to those who embrace the promise of the Gospel. The New Testament is firm in teaching that faith in God as revealed in Jesus is necessary, but it also instills confidence that the *Deus absconditus* of the new covenant is the God and savior of all, and that attempts to narrow the scope of divine love is folly. Time and time again in the gospels it is Roman officials, Samaritans, and prostitutes who experience that saving love while religious officialdom does not. It is common practice to oppose the Pauline Gospel of justification in faith to the Synoptics Gospel of the Kingdom. In fact, the Pauline corpus is shifting from a narrative to extracting the meaning of the narratives, and the meaning of the narratives revolves around encountering Christ and trusting him.

I commend Kaariainen's work to the reader because he shows why Christians are well advised to extend a hermeneutic of generosity toward the religious other while maintaining Christian identity as a Christomorphic, profoundly Trinitarian faith. In particular, I commend the author's careful attention to what the Gospel *is*. He knows that Christian mission revolves around propagating the Gospel within a context in which the Law of loving God and neighbor as oneself is the criterion of human authenticity and justice in a context where God hates "sin" yet wills to save *all* (1 Tim 2:4). That universal will, of course, appears to conflict with John 3:16, where the text has Jesus saying only those *who believe in him*, a statement tempered in the next verse where he is sent not to condemn but that the "world" (in all its ambiguity!) may be saved. Such texts point to important but paradoxical aspects of a single economy of salvation – aspects that are reconciled not theoretically by doctrine but existentially by embracing the promises and person of Jesus the Christ.

In our day—as it is, I suppose, in every age—it is common to pick and choose only the texts that fit one's predilections. Thus one group accents only recitals of God's love and calls for Christians to extend that love by charity and systemic reform. Tutored by Freud, they are reluctant to imagine that someone who abuses sex and drugs could be condemned by God. Another group cites texts that emphasize the absolute import of explicit faith in Christ and the rejection of sin and seem cheerful about the negative fate of the billions who will never turn to Jesus and ask for the gift of the Spirit. Lost to both is a robust biblical realism that recognizes the full panoply of human evil and self-deception, not just at the level of economics and societal oppression of the poor, women, and non-heterosexuals, but also in the battle that goes on in our individual lives to be truly righteous and loving. The person who tries to keep his or her feet on the path of total loving-kindness, personal authenticity, and holiness knows both the impossibility of fulfilling that Law and, nevertheless, that it remains obligatory. But if that is the Law, are we not all in the position of the rich young man who recognizes he cannot leave all his possessions behind? And isn't it also the case that some who do leave all can be insufferably priggish and self-righteous.

In the Markan parable of the eye of the needle, we are told that the impossible is possible with God, which brings us to the paradoxes of the New Testament's revelation of the *Abba-Theos-Pater* of Jesus and his two ways of relating to the world: (1) standing behind the law as judge yet also (2) being in his very nature, *agapaic* love and *hesed* ("loving-kindness"). With the Lutheran tradition of interpreting the Gospel, Kaariainen retrieves the principle of God's hiddenness, the *Deus absconditus*, to name this paradox, showing that we cannot comprehend the operation of God's beneficence in saving the "other." In so doing he articulates a missiology that entails an antidote to theologies of religion and mission that pretend to know more about God than we do.

I do not do justice to the richness and texture of Kaariainen's argument as he discusses the official Catholic position in Vatican II documents and the work of Karl Rahner and Jacques Dupuis. He is ecumenical in the best sense of the word, because he does not merely seek to find areas of agreement by chipping away at particularity, which often results in a tasteless, deracinated academic stew. Instead, he is ecumenical in following a more difficult but finally more satisfying road—accenting what Lutheranism really has right. Although Kaariainen does not develop the theme, such an intensification of particularity leads to humility in the face of the All Holy One. It produce a person in whom, in the words of Cardinal Newman's motto, heart speaks to heart (*cor ad cor loquitur*). And that is the heart of any missiology that is worthy of the name Christian.

Antonio Bellagamba (1923–2011), an ebullient Italian friend, missionary, and member of the Consolata order, once said to me, "In all my travels and meetings with persons of other faiths, no one ever objected to me speaking about my experience of Jesus and life in the Spirit." "Problems," he said, "arise when I try to place these people on a theological map that implies I know them better than they do." Tony Bellagamba embodied the wisdom of both St. Augustine and St. Francis de Sales to whom Newman's *cor ad cor loquitur* is often attributed. One attracts others to the Way of Jesus not by theological schemes but by embodying Jesus and being willing to give an account of his faith when asked (Acts 3:15). With Pope John Paul II an honest Christian must acknowledge that there are many reasons why the follower of another way may not respond to our words by committing to Jesus in faith. In that regard the experience of encountering goodness and holiness in followers of other Ways calls us back to a fundamental hermeneutic that needs to be employed in dealing with God's dealing with the world. God's saving purposes have been revealed in Christ, but paradoxically the height of that revelation is in the cross in which the hiddenness of God confounds every human attempt to judge how God's providence is working in history.

In his book Jukka Kaariainen's *ressourcement* draws us to the wellsprings of a well-deserved humility in regard to the religious "other" and how our missiology must be—in the words of David Bosch—at the service of "bold humility," a humility that knows we Christians carry our treasure in earthen vessels. We are called to mission in the Christ through whom we believe the world is saved, but that does not mean we know everything about God's hidden ways of enacting that salvation in surprisingly unexpected ways. At the risk of tiring the reader with yet another medieval Latin phrase, we know much but what we know reminds us constantly that a great deal of our knowledge is *docta ignorantia* ("learned ignorance"). We are in Jukka Kaariainen's debt for helping us better understand what we know and what we don't know, and the importance of recognizing our *ignorantia* of the *Deus absconditus* ("hidden God") revealed in the paradox of the cross.

Acknowledgments

I WOULD LIKE TO thank the many people without whose help, support, and encouragement this book would not have been possible. First, and foremost, I thank my wife Laura for her tireless encouragement and loving support. I thank her for financially supporting us during my graduate studies at Fordham University, as well as for caring for our young daughters Jemina and Aliina in enabling me to spend the time needed to finish this project.

I thank my parents, Taimo and Raili Kääriäinen, lifelong missionaries to Taiwan (1965–2001), for nurturing me in the way of Jesus and for instilling in me a passion for mission.

I thank my *Doktorvater*, Bradford Hinze, and my two readers, Jeannine Hill-Fletcher and William Burrows. Brad's wise counsel and seasoned mentoring helped guide this project along. Jeannine and Bill, with their expertise in religious pluralism and missiology, respectively, likewise provided constructive critique and helpful suggestions for improvement which vastly improved this project.

I owe a debt of gratitude to my Lutheran mentors. Edward H. Schroeder not only taught me to appreciate the richness of the Gospel as promise, but also planted the seeds of this book in my mind already in 2004. My teacher Robert Kolb gave me invaluable feedback and encouragement as the project progressed.

Finally the people of the Lutheran Church of the Messiah, Princeton, NJ, were gracious enough to give me the time to write this project while serving as their pastor. I am grateful for their accomodation, understanding, and support in making it possible for me to finish. I am also grateful to my editor, D. Christopher Spinks, as well as Pickwick Publications for making it possible to distribute my work to a larger audience.

Soli deo gloria!

Abbreviations

BoC	*Book of Concord*
Apology IV/ Ap. IV	Apology to Augsburg Confession Article IV
FCSD Article I	Formula of Concord Solid Declaration, Article I
FCSD Article II	Formula of Concord Solid Declaration Article II
Gen	Genesis
Exod	Exodus
Ps	Psalms
Job	Job
Jonah	Jonah
Isa	Isaiah
Jer	Jeremiah
Ezek	Ezekiel
Mark	Mark
Matt	Matthew
John	John
Luke	Luke
Acts	Acts
Rom	Romans
1 Cor	First Corinthians
2 Cor	Second Corinthians
Gal	Galatians
Eph	Ephesians
Col	Colossians
Heb	Hebrews
1 Tim	First Timothy
2 Thess	Second Thessalonians
1 John	First John
Rev	Revelation

Introduction

In Search of a Lutheran Missional Hermeneutic

STATEMENT OF THE PROBLEM AND BACKGROUND TO THE QUESTION

THE TERM "LUTHERAN MISSIOLOGY" is viewed by many as an oxymoron. Historically, ever since Gustav Warneck's (the founding father of modern missiology) stinging critique of Martin Luther for lacking a theology and awareness of mission, conventional wisdom has dictated: to the extent that Lutheran theology derives its impetus and motivation from Luther, to that extent it will be missiologically weak and inadequate. In other words, Lutheran theology provides no real resources for a contemporary, relevant Christian missiology and engagement with the world religions and religious pluralism.[1] The late David Bosch agreed with the main thrust of Warneck's critique of Luther, claiming: "We miss in the Reformation not only missionary action 'but even the idea of missions, in the sense in which we understand them today.'"[2]

Beginning with Karl Holl in 1928 and Werner Elert in 1931, a school of Luther scholars arose, opposing and rebuffing Warneck's criticism of

---

1. The distinction between Luther's theology and writings and the theology of the Lutheran confessional writings as expressed in the *Book of Concord* is important. However, as I will argue in this project, I believe Luther's theology and that of the *Book of Concord* are best understood as offering fundamentally complementary, rather than alternative, positions, centered around the notion of the Gospel as promise.

2. Bosch, *Transforming Mission*, 244.

Luther's theology,[3] claiming that to judge Luther's theology as lacking a missionary vision "is to misunderstand the basic thrust of [his] theology and ministry."[4] Warneck anachronistically imposed a very particular, nineteenth-century understanding of mission upon the Reformers. Describing missionary outreach in terms of organized missionary societies sending career missionaries to foreign lands, he judged the Reformers "guilty for not having subscribed to a definition of mission which did not even exist in their own time."[5] While historically speaking it is true that the Reformation resulted in very little missionary outreach, the real issue and question is whether this is due to historical context or to theological deficiency. It is one thing to say that Luther and other Reformers viewed their main theological challenge as reforming the existing Church rather than mission outreach; it is quite another to charge their theology with missiological deficiency.

In contrast to Warneck's pessimistic assessment of Luther's theology, I agree with and wish to develop an argument in support of James Scherer's contention that "For Luther, mission is always pre-eminently the work of the triune God-*missio Dei*-and its goal and outcome is the coming of the kingdom of God . . . [T]he rich but untested potential of Luther and the Reformation for mission practice comes down to the present, not as definitive guidance, but certainly as inspiration and challenge for missiology today. It becomes a calculable 'benchmark' for testing today's missiological axioms."[6] Among Lutheran theologians, Richard Bliese has issued a call for Lutheran missiology to move from "reactive reform" to "innovative initiative."[7] It is the modest, yet ambitious, goal of this project to make a contribution toward such an innovative, missiological initiative.

In addition to the question of whether or not Lutheran theology has missiological potential and, if so, what resources it has to offer, this project will also address a second, closely related question: In light of the *missio Dei* (mission of God), how should the Church's mission be properly

---

3. Öberg, *Luther and World Mission*, 3. This group of scholars includes, but is not limited to, Karl Holl, Werner Elert, E. Danbolt, Wilhelm Maurer, Walter Holsten, Johannes Aagard, James Scherer, Juhani Forsberg, Eugene Bunkowski, Volker Stolle, P. Peters, and Ingemar Öberg.

4. Bosch, *Transforming Mission*, 244.

5. Ibid.

6. Scherer, *Gospel, Church, and Kingdom*, 55, 66.

7. Bliese, "Lutheran Missiology," 13.

understood, in terms of its distinctive shape, content, and emphases? This project will answer these two questions by interrelating them, using four distinctive resources from the confessional Lutheran tradition in addressing both questions: 1) the Gospel as promise; 2) the law/Gospel distinction; 3) a theology of grace as promise of mercy realized; and 4) a theology of the cross utilizing the hiddenness of God.

An introductory remark on terminology is in order before proceeding further. The creedal Christian tradition, as expressed in the classic Christological and Trinitarian dogmas, has always recognized the sin/grace dialectic as a central theme of Scripture. The confessional Lutheran tradition further nuances this classic dialectic, offering the terminology of law and promise (Gospel) as a more precise formulation of this dialectic. A Lutheran terminology seeks to avoid the connotations of the classic "nature/grace" paradigm, whereby grace can potentially be viewed as something quantifiable which fulfills sinful or defective human nature. In seeking to avoid views of grace as either quantifiable or internally enhancing human nature, a Lutheran perspective views grace as a fundamentally relational reality, offer, and external word of surprising mercy.

While contemporary missiology is a multifaceted discipline, embracing many concerns and emphases such as evangelization, inculturation, the promotion of justice, liberation, and peace, and interreligious dialogue, I believe that mission as *missio Dei* is the prevailing, dominant paradigm for missiology today. While it can be variously interpreted, its key features include emphasizing the Trinitarian origin of mission, God's *shalom* as the final, eschatological reign of peace and justice, and the Christian/human participation in that reign. Karl Barth, with his 1932 essay entitled "Theology and Mission," inaugurated contemporary Protestant reflection on mission as *missio Dei* by grounding the theological foundation of mission in the doctrine of the Trinity.[8] Theologically, mission came to be seen as a divine activity and attribute, originating from God himself, rather than the Church's activity.[9] Francis Oborji clarifies the ecclesiological ramifications of this affirmation: "Mission is not primarily an activity of the church but an attribute of God. The church is the movement of God toward the world. The church is an instrument of mission. The church exists because there is *missio Dei*, and not the contrary."[10]

8. Oborji, *Concepts of Mission*, 134.
9. Ibid.
10. Ibid., 135.

While the phrase *missio Dei* has been widely accepted and used by virtually all mission theologians, its actual meaning and content is vigorously contested. Wilhelm Richebacher describes the current quagmire: "It seems that everyone reads into and out of this 'container definition' whatever he or she needs . . . Is such a term of any use at all, if it does not help us establish a clear single interpretation of the central concept? Should we give up this formula altogether . . . ?"[11] The title of his article bluntly asks: "*Missio Dei*: the Basis for Mission Theology, or a Wrong Path?"

While I believe *missio Dei* to be a helpful category, the very "structure of Lutheranism" (Werner Elert) would insist that this term requires nuancing: Does God have one or two missions to the world? This question directs us to the nature of the Gospel as giving Christian mission a distinctively dual or "duplex" shape (Ed Schroeder).[12] A confessional Lutheran contribution to understanding the *missio Dei* insists that the divine mission is *bivocal*. The triune God, rather than saying and doing only one thing, has a dual mission: God's mission always manifests itself in the dual form of judgment *and* salvation, of condemnation *and* forgiveness, of wrath *and* promised mercy. These dual missions roughly correspond to the Lutheran dialectic of law and promise (Gospel), respectively. While these missions are complementary, with the first clearly serving the second, they are also in dialectical tension. In other words: *missio Dei* is shaped by *promissio Dei*, or the promise of God is the secret to mission.[13] Such is the confessional Lutheran claim.

Barth's immense influence is evident in the fact that most of the missiological discussion surrounding *missio Dei* assumes God's mission to be largely *unitary*, that God is doing and saying basically one thing (God's loving salvation universally present). Most contemporary missiologies arising from the basis of *missio Dei*, whether employing a "nature/grace" hermeneutic (traditional Roman Catholic theology) or a "sin/grace" hermeneutic (traditional Reformed theology), end up talking about the Gospel and grace in such a way that it *seems* that God has only one word to say, a word of loving grace. Lutherans find this problematic

---

11. Richebacher, "*Missio Dei*," 589.

12. A debate about the twofold nature of mission is often conducted in terms of the mission of the Son and the mission of the Spirit. This debate will be explored more in-depth in chapter 5, in the section entitled "*Missio Dei*: One Mission or Two?"

13. Bertram, "Doing Theology," 41ff.

In Search of a Lutheran Missional Hermeneutic

as addressing only half of the story, half of revelation, half of what needs to be confessed, trusted, and proclaimed.

Confessional Lutheran theology insists that, to the extent that the first mission of divine judgment is ignored or marginalized, or to the extent that the two missions are conflated under one rubric, to that extent the divine mission as a whole is misconstrued. This project will demonstrate how a clear understanding of the divine, dual mission, expressed in terms of wrath and promise, law and Gospel, leads to a nuanced, dialectical relationship between mission as proclamation and dialogue.[14]

Viewing the Gospel as promise is gaining some appreciation beyond Lutheran circles. For example, Roman Catholic theologian William R. Burrows notes:

> The Gospel is not a new law, not even a new law of love, nor is it a social program. The Gospel of the New Covenant is, rather, an intensification and realization of the dominant theme of the Gospel of both Testaments—God is a God of promises. Concretely, God promises to save his people, and in Jesus we Christians believe we have the clearest revelation, indeed, the accomplishment of that promise, in the paschal mystery of Jesus of Nazareth—his *transitus* or passage from life through death to new life as he becomes the sender of the Holy Spirit, who is the inner witness to us that our sins indeed are forgiven and the first fruits of the realization that God's promises to us will be fulfilled.[15]

---

14. My use and contrast of the terms "wrath" and "promise," "law" and "Gospel," may cause some to wonder whether I am designating and caricaturing all religions other than Christianity, especially Judaism, as "religions of the Law." While I will offer a more in-depth and comprehensive definition of law, its implications, and its relationship to the Gospel, in chapters 1 and 2, some preliminary remarks at this time serve to clear up any misunderstandings and to give a working understanding of how I intend to use the term "law." First of all, in addressing concerns related to a Christian caricature of Judaism as a religion of the law and a Christian supercessionist view of Christianity fulfilling Judaism by replacing it, the Easter event (the resurrection of Jesus) is the culmination, intensification, clearest revelation, and final realization (using William Burrows' terminology) of the same promises that the God of Abraham, Isaac, and Jacob made with the people of Israel. The theme of God's promises runs throughout both testaments of Scripture, unifying them. Second, while some Christians would understand the promise of God fulfilled in Christ in supercessionist terms, it need not be taken that way. Compelling arguments, centered on interpreting Paul's argument in Rom 9-11, have been made for both one covenant and two covenants in Scripture.

15. Burrows, "Participation."

Mission Shaped by Promise

This project's view of the *missio Dei*, stated in terms of an "economy of salvation,"[16] will draw from the work of Oswald Bayer, Robert Bertram, Robert Kolb, Gerhard Forde, Edward Schroeder, and other confessional Lutheran theologians. As an alternative to the prevailing missiological models, an "economy of salvation" model situates itself between and contrasts itself with an uncritical acceptance of the salvation history model (epitomized by fellow Lutherans who see no need for missiological renewal and vision), on the one hand, and the inclusive pluralist model of Jacques Dupuis, on the other. A constructive Lutheran critique insists that an insufficient view of the nature of the Gospel as promise, articulated and preserved by the law/Gospel distinction, leads to an insufficient theology of grace, one which marginalizes the centrality of the promise of mercy in Christ and therefore overly optimistically views the saving grace of God as operative throughout the world religions. Rather than a notion of the Gospel and grace which leads to a view of interreligious dialogue as a conversation between those already belonging to the reign of God, attributed to the power of the grace of Christ and the work of the Spirit (Dupuis), a Lutheran proposal insists that an interreligious dialogue, employing the Gospel promise of "loving mercy" in Christ and a theology of the cross utilizing the hiddenness of God, is both more faithful to the broad Christian tradition and Scriptures as well as more honest to our lived experience, accurately reflecting both commonality and difference of religious experience. By articulating four Lutheran resources (the Gospel as promise, the law/Gospel distinction, a theology of grace as promise of mercy realized, and a theology of the cross utilizing the hiddenness of God) for constructing a nuanced, "economy of salvation" model of the *missio Dei*, I will delineate how a particular view of the Gospel (as promise) undergirds a particular model of the *missio Dei*, culminating in a very particular, dialectical relating of proclamation to interreligious dialogue.

The historical lineage of this approach can be traced from the confessional movement within late sixteenth-century German Lutheran theology, through the Erlangen school in the mid-twentieth century (Werner Elert), to contemporary theologians such as Oswald Bayer (professor emeritus, University of Tübingen), the late Robert Bertram (Christ Seminary-Seminex, St Louis), Robert Kolb (professor emeritus, Concordia

---

16. Hinze, "End of Salvation History," 242. In contrast to my proposal, Hinze emphasizes that fragments and traces of the economy of salvation and destruction are found in the diverse voices of the Christian Scriptures and beyond.

Seminary, St Louis, MO), Edward Schroeder (professor emeritus, Christ Seminary-Seminex, St Louis, MO), Carl Braaten (professor emeritus, The Lutheran School of Theology in Chicago), Richard Bliese, Gary Simpson, Patrick Kiefert, and the late Gerhard Forde (Luther Seminary, St Paul, MN).

LUTHER'S CONTEXT AND OUR CONTEMPORARY CONTEXT: RECOGNIZING THE DIVIDE

In many ways, Martin Luther's thought and theology stands at the juncture between the medieval and modern eras. It is important to situate Luther's thought within his societal and ecclesial context, in order to properly recognize both the limits and potential fruitfulness of his theology for our contemporary context.

Luther's immediate concern and agenda was to "Christianize Christendom," centered on internally reforming the Church, rather than a theology of mission intentionally engaging other religions.[17] This is highly significant for two reasons. First, the issue of religious pluralism and the need to theologically address it never arose for him. In his lifetime, Luther probably met fewer than twenty people who were not baptized Christians. Luther, in step with the Church of his day, viewed Muslims primarily as "infidels" and a political threat to the Holy Roman Empire, rather than as prospective converts to Christianity.[18] This means, secondly, that a theology of religions simply was not on his intellectual horizon

---

17. For a fuller treatment of this point and an excellent overview of the various Christian agendas at play in the Reformation era, see Scott Hendrix, *Recultivating the Vineyard: The Reformation Agendas of Christianization*. Hendrix addresses Luther's specific context and concerns in chapter 2.

18. Some inflammatory statements and prejudicial writings by Luther regarding Muslims and Jews in his later years are well known and documented. Perhaps the best known such work is *On the Jews and Their Lies* (1543). I readily acknowledge such problematic writings and condemn them as unacceptable hate speech. Luther's problematic outlooks and hermeneutical assumptions regarding other religions are partly attributable to their being rooted in his limited life experience with those religions. I wish to claim that such statements do not render Luther's theology missiologically useless, but rather that the fruitful missiological resources within that theology are retrievable and applicable in today's pluralistic context, his inflammatory writings notwithstanding. When it comes to Luther's potential as a missiological resource and thinker, I will be cautioning us not to "throw the baby out with the bathwater." For a balanced, insightful study of Luther on these matters, see Adam Francisco, *Martin Luther and Islam: A Study in Sixteenth-Century Polemics and Apologetics*.

in the same way it is in our pluralistic context today. However, this does not mean that Luther's theology, or that of the confessional Lutheran tradition, does not have valuable resources that can be legitimately retrieved and applied to today's context. What it means is that these resources are not self-evident, and that their identification, creative retrieval, and critical appropriation to our context necessitates a creative, critical process. I will outline how I believe this can be done in the hermeneutical section.

In sharp contrast to Luther's context, our contemporary social, ecclesial, and theological context is characterized by a recognition and appreciation of ambiguity and pluralism. As Francis Schüssler Fiorenza notes, our contemporary scene exhibits deep ambiguity in relation to appreciating the nuanced relationships between pluralism and unity, rationality and its critique, and power and its potential oppressiveness.[19] This situation necessitates that theological systems and statements be made with greater humility, nuance, and provisional certitude. As Schüssler Fiorenza notes, "If one expresses Christian belief in particular philosophical [or theological] categories, then one has not *eo ipso* made that belief more public or more warranted."[20] This means that "theology then seeks to articulate the Christian faith as existing within a pluralistic culture," being unable to "appeal to a particular philosophy as a link between faith and rationality."[21] Schüssler Fiorenza eloquently articulates the contemporary challenge facing theology: "The task for theology is both to take pluralism seriously and to explore the particularity and significance of the Christian vision without reducing religious language to an isolated language-game that neglects other religious visions and the global situation of humanity."[22] While deeply mindful of the significant divide between Luther's and confessional Lutheran theology's original context (16th and 17th centuries) and our contemporary social, ecclesial, and intellectual context, a confessional Lutheran approach asserts the possibility and validity of approaching theology's contemporary challenge via responsible, critical retrieval and appropriation of key insights from the confessional Lutheran tradition, especially the Gospel as promise, to today's context. Retrieving the Gospel as promise and articulating its subsequent implications for shaping a contemporary, Christian vision of the

19. Schüssler Fiorenza, "Systematic Theology," 66–70.
20. Ibid., 66–67.
21. Ibid., 67.
22. Ibid., 68.

In Search of a Lutheran Missional Hermeneutic

Church's mission in a pluralistic setting is a unique offering the confessional Lutheran tradition seeks to make for the sake of the wider Church. Such an approach focuses specifically on reconstructive hermeneutics as a means of articulating the integrity and fruitful authority of a Christian, confessionally Lutheran tradition, employs a theology of the Word of God as a primary background theory, and seeks to ground the theological task within and for the sake of the community of the Church.[23] In other words: a confessional Lutheran approach grounds the theological task primarily, while never exclusively, in the "public" of the Church.[24] Before turning to elaborate a confessional Lutheran methodology more in-depth, my thesis and its fundamental convictions will be clearly stated.

STATEMENT OF THE THESIS AND FUNDAMENTAL CONVICTIONS

In contrast to much of contemporary missiology, this project will argue for the following thesis. The following features of a confessional Lutheran approach mandate the construction of a missiology as promise formulated in terms of an economy of salvation: 1) the Gospel as promise; 3) the law/Gospel distinction; 3) a theology of grace as the promise of mercy realized; and 4) a theology of the cross utilizing the hiddenness of God.

Confessional Lutheran theology has unique resources with which to build a robust, dialogical, Christocentric, Trinitarian missiology. In order to address contemporary missiology, confessional Lutherans believe one must understand God's mission and the Church's mission. This requires understanding how mission is rooted in God's promise as revealed in Scripture. The overall logic for this project's argument is the following: 1) For Luther and the Lutheran Confessions, the nature of the Gospel is pure promise. 2) The nature of the Gospel should determine the nature and shape of Christian mission. 3) Therefore, promise becomes a central

---

23. While placing primary emphasis and attention on reconstructive hermeneutics, background theories, and engaging the theological task within the community of the Church, a confessionally Lutheran approach is mindful of and recognizes the importance of the hermeneutical role of the oppressed as emphasized by various schools of liberationist theology. However, it maintains that an adequate theological method must seek to balance these various factors, while paying sufficient attention to the hermeneutical significance of the Gospel as promise. For a treatment of these various elements, see Schüssler Fiorenza, "Systematic Theology," 70-84.

24. For a fuller treatment of the tripartite schema of the "publics" of the academy, society, and church, see Tracy, *The Analogical Imagination*, 3-46.

category for shaping Christian mission. In other words: a confessional Lutheran approach insists that clarity about the *nature* of the Gospel is crucial both for shaping Christian mission and constructing a faithfully relevant missiology for the twenty-first century. As Robert Bertram put it, "*Promissio* is the secret of *missio*."[25]

Given this project's goal of articulating a theological foundation for a confessional Lutheran missiology, such a goal will be pursued in two parts: 1) articulating a theologically foundational argument, drawn from Luther and the Lutheran Confessions' interpretation and formulation of key Scriptural themes, and 2) further augmenting this foundational argument in order to apply it to the missiological challenge of approaching religious pluralism, specifically in terms of relating proclamation to interreligious dialogue.

CONFESSIONAL LUTHERAN METHODOLOGY: APPROACHING THE CONTEMPORARY THEOLOGICAL CONTEXT

Before outlining a confessional Lutheran methodology within the contemporary theological context, an important, preliminary observation concerning God's relationship to history and the world prefaces my delineation of such a method. In approaching the issue of how the divine relates to the world, a confessional Lutheran method anchors itself in the traditional dogmatic framework by navigating this question within the framework of immanence versus transcendence. While recognizing that many contemporary theologies "historicize" God and salvation, construing the divine relationship to the world as largely immanent, a Lutheran approach affirms the classical, creedal tradition's emphasis on divine transcendence as a source of God's critical stance, vis-a-vis judgment and wrath, toward the world.[26] This fundamental difference of approach has profound implications for understanding what constitutes sin, grace, salvation, and the gospel, among other matters. Exploring this difference sufficiently, however, is beyond the scope of this study.

For the purposes of this project, I will bracket the issue of the world being in the seriously broken state the Scriptures describe as "sinful" or

---

25. Bertram, "Doing Theology," 41ff.

26. For helpful overviews and insightful treatments of the issues involved in this debate, see Gilkey, *Reaping the Whirlwind* and Hodgson, *God in History*.

"fallen." Confessional Lutheran theology does not intend to prove that the need to be saved from the results of a sinful condition is the fundamental problem that the person and work of Jesus Christ are meant to resolve. Instead, it merely stipulates this, as do Martin Luther, Jacques Dupuis, and the respective dogmatic traditions they represent. My aim is to compare and contrast Dupuis and the confessional Lutheran tradition on dealing with the issue of how the categories of "gospel" and "grace" are construed and how, to what extent, and on what grounds one can assert the active, implicit influence and work of the "gospel" and "grace" within the horizon of other religions. This means I will engage in a historical-theological mode of discourse through chapters 1 through 5, while moving into a more constructive, contemporary mode in chapter 6.

"The Christian, while knowing where Christ is, can never be certain where he is not," provides a helpful way of expressing the differences between a Lutheran, "law/promise" approach, and those based on the "nature/grace" paradigm.[27] While Lutheran theology offers a robust rationale for where and how Christ can be known and embraced-in the Gospel promise of forgiveness and loving mercy, and its attendant invitation to trust that promise in faith-it remains cautiously skeptical regarding the "nature/grace" paradigm's optimistic attempts, by those indebted to transcendental Thomism such as Rahner and Dupuis, to assert the saving presence of Christ in the world religions.[28] While Lutheran theology emphasizes where Christ can be known, Roman Catholic theology in general and those that subscribe to Spirit Christologies or robust pneumatologies in particular focus their creative energy on delineating how Christ and the Spirit are potentially present, in and through the world religions, in unexpected ways.

In light of the above-mentioned preface, will this project be a historical study of Luther's thought, or a systematic presentation of his key insights relating to mission? Yes. I intentionally answer this question ambiguously due to the complexly nuanced nature of Luther's thought. Did his theology develop over time? Certainly, as the well-known references to the "early" and "later" Luther indicate. Was Luther a

---

27. Oleksa, "Orthodox Missiological Education," 86.

28. It is worth noting that Roman Catholic theologians such as Henri de Lubac, Hans Urs von Balthasar, and Joseph Ratzinger, while also subscribing to the nature/grace paradigm, would not be open to the accusation of being optimistic in their assessment of salvation in history, unlike the "presence of Christ in the religions" school of thought represented by Rahner and Dupuis.

systematic theologian in the contemporary sense of the word? No. Unlike both Thomas Aquinas and Luther's own colleague Philip Melanchthon, both of whom systematically organized their theology into the famous *Summa* and *Loci*, respectively, Martin Luther never wrote a comparable systematic theology.[29] While recognizing that "Luther's thought, as complex as his perception of human life, as nuanced as he believed the biblical message to be, defies adequate summary," I nonetheless wish to argue that one can indeed identify a foundationally central motif to his theology, something which both unifies and clarifies his otherwise unsystematic, occasional theology.[30] The Scriptural motif of *promise*, nuanced and articulated by the law/Gospel distinction, provides such an animating center, not only for Luther's theology in general, but specifically as the key to unlocking his contemporary relevance for and contribution to mission. I will substantiate this point as this project unfolds. I will now proceed to situate a confessional Lutheran methodology in relation to contemporary theologies of religion, contemporary paradigms of theology, contemporary hermeneutical considerations, and the spectrum of contemporary Lutheran theological positions, in addition to describing its defining characteristics and its nuanced appropriation of the cultural-linguistic model in utilizing specific theological resources.

Contemporary Theologies of Religion

Paul Knitter's typology of theologies of religions distinguishes four approaches to religious pluralism, identifying them as replacement, fulfillment, acceptance, and mutuality models, respectively.[31] Within this scheme, a confessional Lutheran proposal for "inclusive exclusivity," as will be developed in subsequent chapters, incorporates elements from the replacement, fulfillment, and acceptance models. Such a proposal differs sharply from Karl Barth's "strict" exclusivism, viewing all revelation as concentrated in Jesus Christ and the religions as expressions of human unbelief, devoid of divine grace and objects of divine wrath. As a "partial replacement" model, a Lutheran proposal vigorously affirms God's benevolent, loving care and presence in the other religions, qualified by

---

29. Bayer, *Martin Luther's Theology*, xv.
30. Kolb, *Martin Luther*, 10.
31. For a fuller treatment of this schema, see Paul Knitter, *Introducing Theologies of Religions*.

a nuanced distinction between revelation and salvation. It affirms the centrality of Scripture as an important source, the radical reality of evil and sin in the world, and Jesus Christ as the "one and only" savior of the world.[32] It views the divine law, not only as revealing human sin and brokenness, but also as structuring human existence in relation to God in various ways. Along with the fulfillment model, it affirms insights on truth and mercy present in other religions, the importance of dialogue, and an eschatological vision of "all things being united under Christ (Eph 1:10)."[33] Lastly, with great affinity for the acceptance model and its post-liberal foundations, it affirms insights from the cultural-linguistic approach such as language and culture radically shaping experience, deep, abiding differences between the religions, the (almost) practical inevitability of an inclusivist orientation toward others, and the central role of the "deep grammar" of Christian Scriptures. Its nuanced appropriation of George Lindbeck's model will be elaborated momentarily.

Contemporary Approaches to Theology

A confessional Lutheran methodology can be characterized as incorporating elements and concerns from hermeneutical, neo-orthodox, and cultural-linguistic approaches to theology.[34] In sharp contrast to and critique of Rahner's transcendental approach, it asserts that "language does not just express but also constitutes experience."[35] As a broadly neo-orthodox approach, it insists that the theological task involves "not only 'criteria of adequacy' to human experience but also 'criteria of appropriateness' to the central meanings of the Christian tradition."[36] In sympathy with Hans-Georg Gadamer's opposition to the Enlightenment's prejudice against tradition, a Lutheran approach affirms several critical insights

---

32. Knitter, *Introducing*, 50–55.

33. Ibid., 100–102.

34. Francis Schüssler Fiorenza and David Tracy offer helpful typologies for describing contemporary theological approaches. Schüssler Fiorenza describes and differentiates between transcendental, hermeneutical, analytical, correlational, and liberationist theological approaches (*Systematic Theology: Roman Catholic Perspectives*, Volume I, 35–65). Tracy's typology outlines orthodox, liberal, neo-orthodox, radical, and revisionist theological models in his *Blessed Rage for Order: The New Pluralism in Theology*, 22–42.

35. Schüssler Fiorenza, "Systematic Theology," 44.

36. Tracy, *Blessed Rage*, 29.

from Gadamer and David Tracy's work: 1) The Christian Scriptures and confessional Lutheran writings, as "classics" of the broad Christian and confessionally Lutheran traditions, encounter us with a certain authority and claim."[37] 2) "The interpretive retrieval of the meaning and truth claims of the Christian classic" constitutes a primary challenge and task of systematic theology.[38] 3) A Lutheran approach is open to "the explanatory modes of historical-critical, literary-critical, and social-critical analysis" as complementing and enriching its method, properly understood.[39] 4) As a result, the challenge of reconstructive hermeneutics, delineating the authority, integrity, and critically appropriate retrieval of key theological resources from the tradition, becomes a central task.[40]

Defining Characteristics and Contemporary Hermeneutical Considerations

Given the preceding survey, we are now better positioned to describe definitive characteristics and hermeneutical emphases of a confessional Lutheran methodology. To begin with, given its view of the confessional Lutheran writings as "classic" expressions and summaries of the broad Christian tradition, such a methodology is largely historical-theological in spirit and emphasis. This means that its chief mode of operation is one of *ressourcement*, focused on retrieving from the tradition key, theological resources for engaging the contemporary scene.

Not only does such a method prioritize the paradigmatic character of the Christ event but, secondly, it also affirms the *importance of engagement and dialogue* with the present context in order to critically appropriate classic, Christian resources such as the categories of promise and the law/Gospel distinction. Such a spirit of engagement and dialogue takes its cue from Luther, whose "sustained engagement with the more prominent writers of the *via moderna* expresses an important element of his theology: the need to engage in dialogue with the present concerning the heritage of the past."[41]

---

37. Schüssler Fiorenza, "Systematic Theology," 44.
38. Ibid., 45–46.
39. Ibid., 46.
40. Ibid., 71–74.
41. McGrath, *Genesis of Doctrine*, 124–5.

In Search of a Lutheran Missional Hermeneutic

Third, confessional Lutheran method is self-consciously a particular *theology of Scripture*, rooted in, while creatively utilizing, Luther's reformation hermeneutic of reading Scripture via the law/Gospel distinction.[42] As previously noted, this necessarily entails a hermeneutical approach to the theological task. Three central points merit attention. First, while affirming the nature of Scripture as the "Word of God," confessional Lutherans view the Scriptures as exhibiting both divine and human authorship, analogous to affirming the divinity and humanity of Jesus Christ. In rejecting fundamentalist notions of Scriptural inspiration and authority, such an approach, while affirming the ultimate, divine authorship of Scripture, nevertheless is open to judiciously incorporating historical-critical, literary, and social-critical analysis and insights as illuminating the dynamics of human authorship. Second, its theology of the Word of God, explicated as a performative Word in terms of speech-act theory, serves as a critical background theory in undergirding a Lutheran hermeneutic. Such a theology of the Word of God advances a dual understanding of God's relationship to humanity, both nuanced by the law/Gospel distinction. In terms of approaching Scripture, it interprets the Scriptures as a broad witness of God relating to the world in fulfilling

---

42. For excellent treatments of the diversity of Christian theologies of Scripture, see Justin S. Holcomb, ed., *Christian Theologies of Scripture: A Comparative Introduction* and David H. Kelsey, *Proving Doctrine: The Uses of Scripture in Modern Theology*. I am acutely aware of the diversity of theologies operative in the Hebrew and Christian Scriptures. Theologians inevitably select certain metaphors, motifs, themes, narratives, and dialectical paradoxes based on their own presuppositions and commitments. Recognizing this fact does not settle the debates concerning the meaning of texts, their dominant motifs, or their interrelationships, but it does help illuminate the fact that claims to objective or unbiased interpretations, given our pluralistic context, are naive. In this project, I will use "theology of Scripture" to refer to the "diverse discussions about the nature, authority, interpretation, and uses of Scripture . . . as well as the relationship between Scripture and tradition" (Holcomb, *Christian Theologies of Scripture*, 2). Holcomb suggests some central issues any Christian theology of Scripture must adequately address: "What is the nature of scripture? Is it divine? Human? Both? Is scripture authoritative? If so, how and for whom? What is the scope of its authority? Is scripture inspired by God? What about scriptural interpretation-is that inspired? Does God illuminate humans to understand scripture? Is there an appropriate method of interpreting the words of scripture? Who can interpret scripture? What is its purpose? How *is* scripture interpreted? How *ought* scripture to be interpreted? How do scripture and tradition relate? Does scripture interpret tradition or does the tradition interpret scripture? Or both? What does it mean for a Christian to call the Bible 'the Word of God'? And if Jesus is also called the Word of God, how does Jesus as the Word of God relate to the Bible as the Word of God?" (Holcomb, *Christian Theologies of Scripture*, 1–2).

God's promise to love the world despite its brokenness and refusal to receive that love. In terms of approaching the world, it distinguishes the divine work of benevolently caring for and preserving creation ("left hand" work) from the work of restoring, repairing, and healing the world's brokenness through the ministry of Jesus Christ ("right hand" work). Third, the motif of promise, in light of its theoretical and practical fruitfulness (argued in chapter 1), functions as a retroductive warrant.

Fourth, a confessional Lutheran method is necessarily and fundamentally a *hermeneutical theology*. What are the distinctive, hermeneutical emphases of such an approach in relation to options within contemporary Biblical scholarship? I will use Manfred Oeming's schema of authors and their worlds, texts and their worlds, readers and their worlds, and the subject matter as the reality behind the text to briefly identify confessional Lutheran emphases.[43]

First, in terms of authors, texts, and their respective worlds, James Voelz summarizes a Lutheran perspective on the relationship between Biblical author and text: "Does a text 'have' a meaning which reflects the intention of its author? Yes. Does the intentional meaning of the author exhaust the meaning of the text? No. Can the intentional meaning of the author be determined? To a certain extent . . ."[44] Without denying the postmodern insight that meaning is largely constructed by the individual reader and interpreter, such an approach, while recognizing concerns expressed by linguistic-structuralist and "new" literary criticism methods, nonetheless asserts the primacy and potential of discerning an author's original intent.[45] Emphasizing the value of canonical interpretation of Scripture (Brevard Childs and James A. Sanders) and engaging in biblical exegesis via speech-act and word-act theories, this method remains open to insights from the historical-critical method, historical sociology, and archaeology, as these serve to further articulate a given text's "excess" of meaning. In terms of biblical exegesis, a confessional Lutheran approach generally builds upon the work of Ernst Fuchs, Gerhard Ebeling, and the application of their work in George Lindbeck's cultural-linguistic model. Agreeing with Gadamer's claim that "All being that can be understood is language," a Lutheran approach recognizes the importance of Fuchs'

---

43. Oeming, *Contemporary Biblical Hermeneutics*.

44. Voelz, *What Does This Mean?*, 215.

45. For a further elaboration of this position, see Voelz, *What Does This Mean?*, 207–29.

point that "God's salvation occurs primarily in believing his words of promise and forgiveness"[46]

Moving on to readers and their worlds, a Lutheran approach commends "a reading which is at all times utterly aware of the 'personal text' of the interpreter, especially his beliefs and opinions relative to doctrine and morals, and which takes seriously the fact that his own life can and will be illuminated by the text."[47] A Lutheran method is therefore highly attuned to the history of effects (*Wirkungsgeschichte*), recognizing the contextual and situational aspect of truth claims. While sensitive to the concerns of liberationist and feminist exegesis,[48] it asserts that a missiology of the cross that is reticent to be triumphalistic and open to irony and paradox, is possible, defensible, and fruitful. Especially as an elucidation of "broken power," a missiology of the cross articulating a vision of "loving mercy" offers a nuanced way to transcend the critique that all truth claims, especially those grounding themselves in the authority of the past, are *de facto* oppressive expressions of domination and power.

Finally, in terms of the subject matter as "reality behind the text," a Lutheran approach affirms the hermeneutical principle that "a text can only be read and understood in light of the reality or subject matter that lies behind the text."[49] It deems "methods that merely strive to understand human aspects of the biblical text (authors, languages, readers)," as well as fundamentalist and exclusively existentialist biblical interpretations, as insufficiently grappling with both the "transcendent" and historical character of Scripture.[50] As a broadly "dogmatic" approach to interpretation which seeks to constructively, responsibly interrelate the fields of exegeti-

---

46. Oeming, *Contemporary Biblical Hermeneutics*, 70–74. While affirming valuable insights from Fuchs' and Ebeling's theology of "language event" and "word event," a confessional Lutheran approach nonetheless recognizes the limitations of such an approach, especially as insufficiently incorporating the hermeneutical significance of history for Christian theology. As Carl Braaten notes, "In Fuchs and Ebeling all theology shrinks to the linguistic exchange between the Word and faith. The concept of language event cannot by itself span the wide chasm of the centuries between the history of salvation recorded in the Bible and the times in which we live. The actual bridge is history itself . . ." See Braaten, *Because of Christ: Memoirs of a Lutheran Theologian*, 62.

47. Voelz, *What Does This Mean?*, 340.

48. I have in mind here especially the hermeneutical emphasis on praxis and the role of the oppressed, as well as the hermeneutics of suspicion and condemnation.

49. Oeming, *Contemporary Biblical Hermeneutics*, 113.

50. Ibid.

cal and dogmatic (systematic) theology, a Lutheran approach, following Luther's lead, self-consciously grounds the interpretive task in Scripture (*sola Scriptura*) Christologically understood and concentrated:

> Theology is concerned with the significance of *Deus pro nobis* [God for us], rather than *Deus in se* [God in Godself]--and for Luther, "God" is defined Christologically . . . God can be fully known (in both the cognitive and personal senses) only through Jesus of Nazareth. The proper subject of theology is thus "God," as defined in the saving event of Jesus Christ. Given Luther's theological premise that theology is obliged to wrestle with Jesus Christ rather than with general principles or universal *a priori* concepts of divinity, the priority of the New Testament is thus secured on historical and literary grounds.[51]

Lutheran theology contends that this Christocentric core of Scripture is further illuminated through the use of three Scriptural dialectics: letter and spirit, law and gospel, and promise and fulfillment.[52] This project will argue for the fruitfulness of the category of promise, advanced and nuanced by the law/Gospel dialectic, as a useful resource for illuminating the missiological implications of this Christocentric core.

A central concern of a confessional Lutheran approach is to safeguard, preserve, and clearly articulate the Gospel as promise. This concern leads to a stance toward Church tradition, "not [as] criticism of tradition per se, but rather a demand that the proper criterion [of Gospel as promise] be used for judging the whole tradition or any part of it."[53] In other words: "The tradition's legitimate authority in the church is fundamentally the authority of promise rather than of law."[54] Such a concern is expressed in the following three emphases and advanced by them as distinct modes or strategies: by 1) the law/Gospel (promise) distinction, 2) a distinctive theology of grace as the promise of loving mercy fulfilled rather than nature fulfilled, and 3) a theology of the cross utilizing the hiddenness of God. These three strategies will be further articulated in chapters 1, 2, 5, and 6, respectively. What is noteworthy at this point of this project is that each strategy both helps preserves the foundational motif of Gospel as promise, while further augmenting and applying it.

51. McGrath, *Genesis of Doctrine*, 125.

52. For a fuller treatment of these dialectical principles, see Gerhard Sauter, *The Question of Meaning: A Theological and Philosophical Orientation*.

53. Horton, "Theologies of Scripture," 92.

54. Gritsch and Jenson, *Lutheranism*, 9.

A Nuanced Appropriation of the Cultural-Linguistic Model

As a hermeneutical theology, a confessional Lutheran method intentionally utilizes a nuanced version of George Lindbeck's cultural-linguistic model, employing its insights while seeking to overcome its deficiencies.[55] It is self-consciously a theology of the Word of God, asserting that "both as Law and as Gospel, the Word of God speaks the truth about the human creature."[56] It advances a nuanced understanding of Christian doctrine as an integrative, complex, and historical phenomenon. Lindbeck's model is vulnerable to criticism on at least three fronts: as an idealized approach which insufficiently engages history (mainly for illustrative purposes), as asserting a singular grammar for Scripture as a whole (insufficiently recognizing the polyvalence of Scripture), and as denying the possibility of some commonly shared human experiences (thus making interreligious dialogue impossible). While affirming with Lindbeck that religion is helpfully viewed as "an external word, a *verbum externum*, that molds and shapes the self and its world,"[57] I view this sole emphasis of Lindbeck's as unnecessarily reductionistic and idealized. While affirming and utilizing cultural-linguistic insights such as the stress on the priority of language over experience, as well as a religion comprising "a vocabulary of discursive and nondiscursive symbols together with a distinctive logic or grammar," correlated with and articulating a particular form of life, confessional Lutheran theology affirms a more nuanced, dialectical relationship between doctrine and experience.[58] Not only do doctrines shape and articulate experience, but certain doctrines or categories have the potential to meaningfully describe a broad range of common, shared human experience.

The methodology of this project will employ a historically conscious view of doctrine, affirming a fourfold understanding of doctrine: 1) functioning as a social demarcator, 2) generated by, while subsequently interpreting, the generative Christian narrative of the history of Jesus of Nazareth, 3) interpreting experience, and 4) making truth claims.[59]

---

55. For an excellent overview of contemporary paradigms of theology, see John Galvin and Francis Schüssler Fiorenza, eds., *Systematic Theology: Roman Catholic Perspectives Volume I*, 1–88.

56. Mattox, "Martin Luther," 101.

57. Lindbeck, *Nature of Doctrine*, 34.

58. Ibid., 33.

59. McGrath, *Genesis of Doctrine*, 37. For a fuller discussion of this model for understanding doctrine, see McGath, *Genesis of Doctrine*, 35–80.

While recognizing that "no single paradigm may be identified which adequately accounts for the phenomenon with which the 'total history of doctrine' is encountered," I will argue for the validity and fruitfulness of retrieving and appropriating Luther's hermeneutic of distinguishing law and gospel as a helpful vehicle for articulating and preserving the nature of the Gospel as promise.[60] Cognizant of other methodologies and alternative paradigms, confessional Lutherans maintain that understanding the Gospel as promise provides a fruitful avenue, not only for accessing a central theme of Scripture, but also for engaging the religiously other through the categories of divine mercy and divine hiddenness.[61]

The theoretical underpinning of this approach draws upon Walter Benjamin's "theoretical account of history [which] allows *Historie* (history as that which is past) to become *Geschichte* (history as that which is existentially relevant and personally appropriated)," thus making possible "the creative and critical reappropriation of the doctrinal heritage of the past."[62] Furthermore, this project builds upon the basic insights of Anders Nygren's "motif-research" approach to advance the motif of "promise" as central.[63] In delineating an "economy of salvation" approach concentrating on the Gospel as promise, such a confessional Lutheran method advances the following affirmations: 1) "The history of Jesus of Nazareth may be regarded as the precipitating or generative event of Christian doctrine."[64] 2) Narratives require interpretation. 3) The history of Jesus "represents an initiative which is not ours . . . and invites us to enter into a conceptual world which we ourselves did not fashion."[65] 4) While not denying the significance of Jesus' life and ministry, the events of his death and resurrection are, for Lutheran theology, of primary importance for adequately interpreting the theological significance of his

---

60. McGrath, *Genesis of Doctrine*, 165.

61. Postmodern, feminist, and liberationist paradigms of theology highlight the potential hazards of covert, ideological influences distorting Scriptural traditions and marginalizing or subjugating alternative voices.

62. McGrath, *Genesis of Doctrine*, 169. Benjamin articulates his theory in "Theses on the Concept of History." My use of Benjamin's model is indebted to McGrath's description of its salient features in *Genesis of Doctrine*, 165–71.

63. The main contours and insights of this approach are outlined in Anders Nygren, *Meaning and Method: Prolegomena to a Scientific Philosophy of Religion and a Scientific Theology*. For a systematic theology written from Nygren's "motif-research" perspective, see Gustaf Aulen, *The Faith of the Christian Church*.

64. McGrath, *Genesis of Doctrine*, 35.

65. Ibid., 174.

life. 5) The category of promise has an intratextual, integrative function for interpreting Christian Scripture for Lutheran theology. 6) Promise, utilized within an "economy of salvation" model, affirms the intelligibility of claiming that the divine promise of salvation, offered from the very beginning of the Hebrew Scriptures, finds its fulfillment in the Christ event.[66] This means that, for all their internal tensions, conflicts, apparent contradictions, and resistance to harmonization, the Scriptural texts taken together "are about God's will for salvation in election, judgment and redemption."[67] 7) Lutheran theology affirms an understanding of revelation as incorporating both intratextuality and intertextuality. Within the hermeneutical spiral, the generative event of Jesus of Nazareth, the Scriptural text bearing witness to that event, and the reading community are interrelated in a manner that "allow[s] for what comes to us from beyond and between the texts we inhabit, as well as from within them."[68] 8) The most significant similarities and overlaps concerning human religious experience are aptly described, not by categories of being, existence, or human nature (ontology or anthropology), but rather in cultural-linguistic terms as the paradoxical relationship between divine wrath and promise, sin and grace, law and Gospel, human brokenness and divine healing. 9) Based on doctrine interpreting experience as one of doctrine's functions, a broad range of common, overlapping human experiences can be intelligibly described and meaningfully compared under Luther's category of divine hiddenness (*deus absconditus*).[69] By choosing these classic Lu-

66. What is important is not the term "economy of salvation" (one could just as well use promise-history, covenant-history, revelation-history, etc.), but rather the critical insight and central conviction it conveys regarding God's relationship to the world and humanity: the promise of reconciliation centered on and realized through the Christ event.

67. Hengel, "Salvation History," 240. Hengel summarizes the basic contours of such a Christocentric view of the economy of salvation, emphasizing a theology of the cross: "God, the creator of the world, is also the Lord of its history. However, we must speak of *God's action* as *hidden action* . . . History in itself does not yield any deeper meaning, and for human eyes it does not contain any saving goal. This goal becomes visible only because God . . . has revealed himself in history, i.e. *in concrete places in space and time* [namely, the Christ event] . . . *[T]his history receives its unity and its foundation from its centre and its goal, the person of Jesus Christ* . . . God's 'salvation history' for the whole of humankind is disclosed in the fate of this one man . . . The way from the promise of Abraham, from the God who justifies the godless, to Golgotha, and the way of the message of the cross to the peoples, is 'salvation history'" (Hengel, "Salvation History," 238–43).

68. Loughlin, "Postmodern Scripture," 301.

69. While recognizing the "hiddenness of God" as a category recognized and

theran motifs as central to a confessional Lutheran hermeneutic, I am not denying that other theologians, even other Lutheran theologians, find other motifs as more illuminative or important. Taken collectively, these nine affirmations underscore the hermeneutical importance of the ecclesial community as a living, interpretive tradition, while necessitating the task of critical reappropriation of the Church's doctrinal heritage. Gerard Loughlin states this well:

> Christ is the rule for the Church's reading of scripture. He is the norm by which the text is judged, the reading context in which the sense of God's writing is discerned. But Christ himself is given in the Church's reading or performance of the text. Christ, as the norm of Christian reading, is realized only in the practice of faithful reading. He is not given apart from that for which he is the rule. The Church is better able to read scripture the more scripture is faithfully read and performed in the Church. And when we read in faith we read in truth, and the truth itself appears.[70]

Alister McGrath succinctly outlines the interrelationship between history, tradition, and the development of doctrine this project will employ:

> Christian doctrine is a response to the history of Jesus of Nazareth. Its achievements and successes, its failures and weaknesses, are all to be judged with reference to that history. That history is mediated through a tradition, and socially embodied in a tradition-orientated community, whose *anamnesis* of its foundational and legitimizing event shapes its sense of identity, commitment, and purpose . . . Outside the community of faith, Jesus of Nazareth will continue to be interpreted according to rival theories of truth and reason; within the community of faith, however, Jesus of Nazareth remains the central object of worship, adoration, and wonder. And in that sense of wonder lies the genesis of doctrine.[71]

---

claimed by the broad Christian tradition, I will be utilizing Luther's treatment of and distinction between the hidden God and the revealed God in constructing my argument.

70. Loughlin, "Postmodern Scripture," 310.

71. McGrath, *Genesis of Doctrine*, 193.

Contemporary Lutheran Theological Approaches

In terms of the spectrum of contemporary Lutheran positions today, how do I situate a confessional Lutheran approach? At least six, formative influences shape Lutheran theology today: evangelicalism, liberalism (seeking divine revelation and truth wherever it is to be found, similar to Avery Dulles' classification of Rahner and Haight's position on revelation as "new awareness"), liberationist, confessional (seeking to harmonize classic Lutheran theological concepts with current mission trends), pragmatist (incorporating sociological insights from the church growth movement), and pentecostal.[72] In finding no current, unified theological basis for Lutheran missiology today, Richard Bliese argues that such a common foundation is desperately needed.[73] He wonders if, and to what extent, the theology of the Reformers, especially Luther's, may serve as such a theological basis.[74] Confessional Lutheran theology contends that the *missio Dei*, understood in terms of an economy of salvation and the Gospel as promise, is indeed a helpful theological basis for constructing a Lutheran missiology, precisely because such a view finds strong support in confessional Lutheran resources.

In terms of Bliese's typologies of Lutheran theology, this project self-consciously argues for the value of utilizing the following sources and convictions for doing Lutheran missiology. First, viewing the Lutheran confessional writings and the entire Reformation from a corrective rather than constitutive perspective is not only faithful to their original intent, but is also most ecumenically and interreligiously fruitful.[75] Second,

---

72. Bliese, "Lutheran Missiology," 22–23.

73. Ibid., 23.

74. Ibid., 26.

75. In terms of the intent and continuing relevance of the Lutheran reformation, Carl Braaten describes the constitutive and corrective orientations articulated by George Lindbeck (Braaten, "Confessional Lutheranism in an Ecumenical World," 225). The constitutive approach views Luther as the founder of a new denomination, Lutheranism, and the Reformation as the beginning of the Protestant movement. In contrast, the corrective approach to the Reformation views Luther and the Lutheran Confessions as standing firmly within and in continuity with the western, Christian tradition, rejecting the concept of denominationalism as completely alien to the spirit and intent of the *Augsburg Confession*. Rather than a denominationally Lutheran identity, the corrective view embraces an "evangelical catholic" identity. The Lutheran confessors articulated this very stance, insisting that "they were the true catholics, in no way teaching anything new or different from classical Christian doctrine." The *Apology of the Augsburg Confession* explicitly states this: "We have clear consciences

Luther's theology and *The Book of Concord* are best understood as offering fundamentally complementary, rather than alternative, positions. Third, a confessional approach within Lutheranism provides the best theological basis, not only for safeguarding and passing on Luther's own missiological insights, but also for articulating a robust, theologically distinctive Lutheran missiology. Fourthly, in order to avoid the twin errors of historical relativism and ahistorical dogmatism, the nature of the Lutheran confessions as problem-solving, "exemplary confession and witness" should be honored, preserving both their status as a "classic" and contemporary relevance.[76] Finally, in the relationship between mission (proclamation) and interreligious dialogue, the distinctive nature of the Gospel as promise should take priority in any articulation or configuration of the mission-dialogue relationship.

Balancing Deductive and Inductive Considerations

Paul Knitter, among others, expresses the concern that a confessional Lutheran methodology, especially in utilizing the law/Gospel distinction, is overly deductive, insufficiently inductive, and therefore lends itself to an inevitably negative assessment of and approach to other religions. Commenting on how C. H. Ratschow employs the law/Gospel distinction, Knitter writes:

> The basic difference between religions and Christianity would therefore seem to be that between *Law and Gospel* . . . Even the so-called Religions of Grace remain within the precincts of the Law . . . Ratschow does not explicitly say that the religions contain only questions. Yet if they can never understand justification *"sola fide,"* if they remain within the order of the Law, then, it seems, all they possess are questions and searchings. Salvation-the answers-come only in the Gospel. The religions

---

on this matter since we know that our confession is true, godly, and catholic" (*Book of Concord*, 222). Furthermore, in articulating the relationship between Luther's thought, the confessional writings, and lived Christian experience, Lindbeck identifies the following four positions: "those committed to *The Book of Concord* as a whole [;] . . . those [like himself] particularly committed to the 'evangelical catholicity' of the Augsburg Confession within *The Book of Concord*; those who gave priority to Luther's theology over *The Book of Concord*; and those who gave priority to 'experiential' or 'service-oriented' perspectives over any of the previous three" (*The Church in a Postliberal Age*, ix).

76. Truemper, "Lutheran Confessional Writings," 134–37.

seem to be left with only a preparatory role-a negative preparatory role: to express questions and needs.[77]

While primarily deductive in emphasis, employing key resources from its tradition, a confessional Lutheran methodology, in encountering the world of religious pluralism, readily incorporates inductive elements. It recognizes and appreciates the real, lived affirmations of divine mercy, loving care, and benevolence within Islam and Judaism, as well as and possibly in other religions.[78] As Paul V. Martinson notes how the concept of divine mercy is shared by both Christianity and Islam: "What a deep affinity we have. The most common reference to God in the Qur'an is of God as gracious and merciful."[79] Similarly, God's covenant faithfulness toward Israel, expressed as mercy, is central to Judaism's vision of God.

While inductively affirming these similarities and overlaps regarding divine mercy, confessional Lutheran theology nevertheless insists that there remains a significant difference between the divine mercy affirmed in Islam, for example, and the loving mercy expressed in and through Jesus Christ. It maintains that, while mercy is a prerogative of power, the divine love expressed in Christ demonstrates two vital aspects of a confessional Lutheran understanding of "loving mercy," aspects that make it a unique view of mercy among the world religions. First, such an approach adequately recognizes and attends to the destructive power of sin and the reality of divine wrath. Second, such a view of loving mercy entails and is enacted, not merely through a decree or pronouncement of forgiveness, but specifically through divine vulnerability, self-emptying, self-condescension, suffering, death, and resurrection. Such an articulation of vulnerable, "cruciform," loving mercy is virtually unparalleled in world religions and constitutes a Christian contribution to interreligious understanding and dialogue. Without denying the presence and affirmation of divine love in Islam and Judaism, Martinson delineates how a Christian view of "loving mercy" differs from Muslim conceptions of mercy (and one might wonder whether this applies to Jewish views as well):

77. Knitter, *Towards a Protestant Theology of Religions*, 190–91.

78. Paul Varo Martinson documents how, in the Jodo Shinshu form of Pure Land Buddhism and Vaisnava schools of piety within Hinduism, there appear to be striking similarities to the Christian doctrine of justification by grace or mercy. See Martinson, "Justification—Learning Its Meaning Amidst the Religions." In Stumme, *Gospel of Justification in Christ*, 142.

79. Martinson, "Justification," 151.

> But mercy is not yet love. Wherein lies the difference? Mercy is always the prerogative of power. Love never is . . . Only the one who has power over another can extend mercy. Mercy is never given on demand but only freely by the one in power. It can also be withheld. Such is not the case with love. Love is never free, for it is by nature a self-imposed bondage, so to speak. And it is never the prerogative of power. It is always at risk, vulnerable, active only in weakness . . . Herein lies the issue of the referents in Islam and Christianity. In Islam, God is always power and therefore always free to exercise mercy as he so wills. In the Christian faith God is power, yes, but also broken power—love. God's power is made perfect in the weakness of the cross. Here was displayed the divine love at its riskiest and weakest. Such a conception of divine condescension is not possible in Islam.[80]

A confessional Lutheran incorporation of inductive and deductive elements means that, while recognizing and affirming the presence of divine, benevolent care and mercy in other faiths, understood on their own terms, nevertheless a nuanced, Christian view of "loving mercy" offers the incarnate, vulnerable, "cruciform" mercy and love achieved in Jesus Christ as a unique offering within religious pluralism. Within Christianity, such a Lutheran view critiques notions of "grace" as God's undifferentiated self-manifestation, especially ones arising from transcendental theologies based upon the "nature/grace" paradigm, as paying insufficient attention to the dimensions of sin and mercy as "broken power." This point will be argued in chapter 3. The theological foundation for such a critique will be laid in chapters 1 and 2, as the Lutheran view of the Gospel as promise, the importance of the law/Gospel distinction, and the distinctive shape of a theology of grace as "loving mercy" is articulated. Interreligiously, such a view of "loving mercy" not only establishes a point of commonality and contact in interreligious dialogue, but also forms the basis for proposing "the hiddenness of God" as a fruitful avenue for such dialogue. This will be further delineated in chapter 6. In chapters 4 and 5, a missiologically creative version of the "nature/grace" paradigm, Jacques Dupuis' theology of religious pluralism, will be articulated and constructively critiqued from a confessional Lutheran perspective.

Before concluding this introduction, two points regarding a Lutheran view of the law are in order. First, "law" designates a particular way God applies pressure, expectation, and structure across the religious

---

80. Ibid., 151–2.

spectrum, including and beginning within Christianity itself. Christianity must always be vigilantly self-critical and self-aware of the ever-present temptation to misplace its confidence in the law, at the expense of the Gospel promise. Its abysmal history of the Crusades, imperialism, and anti-Semitism makes this task all the more urgent. Second, rather than Christianity being a pure "religion of the Gospel," in contrast to all other religions as "religions of the law," the "law" of God is a universal phenomenon operative in all religions, whether or not they recognize it, and serving a specifically theological function. This function is crucial as a springboard and stepping stone toward a recognition of and engagement with divine hiddenness in all religions, and will be further delineated in chapter 1. A Christian theology of the cross employs various resources, including the category of law, to approach other religions and engage them in interreligious dialogue around the topic of divine hiddenness. A distinctively Lutheran contribution to mission and interreligious dialogue is its use of a distinctive understanding of mercy as "broken, vulnerable power" and a theology of the cross to explore the hiddenness of God. The rest of this project will delineate and defend this Lutheran contribution.

CONCLUSION

"The Christian, while knowing where Christ is, can never be certain where he is not."[81] For confessional Lutheran theology, the Gospel as promise, safeguarded by the law/Gospel distinction, seeks to offer a robust account of where Christ can be known and embraced: in the Gospel promise of forgiveness and loving mercy, and its attendant invitation to trust that promise in faith. While hopeful concerning and open to being surprised by Christ's presence in unexpected places, it nonetheless cautions transcendental theologies based on the "nature/grace" paradigm as insufficiently attending to the deep reality of sin and brokenness in their articulation of Christ's presence being extended, by the Spirit, amidst the religions. Such a proposal offers a missiologically fruitful nuance to the *missio Dei*. This claim will be further explored in chapters 1, 2, and 5. Not only are law and gospel constitutive of the divine/ human relationship, but Bayer further asserts divine hiddenness as its third feature:

---

81. Oleksa, "Orthodox Missiological Education," 86.

Mission Shaped by Promise

> When the subject of theology is taken to be the justifying God and the sinful human being, this "subject" as a dramatic event and encounter takes place within the following three spheres: a. in the conflict with the *law* that judges me, that convicts me with regard to my sins, that accuses me, and that delivers me over to the final judgment of death; b. in the promise of the *gospel*, in which God himself speaks by means of Jesus Christ on my behalf, indeed takes my place; and c. in the assault of the *hiddenness of God*, which cannot be understood merely as the effect of the law and which so radically contradicts the gospel in an . . . incomprehensible way.[82]

What is distinctive about such a confessional approach to Lutheran theology, and why do I believe it provides the best potential for constructing a Lutheran missiology? Based on the conviction that "mission is the mother of theology" (Martin Kähler), a confessional Lutheran approach proceeds with a dual conviction. 1) Lutheran theological insights, as articulated in the Lutheran confessional writings, offer the enduring value of a classic for missiological praxis. These include the Gospel as promise of loving mercy in Christ, the law/Gospel distinction, and a theology of the cross utilizing the hiddenness of God. 2) This rich theological heritage should be further advanced and developed by engaging and interacting with contemporary mission and global trends such as the new awareness of religious pluralism, etc. It intentionally seeks to correct historic deficiencies in the confessional Lutheran tradition, especially in terms of 1) a lack of missiological vision and 2) insensitivity toward the necessity of interreligious dialogue.

---

82. Bayer, *Martin Luther's Theology*, 42.

1

The Gospel as Promise of God

NOT ALL WORDS ARE created equal. Some are more important than others. The Christian tradition has been decisively shaped by, while also bequeathing us, many important words, words without which it would be unrecognizable: salvation, reconciliation, law, Gospel, covenant, sin, grace, trust, mission, and witness, to name but a few. In considering more specifically the topic and task of the church's "mission," a dazzling array of words is likewise used to describe what Christian mission is or should strive to be: proclamation, evangelism, common witness, *missio Dei*, liberation, work for peace and justice, prophetic dialogue, inculturation, contextualization, etc.[1] Such an abundance of definitions of mission led Stephen Neill to comment incisively, "If everything is mission, nothing is mission."[2] Analogously, the same concern could be expressed regarding the nature of the Christian Gospel itself: If everything is Gospel, nothing is Gospel.

A fundamental Lutheran conviction is that, in the Christian lexicon, not all words are created equal. Some are more important than others. Thoughtful Christians throughout the ages have always emphasized certain words as more essential and centrally illuminative than others for

---

1. David Bosch, in chapter 11 of his missiological masterpiece *Transforming Mission*, lists at least thirteen different elements of an "emerging ecumenical missionary paradigm," namely mission as: the Church-with-others, *missio Dei*, mediating salvation, the quest for justice, evangelism, contextualization, liberation, inculturation, common witness, ministry by the whole people of God, witness to people of other living faiths (including dialogue), theology, and action in hope.

2. Neill, *Creative Tension*, 81.

Christian identity. While the consensus regarding which words are central, and on what grounds, has shifted throughout Christian history, the history of the Christian tradition could arguably be viewed as a struggle over this very question. Being ever mindful of the twin dangers of inflation and reductionism, of *either* overloading Christian terms with more weight than they were meant to bear, thus inflating them to the point of losing meaning, *or* reducing a given term too narrowly to a one-dimensional meaning, the Christian church cannot help but engage in the perilous venture of identifying which words are central to understanding the Church's identity and mission if it is both to remain faithful to its tradition and relevantly engage the wider culture. This task, fraught with pitfalls, is inevitable. Since all Christians take the canonical Scriptures as authoritative, as the Word of God (in some sense), Scripture is a natural place to ground this task. Which words of Scripture are most essential, most centrally illuminative, which words serve as a roadmap, helping clarify the multitude of other words and the overall sense of Scripture?

This project will demonstrate how, for confessional Lutheran theology, "Gospel" and "mission" are essential to Christian self-identity and vocation, and that "promise" is a fruitful vehicle for relating the two, since the nature of both the Gospel and Christian mission are grounded in the promises of God. A study of Luther and the Lutheran Confessions shows that they are convinced that the category of promise is the best means by which to illumine, not only the nature of the Gospel, ensuring fidelity to the Christian tradition, but also for understanding and directing Christian mission as the Church seeks to relevantly engage the world. In other words: the notion of "promise" not only holds faithfulness with the Christian tradition and relevant contemporary engagement in mission together, but it is able to do so precisely because "promise" illuminates a fundamental dimension of both the Gospel and Christian mission. I will argue and substantiate these three claims: 1) For Luther and the Lutheran Confessions, the Gospel is a promise; 2) The nature of the Gospel should shape/direct the nature of mission; 3) Therefore, promise should be a central category in defining and understanding mission. I will seek to analyze the significance and various theological implications of these basic convictions. In subsequent chapters I will explore how the Gospel as *promissio Dei* relates to and clarifies the mission of the Church.

Martin Luther, in positing the Gospel as fundamentally a promise of God, understood that such a claim had momentous implications for the entire theological enterprise. As Luther put it in *The Babylonian Captivity of the Church*: "For God does not deal, nor has he ever dealt, with us except through the word of promise. We, in turn, cannot deal with God except through faith in the word of his promise . . . These two, promise and faith, must necessarily go together."[3] In such memorable words, Luther placed the theme of the promise of God at the center of the theological agenda, inviting further exploration of the issues at stake in understanding the Gospel as *promissio Dei*. This quote also underlines the fiduciary character of faith, the radically personal nature of God's relationship with humanity as one of promise and trust, and the very nature of the Gospel as promise. For Luther, Gospel as *promissio* became the lens through which he read the entire Bible, "including the story of creation, which Luther understood as a promise . . . 'what he [God] promises, that he certainly does.'"[4] While many other themes—such as Christian freedom, justification by grace through faith, *simul iustus et peccator*, and a theology of the cross, to name but a few—are also important in Luther's thought and Lutheran theology, I wish to argue for and demonstrate how the category of *promissio Dei* is the most compelling, unifying touchstone around which all the other themes in Luther's theology coalesce. In other words: while "Luther's theology is too lively and too complex to be summarized by a single concept,"[5] the category of *promissio Dei* serves as a heuristic device, illuminating what is distinctive and missiologically creative in Luther's thought and the Lutheran Confessions. Rather than oversimplifying or being reductionistic, a clear emphasis on the *promissio Dei* achieves the very opposite: it opens up new insights into and possibilities for applying Luther's thought, especially missiologically, which were previously overlooked or underappreciated.

What are the significant issues at stake in positing the Gospel as promise? Viewing the Gospel as the promise of God unifies and clarifies six important topics, laying the groundwork for constructing a Lutheran missiology: the relational matrix created by the promissory Word of God, the nature of God, human nature, pastoral issues related to lived Christian experience, the nature of faith, and the law-Gospel distinction or hermeneutic. I will now briefly introduce these issues, before delving into them in greater detail later. First, the trustworthy character of God is grounded in God's faithfulness to His promises. Secondly, the nature of faith is fundamentally trust in God's promises. Thirdly, humans are

---

3. Luther, *Luther's Works*, 36:42.
4. Bayer, "Martin Luther as an Interpreter of Holy Scripture," 75.
5. Bayer, *Martin Luther's Theology*, xvii.

fundamentally trusting creatures, with faith as trust constituting an inevitable feature of human life. Fourthly, the Gospel as promise is most clearly understood when it is contrasted in dialectical tension with the demands of the divine law. The law/Gospel distinction is intrinsic, rather than peripheral, to understanding the Gospel as promise. Fifthly, in order for humans to fully and freely trust in God's faithfulness to God's promises, it is imperative that their consciences be comforted. This happens when the benefits of Christ are fully utilized. It is precisely the law/Gospel distinction which assists in such usage and application of the benefits of Christ. In other words: because the theme of promise captures the core nature of the Gospel, it has far-reaching implications for Christian faith and mission. Since the Word of God as God's promissory, creative speech is foundational for understanding the rest of my argument, we now turn to examine this topic, and the related topic of promise as a "linguistic rule" for Gospel talk, before returning to clarify the five other significant issues.

PRELIMINARY MATTERS

The Word of God: God's Speech Creates Relational Reality

A confessional Lutheran reading of the creation narratives of Genesis chapters 1 and 2 views God's speech as, not only creative, but also creating an inevitably relational matrix with humanity. Not only does creation come into existence through God's creative speech, but God's speech directed toward humanity, comprised of command and promise, sets forth the subsequent trajectory of the divine-human relationship throughout the rest of Scripture.

Luther on the Creative Word of God

As an astute Biblical scholar, Martin Luther picked up on the significance of God's mode of action being primarily through his Word. For Luther, that Word is always creative, performative speech which "accomplishes his will and actualizes his presence in human lives."[6] His emphasis on God's Word creatively realizing its purposes permeated his Genesis lectures: "God does not speak grammatical words; he speaks true and

---

6. Arand and Kolb, *Genius of Luther's Theology*, 135.

existent realities. Accordingly, that which among us has the sound of a word is a reality with God . . . By speaking God created all things and worked through his Word. All his works are words of God, created by the uncreated Word."[7]

In other words, Luther claims that God's speech creates and determines reality. As Robert Kolb puts it, "God's utterly reliable promise possesses re-creative power."[8] While "God is always acting, and his action is speaking,"[9] I will contend that the most crucial aspect of that speaking, the part which unlocks and unifies all the other parts, is pure promise.

Oswald Bayer notes how the dynamic of law and Gospel, human sin and divine forgiveness, is intrinsic to this oral, relational matrix: "God and humans coexist in the Word: in the Word of the confession of sins and in the Word of the forgiveness of sins."[10] Since it is fundamental for Luther as the starting point of his theology of the Word of God, let us examine the warrants for claiming that God's Word is creative, performative speech, the first of at least eight particular functions of that Word.[11]

The Theory of Speech Acts

The theory of speech acts, providing the philosophical and linguistic basis for understanding the Gospel as promise, serves as a background theory to a confessional Lutheran theology of the Word of God. First put forward by John L. Austin in the late 1950's and early 1960's, it was further developed by his student, John R. Searle. Much like Ludwig Wittgenstein, who stressed how a given "language game" only makes sense and works within a particular situation or form of life, Austin's theory of speech acts emphasizes how the meaning of a word or phrase is inextricably tied to the specific context of its use. He sought "a new theory that

---

7. Luther, *Luther's Works*, 1:21–22.
8. Kolb, *Martin Luther*, 82.
9. Arand and Kolb, *Genius of Luther's Theology*, 136.
10. Bayer, *Martin Luther's Theology*, 39.
11. Charles Arand and Robert Kolb in their book, *The Genius of Luther's Theology*, have identified at least eight important functions of God's Word for Luther, including (but not limited to) the following: 1) it creates reality, 2) it re-creates sin-distorted reality, 3) it establishes a relationship of conversation between Creator and creatures, 4) it elicits faith, 5) it both reveals and 6) hides God, 7) it kills and 8) makes alive. While functions #5 and #6 will receive further treatment in chapter 5, functions #3, 4, 7, and 8 will be further elaborated later in discussing the nature of faith, pastoral concerns, and the distinction between law and Gospel.

gives a complete and general account of *what we are doing when we say something...*"¹²

Austin and Searle's basic insight sheds light on the notion of Gospel as promise by distinguishing between two different kinds of utterances or "speech acts": constative versus performative.¹³ Oswald Bayer's description of the difference between these two is illuminating:

> ... a constative utterance refers to a state of affairs that has already been constituted. It gives us information about it but it does not itself bring it about. The constative sentence therefore manifests and discloses what already is. It is ... a declarative sentence ... But something different occurs with the performative utterance, which Austin distinguishes from the constative. *It itself constitutes a situation.* It does not simply establish, disclose, and confirm it as already existing, *but it actually brings it about.*¹⁴

A prime example of a performative speech act for Austin, one that Luther had theological insight into, is the promise. What happens when I say to another, "I promise you..."? Such an utterance (speech act) is never merely descriptive, simply describing a preexisting situation. Rather, "through it a relationship is established which previously did not exist."¹⁵ A new reality is created: a personal, objective relationship dependent upon the promise being kept rather than broken. While a marriage vow would be a prime example of such a promissory utterance, Luther came to view the Gospel itself as such a performative speech act, one whose reliability was directly contingent upon God's faithfulness to such divine promises.

Long before Austin and Searle articulated their theory of speech acts, Martin Luther already grasped one of its central insights, applying it to the Gospel. The controversy over indulgences and the sacrament of penance illustrates how Luther's understanding of the Gospel changed from viewing the words of absolution as a constative, descriptive utterance

---

12. Austin, "Performative-Constative," 13.

13. Ibid. Austin used the paired terms locutionary/constative and illocutionary/performative, interchangeably. Some philosophers of language may be more familiar with or prefer the terms locutionary and illocutionary. Searle went on to further develop the theory of speech acts, most notably in his book, *Speech Acts: An Essay in the Philosophy of Language.*

14. Bayer, *Theology the Lutheran Way*, 127. Italics added for emphasis.

15. Ibid.

The Gospel as Promise of God

conveying information to a promissory, performative utterance.[16] Initially, Luther understood the priestly words of absolution as a declarative statement--the priest sees the sinner's remorse, interprets it as a sign of repentance and divine justification, and simply reconfirms this reality to the penitent as a matter of fact. Understood this way, the words of absolution are a declarative "description of a present state of affairs, rather than the actual performance of forgiveness."[17] However, Luther gradually came to view the words of absolution and the entire Word of God as an active and effective word (*verbum efficax*), creating a new reality and state of affairs. By realizing that the sign (*signum*) is itself the reality (*res*), that the sign means what it says, Luther came to view absolution as an efficacious word "that first constitutes, brings about, a state of affairs, by creating a relationship between the one in whose name it is spoken and the one to whom it is spoken *and who believes the promise*."[18] Its effect is to communicate, liberate, and give certainty. In other words, Luther came to see, not only the words of absolution, but also the sacraments of Baptism and the Lord's Supper, the Christmas narrative ("Fear not! Unto you is born this day a Savior!"), the Easter narrative, the conclusion of Christ's Great Commission ("Lo, I am with you always to the end of the age."), and many other scriptural statements as effective promises, constituting the reality which they offer.[19]

In a spirit similar to Luther's, the defining feature of Lutheran theology is its definition of the Gospel as promise, a performative word in which the promise of the Gospel is powerfully efficacious and serves as the very ground of faith.[20] Oswald Bayer describes the Gospel as such an efficacious Word (*verbum efficax*), doing what it says and saying what it does:[21]

> [T]he Word of Jesus Christ the Crucified . . . is *verbum efficax*; it is "promise" in the categorical sense, *promissio*. It does not make a promise in the sense that it sets something forth as an expectation and thereby puts you off until later. *This promise is much more; it is its own fulfillment; it fulfills itself, and this actually does not take place at a later time, but at the very moment it is uttered;*

16. Ibid., 129.
17. Ibid.
18. Ibid., 130. Italics added for emphasis.
19. Ibid.
20. Ibid., 138.
21. Bayer, "Martin Luther as an Interpreter of Holy Scripture," 76.

> *it is* promissio *as a valid promise that takes effect immediately.* The ear and the mouth open up right when Jesus Christ speaks ... In this way the Word is an active, efficacious Word.[22]

By claiming that the heart of the Christian faith involves such a speech act, a Lutheran approach asserts that the Church's identity and mission are best illumined, interpreted, and explained, "not primarily by an analysis of existence, but by an analysis of language."[23] It is for this very reason that the particular relationship of law and promise, providing a deep grammar of the various biblical genres, is of central importance in constructing a Lutheran missiology.

Promise as a "Linguistic Rule" for Gospel Talk

Lutheran theology posits that both the form and content of the Gospel are best understood as pure promise. Eric Gritsch and Robert Jenson offer an incisive definition of what Lutherans mean by the Gospel as promise:

> [T]he gospel is a wholly unconditional promise of the human fulfillment of its hearers, made by the narrative of Jesus' death and resurrection. The gospel, rightly spoken, involves no ifs, ands, buts, or maybes of any sort. It does not say, "If you do your best to live a good life, God will fulfill that life," or, "If you fight on the right side of the issues of your time ...," or, "If you repent ..." or, "If you believe ..." It does not even say, "If you *want* to do good/repent/believe ..." The gospel says, "Because the Crucified lives as Lord, your destiny is good." The Reformation's first and last assertion was that any talk of Jesus and God and human life that does not transcend all conditions is a perversion of the gospel and will be at best irrelevant ... and at worst destructive.[24]

Given the diversity of Christian interpretations regarding the Gospel, even within the Lutheran tradition,[25] what are the grounds for such a claim?

22. Bayer, *Martin Luther's Theology*, 114.
23. Bayer, *Theology the Lutheran Way*, 138.
24. Gritsch and Jenson, *Lutheranism*, 42.

25. In terms of alternative Lutheran positions to the confessional one, Wolfhart Pannenberg and the later Robert Jenson (in sympathy with the Finnish Mannermaa school of Luther studies) are prime examples. Pannenberg rejects the law/Gospel distinction as epochally outdated, insisting instead that the Gospel is best understood eschatologically as the final consummation of God's plan. Jenson, while holding

The Gospel as Promise of God

I wish to argue, as Gritsch and Jenson do, that a Lutheran claim for the Gospel as promise is rightly understood only when it is taken as an ecumenical proposal regarding the proper conditions for the language game Christians call "gospel." Building on Wittgenstein's insight that the meaning of words is largely contingent upon the specific conditions and setting in which they are used, and therefore the same word can have radically different meanings if it is used in different contexts, a confessional Lutheran proposal for the meaning of "gospel" insists that gospel is only truly, authentically gospel under certain, specific conditions of usage, namely the conditions specified by the category of promise.[26] In Wittgenstein's language, I will argue that, for the "Gospel game" to be played in a manner which is congruent with and faithful to its usage and intent in Scripture, the "rule of promise" must be followed. By confessional Lutheran standards: if one plays a game by rules other than "promise," one may be playing an interesting and even important game; however, rather than "doing the gospel," one is playing a different language game.

Proposing the Gospel as promise is a linguistic proposal about the necessary, fundamental conditions for any Gospel talk to remain truly Gospel. In framing a Lutheran approach as an ecumenical proposal rather than as a specific doctrine or dogma, my goal is to avoid the pitfall of a hierarchy of truths and ecumenical arguments over which doctrine or dogma is most centrally important. As Gritsch and Jenson put it: "If justification were a content-item of the gospel, along with other content-items, the question of which was 'most important' would always be a matter of silly debate. But the doctrine is instead an attempt to state the minimal identifying characteristics of the language-activity we call 'gospel.'"[27]

---

to his earlier view that "The Gospel is a promise," now insists that ". . . the gospel promises inclusion in the triune community by virtue of union with Christ . . . That is . . . deification" (*Systematic Theology Vol.* 2, 309, 311). While Mannermaa's Finnish school and Jenson diligently attempt to ground such a theosis view of salvation and the Gospel in Luther's writings, I find such efforts to be an unconvincing critique of the confessional Lutheran view of the Gospel as the promise of divine mercy and external word of forgiveness of sins for Christ's sake. For a fuller engagement with the Finnish school's critique of the law/Gospel distinction, see "Critical Appraisal of the Law/Gospel Distinction" at the end of this chapter.

26. Gritsch and Jenson argue this point in the first chapter of *Lutheranism: The Theological Movement and Its Confessional Writings*, entitled "An Ecumenical Proposal for Dogma."

27. Gritsch and Jenson, *Lutheranism*, 43.

In other words: for Lutheran theology, the Gospel as promise, rather than being one content item among many others in the Christian faith, is actually the only article of faith, the "article upon which the Church stands or falls."[28] Furthermore, because the Gospel is best understood as promise in contrast to the law, Lutheran theology submits the law/Gospel distinction as indispensable for rightly understanding the Gospel and for properly interpreting Scripture. This understanding of the hermeneutical function of Gospel as promise frees Lutherans from claiming a particular, sectarian view of the Gospel. Instead, it frees this tradition by opening it to the many, varied, and rich contributions from the rest of the Christian family. While the Lutheran tradition has some specific things to say about what the *object* of the Gospel promise is—namely justification by grace through faith, the forgiveness of sins, the offer of divine mercy for Christ's sake, etc.—the very formulation and understanding of the Gospel as "promise of X" prevents the Lutheran tradition from sectarianism. Instead, it continues to insist that, whatever one proposes to designate as the *object* of divine promise, all such proposals should be congruent with the overarching, promissory trajectory of Scripture.

THE GOSPEL AS PROMISE IN LUTHER

When we turn to Luther's writings and the Lutheran Confessions as sources, one prominent, indisputable feature of both is that they are saturated with references to the Gospel as promise. "Promise" occurs throughout the *Book of Concord*, 378 times in 82 of its articles. In terms of Luther's massive corpus, occurrences of "promise" number literally in the tens of thousands, including 2901 times in his lectures on Genesis alone! While not all of these references are to the Gospel, the overwhelming majority of them are, indicative of the intimate linkage between Gospel and promise for both Luther and the Lutheran Confessions. In other words: for Luther and the confessions, "the Gospel" and "promise" are practically synonymous terms, and "promise" is by far the most prevalent, comprehensive term for describing both the form and the content of the Gospel. We now turn to a closer examination of how both Luther and the Lutheran Confessions utilize the category of promise to articulate the

---

28. The twenty-eight articles of the *Augsburg Confession* can validly be interpreted as expressions of how various articles of Christian faith and practice relate to the Gospel as promise, analogous to how the spokes on a wheel connect to the hub.

The Gospel as Promise of God

nature, form, and content of the Gospel, starting first with Luther himself before moving to the Lutheran Confessions.

Positing the category of promise as central to Luther's thought requires a rationale and defense from Luther's own writings. Luther himself clearly stated in his *Preface to the Complete Edition of Luther's Latin Writings* (1545) that something happened which alleviated his terror and freed him, producing such a radical turning point and change of direction that it could only be described by the language of being born again and entering paradise.[29] While most scholars identify this breakthrough as the "reformational" turning point in Luther's thought, "what remains [unclear and] contested [is] . . . exactly which of those early perceptions can be identified as that specifically new way of thinking that he mentions in the preface."[30] While scholars remain in disagreement over an early dating versus a later dating for this reformational breakthrough, all seem to agree on the necessity of paying close attention to Luther's personal testimony and of making a textual argument for what the "reformational" breakthrough might be.

Conventional wisdom dictates that what was "reformational" in Luther's thought, as his distinctively unique contribution, was his new discovery of the meaning of "the righteousness of God" (*iustitia Dei*) in Rom 1:17, namely the contrast between God's own righteousness whereby God justly punishes sinners, versus *iustitia Dei* as the gift righteousness whereby God justifies the ungodly. Designating Luther's changing understanding of *iustitia Dei* as his reformational breakthrough, however, is problematic in at least two ways: 1) it fails to adequately recognize how the centrality of Luther's personal testimony in the Preface is tempered and relativized by his writings elsewhere, especially the passages on promise; and 2) Luther's various expositions of Rom 1:17, the classic text on *iustitia Dei*, show too much variation (even contradiction?) to definitively articulate his understanding of the phrase, beyond general observations of its origin in Augustine's thought.[31] The phrase "righteousness of God" is, however, valuable in terms of serving as shorthand or an abbreviation for the relationship between promise and faith. We will turn to examine that relationship momentarily.

---

29. Luther, *Luther's Works*, 5:157–8.
30. Bayer, *Martin Luther's Theology*, 47.
31. Ibid., 48.

Mission Shaped by Promise

I wish to argue that the silver thread unifying Luther's thought, from his earliest writings through his latest, is the category of *promissio Dei*. Two texts stand out in particular in this regard, serving as bookends to Luther's prolific career. First, the earliest text written from the perspective of *promissio Dei* is Luther's fifty theses in the disputation *For the Investigation of Truth and for the Comfort of Troubled Consciences* (1518). In discussing the sacrament of penance, these theses anticipate the discussion of promise in *The Babylonian Captivity of the Church* (1520).[32] Secondly, near the end of his career, around the same time that he wrote the earlier mentioned Preface, Luther specifically mentioned what he considered to be new and "reformational" in his thinking. Rather than being the righteousness of God (*iustitia Dei*) or some other particular doctrine, Luther identified the recovery of the *promissio Dei* in all its clarity and power as the distinctively new element in his thought. In his lectures on Genesis, interpreting the story of Joseph in Gen 48:20–21, he wrote: "Formerly . . . it was by no means customary to speak of a Word or promise. And I give thanks to God that I may live at this time, when this word "promise" resounds in my ears and in the ears of all the godly. For he who hears the Word easily understands the divine promise, which was obscure and unknown to all the theologians throughout the papacy."[33]

Something extremely practical and important for lived Christian experience is at stake in positing the promise of God as central to understanding the Gospel, namely the assurance of salvation. It is precisely the understanding of the Gospel as promise and its direct result, the assurance of salvation, which was a prominent, if not the chief, point of contention in the disputation between Luther and Cajetan in 1518. Relating the *promissio Dei* and faith in such a way as to guarantee the assurance of salvation as something external to oneself, grounded in the person and work of Christ, is thus central to Luther's theological agenda. Later we will examine how, for the Lutheran Confessions, these practical, pastoral concerns constitute a central feature of the argument of the *Augsburg Confession Apology to Article IV* concerning the Gospel as promise. For now, we turn to examine this practical relationship in greater detail in Luther's writings.

Oswald Bayer, in *Promissio: Geschichte der reformatorischen Wende in Luthers Theologie*, has forcefully argued how, for Luther, the relation of

---

32. Ibid., 49.
33. Luther, *Luther's Works*, 8:192.

promise and faith is both theologically central and rooted in the person and work of Christ, resulting in the assurance of salvation. In analyzing Luther's commentary on such diverse scriptural texts as Genesis, the Psalms, Romans, Hebrews, and the Gospels, Bayer shows how, for Luther, the category of *promissio Dei* became a silver thread unifying and making sense of the divine-human relationship. More specifically, in trying to understand the proper relation between promise and faith (Rom 4:4), Luther came to realize that God's promise of mercy, for Christ's sake, is the key to understanding, not only the nature of human faith, but also God's truthfulness and faithfulness in relation to humanity. For Luther, "*misericordia* and *veritas* join together—the mercy of God and the fulfillment of His promise—and meet in the person of Christ. Both terms Luther understands . . . in a salvation-historical, incarnational sense."[34] In other words: all God's promises throughout Scripture find their ultimate fulfillment and meaning in Christ, and it is precisely in and through Christ that God demonstrates both his faithfulness and truthfulness; not through power and glory, but through humble suffering and mercy. By fulfilling his promises in Christ, the assurance of human salvation is safeguarded and guaranteed.

I concur with Bayer in claiming that, while not always an explicit theme or category, the notion of promise provides the clearest, most comprehensive perspective through which to understand Luther's unique, "reformational" contribution. Bayer states:

> . . . it is necessary to examine what is "reformational" [in Luther's thought] on the basis of understanding what is meant by promise, so that one should understand the formulas that have been referred to in Luther's reflections within this framework, even when they do not specifically use the key term *promissio* . . . the concept of promise has come to the fore clearly enough and specifically enough to be used as the criterion [for defining what is "reformational"].[35]

---

34. Bayer, *Promissio*, 117. Translated by Jukka Kääriäinen.
35. Bayer, *Martin Luther's Theology*, 49.

THE GOSPEL AS PROMISE IN THE LUTHERAN CONFESSIONS: ISSUES AT STAKE

Having noted how Gospel as promise is a central, unifying motif in Luther's thought, we now return to a more in-depth treatment of the significant issues at stake in claiming the Gospel as promise, grounding this discussion in the Lutheran Confessions. It is imperative to keep in mind the practical intention of the Lutheran Confessions. Having experienced the Gospel as promise, the authors proceed to articulate the doctrinal implications of that experience and conviction. Their thoroughly practical motivation will be demonstrated in the rest of this chapter. The following five issues are at stake and fundamentally shaped by the claim that the Gospel is *promissio Dei*: the nature of God, human nature, the nature of faith (in general and justifying faith specifically), pastoral concerns of lived Christian experience, and the law-Gospel distinction as a hermeneutical approach which serves the Gospel promise by both safeguarding it and clarifying the content of Scripture.

The God of Promise

Not only is the Gospel itself a promise, but the very nature of God as the God of covenant faithfulness who makes and keeps His promises is crucially important. Jesus Christ is the very promise of God incarnate, in whom "No matter how many promises God has made, they are 'Yes' in Christ."[36] This view of a personal, promissory God creates a dialogical relationship between believer and God, one in which the person can confront, question, challenge, remind, and hold God accountable to God's own promises.

"The gospel, in anyone's version, is a promise that our life will be fulfilled by Christ."[37] Ronald Thiemann further specifies this Lutheran claim in terms of the nature of God: "God is identified primarily as the *God of promise* whose promises receive *narrative enactment and fulfillment* in the history of Israel and in the life, death, and resurrection of Jesus."[38]

---

36. 2 Cor 1:20.

37. Gritsch and Jenson, *Lutheranism*, 38.

38. Thiemann, *Revelation and Theology*, 100. In this book, Thiemann explores the particular, narrative form and content of the Gospel as promise, arguing how the logic of such form and content necessitate a view of God as prevenient in grace. Gerhard Sauter has elaborated a similar argument.

The Gospel as Promise of God

Thiemann demonstrates how, for Lutheran theology, promise-making and promise-keeping as constitutive of God's identity is a centrally unifying motif in interpreting Scripture. Not only is God identified as Yahweh, the God of promise, but this God who is the Father of Jesus Christ is uniquely prevenient in fulfilling his intentions for humanity:

> As God of promise, Yahweh is the one who specified his intention to save through his prophets, who designated Jesus' death and resurrection as the acts whereby he would enact his intention, who in his declared unity with Jesus identified himself as Father and undertook the obligation implied in his promise, and who, when he raised Jesus from the dead, uniquely fulfilled the conditions of his own promise. God as identified in Matthew's narrative is alone the gracious initiator, actor, and fulfiller of his own promises.[39]

A Lutheran Christocentric, promissory view of the Gospel naturally lends itself to a typological view of Scripture as promise and fulfillment. For example, the case study of Abraham wrestling with the promise of God (Gen 15–17) and Paul's analysis of the fulfillment of that promise in Jesus Christ (Rom 4) provides one concrete, scriptural example of God's identity as faithful promise-keeper and the central motif of promise and fulfillment. As God swears an oath of fidelity to his covenant promises to Abraham, God unilaterally seals this covenant promise by passing through the severed halves of animals alone in Abraham's strange vision (Gen 15:12–21). This signifies that "the fulfillment of God's promise of salvation . . . will not depend on them, but on *God*, who assumes the curses of his own covenant should the promise fail to be realized."[40]

Apology IV identifies the divine, promissory character of this account: "Abraham realized that he had a gracious God only on account of God's promise. He assented to the promise and . . . realized that God keeps a promise on account of his faithfulness, not on account of our works or merits."[41] In analyzing this covenant with and promise to Abraham, St Paul notes how the category of promise applies *both* to God's promissory character *and* to the required response of hope and trust: "Therefore, the promise comes by faith, so that it may be by grace and may be guaranteed . . . [Abraham] did not waver through unbelief regarding the promise of

---

39. Thiemann, *Revelation and Theology*, 137.
40. Horton, *The Gospel-Driven Life*, 136.
41. Kolb and Wengert, *Book of Concord*, 129.

God, but was strengthened in his faith and gave glory to God, being fully persuaded that God had power to do what he had promised."[42]

While much more could be said regarding God's identity and character as the God of promise, Bayer stresses how God's concrete words of Gospel promise and comfort underscore the identity of God as the faithful promise-maker worthy of human trust: "'God' is grasped as the one who in the oral word promises himself to a person in such a way that this one can rely on him. God's truth lies in his faithfulness, with which he stands to his given word."[43] The pastoral significance of this emphasis will be underscored later. For now, let us note that emphasizing God's promissory nature from both Scripture and the Lutheran Confessions leads Lutheran theology to affirm as a vitally important theological task "simply analyzing the form and content of God's promises, which serve as the ground of Christian faith and hope."[44]

Humans as Trusting Creatures

What is at stake for the Gospel as promise in Lutheran anthropology? In contrast to Karl Rahner's foundational, transcendental anthropology (elaborated in chapter 3), a Lutheran anthropology centers on the nature of humans as fundamentally trusting creatures. Faith as trust is a constant, inescapable feature of our daily experience. We trust that the buildings we live and work in are structurally sound and will not collapse on us, that our car or public transportation will reliably get us where we need to go, that our means of communication (from the postal service to cell phones and the internet) will facilitate our communication needs. More relevantly to my argument, we trust that our loved ones, colleagues, and others are dependable, honest, and trustworthy. Not only do we live our lives often implicitly, unreflectively trusting in others to be there for us, to do what they say they're going to do—in other words, to keep their promises, personal or contractual—but our very lives depend on God being faithful and trustworthy.

In terms of a Lutheran view of human nature, all humans trust in some source to deliver ultimate meaning and fulfillment to their lives. We all inevitably "hang our heart on" something or someone which promises

---

42. Rom 4:16a, 20–21.
43. Bayer, "Martin Luther as an Interpreter of Holy Scripture," 77.
44. Thiemann, *Revelation and Theology*, 96.

The Gospel as Promise of God

to fulfill our lives. Luther's view of what constitutes a 'god' captures this dynamic: "Therefore, to have a god is nothing else than to trust and believe in that one with your whole heart . . . it is the trust and faith of the heart alone that make both God and idol."[45] The key question then becomes the nature of the promise(s) one is trusting, and whether or not those promise(s) are trustworthy and can actually deliver what they promise.

The Logic of the Lutheran Argument

Before delving into the next three issues—the nature of faith, pastoral concerns of lived Christian experience, and the law/Gospel distinction—and demonstrating how, for the Lutheran Confessions and Luther, an inner logic intertwines them, we are now well positioned to delineate the key features of the overarching Lutheran argument on Gospel as promise.

I will now unfold the argument of Luther and the Lutheran Confessions concerning the Gospel as promise in a series of theses. In doing so, I hope to clarify and unpack the core meaning of the Reformation "solas": *sola gratia, solus Christus, sola fide*. 1) The righteousness of God that Luther rediscovered was a gift righteousness, the righteousness of God himself rather than a righteousness humans must produce themselves. Humans are saved by God's grace alone (*sola gratia*). 2) This gift righteousness is on account of Christ (*propter Christum*, or *solus Christus*). 3) As indicated earlier, the mode by which this free gift of grace becomes my possession is the promised faithfulness of God, which in turn evokes my trust (*sola fide*). 4) Therefore, for Luther and the Lutheran Confessions, "righteousness of God," "justification by grace through faith," "forgiveness of sins," and "promise of mercy fulfilled on account of Christ" are practically synonymous terms and are used interchangeably. 5) As the Gospel itself, the apostolic Word of God is a central means of grace, the vehicle whereby the promised gift is transmitted to people and the benefits of Christ reach their intended goal. 6) Because Christ himself is the Lord and center of the Scriptures, this promissory Word of God centers on the person and work of Christ. 7) This Gospel promise of Christ is received and appropriated through faith, as the Word of God reaches people in its written, oral, and sacramental forms. In conclusion: the basic Lutheran

---

45. Kolb and Wengert, *Book of Concord*, 386.

conviction is that "the ultimate Word of God is promise and therefore must be present in the written Word."[46]

Building on what has come before, I will now explicate what is at stake for the Gospel as promise in each of the remaining three issues: the nature of faith, pastoral concerns, and the law/Gospel distinction. While I will selectively employ Luther's own writings and other parts of the Lutheran Confessions, in arguing my case I will mainly employ the Apology IV due to its unsurpassed rhetorical force and clarity in relating these issues. I will demonstrate how the Gospel as promise is at stake in each of these issues, and how, as for Paul in his argument in Rom 4, this entails a view of the entire Scriptures as centering on Christ the *promissio Dei*.

Faith as Trust in the Gospel Promise of God

As we noted earlier, human beings are fundamentally "trusting creatures." We live by faith, whether we like it or not, trusting in various promises. Lutheran theology insists first of all that, for such human faith to be specifically Christian in nature, it must be "trust in the mercy promised on account of Christ" (*fiducia misericordiae promissae propter Christum*).[47] Rather than mere intellectual knowledge of the historical facts of the life of Jesus, Christian faith is fundamentally "assent to [trust in] the promise of God, in which forgiveness of sins and justification are bestowed freely on account of Christ."[48] Apology IV describes the relationship between the Gospel and faith in terms of offer and reception: "For faith saves, because it takes hold of mercy or the promise of grace," and "as often as mercy is mentioned, it must be understood that faith is required."[49] Repeatedly, Apology IV reiterates that "the promise cannot be grasped in any other way than by faith."[50]

Secondly, the very nature of a promise requires an attitude and response of trust for the promise to become actualized. As Edward Schroeder states, "The Christ-gospel is a promise, not a doctrine, a promise from God. All promises—Christ's too—don't "work" just because they

---

46. Schroeder, "Is There a Lutheran Hermeneutic?," 118.
47. Elert, *Structure of Lutheranism*, 108.
48. Kolb and Wengert, *Book of Concord*, 128.
49. Ibid., 168, 167.
50. Ibid., 127, 134, 139.

are held to be true and given assent. No, all promises, both human and divine, call for trust."[51]

Not only is Christian faith defined by trust in the promise of loving mercy in Christ, but, thirdly, such faith gains a freeing certainty because it is based solely on the external reality of God's promised faithfulness. Because "I cannot give the promise to myself. It must be given to me,"[52] and because of the covenant faithfulness of the divine promise-maker, faith can rest assured. As Luther states in his *Large Commentary on Galatians,* "And this is the reason why our theology is certain; it snatches us away from ourselves and places us outside ourselves, so that we do not depend on our own strength, conscience, experience, person, or works but depend on *that which is outside ourselves, that is, on the promise and truth of God, which cannot deceive.*"[53] Jorg Bauer further emphasizes how trust in the external Word of promise in Christ transforms human existence: "This transfer of the human ground of existence into Christ and into the triune [God] happens *"solo verbo,"* through God who always comes in a concrete way as one who addresses and makes promises, who takes away from the person the trust that he had up to this point that was grounded in the self and thus awakens faith . . ."[54]

Pastoral Issues Involved in the Gospel as Promise

For Luther and the Lutheran Confessions, especially in Apology IV, the struggle for the truth about God was never merely an abstract, academic exercise, it was inextricably linked to an understanding of the theological task as the practical outworking of the relational matrix of "the sinning human being and the justifying God."[55] In the opening argument of Ap. IV, the Lutheran confessors forcefully lay out two pastoral concerns related to lived Christian experience at stake in claiming the Gospel as promise. Positively stated, the first concern is the Gospel's practical ability to comfort troubled consciences, that which "brings the abundant consolation that devout consciences need."[56] Negatively stated, obscuring the

51. Schroeder, "Luther's Missiology," lines 34–37.
52. Bayer, "Martin Luther as an Interpreter of Holy Scripture," 76.
53. Luther, *Luther's Works,* 27:387. Italics added for emphasis.
54. Quoted in Bayer, *Martin Luther's Theology,* 236–7.
55. Bayer, *Martin Luther's Theology,* 29.
56. Kolb and Wengert, *Book of Concord,* 121.

Gospel as promise leads one to "tear away from devout consciences the consolation offered them in Christ."[57] Luther's *For the Inquiry into Truth and for the Comfort of Troubled Consciences* (1518) already reflected this concern.

The second, more systematically comprehensive concern, was for the Gospel specifically and Christian discourse more generally to "illumine and magnif[y] the honor of Christ" rather than "obscure the glory and benefits of Christ."[58] The Gospel as promise, according to the Lutheran confessors, has an irreducibly practical goal and concern: that the benefits and merits of Christ be put to use rather than wasted. As Melanchthon put it, "To know Christ is to know His benefits," or "In this way commendations of works and the law must be understood, so as not to detract from the glory [benefits] of Christ and the gospel."[59] Melanchthon repeatedly echoes this concern: "for how will Christ be mediator if we do not *use* him as mediator in our justification?" "The Gospel . . . compels us *to make use of* Christ in justification." "Christ's glory becomes brighter when we teach people *to make use of* him as mediator and propitiator."[60] In other words: receiving and appropriating the Gospel as promise helps people "use" and apply the benefits of Christ, while overlooking the Gospel as promise "buries" and "wastes" these benefits of Christ. "So what he [the Christian] needs to have, and what God wants him to receive from the Scriptures, is help on how to *use* Christ."[61] If "systematic theology is [indeed] for proclamation,"[62] then the (Aristotelian) final cause or goal of such theology must always be to deliver the Gospel as a comforting, reassuring promise of divine mercy for Christ's sake, utilizing his benefits.

After introducing the twin pastoral concerns of comforting troubled consciences and making use of the benefits of Christ in Apology IV, the Lutheran confessors go on to show how the law/Gospel distinction is an indispensable tool for addressing these concerns. As the *Formula of Concord, Solid Declaration*, Article V "Concerning Law and Gospel" puts it:

> The distinction between law and gospel is a particularly glorious light. It serves to divide God's Word properly [cf. 2 Tim 2:15]

57. Ibid.
58. Ibid.
59. Ibid., 149.
60. Ibid., 131ff.
61. Schroeder, "Is There a Lutheran Hermeneutic?," 118.
62. Forde, *Theology is For Proclamation*, 1.

and to explain correctly and make understandable the writings of the holy prophets and apostles. Therefore, we must diligently preserve this distinction, so as not to mix these two teachings and make the gospel into a law. For this obscures the merit of Christ and robs troubled consciences of the comfort that they otherwise have in the gospel when it is preached clearly and purely. With the help of this distinction these consciences can sustain themselves in their greatest spiritual struggles against the terror of the law.[63]

In other words: the *purpose* of the law/Gospel distinction *directly addresses* the pastoral concerns, it is absolutely necessary in order for troubled consciences to be comforted, the benefits of Christ to be fully used, and the Gospel as promise to be clearly preserved. Therefore, the Gospel as promise necessitates a particular hermeneutical approach to Scripture in order that the promise is not lost or "buried," but rather highlighted, utilized, and applied. That is why the law/Gospel hermeneutic is indispensable; I will now clarify how it serves the Gospel as promise.

How the Law/Gospel Distinction Serves the Gospel as Promise

What is at stake in positing the law/Gospel distinction as indispensable for understanding the Gospel as promise? While non-Lutherans readily understand the Lutheran emphasis on the Gospel as promise, based on abundant scriptural evidence, they often puzzle why Lutheran theology insists upon the law/Gospel distinction as being intrinsically related to that Gospel promise. I will now seek to address this confusion. First of all, the Lutheran claim is that the Gospel is fully understood as promise only as it is distinguished from the law; therefore the law/Gospel distinction is crucial for getting the Gospel right. Secondly, the law/Gospel distinction, as a living, dynamic tension and hermeneutic, clarifies God's dual mission and promises throughout the Scriptures. As Apology IV insists, "All Scripture should be divided into these two main topics: the law and the promises. In some places it communicates the law. In other places it communicates the promise concerning Christ . . . We acknowledge that in some places Scripture presents the law and in other places it presents the gospel, the free promise *of the forgiveness of sins* on account of Christ."[64]

---

63. Kolb and Wengert, *Book of Concord*, 581.
64. Ibid., 121, 150.

Mission Shaped by Promise

The Law/Gospel Distinction Defined

For Luther and the Lutheran Confessions, the law and the Gospel are diametrically opposed. In stark contrast to the law, which accuses and leads to a knowledge of sin, the Gospel comes to us as a "second, decisive, final, [utterly] different Word of God,"[65] one in which God speaks on our behalf and for us (*pro nobis*), being on our side. Gritsch and Jenson offer an insightful description of how radically different the promise (Gospel) is from the law, highlighting its freeing, unconditional, and future dimensions:

> The "law" is the totality of all human communication, insofar as what we say to each other functions in our lives as *demand*, or, what is the same, poses the future *conditionally*. Literal laws say, "If you do such-and-such, such-and-such will happen" . . . The direct counterpole to "law" is "promise." If law-communication imposes an "If . . . then . . ." structure on life, a promise grants the pattern "Because . . . therefore . . ." The trouble is that . . . our promises are implicitly conditional; for by every promise I commit my future, and my future is not altogether mine to commit. Death can always take it from me and turn my promises into law just when they are most needed. "The gospel" is the Reformation label for that promise which, if true at all, is unconditional: the promise made in the name of one who has already satisfied the condition of death and therefore has all the future in his gift . . . The gospel tolerates no conditions. It is itself unconditional promise. Law and gospel are God's ways of dealing with the world . . . The law reveals sin, the gospel discloses salvation. They *appear* to be two distinct forces . . . yet the "mask" of history hides the one God behind both. Thus law and gospel are the ways in which God reveals himself as the god who justifies the ungodly.[66]

Rather than an abstract, a-historical principle, the law/gospel distinction seeks to capture the tension and ambiguity of God's concrete speech to humanity, God's specific dealings with humanity, as well as the deeply interpersonal, inextricably intertwined nature of the divine-human relationship. Having articulated its hermeneutical significance for interpreting Scripture, we now turn to appreciate its fundamental significance for an economy of salvation.

---

65. Bayer, *Martin Luther's Theology*, 61.
66. Gritsch and Jenson, *Lutheranism*, 43–44, 48.

The Gospel as Promise of God

First of all, the law/Gospel distinction corresponds to a New Testament testimony concerning the dual, two-fold nature of divine revelation. A few, brief examples are in order. As the prologue to John's Gospel puts it: "For the law was given through Moses; grace and truth were given through Jesus Christ (John 1:17)." In Rom 3, Paul contrasts the nature of the gospel as a gift of righteousness, appropriated by faith, as distinct from the law bearing witness to it: "But now a righteousness from God, apart from law, has been made known, to which the Law and the Prophets testify. This righteousness from God comes through faith in Jesus Christ to all who believe. There is no difference, for all have sinned and fall short of the glory of God."[67]

Such a two-fold revelation has been variously described as "natural" knowledge of God versus faith's knowledge of God, the law of creation vs. the gospel of Christ, and the distinction between revelation and salvation.[68] The significance of this distinction for the purposes of revelation is that it affirms genuine, divine revelation throughout creation and in the world's religions (contra Barth),[69] while insisting on Christ's singularity as God's instrument of salvation for all. In doing so, it holds in creative tension the universality of revelation, on the one hand, and the uniqueness of Christ, on the other. As Carl Braaten puts it: "Jesus Christ is sole Savior, not the sole revealer."[70]

Secondly, law and gospel are diametrically opposed realities, deeply resistant to both coordination as two different phases of a historical sequence (the law pertaining to the Old Testament, but now superseded by the Gospel in the New Testament) and a dialectical, complementary relationship (contra Barth). Although in Scripture the concept "revelation"

---

67. Rom 3:21–23.

68. Various Lutheran theologians have subscribed to this basic schema of revelation in varying forms, including J. C. Hoffman, C. H. Ratschow, Nathan Söderblom, Oscar Cullmann, Paul Althaus, Paul Tillich, Wolfhart Pannenberg, Carl Braaten, and Edward Schroeder, to name but a few. It should be noted that, while all subscribe to the formulation of distinguishing revelation from salvation, some (such as Pannenberg) object to the law-gospel distinction as the most helpful articulation of this distinction. Pannenberg's concerns center on his view that the law-gospel distinction has become outdated and is no longer relevant in the postmodern world, assuming a sense of guilt which postmodern people largely dismiss.

69. Karl Barth's view of the Christian Gospel as being diametrically opposed to and standing in judgment of human religion in its various forms is articulated, among other places, in his "The Revelation of God as the Abolition of Religions," in *Church Dogmatics* 1/2, 280–361.

70. Braaten, *Justification*, 77.

is used of both, this should not be construed as suggesting that they are complementary or the same, and therefore not contradictory in their message and function. As Elert puts it, "The term revelation cannot eliminate the contrast between law and Gospel, cannot even bridge it, even when understood exclusively as the becoming revealed of God."[71] Instead, both law and Gospel are enduring realities that have applied to the divine-human relationship through all ages, whereby people live life either under the law or under the Gospel.[72] As two opposite revelations, law and Gospel stand in substantive, dialectical opposition to each other, saying opposite things about the same subject: "When the one is revealed, the other is veiled; and when the second shines forth, the first one is darkened."[73]

Thirdly, in each of these two words, important, opposing realities in both God and humanity are correlated, affirming the inevitable, mutual entanglement of God and humanity: "Wrath and grace become revealed in God, sin and faith in man . . . The revelation of God's wrath corresponds with the revelation of man's sin, the revelation of his grace with the revelation of man's faith . . . This also demonstrates the contrast between law and Gospel . . . two things become manifest both in God and in man, which contradict each other, wrath and grace in God, sin and faith in man. With regard to both we must thus speak of a twofold revelation."[74]

A Confessional Lutheran View of the Law

Moving from the law/Gospel distinction to elaborating the divine law, confessional Lutheran theology makes a fundamental distinction between the first use of the law (the "civil" law which all must obey or face punishment) and its second, properly theological use of illuminating a knowledge of sin and accusing of sin.[75] Such a fundamental, two-fold

---

71. Elert, *Christian Faith*, 87.

72. In his various writings (*The Christian Faith, The Christian Ethos, Law and Gospel, The Structure of Lutheranism*), Werner Elert contrasts these two states of being as "ethos under law" versus "ethos under grace."

73. Elert, *Christian Faith*, 88.

74. Ibid., 87–88.

75. From its earliest days, Lutheran theology has debated whether or not there is a "third use" of the law: whether the law, in the form of moral guidance, applies to Christians, or whether its use is restricted to convicting the sinful self of sin. While

The Gospel as Promise of God

understanding of the divine law leads Lutheran theology to affirm the divine law as a universal existential, as permeating all creation. This means that a certain kind of naming of God makes sense universally across all human experience: one that identifies God as applying pressure against humans ambiguously with judgment in the midst of promise.[76] While contemporary people do not recognize the divine law as such, its influence is an inescapable feature of life. As Oswald Bayer describes it:

> Our contemporaries do not experience the law anymore as the law of God. Rather, the law is experienced as anonymous, or, in the best case scenario, as the "categorical imperative." A sense of inescapable duty weighing heavily on every human heart is revealed to us by this anonymous law. Duty becomes deadly when the law coincides with the gospel, when they are not distinguished from each other.[77]

---

traditionally Lutherans have affirmed the necessity of the third use of the law, Werner Elert (among others) has vehemently rejected the third use of the law. Elert insisted that the title of the *Formula of Concord*, Article VI, "Third Use of the Law," misrepresented the true intent and affirmation of that article. Instead, Elert asserted that, while the law rightly applied to and accused the "old sinful self" in Christians, the "new self" in Christ could and should only be governed by the Gospel. Elert understood the ethical imperatives in the New Testament as "grace imperatives," as invitations to live the Christian life in its radical freedom. For a fuller treatment of Elert's view, see his *The Christian Ethos*, 294–303. This debate continues within contemporary Lutheran theology.

76. I am cognizant that this claim is made from within a framework of "confessional ultimate reality." Catherine Cornille describes its nature well: "*The natural tendency of any religious tradition is to situate the origin or basis for interconnection between religions in their own particular conception of ultimate reality.* Religions indeed presuppose that the fullness of truth is concentrated in their own conceptions of ultimate reality and that whatever form or degree of truth is found elsewhere will be derived from or oriented toward this truth . . . And though it is true that such an understanding of other religions from within one's own conception of ultimate reality entails a certain degree of domestication of the other, it may fairly be said that *this is an inevitable condition of the irreducible particularity of all religious perspectives.* It is the recognition that . . . *each engages the other from within their own hermeneutical framework*, which forms the basis for the balanced and sincere exchange that occurs in genuine dialogue. Moreover, the fact that all religions enter dialogue *from a distinct understanding of how the truths of all religions cohere within their own perspective does not rule out considerable overlap between them even on the matter of ultimate reality itself . . .*" (*The Im-possibility of Interreligious Dialogue*, 127, 132–33, italics added for emphasis). My nuanced use of this perspective and its application to interreligious dialogue will be further articulated in chapter 6.

77. Bayer, "Justification as Basis and Boundary," 285.

Extending beyond mere moral legislation or prohibitions, such as the Decalogue, the divine law itself constitutes a further, three-fold structure in describing three, distinct orders through which God and humanity relate to one another. These three orders or connective spheres can be described as the orders of creation, the moral order, and judgment, wherein God relates to humanity as its creator/preserver, legislator, and judge, respectively.[78] Werner Elert delineates these orders, constituting life under the law:

> The divine law as a compulsory order contains different kinds of bonds. In the first place, as Creator and Ruler, God places man in distinct though different categories . . . In the second place, God acts as lawgiver . . . He issues commands and prohibitions. In this manner, rules- a system of "oughts" comes into existence. In the third place, God acts in a judicial capacity . . . like a human judge in a court of law . . . This makes for a system of qualitative judgments by which men are divided into just and unjust, saints and sinners. And perhaps they . . . all are assigned to the same category [of sinner]. This threefold bond constitutes ethos under law.[79]

First of all, by virtue of creation, God is the creator, source, and manager of our lives, whether or not people acknowledge it. As our creator, God gives us the gift of life and places us in specific contexts of space and time, plunging us into a multitude of relationships that we did not choose, which are simply given to us.

Second, God as the author of the moral order and "legislator" conveys expectations, commands, and guidelines for how we ought to live our lives as God's creatures. This places humanity under obligation to God, to fulfill such divine expectations and obey such commands. As Luther put it in his Small Catechism: "For all of this [the gifts of creation] I owe it to God to thank and praise, serve and obey Him."[80] The law as God's legislation reveals a vast web of expectations and obligations, grounded in the broader context of creation, to which humanity is inextricably bound.

Extending the previous two spheres, the third order connects God to humanity as its final judge, delivering an ultimate, total verdict upon our

---

78. Elert, *Christian Ethos*, 49–56.
79. Ibid., 56.
80. Kolb and Wengert, *Book of Concord*, 355.

lives.[81] As the language concerning forensic justification that Lutherans believe the New Testament makes clear, God as judge passes a sentence and verdict upon our lives. This juridical sphere reveals to sinners the ultimate value and worth of their lives: "God's law makes sin manifest. It makes man guilty."[82]

A confessional Lutheran claim regarding God's law asserts that, long before humans explicitly learn about the divine law and its functioning within these three spheres, they have already encountered the reality of it in the universal human experience of not being in complete control of their lives, of an external "other" opposing and controlling them, frustrating their plans by applying pressure upon their lives. Such a claim is made with epistemic humility and provisional certitude. Rather than naming it the divine law, contemporary people refer to this force in various terms: destiny, fate, karma, one's lot in life, etc. The revelation of divine law enters this experiential matrix, unveiling, specifying, and naming this ambiguous, elusive force as *God's* creative law effecting pressure. In addition, our self-assertive resistance and protest against this pressure is further revealed as rebellion and sin against God himself. Elert explains:

"[P]aradoxically, [God's] hiddenness becomes still darker to us when He is "revealed" to us in the Law. For this becoming revealed of God simultaneously marks the becoming revealed of man. It teaches that the power which forces us into our destiny is God himself, that our opposition to our fate . . . is opposition to God Himself, that we are thus forced into conflict with God, and that all of this together makes us guilty."[83]

Theologies which either overlook the significance of this accusatory function of the law, subsume the law under the gospel, or view the gospel as something other than the promise of mercy fulfilled, fail to sufficiently distinguish between law and gospel in three significant ways. First, while the divine law does promise blessings, such blessings are not unconditional but radically conditional. The prologue to the Decalogue makes this abundantly clear: "I the Lord your God . . . will show steadfast love to thousands of those who love me and keep my commandments" (Exod 20: 5-6). Paradoxically, "the law promises mercy to the righteous who have fulfilled it, the gospel to sinners who have not fulfilled it."[84] Sec-

---

81. Elert, *Christian Ethos*, 49–56.
82. Elert, *Christian Faith*, 183.
83. Ibid., 190.
84. Elert, *Law and Gospel*, 8.

ondly, the law not only promises blessings, but as a law of retribution it threatens punishment. This understanding of the Old Testament Torah is pervasive throughout Scripture. Not only is the law of retribution (Exod 21:24ff.) explicitly God's law, but the New Testament validates it as the valid, divine law (Rom 12:19, Heb 10:30ff., 2 Thess 1:8, Rev 6:10).[85] Life under this law of retribution is characterized by being under the curse and wrath of God (Gal 3:10, Rom 4:15). Thirdly, when the divine law is restrictively understood as merely moral law, as God's legislation and guidance for godly living, it is fundamentally misunderstood. The confessional Lutheran claim is that, in order to give full weight to the divine law and let it do its proper work, the law as legislation is always secondary to and serves the law's primary function of accusing of and judging sin.[86]

Highlighting and Accessing the Benefits of Christ

Having clarified the law/Gospel distinction and the functioning of divine law, we now turn to examine its intrinsic relationship to the Gospel as promise. Before doing so, it is helpful to clarify the interrelationship between the Gospel, promise, and faith. As our opening quote from Luther made clear, Lutheran theology posits an intrinsic relationship between the categories of Gospel, promise, and faith, which is this: The Gospel is a promise which requires faith (trust) in order to be received, in order for the benefits of Christ to be applied and used in a person's life.

Just as faith as trust is required to make full use of the benefits of the Gospel as promise, analogously, the law/Gospel distinction is required to read Scripture (i.e., the Biblical history and the history of Jesus) in such a way as to properly "use" that history for its intended purpose and not waste it. Melanchthon charged his opponents as doing precisely this: by obscuring the *sola fide,* they let Biblical history go to waste. When the *sola fide* is thus obscured, the Biblical history as the history of God's promises is wasted and there is no need for Christ. The law/Gospel distinction helps ensure that Scripture is read and understood as the history of God's promises overcoming God's law, as the history of the God who freely promises to justify the ungodly. Robert Bertram spells out how faith as trust in the Gospel promise and the law/Gospel distinction in

---

85. Ibid., 9.
86. Ibid.

reading Scripture share the same goal of highlighting and explicitly using the benefits of Christ:

> To have the promised Christ altogether by faith is the only way to "use" Him for what He historically was and is: the coming true of sheer merciful promise. Any other way than the *sola fide* is to render Him and His whole history "unnecessary." For what else was that whole long Biblical history, both fore and aft, but the history of God's *promissio*--not only His revealing of it but His making the promise and keeping it, historically—the historic judgments of His *lex* to the contrary notwithstanding? Throughout that Biblical history, as in human experience generally, promises are made to be trusted. Not only does faith need the promise, but as Melanchthon adds, the promise also needs faith. This is the only way to benefit from a promise at all and still honor it as the promise it is: by trusting the promissor's own goodness, especially when he is known to have no illusions about ours. To try instead to insure his promise by realizing it on our own is to make his promise needless.[87]

Melanchthon, in Apology IV, emphasizes the importance of which source one chooses as one's starting point in reading Scripture, the law or the Gospel. "Of these two topics," he says, "[our] opponents single out the law . . . and through the law they seek the forgiveness of sins and justification."[88] His concern is eminently practical: to preserve and highlight the Gospel promise so that consciences be comforted and Christ be used and glorified. If one starts with the law, one will inevitably lose and bury the Gospel promise. Only if one starts with the principle of promise can one properly appreciate, recognize, and utilize both law and promise. Edward Schroeder clarifies what is at stake in these competing hermeneutical approaches: "So a promise-centered hermeneutics opens up both the legal and the promissive material in Scripture. A Law-centered hermeneutics actually destroys both. Not only does it bury the Promise, but in burying the Promise it makes impossible the keeping of the Law as well. Thereby both words of God are wasted. In Melanchthon's recurrent phrase, they are 'in vain.'"[89] Melanchthon's answer to his opponents, by utilizing the law/Gospel distinction, is to "recover within that [Biblical] history its basic 'need' of having happened at all: Jesus Christ, God's

---

87. Bertram, "Hermeneutical Significance," 5.
88. Kolb and Wengert, *Book of Concord*, 121.
89. Schroeder, "Is There a Lutheran Hermeneutic?," 117.

promise kept, who is ours only by faith."[90] Only in this manner is the goal of the entire Scriptures, and the benefits of Christ in particular, properly realized and appropriated.

How the Law/Gospel Distinction Undergirds the Gospel as Promise

Building on the preceding definition of the law/Gospel distinction, a more systematic articulation of how the law/Gospel distinction is indispensable to the Gospel as promise is now called for. Seven main points clarify what is at stake in this relationship. First of all, the law/Gospel distinction protects and preserves the Gospel as unconditional promise. It addresses the central issue of whether the promise is being highlighted, promoted, and used, on the one hand, or whether it is being marginalized, hidden, and unused, on the other. Secondly, not only does the distinction preserve the purity of the Gospel, it also preserves the law and ensures that it always carries out its theological function of accusing of sin. The law always accuses (*lex semper accusat*). A failure to practice this distinction inevitably distorts the Gospel into law, while maintaining the distinction serves to clearly preserve the promissory, gratuitous nature of the Gospel. Furthermore, the distinction prevents the law from being eviscerated and shrunk into legalistic moralism by maintaining its theological function of accusing of sin. As Melanchthon reiterates, "For the law always accuses since we never satisfy the law," "the law always accuses them and brings wrath with it," and "there is no law which accuses us more . . . than this summary of the whole law, ''Love the Lord your God with all your heart.'"[91]

Thirdly, this dynamic is indispensable for identifying the benefits of Christ. As Melanchthon notes, "For one has to distinguish the promises from the law in order to recognize the benefits of Christ."[92] Helping ensure that these benefits of Christ are utilized and used rather than wasted, the law/gospel distinction directly addresses the second of pastoral concerns, that the benefits of Christ be put to use. Such identification and use of the benefits of Christ is never merely a one-time event, but rather a defining, enduring feature of the Christian life. On a confessional Lutheran view of the structure of existence, Christians need to continue to use Christ as

---

90. Bertram, "Hermeneutical Significance," 4.
91. Kolb and Wengert, *Book of Concord*, 148, 151, 154.
92. Ibid., 149.

The Gospel as Promise of God

mediator, they "need to learn how to let both the Law and the Promise move into the Christian life—the Law to expose those areas where his idolatry is still thriving, the Promise to have Christ take over those areas and have them function as sectors of redeemed creation."[93] Fourthly, this distinction helps clarify the nature of justifying faith. As the Law forces us to give up on our own efforts and righteousness, the Gospel directs us to faith as trust as the only means by which we "have" Christ and "use" Him for what He was and is—the Word and promise of God incarnate. Fifthly, it facilitates the comfort of troubled consciences. As mentioned earlier, "With the help of this distinction these consciences can sustain themselves in their greatest spiritual struggles against the terror of the law."[94] Sixthly, the law/Gospel distinction is an indispensible hermeneutic for ensuring that the scriptural history and the history of Jesus are read in such a way that they come out as the good news of promise, of God justifying the ungodly, by grace, through faith alone. Finally, as a practical summary and application of the preceding six reasons, the law/Gospel distinction enables Lutheran theology to properly commend good works without losing the promise. As Melanchthon puts it, "We must see what Scripture attributes to the law and what it attributes to the promises. For it praises *and teaches good works* in such a way as not to abolish the free promise *and not to eliminate Christ*."[95] Clarifying the role of the law/Gospel distinction in relation to the Gospel as promise will also lay the groundwork for spelling out its missiological implications later on.

THE LAW/GOSPEL DISTINCTION IN LUTHER AND THE LUTHERAN CONFESSIONS

Having examined how the law/Gospel distinction is a central feature of Apology IV's argument for the Gospel as promise, we now turn to document how this distinction is grounded, not merely in one, albeit the most centrally important, part of the Lutheran Confessions, but rather how it permeates Luther's theology and the rest of the Confessions as well. This claim will be further substantiated and clarified in chapter 2's discussion of a Lutheran theology of grace as promise of mercy realized. Oswald Bayer describes how the law/Gospel distinction functions as the

---

93. Schroeder, "Is There a Lutheran Hermeneutic?," 117.
94. Kolb and Wengert, *Book of Concord*, 581.
95. Ibid., 150.

Mission Shaped by Promise

"chromosomal structure" permeating Luther's thought and serving the Gospel as promise: "Luther's theology is too lively and too complex to be summarized by a single concept. It was not conceived a priori as a system, but maintains its internal coherence only because of the way it is concerned to articulate, at every stage, the dynamic that differentiates the gospel—the promise (*promissio*) of God—from the law. One might say that the interrelationship between law and gospel forms the chromosomal structure within every cell of Luther's theology."[96]

In a classic passage from *The Freedom of the Christian*, Luther elucidated both the irreducible difference between law and Gospel and how this distinction actualizes the Gospel, through faith in the promise, in Christians' lives:

> [T]he entire Holy Scripture is to be divided into two words: the commandments or the law of God and the assurances or the promises. The commandments teach and prescribe for us various good works . . . They indeed do give direction, but they do not help; they teach what a person ought to do, but furnish no power to make something occur . . . When the human being learns about and has discovered his own powerlessness on the basis of the commandments . . . He does not find anything in himself by means of which he can be righteous. Following upon this comes the other Word, the divine assurance and promise, which says: If you want to fulfill all the commandments . . . look here, believe in Christ, through whom I promise you all grace, righteousness, peace, and freedom. If you believe, you have it; if you do not believe, you do not have it: For what is impossible for you . . . is made simple and easy for you through faith . . . This is what the promises of God provide, what the commandments demand; they fulfill what the commandments demand, so that

---

96. Bayer. *Martin Luther's Theology*, xvii. The phrase "chromosomal structure" requires explanation. While Bayer identifies three foundational motifs in Luther's theology—Christian freedom, justification by grace through faith, and the distinction between law and Gospel—he argues that the law/Gospel distinction forms the central hub or touchstone which all other loci of Luther's theology relate to. Rather than being able to delineate Luther's thought in a linear progression, Bayer argues that all aspects of Luther's thought—whether it be Scripture, Christology, anthropology, ecclesiology, ethics, etc.—dynamically relate to the law/Gospel distinction. Similar to how the genetic code encapsulated in chromosomes finds ultimate expression in cells, likewise the law/Gospel distinction finds dynamic expression and application in the various dimensions and facets of Luther's theology.

everything is from God himself, both commandment and fulfillment. He alone commands; he alone also fulfills.[97]

What is true of Luther also applies to the Confessions as a whole: the theology of the Lutheran Confessions is permeated by the "chromosomal structure" (Bayer) of the Gospel as promise in contrast to the law. For instance, the *FCSD Article II* contrasts the preaching of the law with the preaching of the gospel: "[T]hrough the preaching of the law [people] feel real terror, regret, and sorrow in their hearts. Through the preaching of the holy gospel of the gracious forgiveness of sins in Christ and through meditating upon it, a spark of faith is ignited in them, and they accept the forgiveness of sins for Christ's sake and receive the comfort of the promise of the gospel. In this way the Holy Spirit, who effects all of this, is sent into their hearts."[98]

As noted earlier, the law/Gospel distinction has immensely practical implications for addressing pastoral concerns of lived Christian experience. Luther held the distinction between law and Gospel in the highest regard, viewing the ability to discern and practice this distinction as the mark of a true, practical theologian: "Therefore, whoever knows well how to distinguish the Gospel from the Law should give thanks to God and know that he is a real theologian."[99]

Interestingly, Luther identified this dynamic distinction, rather than understanding the righteousness of God, as his great Reformation discovery. In his *Table Talk*, Luther writes: "I learned to distinguish between the righteousness of the law and that of the gospel. Prior to that I lacked nothing except that I made no distinction between law and gospel. I considered them to be one and the same, and spoke of no difference between Christ and Moses except their location in historical time and (their different) degrees of perfection. But when I discovered the difference, that the law is one thing and the gospel is another, *that was my*

---

97. Luther, *Luther's Works*, 31:358ff.

98. Kolb and Wengert, *Book of Concord*, 554.

99. Luther, *Luther's Works*, 26:342. Interestingly, Luther understood the skill of distinguishing law and Gospel as a spiritual charism and gift, something which ultimately could only be cultivated by God's Spirit. As he put it, "There is no person on earth who rightly knows and understands how to distinguish between gospel and law . . . Only the Holy Spirit can work with this skill. It was even lacking for Christ in his human nature on the Mount of Olives, so that an angel had to comfort him . . . I would have thought with all certainty that I could do it, because I have written about it for such a long time and so often . . . Thus God alone ought to be and must be the most holy master and teacher" (*Luther's Works* 54:127).

breakthrough."¹⁰⁰ In other words: "For Luther, to do theology . . . meant constantly to distinguish between the history of salvation, heralded in the gospel, and the history of condemnation, proclaimed in the law." ¹⁰¹ Having examined the significance of the law/Gospel dynamic in relation to the Gospel as promise, we conclude this chapter by noting criticisms leveled against it and offering confessional Lutheran responses to such criticisms.

CRITICAL APPRAISAL OF THE LAW/ GOSPEL DISTINCTION

While confessional Lutheran theology views the law/Gospel distinction as indispensable for safeguarding the integrity of the Gospel as promise, it acknowledges and seeks to respond to criticisms of this distinction from Roman Catholic, Reformed, and even other Lutheran perspectives. I will now identify seven broad areas of critique, seeking to address them while mindful that a sufficiently robust response is beyond the limited scope of this study.

First, Lutheran theologian Wolfhart Pannenberg criticizes the law/Gospel distinction as being epochally outdated, rather than constitutive.¹⁰² Viewing justification as "a historical transition, the epochal succession of Mosaic law to apostolic parenesis within salvation history,"¹⁰³ Pannenberg claims: "The eschatological turn from law to gospel is not something that takes place again and again in the church in the pro-

---

100. Luther, *Luther's Works*, 54:442–3. Observing that Luther identifies this as his breakthrough does not negate the fact that the category of promise was comprehensively central to his thinking, as noted earlier. As I have argued in the preceding section, the law/Gospel distinction undergirds and serves the Gospel as promise. For Lutheran theology, the two are inextricably intertwined and mutually condition each other. The Gospel is ultimately Gospel as promise only in contrast to the law.

101. Gritsch and Jenson, *Lutheranism*, 48.

102. In Pannenberg's *Systematic Theology*, the treatment of law and gospel is separated from his treatment of justification by faith. His view of justification entails a historical transition from the Mosaic law to Spirit-led, parenetic love within salvation history. Such a position views law and gospel as epochally sequential: "As concerns the distinction between law and gospel, however, the finality of the turn that for Paul came with Christ's coming did not make its full impact because Luther, unlike Paul, viewed Christian life in the flesh as a life still subject to law. Paul precisely did not say that Christian life 'in the flesh' is still under the law. For him believers are already to let their earthly life be determined by the Spirit" (Pannenberg, *Systematic Theology* 3:86).

103. Mattes, *Role of Justification*, 59.

nouncing of forgiveness. It has taken place definitively [understood as God's eschatological future already present] in Jesus Christ."[104]

A confessional Lutheran response to Pannenberg is multifaceted. First, Pannenberg's prior commitment to metaphysical presuppositions that prioritizes transformation and his overall eschatological framework move him to critique Luther as having fundamentally misread Paul. "The Reformation failed to unfold the 'finality' of the eschatological turn in its implications for the theological understanding of law. Luther does not do justice to the breadth of the gospel. He individualizes Paul."[105] With this view, Pannenberg seems unable to sufficiently grapple with the Lutheran affirmation of *simul iustus et peccator*, classically grounded in Rom 7. Confessional Lutherans view Paul and Luther as "acknowledging the impact of a new cosmic reality upon an old . . . an interactive struggle between cosmic epochs that constantly impinges—personally, socially, and even in nature—upon our lives."[106] In addition to the "simultaneously saint and sinner" paradox, Pannenberg's approach, in affirming God *in se* as the object of theology, seemingly supplants faith understood as trusting God's promise with metaphysical theories for mapping the reality of God. In pursuing a theoretical delineation of the "intelligible transparency of all life in the triune life" within an overarching framework of the fulfillment of divine history, Pannenberg seems to subsume such central Lutheran categories as *simul iustus et peccator*, *deus absconditus*, and the hiddenness of the church under more pressing philosophical concerns.

Mark Mattes summarizes three ways confessional Lutheran theology critiques Pannenberg's objection to the law/Gospel dialectic:

> First, his view of law and gospel as epochal misconstrues the unavoidable, though often denied, encounter of all people with God as accusing and hidden in daily experience . . . Second, his affirmation of the imputative judgment as analytic, not synthetic, sidesteps the performative aspect to the words of promise uttered in the present. The proclamation "Your sins are forgiven for Jesus' sake" grants life and salvation—delivering us from God's wrath . . . [and] promising a hopeful, reconciled future . . . Our union with Christ depends on the word which delivers it, not vice versa! Third, there is transformation—even progress to a degree—in the Christian life. But it is not one "upward,"

---

104. Pannenberg, *Systematic Theology*, 3:87.
105. Mattes, *Role of Justification*, 62.
106. Ibid., 61–62.

as Pannenberg maintains, but one outward--an incarnation as service.[107]

Secondly, Pannenberg asserts that the law/Gospel distinction unnecessarily ties the doctrine of justification to a consciousness of guilt. A confessional Lutheran response asserts that, whether people are consciously aware of it or not, the experience of God's law is a universal reality significantly coloring humanity's ambiguous experience of the divine—personally, interpersonally, socially, and in creation. As Bayer previously noted: "Our contemporaries do not experience the law anymore as the law of God. Rather, the law is experienced as anonymous, or, in the best case scenario, as the 'categorical imperative.' A sense of inescapable duty weighing heavily on every human heart is revealed to us by this anonymous law. Duty becomes deadly when the law coincides with the gospel, when they are not distinguished from each other."[108] The blurring or marginalizing of the law/Gospel distinction, confessional Lutherans contend, leads to a corollary blurring of the distinction between God hidden and revealed, sapping Lutheran missiology of a crucial contribution to interreligious dialogue.

Thirdly, another Lutheran challenge to the law/Gospel distinction comes from the "new Finnish school" of Tuomo Mannermaa. Mannermaa and his colleagues critique confessional Lutheran theology as failing to sufficiently appreciate the diverse, New Testament understandings of justification and as fundamentally misinterpreting Luther's view of justification, emphasizing the indwelling presence of Christ as gift as the basis of justification (effective justification) over the promise of mercy reconciled in Christ (forensic justification).[109] Such a view pits Luther,

---

107. Ibid., 83–84.

108 Bayer, "Justification as Basis and Boundary," 285.

109. Olli-Pekka Vainio, in his *Justification and Participation in Christ: The Development of the Lutheran Doctrine of Justification from Luther to the Formula of Concord* (1580), shows the diverse views concerning justification within the Lutheran movement. The five Lutheran models of justification Vainio identifies include: 1) participation in Christ and His merit, 2) renewal of faculties of the soul by the Holy Spirit, 3) connection with Christ's divine nature, 4) a causal effect of the Holy Spirit, and 5) participation in the person of Christ and His merit, effected by the Spirit. While such diversity can be recognized and appreciated, the critical issue raised by the Finnish school of Luther studies is how the relationship between forensic justification (justification as the external word of forgiveness) and effective justification (the indwelling Christ and the believer's union with this indwelling Christ as the basis for justification) should be properly construed. While both views of justification are present in Luther,

The Gospel as Promise of God

as emphasizing the indwelling presence of Christ, against the Lutheran Confessions' emphasis on justification as the forensic declaration of God's forgiveness. The chief claim is that the indwelling presence of Christ grounds and guarantees the forgiveness of sins: effective justification grounds forensic justification. As Mannermaa states:

> Luther's notion of the "righteousness of faith" is permeated by Christological thinking. He does not separate the person (*persona*) of Christ and his work (*officium*) from each other. Instead, *Christ himself*, both his person and his work, *is* the Christian righteousness, that is, the "righteousness of faith." Christ—and therefore also *his entire person and work*—is really and truly present in the faith itself (*in ipsa fide Christus adest*). The favor (*favor*) of God (i.e., the forgiveness of sins and the removal of God's wrath) and his "gift" (*donum*; God himself, present in the fullness of his essence) unite in the person of Christ.[110]

I agree with Mark Mattes' critique of this view as confusing the order of important aspects of Luther's view of justification:

> Luther emphasizes Christ in us because it is the strongest scriptural affirmation to support the truth that Christ is for us. The efficacy of Christ in us is logically subordinate to the forensic declaration that Christ is for us. It serves to substantiate the latter which is pivotal in securing assurance for the terrified conscience in light of the accusing law . . . In the *Lectures on Galatians* (1535), Luther emphasizes that faith is "taking hold" of Christ. Such taking hold of Christ is not so that our nature might be perfected but so that the conscience, terrified since it is under attack by law, might be free. Here is affirmed not the continuum between nature and grace, but the opposition between law and gospel. Christ defends the conscience against the law. Indeed, Luther's metaphor is that the conscience is a "bride" who is to be ruled by Christ, the gospel. The law's place is to rule the body. We might say that Christ is *so for us* that he becomes

---

the Lutheran confessional writings clearly prioritize forensic over effective justification, viewing the latter as the logical result and fruit of the former. The forensic view of justification, confessional Lutherans argue, is more fruitful missiologically because it better facilitates the proclamation and application of the law/Gospel distinction, allowing for a fully robust theology of an external Word of God. To the extent that the effective view of justification undermines the necessity of the law/Gospel distinction and a strong emphasis on the *verbum externum*, to that extent I deem it missiologically deficient and lacking.

110. Mannermaa, *Christ Present in Faith*, 5.

> *one with us* in this marriage of the conscience to Christ. Christ and the conscience are then "one body." The reason that Christ lives in me is not to accentuate a mystical teleology of ascent into the triune life but to "abolish the law."[111]

In other words: God's external, justifying Word shapes human ontology more decisively than any ontological category. While the notion of Christ's indwelling presence as gift is certainly present in Luther, I would argue that it is a relatively minor emphasis compared to Luther's strong emphasis on forensic justification and his criterion for understanding the gospel as promise in contrast to the law. The Finnish school, in my view, turns a relatively minor emphasis in Luther into the foundation for defining grace. Given that the Lutheran tradition has always understood Luther's theology as subordinate and complementary to that of the Lutheran Confessions, it is puzzling why the Finnish school insists on prioritizing Luther's (alleged) theology and driving a wedge between Luther's theology and that of the Confessions. A clue to that may be found in the historical context and motivation for Mannermaa's developing theology: the Finnish Lutheran Church's ecumenical dialogues with the Russian Orthodox Church. Ironically, in their emphasis upon grace as the indwelling gift of Christ enabling spiritual transformation, the Finnish school ends up with an understanding of grace as human nature fulfilled, similar to the Roman Catholic "nature/grace" model. As Mattes states:

> Those authors in the Finnish line, along with Thomas Aquinas, present grace and justification from within the framework of a nature/grace distinction in which grace is seen as perfecting nature, permitting the temporal to achieve its goal in the eternal, the final deification of the human in the harmonious beauty of the triune life. The human is healed from the wound of sin and is granted the gift of the infusion of God's love as the indwelling Christ in order to make this heavenly pilgrimage possible. This development is intentionally in contradistinction to the confessional Lutheran perspective that contrasts grace to law, in which the gospel liberates terrified consciences from the law's accusations and helps liberate sinners from self-righteousness so that they can honor God on God's own terms and serve creation as God intends. From this latter perspective, it is not that grace perfects nature but instead liberates it from sin [like Augustine] . . .[112]

---

111. Mattes, "Future for Lutheran Theology?," 445–6.

112. Ibid., 440.

The Gospel as Promise of God

In contrast to both schools of grace as nature fulfilled, the broad Roman Catholic tradition as well as the Finnish school, a confessional Lutheran model insists on prioritizing grace as the promise of mercy fulfilled, a promise that, far from being a legal fiction, is guaranteed and actualized by the faithfulness and power of the Promise-maker himself. The debate between effective and forensic justification is a false dichotomy, given Luther's understanding of the Word of God as God's performative, creative agent for determining reality. As Robert Kolb notes, citing Gerhard Forde's insight, "the more 'forensic' Luther's teaching becomes, the more 'effective' it is, because nothing can be more real than that which God's Word declares."[113] A confessional Lutheran response to the Finnish school affirms the "unity in distinction" of God's favor and gift, asserting the importance of the external origin of both:

> God's *favor* is not a possession or essence of God's own, but *is* precisely the *gift*, applied to the unrighteous while they are unrighteous. Only on this truly objective foundation of imputation as forgiveness on account of the cross of Christ which is once and for all, is the gift (*donum*) of the present Christ preached for one and so given ... *God's favor and gift are not distinguished as object and subject; they are both objective and external to the sinner*, and they both work the only truly subjective change that matters for sinners--the end to the old and the beginning of the new ...[114]

Similar to its response to Pannenberg, confessional Lutheran theology insists that what is at stake is preserving the comforting power of the Gospel as an external word of promise:

> This new Finnish view jeopardizes the centrality and objectivity of the "external word" (*verbum externum*), God's means to comfort anxious consciences threatened by the accusatory function of the law. Luther's view of the indwelling Christ and the happy exchange are grounded in this external word, which comes to humans from *outside* of themselves. Christians are directed to trust this external word that defines their very being, and not their own intuitions about this new being. Only by clinging to the external word of the promise is the sinner liberated from incurvation and allowed selflessly to serve the neighbor. While Jenson and the new Finns are apt to emphasize a reciprocity

---

113. Kolb, *Martin Luther*, 128.
114. Mattes, Review of *Justification and Participation in Christ*, 116–17.

between the justifying word and the indwelling Christ, only the logical and rhetorical prioritizing of forensic over effective justification (which may both be temporally simultaneous) can address Luther's chief pastoral concern to console the anxious conscience in his formulation of the doctrine of justification.[115]

Fourth, the so-called "new perspective" on Paul accuses Lutheran theology of fundamentally distorting the category of law as it was used within second temple Judaism.[116] It claims that Lutheran theology articulates and advances a "Lutheran" view of Paul and his understandings of law and justification, rather than wrestling with the "historical"

---

115. Mattes, *Role of Justification*, 129–30.

116. The so-called "new perspective" on Paul is championed by E. P. Sanders (*Paul and Palestinian Judaism: A Comparison of Patterns of Religion; Paul: A Very Short Introduction*), James G. Dunn (*The New Perspective on Paul*), and N. T. Wright (*Paul: In Fresh Perspective, Justification: God's Plan and Paul's Vision*), among others. Its contributions include a renewed emphasis on the significance and implications of Jesus' and Paul's Jewish heritage, as well as a deeper understanding of the significant issues pertaining to Second Temple Judaism. It is critical of the classic, Lutheran law/Gospel distinction as a Pauline distortion of the Jewish understanding of law within "covenant nomism." Such alleged distortion of what is meant by "law" has led to a subsequent reduction of justification to merely personal salvation, rather than understanding salvation more broadly as incorporation into the people of God and "law" as the markers delineating the boundaries demarcating the people of God. Two examples of works critical of the new perspective include Peter Stuhlmacher's *A Challenge to the New Perspective: Revisiting Paul's Doctrine of Justification* and John Piper's *The Future of Justification: A Response to N. T. Wright*. The confessional Lutheran response to and critique of the new perspective is as follows: For the new perspective, the gospel is understood in terms of covenant. As Richard Koenig puts it, "Righteousness for humans is to be in God's covenant. God's own righteousness is the same as covenant faithfulness. Therefore "the imputation of God's own righteousness [to sinners] makes no sense at all." No new action on God's part is needed to get sinners justified. Needed only is the correction of some Jewish voices on how Gentiles can get in. Jesus is the agent for this clarification, and Paul is the instrument for carrying it to the Gentiles ... On justification, Wright says it comes as the end of a process on the Day of Judgment when the verdict will be rendered on us on the basis of the "complete life lived." Piper puts it at the very outset: when sinners begin trusting Christ, they ARE justified and their works follow. Wright [claims] that "Paul, in company with mainstream Judaism, affirms God's final judgment will be in accordance with the entirety of a life led—in accordance, in other words, with works" (111) ... Concerning justification, therefore, Wright's new perspective on Paul appears to yield nothing but the old perspective of justification by faith and works" (Koenig, "Future of Justification," lines 51–66). In other words: N. T. Wright and the new perspective on Paul are closer to Dupuis than to a confessional Lutheran view in terms of emphasizing the centrality of one, divine covenant into which we are included through Christ.

Paul and his understanding of Judaism in terms of covenantal nomism. While acknowledging that "Judaism, described in its own terms, knew and depended on God's grace and did not promote a self-righteous pursuit of salvation by works," confessional Lutheran theology nonetheless maintains that "the operative principle of the law, for Paul, *was* its demand for works; a principle that merely made explicit God's requirement of all human beings to *do* what is good and right."[117] When competing definitions of grace are posed in terms of "grace abounding to sinners" versus "erasing ethnic boundaries," a confessional Lutheran stance readily acknowledges that "critics have rightly defined the occasion that elicited the formulation of Paul's doctrine and have reminded us of its first-century social and strategic significance; the 'Lutherans,' for their part, rightly captured Paul's rationale and basic point."[118] While recognizing the social-historical context within which Paul's doctrines of law and justification arose, Lutheran theology maintains the validity of the law's theological use of illuminating sin and necessitating the grace of Christ.

Fifth, given the immediate context of Paul's articulation of law and Gospel—his struggle with the Judaism of his day—does confessional Lutheran theology use this distinction too broadly? Does it overextend its valid application in seeking to apply it to the world of religious pluralism? This substantial concern, raised in the introduction and provisionally answered there, will be further addressed in chapter 6.

Sixth, Karl Barth, the most famous twentieth-century critic of the law/Gospel distinction, critiqued the Lutheran view of law as misguided, failing to appreciate its true character as "the very specific unity of authority and freedom which is given in Jesus Christ and apprehended only by faith."[119] Advocating a reversal of the law/Gospel dialectic, namely Gospel/law, as a more accurate articulation of the Word of God as a unified, gracious word, Barth insisted on distinguishing, without separating, the gospel and law:

> The Word of God, when it is addressed to us and when we are allowed to hear it, demonstrates its unity in that it is always grace; i.e. it is free, non-obligatory, undeserved divine goodness, mercy, and condescension. A gospel or a law which we speak to ourselves, by virtue of our own ability, would as such, not be *God's* Word; it would not be his *Gospel* and it would not

---

117. Westerholm, *Perspectives*, 444.
118. Ibid., 445.
119. Forde, *Law-Gospel Debate*, 144.

> be his law. The *very fact that* God speaks to us, that, under all circumstances, is, in itself, grace . . . The traditional order, "Law and Gospel" . . . must not, however, define the structure of the whole teaching . . . Anyone who wishes correctly to approach our subject must speak first of the *Gospel* . . . And the Gospel, too, is only the Gospel if the Law . . . is *hidden* and *enclosed* in it as in the ark of the covenant. The Gospel is not law, just as the Law is not Gospel; but because the Law is in the Gospel, from the Gospel, and points to the Gospel, we must first of all know about the Gospel in order to know about the Law, and not vice versa.[120]

As the concrete shape of lived Christian experience created by the Gospel in the world, the law could be called a "form" of the Gospel. In other words, "God's grace . . . does have the form of Law, of commandment, of requirement, of claim."[121] "The grace of God commands, and the command of God is gracious."[122]

Situated within Barth's larger, overarching concern that the Word of God be clearly contrasted with human words, Barth's criticism and this debate "centers around the problem of the knowledge and use of the law."[123] While sharing such common, theological concerns as the necessity of breaking the continuity of the law (Lutheran through rejecting the "third use" of the law, Barth through rejecting the first two uses of the law) and, through the gospel, excluding the law which accuses (for Lutheran theology, the law as such; for Barth, the "misused" law), the vehemence of the debate suggests that the differences are more than terminological. Gerhard Forde captures the heart of this debate nicely:

> Barth cannot rid himself of the suspicion that the Lutheran concept of law, distinguished as it is from the gospel, not only sanctions the fateful idea of a *Volksnomos* as a revelation of "God's will" apart from the gospel but also leads to a perversion of the gospel itself. For a law understood apart from the gospel leads inevitably, for Barth, to a gospel which merely becomes a crutch for man's attempts at self-justification. On the other hand, the Lutherans see in Barth's idea of the law as the form of the gospel

---

120. Barth, "Gospel and Law," 72, 71.
121. Ibid., 85.
122. Busch, *Great Passion*, 152.
123. Forde, *Law-Gospel Debate*, 203.

The Gospel as Promise of God

a fatal tendency to unify law and gospel which threatens to destroy the dialectic . . .[124]

Let us further unpack Barth's charge that Lutheran theology, in misinterpreting the nature and role of the law, inevitably misconstrues the gospel. Barth's main assertion is this: because God's first Word to humanity, the Gospel, expresses divine grace, therefore the subsequent law is intrinsically connected to that Gospel in a positive manner that shapes Christian experience. Barth insists that a proper understanding of God's initial encounter with humanity is crucially important: does God first address humanity in a word of critical accusation and judgment (Lutheran), or rather as a gracious God whose Gospel word of forgiveness contains within it a condemnation of sin and command to obedience (Barth)?

Within the historical context of "the modern emancipation of ethics from the gospel of grace" and the appeals of the Nazi regime to allegiance based upon views of natural law and the natural orders,[125] Barth vigorously maintains the inseparability of the law from the gospel: since the law must always remain the law *of God*, it can never become an independent norm or principle. Only if its origin is clearly affirmed in God's revelation can the law be considered the law of God. This affirmation seeks to exclude all other sources for the law, including natural law, human autonomy (self-determination), and worldly authorities, while maintaining God's sovereign freedom to determine the human.

From the above-mentioned central affirmation , Barth critiques the Lutheran law/Gospel formulation in various ways. First, the *nature* of the law is not abstract demand/command, but rather the concrete expression of the will of God. The law of God is constituted, not by its commanding or demanding character (contra Lutheran theology), which could be filled by various content, but rather by the fact that God commands it.[126] Barth's concept of the "fulfilled law," that humans should acknowledge that the law has already been graciously fulfilled (on both the divine and human side, by Jesus Christ), critiques the Lutheran view of law as the mere form of demand. Barth charges Lutherans as misconstruing the law as "an ideal that the human must fulfill because it has not been fulfilled in

---

124. Ibid., 202.
125. Busch, *Great Passion*, 154–57.
126. Ibid., 158.

itself."[127] His concern is to avoid all forms of self-righteousness whereby humans misconstrue the law as either unfulfillable or humanly fulfilled.[128]

Second, Barth fears the Lutheran view, taken to the extreme, could regard the law as an eternal principle of retribution, originally definitive of the divine-human relationship. If that were the case, then "the original relationship between God and man was not one of love, and therefore . . . the gospel could not be the reestablishment of that original relationship."[129] Third, Barth's formulation of the *proper use* of the law seeks to combat the lurking antinomianism and seemingly inevitable "cheap grace" he detects in the Lutheran position. While Barth insists that "the law apart from the gospel and faith is necessarily 'misunderstood' and 'misused' by man, so that only the use of the law in faith can be considered its proper use," Lutheran theology maintains the law "can find its proper function only *prior* to the gospel."[130] Fourth, "he does not see how one could ascribe to Paul a concept of divine law which runs contrary to the Old Testament view of the positive relation of law and covenant as evidenced by contemporary Old Testament scholarship."[131] Fifth, in homiletically applying his main assertion, Barth insists that Christian preaching should reflect the reality of the Gospel encountering people before the law: rather than the Lutheran, law/Gospel structure, Christian proclamation should prioritize the Gospel before the law.[132]

Lutheran theology responds to Barth's critique on at least four fronts.[133] First, while affirming the "distinction without separation" of law and Gospel, it nevertheless insists that only the clear distinction of the law prior to the Gospel preserves the proper character of each: the accusatory character of the law and the promissory character of the Gospel. As Ebeling states: "Only when the gospel of justification by faith alone is free of any legal provisos . . . can it grant the peace and freedom that it

127. Ibid., 163.
128. Barth, "Gospel and Law," 85.
129. Forde, *Law-Gospel Debate*, 153.
130. Ibid., 203.
131. Ibid., 167.
132. For a recent, in-depth study of Barth's sermons on this very point, see Andre Demut, *Evangelium und Gesetz. Eine systematisch-theologische Reflexion zu Karl Barths Predigtwerk*.
133. Lutheran theologians such as Werner Elert, Helmut Thielicke, Gustaf Wingren, Hans-Joachim Iwand, and Gerhard Ebeling have written specific responses to Barth's critique of the law/Gospel distinction.

promises."¹³⁴ The fact that God speaks two, diametrically opposed words in law and Gospel, contra Barth, does not mean they are separated or unrelated in Lutheran theology, since they both originate from God.¹³⁵ Second, it counters Barth's critique that God's initial word to humanity is one of grace by affirming God's initial involvement with people by virtue of creation, while nevertheless insisting that such a relationship falls under "ethos under law." A first-article relationship with God the Creator is substantially and qualitatively different from a second-article relationship with God through Jesus Christ. Third, Lutheran theology wonders whether Barth's theology fails to do justice to and maintain the divine dialectic of wrath and mercy: is divine wrath real, or only apparent?¹³⁶ This point is central to the Lutheran argument. To the extent that "God's action [seemingly] loses its double character as judgment and grace," Barth's theology seems open to the critique of "a timeless monism which would lead necessarily to universalism."¹³⁷ Fourth, a Lutheran understanding of "ethos under law," articulated earlier, would challenge Barth's understanding of law to account more broadly for God's dealings with humanity beyond the scope of God's revelation in Jesus Christ.

In my judgment, the heart of the disagreement between Barth and Lutheran theology lies in differing understandings of the proper place of the law in the economy of salvation. The differences, while methodological, are not merely methodological: they are material and substantive. As Gerhard Ebeling notes: "It is a fundamentally different way of doing theology if one reasons from a standpoint where law and gospel form a self-evident unity rather than from a standpoint where this unity can be maintained only in the face of anxiety (*Anfechtung*). In these two instances, quite obviously, the concept of law will then be very differently defined."¹³⁸

---

134. Ebeling, *Lutherstudien Vol. 3*, 566.

135. It is important to distinguish, without separating, the theological use of the law, as accusing of sin and necessitating Christ, from the tripartite scheme of the orders of creation, moral order, and judgment, whereby God relates to humanity as its creator/preserver, legislator, and judge, respectively.

136. While Barth would disagree with this criticism, asking whether divine wrath exists autonomously and independent of divine love, Lutheran theology would maintain this critique as valid.

137. Forde, *Law-Gospel Debate*, 158. Barth's theology of reconciliation, like Rahner's and Dupuis' theology, would be very optimistic about the salvation of most (all?) people.

138. Ebeling, *Word and Faith*, 270. "For the letter kills, but the Spirit gives life"

Enduring differences manifest themselves in differing understandings of the nature of the divine address, the grounding of knowledge of God, and the function of law, both within the economy of salvation and in the Christian's life. Two fundamental differences merit particular attention. First, the defining dialectic is located differently for each. "[For Lutheran theology] the decisive and absolute break comes between law and gospel, not between law and law [as it does for Barth]. Only the gospel is the end of the law."[139] Second, the subject of the law is understood differently: "Who really is the one who uses the law. Is it God as the author of the law, or is it man upon whom the law impinges?"[140] From a Lutheran perspective, "even though *man* misuses the law, *God* does not . . . Once it is realized that God, after all, is sovereign over the use of the *law*, the necessity of speaking of another [misused or true] law is removed . . . For the law is not the form of the Gospel; it is rather, the form of *this* [eschatological] *age*. The gospel is its end and *telos*."[141] Paul R. Hinlicky captures what is at stake for each position:

> [F]or Barth, there cannot finally be any true opposition between law and gospel, since as God's Word both alike are expressions of the same eternal election of grace, differing only as form and content . . . For [Lutheran theology], the opposition between the law of God which rejects the sinner and the gospel of God which mercifully receives her, represents more than humanocentric states of religious consciousness. It indicates a real movement in the life of God . . . a passage internal to the life of God . . . It is important [in Lutheran theology] that God's election of sinful humanity be understood as a costly decision, entailing an incalculable struggle and "overcoming" in God, a true miracle of God entering into time to become what He had not been.[142]

Seventhly, the law/Gospel distinction, in its cross-centeredness, is vulnerable to a criticism of paying insufficient attention to the significance

---

(2 Cor 3:6b) serves as a helpful locus for delineating these differing understandings of the law. While Barth concedes, "This is the Law of which it was said and must be said: either entirely the Law and then death, or entirely the Gospel and then life, there is no third possibility," he nevertheless defines it as the Law "dishonored and emptied by sin's deception, which, with the power of the *wrath* of God, nevertheless remains *his* Law" (Barth, *Gospel and Law*, 94).

139. Forde, *Law-Gospel Debate*, 205–6.
140. Ibid., 206.
141. Ibid., 206–7.
142. Hinlicky, *Luther and the Beloved Community*, 112, 111.

and implications of the resurrection. This critique, without denying the significance of the cross, argues that the paradigmatic character of the resurrection for shaping Christian anthropology and discipleship is both more faithful to the broad scope of the New Testament and more expansive in its application to Christian thought and mission than the law/Gospel distinction.[143]

CONCLUSION

"For God does not deal, nor has he ever dealt, with us except through the word of promise."[144] Such a claim for a God of promise who offers a Gospel of promise is met with skepticism and resistance in our postmodern world, which has lost confidence in even the very possibility of making promises. Robert Jenson aptly describes the features of such postmodern skepticism: "Promises . . . should not be made, because they cannot be kept. Promises, in the postmodern world, are inauthentic simply because they are promises, because they commit a future which is not ours to commit . . . Promises can be made only if reality is getting someplace, that is, if it has a plotted story . . . The impossibility of promises is there in our daily experience."[145]

While overcoming such pervasive skepticism is a daunting task for the Church's mission, Lutheran theology offers the Gospel as *promissio Dei*, concentrated in Jesus Christ as the Promise incarnate, as a promising gift, not only to the wider ecumenical world, but to the world at large. Lutheran theology commends the category of promise as crucially illuminative for the Christian Gospel and mission. The notion of "promise" not only holds faithfulness with the Christian tradition and relevant contemporary engagement in mission together, but it is able to do so precisely because it articulates the very essence of both what the Gospel and Christian mission entail. The Gospel promise is trustworthy because "the promise [is] made in the name of one who has already satisfied the condition of death and therefore has all the future in his gift."[146]

Claiming the Gospel as promise has significant, far-reaching implications for at least six areas: appreciating the nature and character

---

143. For an eloquent articulation of this position positively stated, see Anthony J. Kelly, *The Resurrection Effect: Transforming Christian Life and Thought*.

144. Luther, *Luther's Works*, 36:42.

145. Jenson, "How the World Lost Its Story," 23.

146. Gritsch and Jenson, *Lutheranism*, 44.

of God as a faithful, promise-keeping God; a view of human nature as fundamentally "trusting creatures"; the nature of Christian faith as trust in the divine promise to have mercy for Christ's sake; pastoral concerns of comforting troubled consciences and intentionally utilizing all the benefits of Christ; the law/Gospel distinction as safeguarding both the nature of the Gospel as promise and that of the law as fundamentally accusing of sin; and the creative, reality-shaping and reality-determining nature of God's performative Word. God's dual speech of law and Gospel, wrath and promise, creates a relational matrix between God and humanity, confronting and challenging people to respond in faith by trusting the Gospel promise of mercy rather than "wasting" their trust on lesser promises.[147]

As we turn to anticipate the rest of this project, Oswald Bayer's work, especially his identification of three key features of Luther's theology as missiologically significant (the law as accusing, the gospel as promising,

147. As Robert Jenson has demonstrated in *Story and Promise: A Brief Theology of the Gospel About Jesus*, the category of promise, rather than having an exclusively Christocentric focus and application, has fruitful potential for application to many other facets of Christian theology: to Israel and the church as the communities of promise, to Jesus as the fulfillment of the promise and the divine promise incarnate, to the content of the Gospel as the forgiveness of sins and promise of mercy, to Christian ethics and discipleship, to God the Father as the God of promise, to the Holy Spirit as the presence of the promise, and to the world as the arena of God's promise, to name but a few.

The category of promise is also creatively open to insights from other hermeneutical approaches, such as those of covenant theology, narrative theology, theologies of hope with an eschatological emphasis, etc. While my Lutheran law/Gospel hermeneutic emphasizes certain content (the forgiveness of sins, promise of mercy for Christ's sake, etc.) as indispensable to the Gospel promise, and while it is certainly critical of approaches which overlook or marginalize such central content, the theological strength and fruitfulness of promise as an overarching category is by no means limited only to insights from the Lutheran tradition.

While confessional Lutheran theology emphasizes the centrality of forgiveness of sins and divine mercy realized on account of Christ as the indispensible content of the Gospel promise, the category of promise is broad enough to ecumenically encompass the central concerns and convictions of other Christian traditions and approaches as well. For example, the Eastern Orthodox understanding of *theosis* (divinization), the Roman Catholic understanding of justification as the hope of eternal life, covenant theology paradigms of promise and fulfillment, a liberation theology emphasis on the promise of divine liberation based on the paradigm of the Jews' exodus from Egypt, and various theologies of hope with eschatological emphases all incorporate and utilize, to a greater or lesser extent, the theological category of promise. As such, the category of promise has creative, fruitful potential for furthering ecumenical relations and understanding.

and the hiddenness of God as elusively mystifying),[148] forms an overarching outline for constructing a confessional Lutheran missiology.

Bayer asserts that there are "three, irreducibly different ways in which God encounters us . . . which are irreducible and cannot be subsumed under a general concept, not even the self-revelation of God (contra Rahner and Barth)."[149] When the subject of theology is taken to be the justifying God and the sinful human being, this "subject" as a dramatic event and encounter takes place within the following three spheres:

> a. in the conflict with the *law* that judges me, that convicts me with regard to my sins, that accuses me, and that delivers me over to the final judgment of death; b. in the promise of the *gospel*, in which God himself speaks by means of Jesus Christ on my behalf, indeed takes my place; and c. in the assault of the *hiddenness of God*, which cannot be understood merely as the effect of the law and which so radically contradicts the gospel in an . . . incomprehensible way.[150]

Having introduced and elaborated the theologically foundational components for Lutheran missiology thus far, chapters 2, 5, and 6 will articulate how employing the Gospel as promise and the law/Gospel distinction lead to distinctive strategies in approaching religious pluralism, namely a theology of grace as promise of mercy realized (chapter 2) and emphasizing the interreligious potential of the distinction between God simultaneously revealed and hidden in the cross (chapters 5 and 6), respectively.

As we turn our attention to differing theologies of grace in chapters 2 and 3, the roots of these differing visions of grace can be found in the interrelationship between one's understandings of sin, grace, human nature, and the Gospel itself. Stephen Duffy insightfully notes how one's theology of grace is inextricably tied to one's views of sin and human nature: "[The] dynamics of grace become more intelligible the more one's understanding of sin, the correlate of grace, accurately portrays the human predicament. Differences concerning grace reflect differences concerning sin, which in turn are traceable to different images of the divine/human relationship."[151]

---

148. Bayer, *Martin Luther's Theology*, 42.
149. Bayer, *Theology the Lutheran Way*, 105, 102.
150. Bayer, *Martin Luther's Theology*, 42.
151. Duffy, *Dynamics of Grace*, 390.

I will show that in the classic, Lutheran theological anthropology, our human proclivity to trust and build our lives on promises other than the Gospel necessitates an understanding of grace as primarily the promise of loving mercy fulfilled in Christ. Chapter 2 will further substantiate this claim.

2

A Paradigm of Grace as Promise of Mercy Fulfilled

A FUNDAMENTAL AXIOM IN Roman Catholic theology today, implicitly operative in inclusive pluralist proposals, is the formula *gratia non tollit naturam, sed perficit*: grace does not remove or abolish nature, but rather perfects it.[1] Such a "nature/grace" model claims that what God's grace offers (including the Gospel) fulfills what is already naturally present, rather than replacing it. Not only do prevailing models of replacement, fulfillment, and mutuality[2] all build on this "nature/grace" model, but they also connect it to a revelationist framework in which the very fact of God's self-communication is defined as grace.[3]

Before proceeding to delineate, in chapters 2 and 3, Lutheran and Roman Catholic theologies of grace, respectively, it is important to realize that our knowledge of God is always analogical. As David Tracy states: "We understand one another [and God], if at all, only through analogy."[4] This means that any analogy, metaphor, or image for construing and illuminating the divine/human relationship is inherently limited. We may obtain true, adequate, and illuminative, but never comprehensive, knowledge of God through any given set of analogies or metaphors. This does not mean that all analogies are equally valid: a given analogy or

1. This expression by Aquinas is cited in Duffy, *Dynamics of Grace*, 132; see Thomas Aquinas *Summa Theologiae* q. 1, q.1, A.8, ad.2.

2. This terminology is used by Paul Knitter in his book, *Introducing Theologies of Religions*, in place of such traditional terms as exclusivism, inclusivism, and pluralism.

3. Schroeder, "Pluralism's Question," 165.

4. Tracy, *Analogical Imagination*, 454.

metaphor can more comprehensively and adequately account for the data of the Christian tradition and Scriptures, or possess greater theoretical or practical fruitfulness. Whether emphasizing divine healing (the nature/grace model) or divine mercy (Lutheran law/promise model), a given theology of grace should be epistemically humble enough to recognize, not only the polyvalence of grace, but also the inherent limitations of theological, second-order language to mediate faith knowledge. While we can "know" and "experience" God either through divine mercy and forgiveness or through divine healing, we can never fully comprehend God.

This chapter will delineate three main assertions, building on the Lutheran view of the Gospel as promise. First, if the Gospel is understood as an unconditional promise of forgiveness and reconciliation, for Christ' sake, then such a definition of what constitutes Gospel leads to a theology of mercy as promise fulfilled. Secondly, such a theology of mercy as promise fulfilled serves a crucial function of preserving and safeguarding the Gospel as unconditional promise. Thirdly, instead of using the pairing "sin and grace," a confessional Lutheran approach prefers the pairing "law and [Gospel] promise [of mercy]." These three building blocks of a confessional Lutheran theology of mercy will be articulated and argued as the answers to three key questions are formulated: 1) What is the nature of sin? 2) How does such an understanding of sin relate to the nature of the Gospel and grace? 3) What role does faith play in interrelating the two?

I will argue how a confessional Lutheran, "law/promise" paradigm radically differs from a Roman Catholic, "nature/grace" paradigm. By exploring this difference, building upon what has come before, this chapter lays an important foundation toward formulating a confessional Lutheran missiology. "Why Jesus? Why is Jesus necessary for anybody?" is the question which a confessional Lutheran approach insists must remain central to any theology of grace or mercy (the Lutheran preference for 'mercy' rather than 'grace' will be clarified later). It offers a decisively different answer to that question from revelationist theologies (like those found in both Roman Catholic and alternative Lutheran theologies), one which I submit is more closely tied to the biblical grammar of sin and grace, law and promise.

While Lutheran theology never directly disputed the Catholic, scholastic "nature/grace" model, the Lutheran confessional writings essentially replaced it with the "sin/mercy" dialectic, insisting that a more

A Paradigm of Grace as Promise of Mercy Fulfilled

biblically accurate counterpart to "grace" is "sin," rather than "nature." This was done for two basic reasons: 1) there was no Biblical (Hebrew or Greek) term equivalent to the Greek, philosophical notion of nature, and 2) The grace which perfected such nature was not what the New Testament calls the "grace of our Lord Jesus Christ."[5] In fact, if you read Apology IV on justification, Melanchthon begins by using the term "grace," but ends up preferring the synonymous terms "mercy" or "favor of God." Therefore, confessional Lutheran theology submits that grace is best understood, not merely as the power to perfect or fulfill nature, but rather as the promise of God's *mercy and favor* realized in Christ. The former leaves the focus on the creation or creature, whereas the latter properly focuses on the Creator's work for us (*pro nobis*).

In response to this 'nature/grace' paradigm, a distinctively Lutheran contribution to a theology of religions is its insistence that, not only must the question, "Why is Jesus necessary for anybody?" remain front and center, but that the answer must account for God's new "economy of salvation" which Pauline theology describes as justifying reconciliation: "that God was reconciling the world to himself in Christ, not counting men's sins against them . . . God made him who had no sin to be sin for us, so that in him we might become the righteousness of God" (2 Cor 5:19, 21). For Luther, this Pauline formulation reveals the 'joyful exchange' between Christ's righteousness and human sinfulness.[6] Righteousness accounted to sinners as the forgiveness of sin, Lutheran theology insists, is not and cannot be properly understood as merely a "fuller revelation" of God as God is encountered in daily life or in the other religions.[7] To treat it as such would be to distort the very essence of the Gospel as promise, to marginalize what is central, to distort its uniquely new and good content, and to essentially "preach another Gospel" (Gal 1:9). Thus, to the extent that justification by faith and forgiveness is marginalized in models of mission, to that extent confessional Lutheran theology deems such models insufficient. In other words: forgiveness of sins is central to the Gospel promise of grace. The practical importance and application of the Lutheran emphasis can be summarized by Luther's distinction, one he used to contrast his approach to the medieval understanding of

---

5. Schroeder, "Pluralism's Question," 166. Whereas the philosophical or ontological category of "nature" does not appear in the Christian Scriptures, references to "sin," "mercy," "forgiveness," "loving kindness," etc., are ubiquitous throughout Scripture.

6. See Luther, *Luther's Works*, 25:280–81.

7. Schroeder, "Pluralism's Question," 169.

natural law: "While 'to know that there is a god' is implied by natural law, it makes a world of difference . . . to know who God is. The first is known by nature and written in hearts, the second is taught through the Holy Spirit alone."[8]

A confessional Lutheran understanding of the nature of sin challenges a Roman Catholic view of original sin as insufficient in scope. To the extent that the "problem" or nature of sin is under diagnosed, confessional Lutherans argue, to that extent the nature of the Gospel itself as remedy to and healing of sin is inevitably and equally underappreciated. When sin is understood primarily as "defective nature needing repair," Christ's merits are "wasted" and the Gospel is downsized from the truly good news it actually is. In other words: to the extent that a model of mission is based upon a "nature/grace" rather than a "law/promise" axiom, to that extent both the reality of sin and the necessity of Christ are reduced in scope; if sin is not such "bad news," Christ's work is not such radically "good news." This chapter will delineate and argue this confessional Lutheran critique.

In contrast to a Roman Catholic, inclusively pluralist model (based on Karl Rahner's theology of revelation defining grace as nature fulfilled), a confessional Lutheran theology of loving mercy bases itself on a theology of revelation centered on an understanding of the divine address as law and Gospel promise.[9] Such a theology of mercy insists that what grace "fulfills" is the promise of mercy for Christ's sake, rather than "defective" human nature.

Martin Luther and the Lutheran Confessions' understanding of how sin, the revealed law of God, the nature of the Gospel, and faith relate to each other forms a foundation for articulating a confessional Lutheran theology of mercy. This matrix and interrelationship sheds light on all our relationships within the world, including world religions, while also forcing a radical division between the law, which constructs a "natural" relationship between God and humanity, and the Gospel, which is inherently unknowable to humankind apart from revelation and comes to it as

---

8. Wannenwetsch, "Luther's Moral Theology," 123.

9. While I am aware that Rahner's model is an inclusivist one, to be distinguished from Jacques Dupuis' model of inclusive pluralism, the point I wish to substantiate is that Dupuis' inclusive pluralism is firmly anchored in, and would be incomprehensible without, an understanding of grace as primarily nature fulfilled. My Lutheran proposal will critique such an approach to grace in this chapter, followed by a further critique of its missiological implications in subsequent chapters.

external good news. Within this framework, given the Lutheran articulation of the devastating depths and extent of sin's corruption, grace cannot merely be an infused ingredient added to inherent, human potentiality. Rather, grace (mercy) is God's *extra nos* intrusion of an external reality (promise of mercy for Christ's sake) we cannot know or intuit apart from Christ. According to classic Lutheran theology: Christ *is* grace and mercy. We know it only in His person and through His promises.

LUTHER AND THE LUTHERAN CONFESSIONS ON THE NATURE OF SIN

When it comes to the nature and essence of sin, Martin Luther and the Lutheran Confessions take as their point of departure Paul's assessment in Rom 14:23, "Whatever does not proceed from faith is sin." They agree that a Biblical understanding of sin is primarily grounded in the fiduciary, promissory framework of trust versus distrust, belief versus unbelief, and only secondarily and derivatively in the performative framework of obedience versus disobedience. In other words: the Biblical notion and definition of sin is first of all a matter of distrust, unbelief, and suspicion regarding the promises of God, which inevitably leads to concrete acts of disobedience manifesting such misplaced trust. If the notion of sin is understood in terms of trust, the object of that trust inevitably becomes an important category in examining the deeper dimensions of sin. Luther, in his explanation of the first commandment in his *Large Catechism*, argues for a definition of sin as fundamentally a matter of trust and placing one's faith in an inadequate "god," as opposed to the true God:

> A "god" is the term for that which we are to look to for all good and in which we are to find refuge in all need. Therefore, to have a god is nothing else than to trust and believe in that one with your whole heart . . . it is the trust and faith of the heart alone that make both God and idol. If your faith and trust are right, then your God is the true one. Conversely, where your trust is false and wrong, there you do not have the true God. For these two belong together, faith and God. Anything on which your heart relies and depends . . . that is really your God.[10]

Luther's definition of sin as a matter of distrust, misplaced trust, and unbelief, rather than being an abstract principle, is firmly rooted in the

---

10. Kolb and Wengert, *Book of Concord*, 386.

concrete example of the account of the Fall (Gen 3). In his interpretation of this account, Luther goes to great lengths to emphasize that the heart of human sin lay, not in the mere fact of disobedience (eating the fruit which God had forbidden them to eat), but rather in calling God's Word into question, therefore doubting God's truthfulness, goodness, righteousness, and faithfulness to His promises. Disobedience is a symptom and result of sin as prior unbelief. As he puts it: "Therefore the root and source of sin is unbelief and turning away from God, just as, on the other hand, the source and root of righteousness is faith. Satan first draws away from faith to unbelief . . . The outward act of disobedience follows sin, which through unbelief has fully developed in the heart."[11]

Another important passage for understanding Luther's view of sin, building on the notion of sin as basic unbelief in God's promises and trustworthiness, compares our faith in fellow human beings and what it means to trust or distrust someone with faith in or distrust of God. In his essay *On the Freedom of a Christian*, Luther writes:

> Faith exercises its power in that it honors the one in whom it believes with the most faithful and highest belief . . . What greater thing can we attribute to an individual than truth, righteousness, and virtually unconditional goodness . . . This is how the soul acts in faith when it believes steadfastly in the God who makes promises . . . This is the highest honor accorded to God . . . because it holds firmly to the promise of God and does not doubt that he is a true, righteous, wise God, who acts, ordains, and gives care according to what is best . . . By contrast, what rebellion, what unbelief, what insult is greater than not believing in his promise? How is this anything other than either to make God a liar or else to doubt that he is true?[12]

From these examples it should be clear how, for Luther, sin is fundamentally a relational category describing human brokenness resulting from the unbelief, distrust, and mistrust of God's promises and truthfulness. Oswald Bayer captures the depth of Luther's view of sin as a constitutive, inescapably inherent human reality: "[for Luther] consideration of unbelief and of sin shows that it does not deal with some sort of quality, as if something were added to the substance of "human" at a later time, but

---

11. Luther, *Luther's Works*, 1:162.

12. Ibid., 31:350–51. I am citing the translation of the Latin text by Oswald Bayer in *Martin Luther's Theology*, 177–78.

that it offers the definition of the entire human. It is not just something about him but rather involves his very nature."[13]

Luther and the Lutheran Confessions on Universal (Original) Sin

The preceding quote directs us to a critical component of the discussion of sin: what constitutes, what is the nature of, original sin? The answer to this question, perhaps more so than any other theological locus, distinguishes a Lutheran theology of mercy as promise realized from theologies of grace as nature fulfilled. Since both Luther and the Lutheran Confessions have important things to say regarding the "depth dimension" of original sin, it is only fitting that we examine the pertinent passages from both. For the Lutheran Confessions, this would chiefly entail the *Apology to the Augsburg Confession Article II (Ap. II)*, "Original Sin,"[14] as well as the *Formula of Concord Solid Declaration (FCSD) Article I*, "Concerning Original Sin."[15] For Luther, the key locations expressing his views on the nature and effects of original sin include the *Smalcald Articles Article I*, "Concerning Sin," his explanation of the first commandment, explanation of the sixth petition of the Lord's Prayer, and commentary on Gen 3, to name but a few. We now turn to examining the main Lutheran assertions, as well as the theological rationale underlying those assertions, in greater detail.

In summary: the Lutheran Confessions seek to strike a delicate balance between the total depravity brought about by sin, on the one hand, and the goodness of human nature. On the one hand, original sin so thoroughly corrupts human nature "that nothing sound or uncorrupted [is] left in the human body or soul, in his internal or external powers."[16] On the other hand, a distinction must be made between human nature, "originally created pure, holy, and without sin," and original sin as a "work of the devil."[17]

---

13. Bayer, *Martin Luther's Theology*, 179.

14. "Apology to the Augsburg Confession, Article II: Original Sin," in Kolb and Wengert, *Book of Concord*, 111–20. Hereafter Ap. II.

15. "Formula of Concord Solid Declaration, Article I: Concerning Original Sin" in Kolb and Wengert, *Book of Concord*, 531–42. Hereafter FCSD Article I.

16. Kolb and Wengert, *Book of Concord*, 488.

17. Ibid.

Having set this overall, paradoxical framework in place, three initial observations frame the way Luther and the Lutheran Confessions approach original sin. First, the term "original sin" is perhaps more accurately named "universal sin" because their main concern, rather than explaining the origin of sin, is to articulate sin's devastating dimensions and "why all human beings in all ages without exception are opposed to God and therefore need a Savior."[18] Secondly, original sin is fundamentally a "meta," relational category emphasizing the disordered, broken nature of the relationship between the entire cosmos and God, rather than a "micro," private category emphasizing personal, private moral performance.[19] The ability of all people, Christian or non-Christian, to achieve a level of civil righteousness is rightly affirmed, but such righteousness operates in a different realm from the realm of salvation. Thirdly, humans are never in a neutral position in relation to God.

If sin is not taken seriously enough, then Christ and his merits are underestimated and "wasted." Conversely, "if sin is taken as seriously as it should be, then Christ cannot be taken lightly."[20] This axiom and logic guides all that Luther and the Confessions say regarding original sin. As Ap. II puts it, "For we cannot know the magnitude of Christ's grace unless we first recognize our malady."[21]

When we turn to Ap. II, we see Melanchthon's twofold intention to demonstrate, not only that the Lutheran confessors' view of original sin was congruent with the church's traditional definition, but also that their opponents' view of original sin was insufficiently deep, failing to account for its devastating power and influence. Ap. II makes two basic assertions regarding original sin. First, original sin is not merely the absence of original righteousness, but such absence is more particularly specified as excluding "not only the obedience of the lower human powers, but also the knowledge of God, trust in God, fear and love of God, or certainly the power needed to produce those things."[22] Human will and reason are prevented from functioning as they were meant to: rightly knowing and trusting God. The intervening obstacle and disruptive force, the Lutheran Confessions claim, is original sin. Secondly, while their opponents viewed

---

18. Gassman and Hendrix, *Fortress Introduction to the Lutheran Confessions*, 162.
19. Ibid.
20. Ibid., 154.
21. Kolb and Wengert, *Book of Concord*, 117.
22. Ibid., 115.

original sin as a tendency, human potentiality, and defect of human nature, Melanchthon argued that it was a serious, deadly condition "full of evil lust and inclination."[23] At stake was the notion of "concupiscence." While both parties accepted the reality of "concupiscence," they vehemently disagreed over whether or not the concupiscence remaining in human nature after baptism could be considered actual sin. The Lutheran confessors insisted it is sin. Their opponents considered this "tinder of sin" (*fomes peccati*) "a 'weakness' or 'inclination' to sin that was not sin in itself unless a person yielded to it."[24]

Far from being a merely technical issue of whether or not concupiscence is sin, the question of how concupiscence is understood raises the larger question of how to properly understand the severity of sin and necessity of baptism. Roman opponents accused Melanchthon of making light of both sin and the necessity of baptism ("If sin remains after baptism, as you insist, then why bother being baptized and becoming Christian?"). Melanchthon returned the charge, insisting his opponents were the ones underestimating the depth dimension of sin. Rather than original sin being wiped out and taken care of at baptism, it is a deeper, more persistently pernicious reality in Christian life than his opponents were willing to admit. Melanchthon, in emphasizing the ongoing influence of sin in Christians' lives necessitating the grace of Christ, cites Luther: ". . . when Luther wanted to expose the magnitude of original sin and human weakness, he taught that the remnants of original sin in the human being are not in their essence neutral, but need both the grace of Christ . . . and also the Holy Spirit, so that they might be put to death."[25]

As noted earlier, the *FCSD Article* I seeks to establish a delicate balance between the deep, pervasive corruption of original sin without claiming that human nature is essentially evil:

> To be sure, original sin has contaminated and corrupted all of human nature like a spiritual poison and leprosy . . . so that in our corrupted nature no one can show or prove what is unmistakably human nature and what is original sin. Nonetheless, the corrupted nature . . . and original sin . . . are not one and the same thing . . . According to Holy Scripture, both propositions

---

23. Ibid., 112.

24. Kolb and Wengert, *Book of Concord*, 113n. 13. For further articulation of this view of concupiscence, see Peter Lombard, *Sentences* II, d. 30, 7 (MPL 192:722) and Thomas Aquinas, *STh* III, q. 15, a. 2; q. 27, a. 3.

25. Kolb and Wengert, *Book of Concord*, 119.

must and can be considered, taught, and believed as distinct from each other.²⁶

When we turn to consider Luther on original sin, his clear concern in the *Smalcald Articles* is that the minimizing of original sin threatens both the necessity of Christ and the very integrity of the Gospel itself.²⁷ In listing seven errors of scholastic theology clearly resulting from underestimating the depth dimension of sin, Luther concludes, "... if these teachings were right, then Christ has died in vain. For there would be no defect or sin in humankind for which he had to die."²⁸ As with his explanation of the first commandment, Luther points to the core of original ("the chief") sin consisting of "not knowing or honoring God,"²⁹ manifesting itself as all the other visible, actual sins. Its seriousness and distorting power is such that it blinds reason; therefore "it must be believed on the basis of the revelation in the Scriptures (Ps 51:[5] and Rom 5[:12]; Exod 33[:20]; Gen 3[:6ff.])."³⁰

In contrast to Rahner's "nature/grace" paradigm, I will articulate a confessional Lutheran, "law/promise" theology of grace as the promise of loving mercy realized in Christ, one which tackles head-on the challenge of adequately addressing the depths of human sin as well as reconciling the paradox of divine wrath and divine mercy.³¹ Rahner's theology of

---

26. Ibid., 537.

27. Gassman and Hendrix, *Fortress Introduction to the Lutheran Confessions*, 154.

28. Kolb and Wengert, *Book of Concord*, 311.

29. Ibid., 310.

30. Ibid.

31. The question of whether or not, and to what extent, the wrath of God is central to a Christian theology of the cross and reconciliation was a much debated, controversial issue in nineteenth and twentieth century theology. The question of the necessity or centrality of divine wrath led directly and inevitably to the controversy over sacrificial, substitutionary theories of atonement. I will now briefly describe the broad contours of the debate concerning the wrath of God in order to historically situate my confessional Lutheran position and critique of Rahner's position. Martin Kähler, in his *Doctrine of Reconciliation* (1898), famously posed the question as, "Did Christ just make known some insights concerning an unchangeable situation—or did he establish a new situation?" In other words: What is the nature of the cross as a salvific event? Is the cross an illustrative event, demonstrating and revealing the unchangeable love of God which is not yet fully evident, or is the cross a constitutive event, creating a new situation by changing both the reality of God (from wrath against sin to reconciling mercy) and of the human condition (reconciling sinful human beings to God by bridging the divide between sinful humanity and a holy God)? These differing views constituted a major debate within Lutheran theology and

A Paradigm of Grace as Promise of Mercy Fulfilled

grace will then be articulated and constructively evaluated in chapter 3. Before proceeding, however, a recognition of the inflation of revelation the broader Reformation tradition. In terms of the illustrative view, Albrecht Ritschl, following in the liberal Protestant tradition established by Friedrich Schleiermacher, rejected the notion that sinners needs to be saved from divine wrath, and therefore that Jesus endured and "satisfied" God's wrath against sin by dying an atoning death as humanity's substitute. Ritschl found it impossible to speak of sinners being objects of God's love and God's wrath at the same time (Brondos, *Salvation and the Cross*, 206). Rather than God needing to be reconciled to humans on account of God's wrath against sin, sinful humans needed to be reconciled to God in their view and understanding of God's eternal love toward them. Instead of reconciliation being an event within *God's* self (the reconciliation of God's wrath with God's love) and justification an event located within humanity (as God imputing Christ's righteousness upon sinners as the promise of forgiveness for Christ's sake), Ritschl located *both* justification *and* reconciliation as changes within the human person's consciousness, awareness, and attitude toward God (Brondos, *Salvation and the Cross*, 123). Ritschl understood Jesus Christ as saving people through the divine revelation of God's eternal love toward them, demonstrated in his life and death. Furthermore, Ritschl insisted that the nature of salvation determines the nature of sin, and not the other way around. In affirming an eternally loving God, the nature of salvation centered on a change in human consciousness in relation to God, and rejecting the penal substitutionary theory of atonement, Ritschl has exercised tremendous influence within the nineteenth and twentieth century liberal Protestant tradition. His seminal works on this topic include the essay *De Ira Dei* (1859) and the three-volume *A Critical History of the Christian Doctrine of Justification and Reconciliation* (1870–1874). In contrast to the liberal Protestant view espoused by Ritschl, Adolph von Harnack, and others, the constitutive view of salvation insists that the cross of Christ is fundamentally an atoning event, constituting both the reconciliation of divine wrath with divine love as well as the forgiveness and acceptance of sinful humanity. A confessional Lutheran approach, building upon the work of such scholars as Werner Elert, Helmut Thielicke, Gustaf Wingren, Gerhard Forde, Oswald Bayer, and Edward Schroeder, argues for the necessity of atonement and the constitutive view of the cross as accounting more comprehensively for the scriptural witness to the life, death, and the significance of the life and death of Jesus Christ, than the illustrative view. I will argue for this view, and its implications for a theology of grace, in the remainder of this chapter. The critique which a confessional Lutheran position lodges against both the liberal Protestant, illustrative view of the cross and Rahner's theology of grace is that neither assigns a significant enough place for divine wrath and the Law within their theological system. It is significant to note that an acceptance or rejection of the wrath of God is intimately (inevitably?) connected to an acceptance or rejection of the distinction between law and gospel. While Ritschl and the theological tradition following him firmly reject both doctrines, a proper recognition of both the Law and wrath of God are essential to my confessional Lutheran articulation, not only of an adequate theology of grace, but also of its missiological implications. While Rahner's theology of revelation and grace is not a participant in this intra-Protestant debate, one can clearly see how his theological approach and method represent the illustrative approach to the cross, reconciliation, and atonement. We will examine Rahner's approach as a distinctive contrast to a confessional Lutheran approach in the next chapter.

89

within theology offers a historical context for my confessional Lutheran missiology.

THE INFLATION OF THE CONCEPT OF REVELATION

From a confessional Lutheran perspective, one concerning development in twentieth century theology has been the inflation of the concept of revelation. Following Immanuel Kant's critique of pure reason and his question, "What can we know?" modern theology has become increasingly preoccupied with the question of revelation. The proliferation of theologies of revelation largely reflects the theological response to this post-Kantian, epistemological crisis. As theologians became weary of battles over differences in soteriology, the category of revelation became increasingly attractive and dominant. To the extent that the question of knowledge has become central in theology ("How and what can we know about God?"), it seems inevitable that revelation as the answer would become the central, theological category.[32] Rahner's transcendental anthropology and theology of grace, as elaborated in chapter 3, is one way of addressing this epistemological crisis.

In contrast to Dupuis' Rahnerian orientation which primarily emphasizes grace and marginalizes the importance of sin and law, a confessional Lutheran approach insists on two crucial points: 1) the question of salvation is always prior to and more central than the question of revelation for Christian theology, and 2) a shift in the overall theological discourse away from soteriology toward theologies of revelation muddies the missiological waters by failing to appreciate the crucial role of divine law and the centrality of a theology of reconciliation. I will clarify and defend this claim as this chapter unfolds. In other words: a primary emphasis on the dynamics of *reconciliation* is always more primary for Christian missiology than the dynamics of *grace*, if such grace is primarily knowledge and revelation of God's presence.

A Lutheran proposal views the relative ascendancy of the category of revelation over soteriology with a healthy dose of caution. Confessional

---

32. Braaten, *Justification*, 71–72. While Dupuis and other proponents of the "presence of Christ in the religions" approach might argue that contemporary theologies of revelation are being interrelated to, rather than shifting away from, soteriology, the practical result and impact of such theologies of revelation is a primary emphasis on explicating the universal presence of divine love and grace, while marginalizing the dynamics of reconciling divine wrath with divine love.

A Paradigm of Grace as Promise of Mercy Fulfilled

Lutheran theology cautions and reminds systematic theology that, for it to remain Christian systematic theology, revelation should properly be understood in service to salvation, not the other way around, and that a proper distinction (never separation!) between revelation and salvation, grounded in the law/Gospel distinction, is fundamental to properly relating revelation and salvation. Carl Braaten summarizes my distinctively Lutheran reservations:

> There is good reason to question the dominant role that revelation plays in modern theology. Revelation is not the supreme category of Christian dogmatics; salvation is! The supremacy of revelation [as a category] assumes that the basic human predicament is the lack of the knowledge of God. However, from a biblical perspective God is engaged in a cosmic struggle over against willful rebellion. The fundamental human predicament is the enslavement of the human will to the powers of sin, death, and the Devil. Then reconciliation—not revelation that answers to the question of knowledge—becomes the key category because it answers to the question of sin as estrangement. Furthermore, when revelation becomes the focal point of dogmatics, it relegates Jesus Christ primarily to the role of revelation . . . Our word of caution is meant to point out that revelation is not the single most important category for interpreting the divine-human relationship . . . We hold . . . a twofold revelation of God—through the law of creation (*lex creationis*) and through the gospel of Christ. There is revelation not only of God's redemptive love in Jesus Christ but also of God's law through the structures of creation. It is essential to draw a proper distinction between revelation and salvation. Not all revelation is salvific; there is also the revelation of divine wrath and judgment through world historical events and personal experiences. Jesus Christ is not the sole revelation of God . . . The truly unique thing that happens in Christ is God's act of reconciliation.[33]

Some American theologians have recognized and elaborated this critique of revelationism (the view that all revelation has salvific value), most notably Carl Braaten, Robert Bertram, and Edward Schroeder. However, due to the fundamentalist Biblicism inherent in some branches of American Lutheran theology and Barthian emphases in other branches, this fundamental axiom in Lutheran theology has been largely ignored in the North American context. However, the prolegomena of Apology

---

33. Braaten, *That All May Believe*, 12–13.

IV clearly evidences this critique (see chapter 1). This emphasis is much better known and more widely embraced and articulated by Lutheran theologians in Europe. One major figure for such a critique of revelationism in the European context has been Werner Elert in his textbooks on dogmatics and ethics, as well as his classic monograph, *Law and Gospel*. Karl Barth has had a tremendous impact upon European theology in the post-World War II era, also among Lutheran theologians, with the result that the debate about revelationism continues among Lutherans. One example of this debate is evidenced in the theological publications of the Lutheran World Federation, where grace is articulated primarily in terms of human nature being fulfilled in and flourishing under divine lordship, rather than as the reconciliation of divine wrath in mercy.[34]

In conclusion: the Gospel (as promise of reconciliation) must serve a critical function in shaping the overall theological framework for Christian missiology. Gustaf Wingren expresses this Lutheran concern in a lament: "It is exactly this framework [of prioritizing revelation] which is questionable. 'Revelation' stands in the place where 'justification' or 'forgiveness of sins,' i.e., the gospel in the essential meaning of that word, ought to stand."[35] Braaten clarifies how confessional Lutheran concerns regarding the concept of revelation center on the human need for reconciliation addressed by the Gospel:

> The picture of the human predicament is very different whether the problem of knowledge and revelation predominates or whether the problem of estrangement and reconciliation. In our view the human being stands under divine wrath and judgment, not without knowledge but without excuse, and thus guilty. The gospel enters a situation in which God and human beings have already been involved with each other, delivering a new righteousness apart from the law . . . through faith in Jesus Christ.[36]

---

34. See, for example, the Lutheran World Federation's *Mission in Context: Transformation, Reconciliation, Empowerment—An LWF Contribution to the Understanding and Practice of Mission*. While this document recognizes that "God's grace, overcoming the consequences of sin—alienation, death, and depravity—extends beyond the individual to all communities, to all creation," it nonetheless subsumes this passing definition of grace under a larger, operational definition of grace as human nature fulfilled in God and under God's lordship.

35. Wingren, *Theology in Conflict*, 28–29.

36. Braaten, *Justification*, 74.

A Paradigm of Grace as Promise of Mercy Fulfilled

More recently, in its efforts to bridge the gap between God and humanity, dialectical theology has employed various contrasts—the ontic contrast between creator and creation, the noetic contrast between divine revelation and human reception of that revelation, etc.—without seriously engaging the classic, Lutheran contrast (distinction) between law and Gospel.[37] My contention is this: to the extent that the main theological problem or human dilemma is defined in terms of relating divine self-communication to human reception of that communication—whether it be through dialectical theology, Rahner's transcendental anthropology, or some other system—to that extent a fundamental dialectic and problem has been overlooked, namely how to interrelate the divine speech of law and Gospel, wrath and promise, and how to resolve the intractable dilemma the divine law creates for humanity.

A CONFESSIONAL LUTHERAN THEOLOGY OF GRACE AS PROMISE OF MERCY REALIZED

Before articulating the key components of a confessional Lutheran theology of loving mercy, we begin by noting its relative absence in the historical discussion regarding nature and grace (see chapter 3). While certainly a minority voice or opinion in the broad scope of Western Christianity, this view of grace as the promise of mercy realized, far from being a Lutheran or Reformation innovation, has solid scriptural (as I will demonstrate shortly) as well as Augustinian roots. Augustine's understanding of sin and grace, articulated in terms of divine wrath and mercy, locates the basis of salvation in the divine promise of grace (mercy) and God's faithfulness to that promise. While it may have been largely buried under the dominant discussion of relating nature and grace, it has at various times throughout church history been recovered and re-utilized. The modest goal of this project is to contribute to precisely such a recovery and renewed appreciation of a crucial, relevant theme for Christian missiology. In place of the "nature/grace" paradigm in its various manifestations (Rahnerian, medieval, or ancient), I submit the "law/promise" paradigm as a more scripturally robust, as well as missiologically fruitful, articulation of grace.

Before delving into the specifics of a confessional Lutheran theology of mercy, it is vitally important to note that Rahner and I share the same

---

37. Elert, *Law and Gospel*, 2.

goal: to have God be the immanently near God of loving grace. How God can honestly, truthfully, and faithfully, to quote Rahner, "be the innermost center of our existence in free grace and self-communication."[38] To press the question even further: How can God be a gracious God and "do mercy" honestly and actually, in a way in which God is faithful *both* to his holiness *and* his justice, both as a God of wrath against sin and a God of love who nevertheless loves sinners with an everlasting love? *That* is the foundational question that this chapter aims to address, and Rahner and my confessional Lutheran proposals go about answering that question in fundamentally different ways.

First of all, a confessional Lutheran theology of grace as "promise of mercy fulfilled" insists that all theologies of grace, and the theologies of revelation which undergird them, must squarely face and answer two fundamental questions: "First, *as what* is God revealed? Only as gracious? Not also as wrathful? Second, is it *only* God who is revealed? Aren't we as well?"[39] Gerhard Forde relates this dual conviction aptly to a theology of the cross: "the cross is not in the first instance a revelation of the love or mercy of God. It is rather the climactic manifestation of God's wrath against sin . . . It is the expression of God's jealousy against a world that will not have this God as a God of mercy."[40] In terms of what God is revealed as, a confessional Lutheran approach explicitly contrasts itself with the Rahnerian, "nature/grace" model. I will follow Bertram's nomenclature in referring to Rahner's "nature/grace" model, and theologies which base their articulations of grace and mission upon it, as "revelationist."[41]

The distinction between divine revelation and salvation, analogous and closely related to the law/Gospel distinction, is central to a Lutheran theology of mercy as promise realized. Carl Braaten articulates this crucial distinction in these terms: "We argue for a twofold revelation of God. There is a universal revelation of God through all the media of creation- through nature, history, moral conscience, and religious experience. But then, in contrast to this, there is a unique revelation of God in Christ that is categorically different in kind, and not only in degree."[42]

---

38. Rahner, *Foundations*, 12.
39. Bertram, *Time for Confessing*, 161.
40. Forde, "Atonement as Actual Event," 90.
41. Bertram, *Time for Confessing*, 160.
42. Braaten, *That All May Believe*, 166.

A brief sketch of the presuppositions of such revelationist theologies helps articulate how the Lutheran, law/promise paradigm is a radical alternative to such theologies. First of all, such theologies of revelation, undergirding the "nature/grace" model, take an illustrative view of the person and work of Christ. What needs to be revealed to humanity, what the work and cross of Christ show, is the fact that the world is already saved, the assurance that humanity is already forgiven and reconciled, that we are in fact already loved. The only change needed is human awareness and acceptance of this graced reality.[43] Since the divine-human relationship is by definition gracious, "the only decisive relation is not our relationship to God but God's to us, which allegedly has never needed changing in the first place."[44]

The Interpersonal Dynamic of Divine Grace and Human Faith

In contrast to such revelationist understandings of what God is revealed as, a confessional Lutheran view emphasizes the inevitably interpersonal, dialogical nature of the Biblical notion of love and grace. From this perspective, the divine initiative of loving and showing grace to humanity, far from being a settled or guaranteed reality, is a perilous venture which can and sometimes is thwarted; not from God's side, but from the human side. In comparing divine love to human love and, specifically, the dynamics of promise-making and promise-keeping, such a view emphasizes the central role humanity plays in appropriating or receiving divine love and grace. As Schroeder, Bertram, and Forde have put it: the divine, loving promise of grace (mercy) is wasted if it is not received and appropriated. Such reception is precisely what faith is all about: namely, trusting and receiving the promise of mercy. As Bertram states: "[I]f those whom God promises to love should disbelieve the Promiser, then they are not in fact "getting" loved. What they are getting—and from God!—is the opposite. Conversely, it is exactly in their trusting the Promiser that the promised love comes true."[45]

Werner Elert further emphasizes the consequences of the Gospel as an offer: "The very meaning of the word "offer" includes the possibility

---

43. This was a central claim of Albrecht Ritschl and the tradition of Protestant liberal theology influenced by him.

44. Bertram, *Time for Confessing,* 160.

45. Ibid., 161.

of rejection. If the offer is rejected, it does not become effective. Then the wrath and the judgment of God remain valid. By making an offer the Gospel becomes a promise. It does not want to instruct; it wants to bestow a gift . . .; it wants to convey forgiveness of sin."[46]

In contrast to revelationist theologies of grace like Rahner's, which view the task of Christian mission as informing the world that it is already forgiven and saved, rather than proclaiming the necessity of "getting" forgiven and reconciled through Christ, a confessional Lutheran view of the first question I posed earlier (As what is God revealed?) posits that the Pauline language of grace is best understood as a relational offer of loving mercy which must be accepted in order to be appropriated. The divine offer of grace can be either accepted or rejected, therefore becoming actualized as grace in a person's life or becoming instead a form of divine judgment.[47] When divine grace is emphasized to the exclusion and neglect of the reality of divine wrath, such "grace" falls short in terms of addressing only half of the scriptural witness to divine revelation.

In other words: God speaks two related, but distinctly paradoxical, words of revelation. God is revealed, not only as gracious (merciful), but also as wrathful. It is precisely this two-fold divine revelation which the Lutheran tradition insists is best preserved and articulated in the law/Gospel distinction. As Paul put it, "For the wrath of God is revealed from heaven against . . . the wickedness of those who by their wickedness suppress the truth" (Rom 1:18). The disturbing aspect of this wrath, one that is overlooked, suppressed, and thus needs revealing, is the "active acquiescence of the Creator" in human wickedness.[48] Paul uses the term "God gave them up" three times in Rom 1: 24, 26, and 28 to emphasize how the divine acquiescence to sin's inevitable course is a form of divine judgment and wrath.

The Divine Dilemma

As the treatment of the law/Gospel distinction in the previous chapter emphasized, the duality of the divine address as both law and Gospel, wrath and mercy, judgment and promise, highlights what is at stake in a confessional Lutheran insistence on the "law/promise" polarity as being

---

46. Elert, *Structure of Lutheranism*, 65–66.
47. Bertram, *Time for Confessing*, 161.
48. Ibid., 162.

more faithful to the deep Biblical grammar and message than the more commonly accepted, "sin-grace" polarity. The central claim of a confessional Lutheran proposal on grace is this: the proper location, main arena, and focal point for articulating a Biblical theology of grace (mercy) is *within God's self, rather than in the divine-human interface*. Why? Because any theology of grace which "solves" the problem of human sin merely by addressing how the human problem of sin is solved by grace, how human nature is fulfilled by grace, fails to address the deeper problematic and paradox of how divine wrath and mercy can be reconciled. Bertram sums up a Lutheran articulation of this problematic: "The starkest theological antithesis is not, as we often pretend, between "sin and grace," namely, between something *we* do (sin) and something *God* does (grace). True, that antithesis would be stark enough . . . But no, starker still is the corresponding antithesis between something *God* does (judgment) and something *God* does (mercy). It is the antithesis, as Paul puts it, between divine Law and divine promise, between God's cursing and God's blessing."[49]

He goes on to describe the source of this paradox, God's divine quandry:

> The opposites are, on the one hand, "the world," which in all honesty God finds infuriating. On the other hand, is God "himself" who, though he yearns to love this world, yearns to love it not cheaply or permissively but in all honesty. That is a quandary. How to reconcile these opposites? . . . God longs to square these two polar opposites, "the world" and "himself," yet to do so honestly. Why? So that in all honesty ("righteousness"), God can love that world.[50]

A confessional Lutheran proposal for how to solve this paradox and apparent contradiction in God's self, by employing the pairing wrath/mercy (law/promise) and taking both terms with utter seriousness, claims to be most faithful to Biblical grammar. Rather than evading the paradox, either by defining wrath as a "passing form of grace" (contra Barth),[51] or by employing a transcendental anthropology which fails to do justice to the scriptural witness of the depth of divine wrath against sin (contra Rahner), a Lutheran proposal seeks to demonstrate how God himself finds a way to "'reconcile' the contradiction (2 Cor 5:18–19), and

---

49. Ibid., 163.
50. Ibid., 167.
51. Ibid., 164.

at immense personal cost... [and] embarrassment... to God's unity and consistency."[52]

While the dynamics of how a theology of mercy plays out will be articulated shortly, an introductory definition of the key terms involved will orient us, at this time, to their subsequent use. What do I mean by terms such as "wrath," "satisfaction," "atonement," and "reconciliation"? Gerhard Forde comments on the interrelationship between atonement, satisfaction, and wrath:

> Atonement occurs when God gives himself in such a fashion as to create a people pleasing to God, a people no longer under law or wrath, a people who love and trust God. When God succeeds in that, God is "satisfied"... The question for atonement is whether God can succeed in doing this. The question is not whether there is blood precious enough to pay God, or even the devil, but whether God has acted decisively to win us... whether God can actually give himself in such a way as to save us. For God is not the problem, we are. Can God actually deliver us from wrath, save us from sin and embittered hostility, and bring something new?... Can wrath be ended? But that is a question of what God gives and not what God gets, for it is... God's wrath, and only God can end it.[53]

From this quote, we can readily see how a Lutheran view of atonement focuses on achieving the goal of human trust in God's promise of mercy. As Forde puts it, "When faith is created, God has reached the goal and is 'satisfied.'"[54] "Satisfaction," rather than operating within the basic structure of payment of a debt to God or substitution for punishment (e.g. theories of vicarious satisfaction), instead emphasizes God's "satisfaction" at Christ's victory over the law and sin in the inevitable collision between sin and righteousness. Such satisfaction has an inevitably fiduciary, promissory framework: "God is satisfied when he is believed, trusted, as the one who has mercy... God is [satisfied] because God's mercy accomplishes its aim... when sins are forgiven, and [when] we finally believe that."[55] The emphasis is on pleasure over the divine mission being accomplished on the cross, over the divine initiative and self-gift being received by and resulting in faith, rather than on satisfaction over a debt

52. Ibid., 163.
53. Forde, "Luther's Theology of the Cross," 50–51.
54. Ibid., 65.
55. Ibid., 76, 74.

paid. As Forde puts it, "If God were the object of satisfaction, there would be no need for incarnation or the cross."[56] Within this context, "wrath" is understood as ending "only in God's self-giving to us . . . But it is not payment to God. It is a gift from God."[57] God's wrath is simply God's loving infuriation at and "burning jealousy" for sinners who insist on playing God and rebuffing the divine gift rather than receive it in gratitude. Such wrath is "satisfied in the sense that God's resolve to have mercy breaks through . . . to create faith."[58] This wrath of God has a dual structure: it is the reality of God's absence (as the hidden God) and "the inescapable reality of God's omnipresence as the God of law."[59] In what follows, the emphasis lies on God's loving initiative and self-gift, rather than on God's anger being appeased by payment.

Resolving the Divine Dilemma: the Centrality of Atoning Reconciliation

A central confessional Lutheran conviction is that an adequate theology of revelation, one that leads to a theology of mercy robust enough to undergird and motivate a theology of mission, must adequately account for and employ the Biblical notions of *atonement* and *reconciliation*. In terms of understanding the "divine dilemma" God faces in dealing with the problematic of reconciling a world God finds infuriating, the following list of scriptural texts provides an adequate, although by no means exhaustive, locus for delineating and grappling with this problematic: 2 Cor 3: 7–18, 2 Cor 5: 17–21, Rom 5, Gal 4, Eph 1, Mark 2, John 1 and 2, Heb 3, 6–10, as well as the juxtaposition of Moses and Jesus throughout the Gospel of John. While the limits of this study prevent an in-depth exegesis of each of these passages, I will examine a representative sampling to demonstrate how they support a theology of reconciliation as the promise of mercy realized.

Before proceeding further, it is important to keep in mind what Paul and the New Testament refer to in using terms such as "ministry of condemnation," "lesser ministry," "lesser or old covenant," and "lesser sacrifices." While such terms may sound like Christian caricatures or

56. Ibid., 52.
57. Forde, "Reconciliation with God," 72.
58. Forde, "Atonement as Actual Event," 98.
59. Forde, "Reconciliation with God," 72.

stereotypes of Judaism as a religion of the law, in contrast to Christianity as a religion of the Gospel, that is a fundamental misunderstanding of what is being conveyed.[60] A confessional Lutheran view designates "the ministry of condemnation" under the rubric of law, while the "ministry that brings righteousness" is defined as the Gospel. "Condemnation" or "lesser covenant" and "righteousness" or "new covenant" refer primarily to the contrast between law and Gospel, *not* to Judaism as a religion of the law versus Christianity as a religion of the Gospel. The promise of God which finds particular concentration, clarification, and culmination in Jesus Christ is the same promise which was made to the patriarchs and the people of Israel, not withstanding a long, complicated history of legalistic distortions, rebellious discursions, and times of alternating clarity and hiddenness regarding the promise motif. The law always accuses, wherever it may be found: in Christian theology, Judaism, or in varying forms in the world religions. While some may draw supercessionist conclusions from the New Testament in general and these texts in particular, a Lutheran theology of mercy centered on reconciliation neither demands nor necessitates such an approach. In other words: the centrality of reconciliation for a Christian theology of grace as the promise of mercy fulfilled in Christ is applicable and relevant to a Christian theology of mission, regardless of one's views on Christianity's relationship to Judaism and the question of one versus two covenants.

With that in mind, a confessional Lutheran theology of mercy as an articulation of the problematic of reconciliation is introduced when two Pauline passages, 2 Cor 3: 7–18 and 2 Cor 5: 17–21, are placed side by side:

> (3:7) Now if the ministry that brought death, which was engraved in letters of stone, came with glory, so that the Israelites could not look steadily at the face of Moses because of its glory, fading though it was, (8) will not the ministry of the Spirit be even more glorious? (9) If the ministry that condemns men is glorious, how much more glorious is the ministry that brings righteousness? (10) For what was glorious has no glory now in comparison with the surpassing glory. (11) And if what was fading away came with glory, how much greater is the glory of that which lasts! . . . (5:17) Therefore, if anyone is in Christ, he is a new creation; the old has gone, the new has come! (18) All

---

60. The "new perspective" on Paul, championed by E. P. Sanders, James Dunn, and N. T. Wright, makes this point especially forcefully.

this is from God, who reconciled us to himself through Christ and gave us the ministry of reconciliation: (19) that God was reconciling the world to himself in Christ, not counting people's sins against them. And he has committed to us the message of reconciliation. (20) We are therefore Christ's ambassadors, as though God were making his appeal through us. We implore you on Christ's behalf: Be reconciled to God. (21) God made him who knew no sin to be sin for us, so that in him we might become the righteousness of God.

Paul's argument in this section of 2 Corinthians juxtaposes two contrasting ministries, those of "condemnation" and "righteousness," with the contrast between "old creation" and "new creation" in Christ. The focal, transition point between both pairings is the ministry and work of Jesus, specifically as agent of divine reconciliation on the cross. A proper appreciation of the dynamics of reconciliation entails a recognition, with Paul, of two covenants, two ministries; in other words, of law and Gospel. While both covenants and ministries (law and Gospel) are glorious and valuable in their own right, how might they be properly related in a way which helps illumine the process of reconciliation and the dilemma it poses for God? I will attempt to unpack that complex issue later in this chapter. For now, what is important to note is that this perspective on the centrality of reconciliation for a sufficiently robust theology of mercy is not merely a Pauline perspective, but is also found in the Gospels and the entire New Testament.[61]

61. In the gospels, especially in the gospels of Mark and John, we find an integral connection between the concept of reconciliation, Jesus' claim to have the authority to forgive sins, and the nature of what is "good" in the "good news," i.e., the Gospel. In Mark's gospel, Jesus begins his public ministry with the call to repentance: "The time is fulfilled and the kingdom of God has come near; repent and believe in the good news" (1:15). What is the nature of that repentance, and how is it related to forgiveness, Jesus, and the temple cult?

While scholarship has traditionally emphasized discipleship and the messianic secret as chief Markan themes, the unique contribution of Lutheran theology has been to highlight the integral connection between the forgiveness of sins, Jesus, and the centrality of reconciliation. While scholars like James Dunn caution "the sparseness of the theme within the Jesus tradition forbids any attempt to make much of the theme (Jesus and forgiveness)," based on their conviction that "it was not so much that Jesus usurped the exclusive prerogative of God to forgive sins which caused offense, as that he usurped the role which God had assigned to the priest and the cult in the established religion of the people." I side with those scholars (Graham Stanton, Vincent Taylor, etc.) who take the opposing view that the offense Jesus caused was *precisely because* he was heard and remembered as *self-referentially* declaring the unambiguous authority to forgive sins. I find this view more compelling because, coupled with

Jesus as Sacrifice "For Us"

In articulating a theology of grace/mercy that deals with the cross, a sufficiently robust view of sacrifice is crucial. Given the prevalence of the theme of sacrifice, not only in the Hebrew Scriptures but also in the New Testament's view of Jesus Christ as the sacrifice *par excellence* (especially in the book of Hebrews), what does a confessional Lutheran proposal do with the central, New Testament affirmation that Jesus' death was a sacrifice "for us"? The controversial status of "sacrifice" in current theories of atonement makes this task all the more pressing. To articulate a new, perhaps even non-cultic or nonreligious concept of sacrifice, a few initial affirmations are necessary. First, "the death of Jesus must interpret and fulfill the nature of sacrifice, not vice versa."[62] Secondly, given that sacrifice, like grace, is a "polyvalent symbol" with an excess of meaning, it would be mistaken and misleading to rigidly restrict it to ideas of penal substitution or propitiation. "Jesus dies for us and not for God."[63] Thirdly, Jesus' sacrifice, in contrast to ritual, cultic sacrifices, is utterly real. "He

---

Jesus' evident authority, it seems to make the most comprehensive sense of the various "forgiveness" passages throughout Mark's gospel. Furthermore, *theologically* it unites and integrates the gospel's beginning ("the beginning of the gospel about Jesus Christ, the Son of God") with its ending (the centurion's confession: "Surely this man was the Son of God") logically and consistently—*if* Jesus was the Son of God, as Mark insists, *then* his authority to forgive sins is logically and theologically plausible.

In terms of an overarching Markan motif: if 1:15 presents Jesus calling people to repentance and believing the good news, can that activity be separated from the authority (*exousia*) by which he claimed to forgive sins? To claim, as Dunn does, that the real source of offense at Jesus was his bypassing the temple cult system of forgiveness, begs the important question of authority: on what *basis*, and by whose/what *authority*, are sins forgiven? Furthermore: whatever one *historically* claims regarding the temple cult and forgiveness, *historically* the Jesus movement came to regard Jesus as offering divine forgiveness, and *theologically* the New Testament portrays Jesus as replacing the temple, *precisely* in terms of offering divine forgiveness. Examples include: the Johannine body of Jesus representing the temple (John 2:19–21), Jesus' high priesthood and sacrifice replacing the temple cult (in the book of Hebrews, which we will consider shortly), the Pauline claim that "in Christ God was reconciling the world unto himself, not counting people's sins against them" (2 Cor 5:19), and Jesus' granting his disciples the authority to forgive sins or withhold forgiveness (John 20:23). While the limitations of space preclude an in-depth study of the relationship between reconciliation, forgiveness, and authority, and *regardless* of one's views on supercessionism, my point is simply this: the forgiveness of sins, as a prerogative claimed by the Markan Jesus, is *organically connected* to Jesus' ministry of reconciliation.

62. Forde, "Atonement as Actual Event," 80.

63. Ibid., 82.

A Paradigm of Grace as Promise of Mercy Fulfilled

bears our sins in his body—actually. The real event occurs. It is not a rehearsal or a cultic substitution."[64] While "the cultic apparatus was only a rehearsal" for the real sacrifice on the cross, what is jarringly unsettling for all theories of sacrifice is that the book of Hebrews places the emphasis in comparing Jesus' sacrifice, not to the temple sacrifices and ritual acts of purifications, but rather to the burning of animal refuse at the city garbage dump: "So Jesus also suffered outside the gate in order to sanctify the people through his own blood" (Heb 13:13).[65] Fourthly, a proper affirmation and understanding of sacrifice helps move us toward a view of atonement as actual and real.[66] Fifthly, in affirming the event of the cross as an utterly shameful, publically humiliating execution, the shocking nature of this sacrifice is preserved and not minimized. Affirming Jesus' death as both execution and sacrifice are not mutually exclusive. Gerhard Forde offers a helpful image for understanding the cross as a real sacrifice: "A child is playing in the street. A truck is bearing down on the child. A man casts himself in the path of the truck, saves the child, but is himself killed in the process. It is an accident . . . The accidental death of the man who saved the child could be called a sacrifice, indeed, even a vicarious sacrifice. He gave his life for another. And the point is that this is all one needs to say."[67]

This analogy, while imperfect, makes some helpful points for a Lutheran view of Jesus' death as a sacrifice. First, "it is not a ritual or cultic sacrifice . . . but a real sacrifice, an actual one." Secondly, the question of "to whom" the sacrifice is offered becomes inappropriate and unnecessary. Thirdly, in addressing the New Testament language of Jesus dying "for us," "one has said all there is to say when one has said [Jesus' death was] 'for us all.'"[68] Fourthly, this analogy illustrates a double emphasis within a Lutheran understanding of atonement. Not only does Jesus' sacrifice save *us* from death (identifying us as the child in danger), but it also underscores the permanently offensive nature of the cross by further identifying us with the truck driver. As such, *we* bear personal responsibility for the sacrificial death of Jesus: he died, not only to deal with the consequences of our sin (our own death), but also to intervene in the

---

64. Ibid., 90.
65. Ibid., 86–87.
66. Ibid., 88.
67. Ibid., 88–89.
68. Ibid., 89.

deadly consequences of our sin upon others. Jesus' sacrifice on the cross, far from an isolated, historically accidental event, instead shows us the necessity of sacrifice: "there is nothing God can or will do but die at our hands: bear our sins."[69] This sacrificial death has universal significance for us because, while Jesus was universally rejected, God vindicated this Jesus by raising him from the dead. Forde encapsulates how forgiveness relates to such an understanding of Jesus' death as sacrifice:

> Jesus had to die because God is forgiving and because God insists on being so. Jesus died precisely because he said, "I forgive you in God's name." He died because we would not have it. The resurrection is his vindication . . . against death, the power of death resident in our legalism. It is the proof that he was right and we are wrong . . . To get [forgiveness] said precisely as forgiveness and not another law, Jesus must die and shatter all opposition even among his own. He must negate the law, the particularization, concretely, so that forgiveness can be said universally to all. Just so did he die for us.[70]

Fundamental Convictions

Having sketched a confessional Lutheran proposal for viewing Jesus' death as vicarious sacrifice, we return to complete the previous discussion of the two covenants and ministries. How might they be properly related in a way that helps illumine the process of reconciliation and the dilemma it poses for God? A confessional Lutheran attempt at doing so operates out of several fundamental convictions, guided by the law-Gospel distinction and grounded in these texts. First, atonement is an actual event. "Jesus came and died because God *is* merciful, not to make God merciful. We killed him because he forgave sins, not to make forgiveness possible."[71] Secondly, going with Paul's allegory of the divine law being veiled, the law's fierce condemnation of humanity, the fact that it always accuses (*lex semper accusat*), has been muted and "veiled" for our sake. We simply could not handle the terrifying truth that we live under a death sentence, that "All who rely on observing the law are under a curse, for . . . no one is justified before God by the law" (Gal 3:10–11).

69. Ibid., 91.
70. Ibid., 92.
71. Ibid., 79.

A Paradigm of Grace as Promise of Mercy Fulfilled

Thirdly, while people may live under the "illusion of a wrath-less, fulfillable Law," the real nature of the law as a "ministry of death" (2 Cor 3:7) forces God into a dilemma: "Can God be party to that deception and still be honest, 'righteous'? On the other hand, can God be 'open' with us (2 Cor 4:2), unveiled, without destroying us?"[72] Fourthly, the Law's veil is lifted in the ministry and death of Jesus Christ by Christ "interposing himself in the Law's line of fire."[73] On the cross, "as God's 'blessing' overcomes God's 'curse,' *both* are revealed for what they are: real curse which in Christ alone is trumped by real blessing" (Gal 3:13).[74] In other words, the reconciliation Paul is talking about involves a real transaction and exchange: the new creation occurs when and because "God . . . not counting [people's] sins against them . . . [instead] made [Christ] who had no sin, to be sin for us" (2 Cor 5: 19, 21). Fifthly, because this change and transaction happens "in Christ," it occurs *to* God and *in* God, with the result that "whatever conflict there may have been in God is now settled." Sixthly, this reconciliation which was accomplished in Christ, rather than automatically or coercively being applied to people's lives, instead must be appropriated by faith in order for it to achieve its intended goal. Acceptance and rejection, trusting or not trusting the promise and offer of reconciliation, are real possibilities, and therefore the church's mission involves extending the offer of reconciliation. Finally, Bertram describes how a confessional Lutheran theology of revelation envisions incorporating the central, Biblical notion of reconciliation: "It is only when and as the divine opposites, curse and blessing, wrath and mercy, are in Christ historically *reconciled* that there is any *revelation* of mercy. Indeed, only then is there any actualized mercy to be revealed. Apart from that and prior to that historic reconciliation, the revelation is at best anticipatory."[75]

While God's reconciliation in Christ was enacted in the death and resurrection of Jesus, that reconciliation is an ongoing, present reality and divine "project." From a Lutheran perspective, two distinct possibilities exist: to accept God's reconciliation in Christ and therefore actually to be reconciled, versus rejecting that reconciliation, in which case the intended goal of reconciliation is not realized, but rather thwarted. The

---

72. Bertram, *Time for Confessing*, 165.
73. Ibid.
74. Ibid., 166.
75. Ibid., 168.

former is what confessional Lutheran theology understands faith to consist of. Within this context, not only is God revealed, but also the nature of saving faith is revealed as that which accepts and trusts the promise of God's reconciliation of the world in Christ.

Resolution of the Tension Between Law and Gospel

Confessional Lutheran theology claims that it is only in the life, ministry, death, and resurrection of Jesus Christ (the Christ event) that the tension between law and gospel is definitively resolved, once and for all. Jesus' death on the cross is the focal point where law and gospel, wrath and mercy, judgment and pardon, curse and blessing, death and new life, converge in a decisive way. Let us first view the cross as an expression of the gospel.

The death and crucifixion of Jesus express three important facets of the nature of the gospel.[76] First, the cross of Jesus, like the divine law, is a revelation and word of God. However, in contrast to the law, it is not merely a spoken word but rather a personal Word, the Word made incarnate. Second, the gospel consists, not merely of the words and teachings of Christ (a speaking Christ), but also of the dying and resurrected Christ. What happened *to* Jesus on the cross is central to the gospel.[77] Third, the rationale for "the word of the cross" (1 Cor 1:18) being termed "good news" or gospel is found in key phrases the New Testament uses to interpret the significance of Jesus' death: it happened "for our sins" and "for our justification" (Rom 4:25).

How, then, can the death of Jesus resolve the tension between law and gospel? How is it simultaneously an act of judgment and mercy? The answer lies in seeing that Jesus died voluntarily, not only *to reveal* the

---

76. Elert, *Law and Gospel*, 17.

77. A Lutheran emphasis on the centrality of Jesus' death on the cross in no way minimizes the importance of his actions of healing, compassion, exorcisms, table fellowship, etc. The classic Lutheran distinction between Christ's active obedience (actively fulfilling the demands of the law for us) versus passive obedience (his suffering and death on the cross) makes this abundantly clear. The point I am making is simply this: the resolution of law and Gospel, divine judgment and mercy, God's righteous holiness and love, is enacted and accomplished in the events of the cross and resurrection. A sole emphasis on Jesus' teaching and acts of mercy, without sufficient treatment of the centrality of the cross and resurrection, fails to adequately elaborate what is involved in the resolution of divine wrath with divine mercy, how God can simultaneously be a righteous God of justice and love.

A Paradigm of Grace as Promise of Mercy Fulfilled

curse of the law, but *to bear it* himself on behalf of sinners. The death of Jesus is the paradigm of divine judgment *par excellence*: God, using the law of the land against the promise, was administering justice according to the law of retribution. God's verdict is that God accepts this one act of pure expiation (the innocent dying for the ungodly), resulting in the curse of life under the law being abolished for all (Gal 3:13, Rom 3:25, 1 John 2:2, 4:10, Heb 9:28).[78] As Elert puts it, "Whereas the promise made by the law applies to those who fulfill it, this promise applies to the transgressors who have not fulfilled it."[79] Jesus fulfills the law (Matt 5:17) as the law of retribution in that, by God performing one act of propitiation, "all share in the righteousness that 'leads to life'" (Rom 5:18). Precisely for this reason the death of Christ is gospel, since "there is therefore now no condemnation for those who are in Christ Jesus (Rom 8:1), since Christ has redeemed us from the curse of the law in order that the promise might be fulfilled (Gal 3:13ff.).'"[80] The promise of forgiveness and new life is validated by God's vindication of Jesus in the resurrection. In the dialectic between law and gospel, the gospel, being God's irrefutable and irrevocable final word of good news, finally reduces the law to utter silence.[81] Elert expresses this final triumph of gospel over law:

> The law "threatens to punish" . . . Christ, on the contrary, forgives all their iniquities. The law erects an insurmountable barrier between the saints and the sinners. Christ tears it down . . . [H]e himself, in his own person, perfectly fulfills the law. But what he here does with sinners goes against the law. The gospel differs from the law, not merely by "the clarity of its manifestation," but as day differs from night, as pardon differs from condemnation. They simply cannot be united. Nor is any compromise between them possible. Sinners are *either* forgiven *or* recompensed.[82]

---

78. Elert, *Law and Gospel*, 29.
79. Ibid.
80. Ibid., 29–30.
81. Ibid., 30.
82. Ibid., 25.

The "Inclusive Exclusivity" of Christ

We now come to the unavoidable problem of the Christian Gospel widely referred to as the "scandal of particularity," the historic Christian claim that the Gospel seemingly limits salvation to those who trust in Jesus Christ. How can God's universal plan of salvation and reconciliation come only through the historically particular life, ministry, death, and resurrection of Jesus of Nazareth? Does not the very exclusive form of the historic Christian claim, "Salvation is found in no one else, for there is no other name . . . by which we must be saved (Acts 4:12)" inevitably raise the disturbing question of "how could God 'save so few and damn so many'—and still be just. Or still be God?"[83] Despite its claim to be a revelation from a just and loving God, doesn't the exclusivity of the Gospel in fact portray God to be either unjust, unloving, or both? Why are some seemingly "saved" and others not?

In addressing this question, the pluralist option (represented by John Hick and Paul Knitter) is immensely attractive. In our religiously plural world, an exclusive claim for salvation by anyone can easily seem arrogant, narrow-minded, embarrassing, and intellectually naïve. One's personal acquaintance and friendship with adherents of other religions who are clearly virtuous, moral, and spiritually vital people of good will makes the pluralist option all the more attractive. The pluralist asks: how could God possibly discriminate against such righteous and morally good people, simply on the basis of their not being Christian? An unspoken assumption inherent to this objection deserves attention: the very form of the question assumes that God must be a God who accepts, loves, and approves of good, religious, moral people. That assumption already sets God up to be more exclusive than the God of Jesus Christ. What about those who don't measure up, who aren't good enough, who are moral failures? Is there no hope for them?

A confessional Lutheran approach to addressing the scandal of particularity could be described as Jesus' own "inclusive universality" or "inclusive exclusivity." While the exclusivity of Christ as the only revealed means of salvation is clearly inferred from the Christian Scriptures, what is equally clear and even more shockingly scandalous than such exclusivity is the radically *inclusive* nature and scope of the Gospel itself. As the "one for all others" (Robert Bertram), Jesus' whole life embodied a deep concern and love for the marginalized and excluded. In order to avoid

---

83. Bertram, *Time for Confessing*, 168.

A Paradigm of Grace as Promise of Mercy Fulfilled

the error of historical anachronism, it is important for us to remember the following. While what causes people the most trouble and embarrassment with Jesus today is the exclusive claims made by and for him, the source of scandalous outrage for his contemporaries was in fact Jesus' *radical inclusivity*. The uniqueness of Jesus lay, not in his exclusivity, but precisely in his inclusivity.

According to the synoptic Gospels, a central feature of Jesus' self-identity and ministry, one that is directly relevant to his "inclusive exclusivity," is summarized in his saying, "It is not the healthy who need a doctor, but the sick. I have not come to call the righteous, but sinners" (Mark 2:17, Matt 9:12–13, Luke 5:31–32). Jesus' inclusive ministry of salvation is literally all-inclusive, excluding no one except those who exclude themselves from the category of sinner by viewing themselves as righteous. As Bertram puts it: "Jesus makes both options available, only those two, and he coerces no one. If under those circumstances 'the righteous' are excluded, it is by their own choosing. So he says."[84]

While the self-exclusion of some from Jesus' inclusivity is a partial answer, addressing the question of those who explicitly reject the offer of Christian salvation, the larger question of those who have never heard the Gospel, who have never been offered the opportunity to trust the Gospel, remains. Is God unjust after all? The problem is not removed by granting the universal scope of original sin and God's right to judge sin. While that is the complaint of some ("It is unfair to categorize all people with the Christian category of 'sinner.'"), the injustice which remains is why some of these sinners, through the death and resurrection of Christ, overcome the divine judgment to enjoy salvation. The question, "Why some and not others?" remains.

Neither is the offense removed by "accusing human beings [ourselves] in order to excuse God."[85] To exercise Christian humility, insisting that Christians, by virtue of their sinfulness, are no more deserving of salvation than others, does not remove the problem. Neither do the pluralist (all are saved) or agnostic (We just aren't in a position to say that some are saved to the exclusion of others, let alone who belongs to which category!) approaches remove the problem. Various human attempts to take the blame for the problem do not succeed in getting God off the

---

84. Ibid., 177.
85. Ibid., 179.

hook.[86] No theological option seems to satisfactorily address the problem and remove the nagging suspicion of God's seemingly unjust partiality.

While the question, "What about those who have not had the opportunity to hear the Gospel proclaimed?" remains challenging and defies easy resolution, Walter Freytag has suggested that the proper emphasis for Christian missiological reflection should lay elsewhere. Rather than the question of divine justice and the fate of those who have not heard the Gospel, Freytag offers the Philippian jailer's question in Acts as pointing us in the right direction, "Sirs, what must I do to be saved? (Acts 16:19)" This question directs our attention to the basis of salvation in God's grace alone, apart from our understanding or lack thereof of the mechanics of how that saving grace may or may not be operative beyond the scope of the proclaimed Gospel.

Letting God's Problem Be God's Problem

In the final analysis, a confessional Lutheran approach commending the importance of faith as trust in God's promise of trustworthiness employs an intentional, theological strategy of leaving this problem in God's hands, refraining from elaborating beyond what the scriptural witness seems to warrant. While our constant temptation is to complain against and attempt to resolve God's apparent injustice, the intentional transition from complaining against God to trusting in God has ample scriptural warrant. For example, when Job was finished with his diatribe against God's injustice, the last four chapters of the book of Job depict God rebuking Job for having the audacity to question him: "Would you discredit my justice? Would you condemn me to justify yourself?" (Job 40:8). In Paul's discussion of the potter's freedom to make some pots for noble use and some for common use (Rom 9:19–24), employing the pairing "objects of wrath" and "objects of mercy," the specific issue of blaming God's wisdom and will for differences between people is not dismissed as unreasonable. While God is ultimately responsible, the real issue is the wisdom differential between Creator and creature, the fact that the pot is not in a position to criticize the potter for being unjust. Regardless of one's views on supercessionism, throughout Rom 9–11, God reserves the executive right and privilege of determining the salvation of both Jew and Gentile.

86. Ibid.

A Paradigm of Grace as Promise of Mercy Fulfilled

In a similar vein, a confessional Lutheran strategy for addressing the question, "Why do so many New Testament texts seem to teach that only those with explicit faith in Jesus Christ will be saved?" intentionally trusts the promises and trustworthiness of God. While such a strategy affirms the "inclusive exclusivity" of salvation in and through Christ, it nevertheless need not "limit our hope born of love and active in prayer that God will win in the end,"[87] trusting that God will find a way to resolve a tension which seems irresolvable to human reason. Bertram summarizes how such trust in God's promises holds in tension the questions of divine justice and salvation. If God is indeed a God of passionate mercy, then "such entrustment . . . does trust that God, all present appearances to the contrary notwithstanding, will in the end emerge as just. For that much, Christians believe, there is explicit promise. But what trust does not prescribe is that, in order for God to be just, all must be saved, even though for now, short of the Last Analysis, there is no conceivable way that both those poles of the dilemma can be harmonized."[88]

While Karl Rahner would approach this problematic differently from his paradigm of grace fulfilling nature, he nonetheless shares a Lutheran emphasis on and hope in God's mercy being God's final word: "We have every reason to think optimistically—i.e., truly hopefully and confidently in a Christian sense—of God who has certainly the last word and who has revealed to us that he has spoken his powerful word of reconciliation and forgiveness into the world."[89] Since Rahner's theology is the most theologically robust and widely accepted example of the "nature/grace" paradigm, it is important to delineate the main features of his theological method and system. In the process of doing so, I hope to clarify how his theology of grace, while overcoming the limitations of traditional western metaphysics, raises other problems which a Lutheran theology of mercy claims to answer more compellingly. As with a Lutheran vision of grace, we will articulate how Rahner understands and interrelates anthropology, sin, and the Gospel in constructing his understanding of grace as human nature fulfilled. Before doing so, however, it is necessary to set Rahner's theology of grace in the broader context of a historical overview of the development of the doctrine of grace in the Western Christian tradition.

---

87. Braaten, *That All May Believe*, 169.
88. Bertram, *Time for Confessing*, 181.
89. Rahner, "Christianity and the Non-Christian Religions.," 123–4.

3

A Paradigm of Grace as Nature Fulfilled

Karl Rahner

IN ORDER FOR RAHNER's theology of grace to be intelligible, it needs to be set in the broader historical context of the development of the doctrine of grace in Western Christianity. This chapter will proceed in the following five parts: a historical overview of the doctrine of grace in the Western church, Karl Rahner's theology of grace as nature fulfilled, a confessional Lutheran, critical engagement with Rahner, how Rahner challenges a Lutheran position, and a conclusion. The first section, a historical overview of the doctrine of grace, will proceed in the following five parts: 1) introduction to grace, 2) Augustine's contributions to a theology of grace, 3) a medieval synthesis of the doctrine of grace, 4) neoscholastic corruption of grace, and 5) further developments. My articulation of this historical overview is indebted to Stephen Duffy's, Robert Jenson's, and R. R. Reno's interpretations.

HISTORICAL BACKGROUND TO THE DOCTRINE OF GRACE IN THE WESTERN CHRISTIAN TRADITION

While "grace never became a focal point of explicit theological reflection until the time of Augustine,"[1] an implicit theology of grace pervades

1. Duffy, *Dynamics of Grace*, 17.

A Paradigm of Grace as Nature Fulfilled

both the New Testament and Hebrew Scriptures (Old Testament). As Stephen Duffy argues, grace (*charis* or *eleos* in the New Testament, *hesed* or *emet* in the Hebrew Scriptures) may well be a polyvalent symbol, with a range of semantic meanings. A confessional Lutheran approach would argue for the primacy of the meaning "mercy realized for Christ's sake." Because, for Lutheran theology, grace is "loving mercy realized," grace takes on the fullness of its meaning only in contrast to its opposite, the divine law. Just as the gospel as promise is best understood in contrast to the law, likewise grace also retains the fullness of its primary meaning only in relation to a robust understanding of the law. To the extent that this contrast and distinction is diluted or marginalized, to that extent the meaning of grace as promise of mercy fulfilled is likewise obscured.

According to Lutheran theology, the distinction between law and gospel is crucial for properly understanding grace. As the "polyvalence" of grace is explored in this chapter, I wish to keep this question front and center: is grace primarily mercy itself, promised and realized in Christ, or is it primarily defined as the impact of that promise of mercy upon the person: either in the various forms of God's gift of self-communication, of the indwelling of Christ or the Holy Spirit, etc., or as a permanent, supernatural structure of grace as thankful response? While the former emphasis develops into a theology of grace as the promise of mercy fulfilled, the latter emphases become variously articulated as a theology of grace as nature fulfilled. These different, although not contradictory, emphases have significant practical implications for a Christian missiology.

Secondly, St. Augustine's contributions to the doctrine of grace are foundational. Dealing with issues of sin, grace, the freedom of the will, and the basis of salvation, Augustine underscored the severity of sin and the gratuitous nature of grace as divine mercy and healing: "For this reason [the corruption of original sin] our guilty nature is liable to a just penalty. For if we are now a new creature in Christ, we were still children of wrath by nature, like everyone else. But God, who is rich in mercy, on account of the great love with which He loved us, even when we were dead through our sins, raised us up to life with Christ, by whose grace we are saved. But this grace of Christ . . . is not bestowed as a reward for merits, but is given freely [gratis], which is why it is called grace [gratia]."[2]

In addition to establishing the etymological link between "freely" and "grace," Augustine offered three analogies for sin, matched by three

2. Augustine, *De Natura et Gratia*, iii, 3—iv, 4. Quoted in McGrath, *Christian Theology*, 366.

parallel analogies for grace. Envisioning sin as 1) a hereditary disease, 2) a power holding human nature in bondage and captive, and 3) guilt (a judicial, legal concept); he correspondingly viewed grace 1) as healing human nature, 2) as a liberating force freeing from bondage to sin, and 3) as forgiveness and pardon.[3] The significance of the second analogy for grace is that it allowed Augustine to argue that, rather than compromising or denying human free will, grace establishes human freedom. This becomes especially important for Rahner, who affirms that divine and human freedom increase in direct proportion: grace establishes and enhances, rather than detracts from, human freedom. The significance of emphasizing grace as healing and perfecting human nature, at the expense of forgiving it, to a large extent shaped, not only the Reformation debates about grace, but also subsequent discussions of grace. These debates, rather than being merely abstract, have deeply practical implications for Christian missiology, which will be spelled out as this project unfolds.

Augustine's famous dictum, "You have made us for yourself, and our hearts are restless until they find their rest in you," set the trajectory for subsequent discussions of grace by raising the attainment of the beatific vision as the central goal of human nature.[4] While Thomas Aquinas concurred with Augustine that, "The soul . . . cannot be happy unless it beholds God directly,"[5] he qualified the human pursuit of the beatific vision by further claiming, "the ultimate goal of a rational creature exceeds the capacity of its own nature."[6] How are these two, the beatific vision as the goal (*telos*) of human nature and this goal exceeding natural human capabilities, to be united? Thomas Aquinas' ambitious synthesis of grace, modifying Augustine's contributions in developing a more precise vocabulary of grace, can be viewed as an attempt to resolve this paradox.

By the thirteenth century, the notion of "nature" had, to a great extent, marginalized the notion of sin as the primary counterpart to grace. Instead, grace became primarily articulated in relation to, and in terms of, nature. Aquinas argued for a mutuality and continuity between nature and grace, based upon the divine purposes and identity of the triune God

---

3. Duffy, *Dynamics of Grace*, 90–95.
4. Augustine, *Confessions*, i.1, quoted in Jenson, *Systematic Theology Vol. II*, 65.
5. Aquinas, *Quodlibetates*, 10–17, quoted in Jenson, *Systematic Theology Vol. II*, 65.
6. Aquinas, *Compendium theologiae*, 144, quoted in Jenson, *Systematic Theology Vol. II*, 66.

as creator, redeemer, and consummator.⁷ As noted earlier, his crucial contribution to a theology of grace can be summed up as '*gratia non tollit naturam, sed perficit*': grace does not destroy nature, it perfects it.⁸ We now further unpack the significance of this claim.

Thomas' context was one in which "a shift in the primary sense of *gratia*" had occurred "from referring primarily to God's merciful action ... to referring primarily to the created gift effected by that active mercy."⁹ In his *Summa Theologiae*, Aquinas delineates three common meanings "grace" had attained in everyday usage:

> First, it can mean someone's love, as when it is said that a soldier has the king's favor ... Secondly, it can mean a gift which is freely given, as when it is said: "I do you this favor." Thirdly, it can mean the response to a gift which is freely given, as when we are said to give thanks for benefits which we have received ... Now if "grace" is understood in either the second or third sense of the word, it will be clear that it leaves something in the one who receives it- whether it is the gift which is freely given, or the acknowledgement of that gift ... To say that someone has the grace of God is to say that there is something supernatural in the soul, coming forth from God.¹⁰

While emphasizing grace as a created, divine effect and gift within a person, one of Thomas' main contributions was the terminology of grace as a "supernatural," a permanent change or supernatural habit (an Aristotelian category) within the person, instead of extrinsic, transitory acts of intervention.¹¹ This directly focused on the issue, "How are nature and grace related?"

Henri de Lubac, developing Blondel's and Marechal's thought, asserted that, until the sixteenth century, "Catholic anthropology viewed human being as the image of God and as constituted by a desire for the vision of God."¹² De Lubac viewed Aquinas as reinterpreting this theme within an Aristotelian framework to produce a natural desire for the beatific vision. Aquinas' use of Aristotelian metaphysics led to an unre-

---

7. Duffy, *Dynamics of Grace*, 122, 132.

8. Aquinas, *Summa Theologiae* 1, q.1, A.8, ad.2.

9. Duffy, *Dynamics of Grace*, 132.

10. Aquinas, *Summa Theologiae*, IaIIae, q. 110, a. 1, quoted in McGrath, *Christian Theology*, 370.

11. Duffy, *Dynamics of Grace*, 150–67.

12. Ibid., 296.

solved anthropological tension between patristic anthropology, centered on the image of God, and Aristotelian anthropology, centered on the concept of "nature."[13] For Thomas, while the desire for the beatific vision is natural, its fulfillment can only be supernatural. However, the enduring ambiguity in trying to harmonize patristic and Aristotelian anthropologies led to a difficulty which opened Thomas up to being misinterpreted: "how could the natural desire stretch toward the vision of God without scuttling the gratuity of the supernatural?"[14] De Lubac criticized Aquinas' use of Aristotelian categories as "intellectualizing" and "naturalizing" Augustine's approach to the beatific vision.[15]

Instead, de Lubac posited that the church's tradition had always conceived of humanity in terms of a single order: "the concrete order of grace in which humans were made for God and human nature could be intelligible only by reason of its sole finality, divinization."[16] Human nature, including its relation to sin and grace, had always been articulated under one, unified order of grace. This unified vision, de Lubac argued, fractured during Catholic scholasticism (seventeenth- to nineteenth centuries). As theologians sought to establish the gratuity of grace, they invoked a theoretical state of "pure nature" in refuting an overly intrinsic view of grace. If God should choose to lead people to reach the beatific vision, such a supernatural gift is in no way indebted to anything "natural" in humanity.[17] Humanity is truly saved by grace alone, in contrast to Reformation critiques of late-medieval Catholic theology as semi-Pelagian.

In neoscholastic theologies of grace, the distinction between uncreated grace (God's own self-giving) and created grace (the practical effect of grace on humans, elevating and perfecting their nature) laid the foundation for a strict separation between the two orders of "nature" and "supernature": while nature was accessible through natural reason, supernature was only available through revelation.[18] A reified, extrinsic, intermittent view of grace as healing human nature and elevating it to perfection predominated. Human nature and grace formed two, distinct orders of being within the human person, related purely externally.

13. Ibid., 298.
14. Ibid., 299.
15. Ibid.
16. Ibid., 296.
17. Jenson, *Systematic Theology Vol. II*, 66.
18. Duffy, *Dynamics of Grace*, 297.

A Paradigm of Grace as Nature Fulfilled

While nature already possessed its own, internal structure, grace came to be viewed as a superstructure added to human nature, which "pure" human nature was neutral toward (neither closed off to nor desiring it). Such created grace changed one's ontological status before God by elevating human acts and nature to a supernatural realm. Nature and grace related dualistically as obediential potency to miraculous gift: connected extrinsically by divine will.

Such neoscholastic corruption of Aquinas' contributions had led, according to Blondel, de Lubac, and others, to the very opposite of its original intention: a "pure nature" complete apart from supernatural grace. While setting out to preserve the gratuitous freedom of divine grace, "the attempt to describe a purely natural human life with its own natural fulfillment had to make this natural order a double of the supernatural order . . . since it is the natural order in which we first find ourselves, the supernatural order becomes in practice 'a kind of shadow of that supposed natural order.'"[19] Rather than protecting the vital centrality of grace, the nature/supernature distinction ended up producing the very opposite: a view of grace as extrinsic, reified, impersonal, superfluous, and largely irrelevant to practical life. The relational, personal dimensions of grace had largely been lost, and "pure nature," rather than a theoretical possibility, became a lived reality. Stephen Duffy's assessment is poignant: "It was a shabby theology that kept the supernatural supernatural by making it superficial."[20]

In sharp corrective to such neoscholastic corruption of grace, *la nouvelle theologie* sought to retrieve the authentic teaching of Thomas as incompatible with "pure nature."[21] If such "pure nature" were internally complete, it would ultimately negate achieving the beatific vision as unnecessary. Such a result would be theologically untenable since the *telos* of human nature, de Lubac concluded, must always be oriented toward the beatific vision. In contrast to neoscholastic assertions of pure nature's self-sufficiency, de Lubac posited that human nature, "as it actually exists, is . . . open to . . . [a] supernatural end."[22] "Nature is made for the supernatural and is unintelligible without it, though having no rights over it."[23]

---

19. Jenson, *Systematic Theology Vol. II*, 66.

20. Duffy, *Dynamics of Grace*, 301.

21. Ibid., 297–98.

22. Lubac, *Mystery of the Supernatural*, 41, quoted in Jenson, *Systematic Theology Vol. II*, 67.

23. Duffy, *Dynamics of Grace*, 300.

The contributions of *nouvelle theologie* return us to Thomas' theorem of the supernatural and habitual grace: "The idea of the possible gift presupposes . . . the idea of a certain fundamental and interior aptitude for receiving that gift."[24] While de Lubac rejected the neoscholastic corruption of Thomism, he was unable to completely abandon the nature/supernature distinction.

In seeking to correct the extreme extrinsicism of neo-scholasticism, *la nouvelle theologie* emphasized the intrinsic character of grace. Precisely this emphasis led many to critique its logical conclusion as an intrinsicism negating the gratuity of grace. While de Lubac contested the charge of intrinsicism, *la nouvelle theologie's* insistence on the graced nature of reality set off an important debate, anticipating and setting the stage for Karl Rahner's theology of grace.

Before examining Rahner's response to *nouvelle theologie*, two contrasting trajectories resulted from the historical development of the nature/grace relationship. Robert Schreiter contrasts these two alternatives:

> If sin totally perverts human nature, then nothing less than an utter transformation, perhaps having little or no continuity with the previous state, will be called for in justification and conversion. If sin wounds human nature but does not destroy it, then grace constitutes a refinement and elevation of human nature. The implications of one's stance on this point will direct one's approach to other religious systems . . . Rahner chooses to emphasize the latter position here more than the former.[25]

While Rahner is certainly concerned to articulate how divine grace transforms the ordinary, he is careful to avoid, not only the neoscholastic corruption of grace as extrinsic, but also the intrinsicist tendency in *nouvelle theologie*. He thus sets out to answer the following questions: "How can human being be such that it is both conceivable without grace and yet able to be fulfilled in the most complete way only by grace? How [can we] preserve divine freedom and the gratuity of grace while avoiding an extrinsicism that makes grace alien to human being? What a priori conditions of possibility lie behind the desire for [the beatific] vision?"[26]

While affirming de Lubac's rejection of extrinsicism, rejection of the radical separation of nature and grace, and the inseparability of nature

---

24. Lubac, *Mystery*, 169, quoted in Jenson, *Systematic Theology Vol. II*, 67.
25. Schreiter, "Anonymous Christian and Christology," 33.
26. Duffy, *Dynamics of Grace*, 301.

and grace in concrete reality, Rahner nevertheless proceeds to distinguish his position from de Lubac's in at least three ways. First, Rahner insists on the importance of maintaining "pure nature" as a necessary construct. While "historical human nature is never pure nature; it stands everywhere and inextricably within the order of grace," nevertheless it is necessary for defending "the gratuity of its correlate, grace, by conjuring up an order that could have been had God so willed."[27] Secondly, while affirming the intrinsic character of grace as necessary, this could not be done at the expense of divine freedom. Rahner critiques de Lubac for endangering "the gratuity of grace by reducing it to the gratuity of creation."[28] De Lubac made the mistake of making grace a constituent part of human nature, thus compromising divine gratuity. Thirdly, Rahner sets out to avoid the twin dangers of neoscholastic extrinsicism and dualism, on the one hand, and the intrinsicism of *nouvelle theologie*, on the other. He set out to complement a "'gratuity from above' with a 'gratuity from below.'"[29] Stephen Duffy explicates the theological challenge Rahner sought to navigate:

> Grace is no alien intrusion, but neither is it owed. Nature is a derivative, inner moment *within* the order of grace. But if grace is to be grace . . . human being must be related to God at some point which is not already grace. The dynamic of grace demands a substratum sufficiently free and autonomous for the recipient of grace to be able to say yes or no to the gift God is not obligated to give. Thus there must be an ontological discontinuity between grace and nature. On the other hand . . . nature finds a basic continuity with grace . . . If God calls human being to a supernatural end, then that being is by that very call always and everywhere interiorly other in structure than it might have been in the absence of such a summons.[30]

---

27. Ibid., 302–3.
28. Ibid., 302.
29. Ibid., 303.
30. Ibid.

KARL RAHNER'S THEOLOGY OF GRACE AS NATURE FULFILLED

Given the preceding historical overview of the development of the doctrine of grace and the relationship between nature and grace, what contribution does Karl Rahner's theology make to the challenge of relating nature and grace? While Rahner's theology addresses many concerns, a helpful starting point is to allow Rahner to describe the problem his theology of grace sought to address in his own words: "There is really only one question, whether God wanted to be merely the eternally distant one, or whether beyond that he wanted to be the innermost center of our existence in free grace and self-communication."[31]

Rahner's theology could be described as universal, transcendental revelation. The locus of revelation is the transcendental human subject, which ultimately is able to adequately accommodate God's self-revelation. The content of revelation is God's self-communication as gracious gift. The mode of revelation is historical mediation, particularly in Jesus Christ as the absolute savior. The goal of revelation is universal salvation through a universal offer of grace as God's self-communication, resulting in human union with and participation in God's being. Rahner describes salvation as the following experience: "[when] man experiences himself as inescapably grounded in the abyss of irremovable mystery, and accepts and experiences this mystery in the depths of his conscience and the concreteness of his history . . . not as consuming judgment, but as fulfilling nearness (for this is what we call faith)."[32]

Rahner's methodology, especially as it emphasizes the modern "turn to the human subject," the transcendental- categorical polarity, transcendental human subjectivity, and historical mediation of divine revelation, situating theology and revelation in human subjectivity and experience, requires further elaboration.

Rahner's Theological Method

While Rahner's method has undergone shifts that have moved it from a more abstract approach toward taking the historical structure of human existence more seriously, from the language of being toward a language

---

31. Rahner, *Foundations*, 12.
32. Rahner, "New Image of the Church," 7.

of mystery, and toward "a reciprocal method by which Christology determines human nature,"³³ his mature method can legitimately be described as centered on a foundational/transcendental anthropology. While Ludwig Feuerbach had criticized theology as anthropology, Rahner audaciously turns the tables on Feuerbach by insisting that all anthropology is theology.³⁴ We now take a closer look at how that claim unfolds into a distinctive, enormously influential theological methodology. We start with the first shift mentioned above.

First, Rahner begins with the "turn to the subject," taking human existence as the starting point for theological reflection because "one must first be in existence before one can reflect on it."³⁵ There are two compelling reasons for doing so. First, basic human experience, unlike faith in God, offers a universally common starting point and shared ground for discussion, regardless of one's background. Everyone supposedly has direct, immediate access to our shared experience. Thus, if human experience reveals, upon study, categories and ways in which 'God talk' becomes intelligible and rational, then theology has a legitimate basis for such God talk in the modern world. Second, if human experience further offers a way of making reasonable sense of the identity of Jesus and the historical Christian witness to his life, then talk of Jesus Christ also becomes intelligible.³⁶

Secondly, central to Rahner's method is the description of reality as being constituted by two poles: a transcendental pole as the universal, unthematic, infinite horizon of being, and a categorical pole which is thematic, concrete, historical, and particular. The relationship between the two can be expressed in terms of the categorical always disclosing, manifesting, and illuminating what is unthematic in transcendental experience. Rahner explains how revelation or knowledge of God is always simultaneously both transcendental and categorical: "What we are calling transcendental knowledge or experience of God is an *a posteriori*

---

33. Schüssler Fiorenza, "Method in Theology," 69–71.

34. Rahner's entire theology exhibits the deep concern that theological discourse and claims "will be taken seriously only if and insofar as they can show the listener that he already has something to do with this question [of human transcendence]" ("Theology and Anthropology" in *Theological Investigations Vol. IX*, 28). In other words, the very structure of human existence is inevitably, intrinsically, and thoroughly oriented toward God.

35. O'Donovan, *World of Grace*, 3.

36. Two of Rahner's works, *Hearer of the Word* and *Foundations of Christian Faith*, can legitimately be viewed as arguing these two points, respectively.

knowledge insofar as man's transcendental experience of his free subjectivity takes place only in his [categorical] encounter with the world and especially with other people . . . The knowledge of God is, nevertheless, a *transcendental* knowledge because man's basic and original orientation towards absolute mystery, which constitutes his fundamental experience of God, is a permanent existential of man as a spiritual subject."[37]

Rahner weaves his transcendental anthropology with a theology of grace to explicate his theology of revelation. I now sketch his transcendental, foundational anthropology in the following five theses: 1) In every act of knowing, willing, and freedom, there is a pre-grasp (*Vorgriff*) of infinite being.[38] In knowing anything concrete, humans are always transcending that concrete object in their self-transcendent, dynamic openness and orientation toward the transcendental horizon of infinite being of God as holy mystery. We are dynamically oriented toward God because God made us that way, and this openness is the "condition for the possibility" of hearing a word from God.[39] As transcendental "hearers of the word," we're open, ready, and ready for God to speak, if He should choose.[40] 2) Humans paradoxically find themselves to be finitely limited, and yet to have infinite questions. The human hope is that reality is ultimately meaningful. 3) A unity exists between human subjectivity and history. Both God's revelation (self-manifestation) and the human hope for that revelation as the ultimate meaning of history must be historically mediated. Because humans are 'spirit in the world'[41] and 'hearers of the Word,' any potential revelation from God must come in a form or mode that they can receive and understand—a concrete, historical Word which can be heard and received. 4) Since all knowledge, even revelation, comes through our sensory engagement of physical creation, where should we expect God's revelation? In history, in the world, in a Word that we can understand and hear, in a historical word. That's where we turn expectantly and hopefully. Therefore human subjects turn to history, searching it expectantly for a revelation and Word from God as their ultimate fulfillment. As Rahner puts it: "Hence our transcendental knowledge or experience has to be called a posteriori insofar as every transcendental

---

37. Rahner, *Foundations*, 51–52.
38. Ibid., 33–35.
39. Ibid., 52–55.
40. Rahner, *Hearer*, 53.
41. Ibid., 127.

experience is mediated by a categorical encounter with concrete reality in our world, both the world of things and the world of persons. This is also true of the knowledge of God."[42] 5) God's revelation can only find fulfillment in a free, exemplary human subject, someone who definitely models and accepts human finitude as well as God's gracious offer of self-presence. Such a person would be an "absolute savior," bridging God's revelation with the human, transcendental hope and goal of active self-transcendence into union with God. When humans search history, they find Jesus Christ to be just such an "absolute savior." Before moving on to address Rahner's theology of grace, let us summarize his view of revelation in his own words:

> In the concrete, then, there remains no other conceivable possibility but a faith which is simply the obedient acceptance of man's supernaturally elevated self-transcendence, the obedient acceptance of his transcendental orientation to the God of eternal life. As an a priori modality of consciousness, this orientation has the character of a divine communication. This transcendental, supernatural experience, which in itself and in the mode in which it takes place satisfies the notion of a divine revelation, and therefore in its history constitutes a history of revelation, does indeed need a historical, categorical mediation. But this [categorical] mediation does not necessarily and everywhere have to make this transcendental experience explicit and thematic *as* the effect of supernatural, revelatory activity by God.[43]

Having sketched Rahner's foundational anthropology, the next key move is to wed that with a new theology of grace, one which preserves both God's freedom and grace as gratuitous.

Rahner's Theology of Grace

In response to the neoscholastic, extrinsic, reified notion of grace, the facts of God's love, power, and universal, salvific will necessitate for Rahner a fresh understanding of grace. His goal is to demonstrate: a God who has a universal will to save, a Jesus Christ who embodies the promise of being truly redeemer of the whole world, and God's loving grace as the final word which ultimately conquers sin, death, and even the possibility

42. Rahner, *Foundations*, 52.
43. Ibid., 152.

of hell itself. Stephen Duffy poignantly describes Rahner's view of grace triumphing over sin:

> Sin, for Rahner, is an existential. However, it is but one vector in life . . . History is not just a story of perdition, but of salvation, and primarily so. Life is drawn by a second vector, grace . . . Sin is no more universal or powerful than Christ's redemptive grace. The existential of sin stands in dialectical (but unequal) relationship to the grace of being redeemed (objectively) in Christ . . . Sin is situated against a graced horizon . . . Grace is in the end more powerful, eschatologically victorious. The mystery of iniquity is swallowed up in the anomaly of the good.[44]

How does he accomplish all that? By making three moves: 1) a new emphasis on uncreated grace; 2) the key concept of supernatural existential; and 3) the real, lived, human life experienced as a dialectic between sin and grace. I will now further unpack the logic of how these moves are linked and build upon one another.

First, Rahner gives renewed importance to uncreated grace as God's self-gift universally given (1 Tim 2:4, etc.). As he puts it, "God does not cause and bring forth in the creature something different from God's own self, but rather makes God's own divine reality, through an act of imparting, into what constitutes the creature's fulfillment."[45] Such a view of uncreated grace positions Rahner's understanding of salvation firmly in the nature/grace paradigm: "the salvation won by Christ [is] the salvation of supernatural grace which divinizes man, the salvation of the beatific vision."[46] By focusing on uncreated grace rather than scholastic created grace, Rahner avoids quantifying and externalizing grace. This lays the foundation for his crucial second step.

Secondly, his concept of the supernatural existential moves grace into the realm of created history, while preserving the gratuity of grace. He posits that the supernatural existential is a universal structure and factor in human life, as the free offer of God's grace (God's self-communication). Given that the supernatural existential is the universal experience (fundamental structure) of offered grace, the offer of grace now constitutes a universal, fundamental feature of human life. As Rahner describes it, "[Man] as subject is the event of God's self-communication

---

44. Duffy, *Dynamics of Grace*, 331.
45. Rahner, *Foundations*, 121.
46. Rahner, "Christianity and the Non-Christian Religions," 122–3.

A Paradigm of Grace as Nature Fulfilled

is a statement which refers to absolutely all men, and which expresses an existential of every person . . . this self-communication is present in *every* person at least in the mode of an offer . . . In this sense everyone, really and radically *every* person must be understood as the event of a supernatural self-communication of God, although not in the sense that every person necessarily accepts [the offer] in freedom . . ."[47]

Rahner insists that such an offer of grace, rather than being an explicitly religious experience, reaches everyone, everywhere, as an unthematic, universal human experience, precisely because the supernatural existential is a fundamental structure of our human nature.[48] The results of this gratuitous offer are clear: God and humans remain free, God's grace is universally offered, it's a grace-filled world, yet grace is not a quantifiable "thing," but rather a living offer calling forth a dynamic response.

Before clarifying Rahner's third move, a brief explication of his theology of sin is in order.[49] In sharp contrast to a Lutheran emphasis on the bondage of the will, Rahner is greatly concerned to affirm and preserve human freedom. This means that his theology of freedom undergirds his theology of sin. While "man's freedom and responsibility belong to the existentials of human existence," original sin is also an existential, but only as "the historical origin of the present, universal, and ineradicable situation of our freedom as co-determined by guilt . . ."[50] Furthermore, the possibility of sin is also a universal existential: "This threat is really a

---

47. Rahner, *Foundations*, 127–28.

48. Ibid., 132.

49. In terms of Rahner's treatment of human guilt and sin, the following include some of his writings on the subject: *Foundations of Christian Faith*, 90–115; "The Sin of Adam" in *Theological Investigations Vol. XI*, 247–62; "The Theological Concept of Concupiscentia" in *Theological Investigations Vol. I*, 347–82; "Guilt, Responsibility, and Punishment within the View of Catholic Theology" in *Theological Investigations Vol. VI*, 197–217; and "Justified and Sinner at the Same Time" in *Theological Investigations Vol. VI*, 218–30. Since Rahner's theology of freedom undergirds his doctrine of sin, his article on human freedom is crucial for understanding his view of sin: "Theology of Freedom" in *Theological Investigations Vol. VI*, 178–96. In the *Encyclopedia of Theology: the Concise Sacramentum Mundi*, see the articles "Original Sin" and "The Punishment of Sin." For relevant secondary sources, see the following: Highfield, "The Freedom to Say 'No?'"; King, *The God of Forgiveness and Healing in the Theology of Karl Rahner*; and Vandervelde, *Original Sin: Two Major Trends in Contemporary Roman Catholic Reinterpretation*.

50. Rahner, *Foundations*, 93, 114.

permanent existential which we can never eradicate in our single, temporal history."[51]

Crucial for Rahner's theology of sin is the distinction between sin in the strict sense, as pertaining to human subjectivity, and sin in an analogous sense. In clarifying this distinction, Rahner describes the human subject by using three terms: "original person," "intermediate reality," and "achieved person."[52] Ron Highfield describes their interrelationship: "The 'original' person is the human being, as it were, before the transcendental decision, as "transcendent spirit and freedom before God." The "intermediate reality" is a partial objectification of the original person in the medium of the world. The "achieved" person is the human person who has subjectively exercised the transcendental capacity to choose what he or she will be definitively."[53]

This scheme has significant, practical ramifications for Rahner's theology of sin: "Venial sin, original sin, and concupiscence point to aspects of this 'intermediate reality' whose objectively evil characteristics mirror only the preexisting evil structures within which the human must make itself concrete; they do not reveal the true subjectivity of the original person. They are not, therefore, sin in the most proper sense of the term, but only in an analogous sense."[54] In other words, "We never know with ultimate certainty whether we really are sinners."[55]

Given such a theology of sin, Rahner, thirdly, deals with the reality of sin by describing the relationship between sin and grace as dialectical. In real life, people struggle with this sin/grace tension. While the supernatural existential never frees anybody from it, grace often triumphs over sin. As a person is faced with original sin (the actual situation of living in this fallen, broken, sinful world), within the dialectic of sin and grace constituting a lived reality of daily life, God's grace nudges and moves people to ultimately say "yes" to God's offer of self-gift and to live in a graced relationship with God rather than rejecting the call of grace to faith. In other words: where sin abounds, grace abounds more. In making these three moves, Rahner unites and synthesizes what had previously been separated: grace and nature, divine freedom and human freedom,

51. Ibid., 105.
52. Rahner, "Guilt and Its Remission," 272–4.
53. Highfield, "The Freedom to Say 'No'?," 495.
54. Ibid.
55. Rahner, *Foundations*, 104.

A Paradigm of Grace as Nature Fulfilled

God's universal will for salvation and the reality that not all are in fact saved. God structured humanity this way in order to be the fulfillment of our lives.

One of the most creative applications of Rahner's theology of revelation is to the question of Jesus Christ's significance and relevance for the world religions. Rahner articulates the dilemma as the challenge of reconciling two seemingly contradictory, incompatible truths: 1) God's universal will of salvation for all, and 2) the absolute necessity of faith in Christ and church membership for salvation.[56] He resolves this dilemma in the following way: if faith in Christ and church membership (#2) are necessary, then they must be universal possibilities for all people. This means that the possibility of faith in Christ and being a Christian must be, not only explicit and historical possibilities, but also implicit and transcendental possibilities. The possibility of implicit Christian faith, an implicit Christology, and implicit church membership is actualized through uncreated grace mediating the efficacy of Jesus Christ anonymously, as well as the supernatural existential in people (mediating God's universal offer of grace).

Rahner's Theology of Redemption and Reconciliation

We have yet to comment on Rahner's views on redemption, reconciliation, and vicarious representation, especially as they relate to his theology of the cross and broader theology of grace. While an in-depth treatment of these topics is beyond the scope of this study, a sufficient understanding of Rahner's view on reconciliation is necessary in order to understand both how it reflects his nature/grace paradigm and how it differs from a confessional Lutheran approach. I will now articulate the main contours of his approach to this cluster of related topics, subsequently highlighting Lutheran concerns in the following section.

Central to Rahner's approach to redemption, reconciliation, and the cross is a clear affirmation of the necessity of the distinction between nature and grace as an overarching framework: "No Catholic doctrine of grace can do away with the distinction between nature and grace even prior to sin."[57] This overall framework of nature/grace is then further explicated and applied by such key elements as a strong incarnational motif;

---

56. Rahner, "One Christ and the Universality of Salvation," 216–7.
57. Rahner, "Christian Understanding of Redemption," 245.

God's prior, loving, salvific will as the cause of both redemption and the cross; God's ultimate solidarity with humanity through Jesus Christ; divine freedom and grace as constituting, necessitating, and enhancing, rather than detracting from, the importance of human freedom; and divine mercy overcoming the realities of human sin and guilt. Rahner begins by affirming the New Testament witness to the concepts of sin and reconciliation in the strongest terms possible. First, the New Testament's use of the term "reconciliation" assumes that people "find themselves in a situation of sin, spiritual peril, discord, and enmity, a situation that determines radically human beings' relationship to God and to one another,"[58] Secondly, "the radical nature of the Christian idea of sin . . . is so radical that the holy and all-merciful God's response to it . . . must be condemnation to that eternal loss which is hell."[59] In further affirming the hopelessness of human guilt and the incomprehensibility of God's forgiveness as realities undergirding a properly Christian doctrine of reconciliation and redemption, both Rahner and confessional Lutheran theology affirm central Pauline insights.

Before delineating the specific features of Rahner's theology of redemption and reconciliation, it is important to note four main concerns driving his proposal. What are Rahner's "non-negotiables"? First, the distinction between nature and grace provides a foundational paradigm for properly relating human sin and guilt, the event of Jesus Christ (his life, death, and resurrection), and the hope of redemption/reconciliation/salvation. Secondly, while "salvation is grace," neither salvation nor grace is simply reducible or equivalent to the forgiveness of sins or removal of guilt.[60] Thirdly, preserving human freedom, as a corollary to divine freedom, in terms of the "ultimate validity of free human decision" is absolutely necessary.[61] Furthermore, penal substitutionary theories of vicarious redemption and atonement are inadequate precisely because they violate such human freedom. In Rahner's own words: "the notion of an exchange of goods or even of guilt being punished in the person of the guiltless Jesus must not be allowed to obtrude itself on the

---

58. Rahner, "Reconciliation and Vicarious Representation," 255.
59. Ibid., 256–7.
60. Rahner, "Christian Understanding of Redemption," 245.
61. Rahner, "Reconciliation and Vicarious Representation," 258.

A Paradigm of Grace as Nature Fulfilled

notion of satisfaction for the sins of the world."[62] We now turn to examine how Rahner applies these concerns in his theology of redemption/reconciliation.

Rahner's starting point for articulating what constitutes redemption/reconciliation/salvation and how it relates to the person and cross of Jesus Christ is a world already graced by God's loving presence: "this world . . . is already encompassed by this forgiving and reconciling love. From the beginning God has made himself the world's innermost heart in such a way that the freely incurred guilt of humankind pierces God's heart."[63] Rahner's description of the goal of redemption and ultimate salvation as "nothing other than the perfection of faith, hope, and love," allowing people to "come to God himself in ecstatic love," affirms the classic notion of the beatific vision.[64] Rather than wrongly focusing on or getting sidetracked by mistaken theories of vicarious satisfaction and substitutionary atonement, Rahner insists that an adequate understanding of redemption and reconciliation must properly integrate the gifts of creation, freedom, and grace. In claiming that redemption is "realized as a gift of this God through creation and grace,"[65] his nature/grace approach is unmistakable.

Such a nature/grace paradigm for understanding redemption and reconciliation can be articulated in five steps. It begins, not only in a world enveloped by God's loving presence, but primarily in affirming the mutual interrelationship between grace and freedom. The gracious act of redemption, rather than being externally imposed, must ultimately validate, undergird, and express human freedom.[66] The free, human act of self-redemption "does not redeem human beings from themselves but unto themselves,"[67] thus overcoming the false dichotomy between extrinsicism and intrinsicism.

Secondly, salvific redemption is holistic, dealing with humanity in all of its dimensions: bodily and spiritual, individual and corporate, historical and transcendental. Since "human transcendentality occurs in concrete historical reality," such holistic redemption rejects as a false

---

62. Ibid., 262.
63. Ibid., 261.
64. Rahner, "Christian Understanding of Redemption," 241.
65. Ibid., 242.
66. Ibid., 241–2.
67. Ibid., 241.

dichotomy the choice between redemption as a purely historical reality or a flight into other-worldly transcendence.[68] Since divine grace embraces, assumes, and redeems everything, the body and concrete human history are dignified as intrinsic to redemption.

Not only does redemption occur within radical freedom and holistically embrace all of human life but, thirdly, it "takes place only when God definitively communicates himself as himself."[69] This axiom is fundamental to Rahner's theology. The basic implication of redemptive grace as the gift of God's self-communication is that "the arrival of the infinite means the life of the finite and not its dissolution."[70]

The remaining two steps, those of redemption preceding human sin and originating from Jesus Christ, complete Rahner's approach to redemption by drawing together important elements, defining them, and drawing them to culmination at the cross of Jesus Christ. The conviction that "the human need of redemption precedes human sinfulness"[71] locates Rahner's view of the cross within the broader framework of an incarnational motif and the priority of God's loving will. Humans prior to sin are "already the ones who can find their perfection only through an absolutely gratuitous self-communication of God which originates from God's free love."[72]

Rahner's description of reconciliation elaborates the implications of such prior divine love for Christian redemption:

> This [forgiving, reconciling, and irrevocable] love has revealed itself in the cross of Jesus Christ who has become our reconciliation. Through Jesus' unconditional solidarity with all sinful human beings, as well as in his unconditional love for the Father, God's forgiving love has reached its historically visible culmination in Jesus' death on the cross, because this love has become irrevocable and has found its acceptance in a human being who was conscious of and who willed his absolute solidarity with all human beings.[73]

---

68. Ibid., 242–3.
69. Ibid., 243.
70. Ibid., 244.
71. Ibid.
72. Ibid., 245.
73. Rahner, "Reconciliation and Vicarious Representation," 261.

A Paradigm of Grace as Nature Fulfilled

This quote serves as a lucid, helpful articulation of how the various strands of Rahner's theology of grace culminate in the cross of Jesus. How is redemption dependent upon the historical event of the cross? The incarnational motif, expressed as God's solidarity with the world, gives the cross its true meaning as the efficacious sign of God's redeeming love which simultaneously establishes that love.[74] In and through the incarnation, God turns toward the world in irrevocable solidarity. This means that the cross, rather than demonstrating vicarious punishment for sin or satisfaction of guilt, is instead the victorious, historically definitive and concrete "seal" of God's loving will.[75] The basis for reconciliation is God's incarnational solidarity with humanity, which involves God making "himself a part of the offense of guilt in order that forgiveness and reconciliation may take place."[76] Rahner insists, "The cross, the reality of Christ, his love, his faith, his hope, his surrender to God's incomprehensibility are . . . the result of a redeeming love of God which itself has no cause outside of itself."[77] In other words: the cross demonstrates a transcendental Christology in which Jesus, by fully embracing solidarity with sinful humanity, fully represents humanity to God and God to humanity, thus actualizing God's loving will. The nature/grace distinction results in this dynamic paradox: while authentic redemption (salvation) must be an event of free, divine love, humans can only reach their intended goal of the beatific vision (which itself transforms and perfects their nature) by accepting precisely that offer of divine love. Salvation truly is grace, which integrates creation, freedom, and love, transforming sinful humanity, in solidarity with the entire cosmos, into "one great symphony of praise to the love of God."[78]

Conclusion

I believe Rahner's enduring legacy includes at least the following. First, his emphasis on God as loving, holy mystery views mystery as not something to be overcome (the neoscholastic distortion). Rather than divine comprehensibility and incomprehensibility being opposing concerns,

---

74. Rahner, "Christian Understanding of Redemption," 250–51.
75. Ibid., 251.
76. Rahner, "Reconciliation and Vicarious Representation," 262.
77. Rahner, "Christian Understanding of Redemption," 249.
78. Rahner, "Reconciliation and Vicarious Representation," 269.

Rahner unites them in emphasizing God's mystery as simultaneously irreducibly concrete and infinitely deep. Reason, rather than removing such mystery, functions in service of such divine mystery. R. R. Reno eloquently captures Rahner's vision of how mystery enfolds the transcendental character of Christian life: "The direction of transcendence is through what we know so well and so clearly, the Christian form of life, to what we cannot possibly understand, the God for us. And if this is the structure of Christian transcendence, then the depth of mystery is infinite and the project of transcendence eternal. For the more we know and understand, the more clearly we grasp the "surface," the more extensive becomes the depth; the more clearly we see God, the more hidden he becomes."[79]

Secondly, by navigating a delicate balance between the radical transcendence of extrinsicism and the pure immanence in intrinsicism, Rahner asserts that divine freedom, grace, love, and mystery are directly related to, and grow in direct proportion to, the human creature as constituted by the mystery of such loving grace and freedom. Thirdly, by showing how Christian doctrines are already internally present in personal experience rather than mythical, external, expressions, he reasserts their intrinsic relevance for the modern person. Finally, Rahner posits that "the 'grammar' of Christianity is structured by the strangeness of grace."[80] Such grace, while not external to the human condition, must remain gratuitous as God's universal, loving disposition to seriously, actually, and concretely reconcile and save the *whole world* to himself. This truly is a graced world. By situating theology in general and revelation in particular in the human subject (transcendental anthropology), Rahner's proposal delineates a particular theology of grace, one which a confessional Lutheran theology of mercy challenges on several points.

CONFESSIONAL LUTHERAN, CRITICAL ENGAGEMENT WITH RAHNER

While on the surface Rahner's renewed theology of grace seems to radically differ from the neoscholastic theology of grace he corrects, my contention is that both theologies of grace can, from a Lutheran perspective, be understood as theologies of grace "perfecting" nature. While the

---

79. Reno, *Ordinary Transformed*, 222.
80. Ibid.

neoscholastic system explicitly makes this claim, defining created grace as elevating and perfecting human nature, Rahner's definitions of grace and the supernatural existential produce a similar, practical result. Rather than making the obvious, refutable error of reified grace, Rahner makes a far more sophisticated, yet similar, claim regarding grace: it is the "key" which fits, fulfills, and therefore perfects the "keyhole" of our human nature. Just as a key and keyhole are mutually complementary and "anticipate" each other, in the same way the shape of Christian revelation (the key) must correspond to the shape of the human situation and subject as its intended target (the keyhole). While the nature of Christian revelation anticipates a certain kind of human subject, one who is able to receive such revelation, likewise the nature of human subjects, as transcendental "hearers of the Word," anticipates the shape of Christian revelation. When the intrinsic, fundamental structure and orientation of human nature is defined as basically and (almost) irresistibly oriented toward God as its final goal and *telos*, grace, while a relational term denoting God's self-communication, serves the practical function of ensuring that humans reach their intended *telos*, that they achieve communion with God and thus have their nature perfected or fulfilled.

Methodological Concerns

Francis Schüssler Fiorenza has identified three broad challenges to Rahner's theological method: 1) as a foundationalist method, it is overly dependent upon certain features of Kantian philosophy (this criticism is leveled by George Lindbeck, Rowan Williams, Hans Urs von Balthasar, Fergus Kerr, and Kevin Hart); 2) it neglects the specific, historically singular shape of Christianity (leveled by Hans Urs von Balthasar and Bruce Marshall); and 3) it reduces salvation to an individual, private reality, failing to recognize the social and political dimensions of salvation history (Johann Baptist Metz).[81] A Lutheran approach and concerns reiterate forms of the first two criticisms. In terms of his use of philosophical resources to support and practically apply his theology, I find his starting point in foundational anthropology and categories of the supernatural existential and anonymous Christian (or anonymous Christianity) problematic due to the way in which they impact and inevitably shape his articulation of the specifically Christian categories of sin, grace (mercy), and recon-

---

81. Schüssler Fiorenza, "Method in Theology," 66–67.

ciliation in light of the cross. While he affirms the necessary relationship between philosophy and theology, from a Lutheran viewpoint his philosophy seems to shape and determine his theological conclusions, saying more than *can* be said about grace and less than *should* be said about sin. In other words: because Rahner's theologies of sin, grace, and the cross are grounded in his transcendental method of foundational anthropology, including the supernatural existential, his treatment of these key, scriptural themes is either insufficient (in the case of sin and the cross) or overly optimistic (in the case of grace and the "anonymous Christian"). While my criticism of his foundationalist method and seeming neglect of the historically specific content and shape of Christianity are intertwined, I will concentrate on the charge of neglecting the historical shape and specificity of Christianity. In echoing von Balthasar's concern, "Does Rahner's method sufficiently attend to the historical singularity of the Christ event and the death of Christ?"[82] I would extend that concern to include the specifically Christian, scriptural categories of sin, grace, and atonement.

In what follows, I will more fully articulate and argue these concerns arising from my law/Gospel (promise) hermeneutic: 1) By starting with foundational anthropology, Rahner treats the reality of the wrath of God insufficiently. 2) Given his method of foundational anthropology and the supernatural existential, Rahner's theology of sin is likewise insufficiently robust and deep. 3) The previous two concerns lead to an inadequate theology of reconciliation that fails to fully appreciate the basis for God's forgiving love, the necessity of atonement, and the crucial role of Christ becoming sin for us (2 Cor. 5:21). 4) Rahner's theology of grace, grounded in his foundational anthropology, supernatural existential, and transcendental Christology, seems to exceed the bounds of what can be scripturally affirmed about grace in his notion of the anonymous Christian. 5) Finally, Rahner's treatment of sin, grace, and the anonymous Christian results in a view of "anonymous" faith. Such a view of faith seems at odds with the scriptural witness for faith as trust in the promises of God. Let us begin with Rahner's foundationalist method, his historical turn to the subject.

When one starts with foundational anthropology, as Rahner does, one will inevitably arrive at a doctrine of God that fails to adequately wrestle with the divine dilemma of reconciling God's wrath with God's

---

82. Ibid., 67.

mercy. Confessional Lutheran theology would argue for the necessity of articulating how divine wrath is reconciled with and overcome by divine, loving grace as a prominent feature of any theology of grace, if not its starting point. The main problem that a Christian theology of grace needs to address and resolve is not fundamentally an anthropological question: Luther's famous question of how a sinful human can find a gracious God. Rahner's method adequately addresses that question. Rather, Lutheran theology insists that the main problem is located in the doctrine of God: how God can be, as Paul puts both "just and the one who justifies" (Rom 3:26).

Secondly, while Rahner challenges Lutherans to wrestle with the implications of the universal extent of God's grace, his category of the supernatural existential and the resulting theology of sin and grace are problematic. Without denying or discrediting what Rahner *does* in fact affirm about sin, one can still ask whether Rahner's emphasis on incarnation and transcendental Christology downplays or minimizes the depth dimension, seriousness, and extent of sin. From a Lutheran perspective, the answer is unequivocally yes. In his own words, "We never know with ultimate certainty whether we really are sinners. But ... we do know with ultimate certainty that we really *can* be sinners."[83] Confessional Lutheran theology deems such a view of the "possibility of sin as a permanent existential" as woefully insufficient and undervaluing the scriptural witness to the depth dimension of sin. As articulated earlier, because sin is a bondage which humanity by its very nature is helpless to extricate itself from, and therefore something which only the liberating, reconciling work of Christ can accomplish, therefore sin, rather than the supernatural existential, should properly be viewed as the "permanent existential" of human nature. It is not that Rahner overlooks the reality and seriousness of sin; he clearly does not. Instead, what is problematic is how he seemingly assigns human sinfulness to a secondary status within his theology of grace, marginalizing it within God's self-communication to humanity. Rahner expresses the concern that sin be given too significant a position in Christian theology, at the expense of God's self-communication:

> [T]he theme of human sinfulness and forgiveness of guilt through pure grace is, in a certain sense, somewhat secondary compared to the theme of God's radical *self*-communication. It is not as if we do not get caught up time and again in our egoism

83. Rahner, *Foundations*, 104.

> because we are sinners. It is not as if we are not in need of God's forgiving grace, something we need to accept as pure grace... It is not as if God's self-communication does not always take place in fact by way of forgiveness. It is not as if our fundamental experience of sinfulness... does not correspond to the actual situation... But today we see how difficult it is for people to accept justification simply as forgiveness of sin. Moreover... God and God's promise of self to humanity... already exists as pure grace prior to sin... If we accept this, then I think we can easily hold that God's self-communication to the creature is more pivotal than sin and the forgiveness of sin. I know that such a claim is highly problematic, especially when placed under the judgment of Scripture. But even if we basically cannot think about sin in any way outside of the framework of God's love for the sinner, there is also at least the danger of *hubris* that we might take sin too seriously.[84]

While I respect Rahner's deeply spiritual concerns and the comprehensiveness of his system, his theology has an overly optimistic view of human nature that minimizes sin, therefore undercutting the Biblical notion of grace (mercy) as well. From a Lutheran perspective, because his supernatural existential is more a philosophical than Biblical category, an improper encroachment of philosophy at this early step results in similarly philosophical conclusions later on. From a Lutheran perspective, this leads Rahner to misinterpret some central scriptural texts, especially those articulating a theology of sin and reconciliation (chapter 2). I concur with Ron Highfield's critique of Rahner:

> I believe Rahner is at least to some degree guilty of this substitution [emptying Christian teaching of its original content and substituting an alien content] in his doctrine of sin. He takes words and phrases, such as "freedom," "offense against God," "sin," and "responsibility," from the [scriptural] sources and pours into them a meaning determined by his transcendental anthropology. For example, his strict definition of sin as a fully free and definitive "no" to God renders many of the central biblical texts on sin incomprehensible. "All have sinned and fall short of the glory of God" (Rom 3:23). Does this text mean that all have sinned in an analogous sense or in the strict sense? The first alternative weakens this classic statement to a triviality, and the second has it proclaim universal damnation."[85]

---

84. Rahner, "Experiences of a Catholic Theologian," 303.
85. Highfield, "The Freedom to Say 'No'?," 500–501.

A Paradigm of Grace as Nature Fulfilled

My previous concerns regarding Rahner's theology culminate in this central concern: while his theology of grace as nature fulfilled is internally coherent and systematically comprehensive, due to his transcendental methodology and view of sin, it ends up failing to do adequate justice to a Biblical theology of grace as the promise of mercy realized in Christ, centered on resolving the dilemma of reconciliation in the cross. It is important to affirm the significant, common ground which exists between Rahner's and a Lutheran view of the cross, namely that what occurred at the cross was not a sacrifice to God understood in terms of changing God's disposition from wrath to loving mercy, but rather that the cross was the result of God's prior, loving will. As Rahner states: "Because God wills salvation, therefore Jesus died and rose again, and not: because the crucifixion occurred, therefore God wills our salvation. God is not transformed from a God of anger and justice into a God of mercy and love by the cross; rather God brings the event of the cross to pass since he is possessed from the beginning of gratuitous mercy and, despite the world's sin, shares himself with the world, so overcoming its sin."[86] Lutheran theology concurs: "If God were the object of satisfaction, there would be no need for incarnation or the cross."[87]

A Lutheran proposal approaches this challenge by affirming the necessity of actual atonement, while simultaneously articulating a renewed understanding of atonement in terms of *promissio Dei*. How can the scriptural notion of sacrifice be synthesized with a sufficiently robust appreciation of God's law, God's promise, and the depths of sin? While I argued this in my earlier account of a confessional Lutheran theology of mercy, in critiquing Rahner's theology of reconciliation and the cross some points require further elaboration.

Having outlined Rahner's view of the cross as the effect of God's prior, loving will to reconcile, redeem, and forgive the world, Lutheran concerns with his overall approach can be articulated in a series of questions: What is the *basis* for reconciliation and forgiveness? What exactly does Rahner mean in stating that God "must make himself a part of the offense of guilt in order that forgiveness and reconciliation may take place"?[88] While Rahner affirms that God overcomes human sin by forgiving it in the cross, how exactly is God's forgiveness and redeeming love

---

86. Rahner, "One Christ and the Universality of Salvation," 207.
87. Forde, "Luther's Theology of the Cross," 52.
88. Rahner, "Reconciliation and Vicarious Representation," 262.

established by and in the cross? Furthermore, what does Rahner mean in claiming that "to experience and understand Christianity's ultimate essence is more necessary than human sinfulness and deliverance from guilt"?[89] In stressing the importance of human freedom resulting in a real act of "acceptance," what is it that needs to be accepted? Is it only the redeeming love of God and God reconciling himself to us in Jesus the crucified? While Rahner concedes the difficulty of how to adequately synthesize "the unmerited grace of divinization prior to sin . . . [and] the remission of *guilt* . . . [into the] conception of vicarious representation,"[90] how does he actually, precisely, and technically achieve such synthesis? Given Rahner's rejection of the cross as a vicarious suffering, satisfaction, and punishment for sin, how does his proposal adequately account for the realities of divine wrath and the vicarious representation of Christ as sacrifice? In other words, can Rahner's approach adequately account for the offensive paradox of the cross, explaining *how* "Christ redeemed us from the curse of the law, having become a curse for us (Gal 3:13a)?"

Rahner's critique centers on a particular, juridical view of vicarious redemption (satisfaction) as payment for sin as compromising the human freedom required for self-redemption: "This misapprehension . . . presumes tacitly that Jesus . . . has done something that is absolutely necessary to redeem the human race from sin, something that human beings themselves cannot do, but that Christ can do . . . A conception of vicarious redemption in which Jesus does for me what I actually ought to do myself but am not capable of doing, and which will then be 'credited' to me is a conception that I consider to be wrong or at least a misleading formulation of the dogmatic truth that my redemption is dependent on Jesus and his cross."[91]

The Necessity of Actual Atonement

While certain passages in Luther and some portrayals of atonement theories may give the impression that an approach to substitutionary atonement as vicarious, penal satisfaction is *the only* Lutheran position, this is not the case. The logic of the Lutheran approach centers on the "question of what the event [of the cross] and the proclamation of it does to us, for

---

89. Rahner, "Christian Understanding of Redemption," 244–5.
90. Ibid., 248.
91. Ibid.

us, to save and reconcile us to God."[92] In affirming how God's Word is performative and active, creating a new reality within us, Gerhard Forde describes how, for confessional Lutherans, the necessity of atonement is rooted in and expressed by the law-gospel distinction: "The necessity of atonement roots therefore in two things: our bondage and alienation, our unwillingness to be reconciled, and God's decision to be true to himself, to be a God of steadfast mercy nevertheless. The cross and the resurrection are . . . the outcome of God's resolve. The cross is God's self-giving to us. Just so, it is revelation and atonement at once. It is the carrying out of God's election to be merciful."[93]

From a confessional Lutheran perspective, Rahner's emphasis on Christ's incarnational solidarity with us does not go far enough: while it is true that Jesus Christ "did not renounce [his predestined solidarity with human beings] even when it meant for him the cross and the death of one forsaken by God,"[94] why not clarify the ultimate, actual cost of such solidarity? In terms of the cross being both revelation and atonement, Rahner readily affirms the cross as revelation of God's forgiving and reconciling love. However, he stops short of articulating deeply enough the *cost* of atonement, what it cost God "to make himself a part of the offense of guilt."[95] What is missing is the crucial emphasis on Christ *becoming sin for us*, on sins attacking Christ and Christ becoming sin on the cross. Martin Luther stresses the necessity of Christ actually becoming a curse for us in order to achieve salvation: "Whatever sins I, you, and all of us have committed or may commit in the future, they are as much Christ's own as if he himself had committed them. In short, our sin must be Christ's own sin, or we shall perish eternally."[96]

In terms of the series of questions on reconciliation I raised, let us address them one at a time. For Rahner, the basis for reconciliation and forgiveness seems to be the eternally loving, salvific will of God. As with Karl Barth, such a prior will of God risks downplaying or minimizing the actual, historical significance of the cross into apparent playacting. Forde expresses the Lutheran concern to emphasize God being for us in the concrete event of the cross: "Only the historical, concrete, suffering,

---

92. Forde, "Atonement as Actual Event," 80.
93. Forde, "Reconciliation with God," 69.
94. Rahner, "Reconciliation and Vicarious Representation," 268.
95. Ibid., 262.
96. Luther, *Luther's Works*, 26:278.

and dying Jesus can save us from the wrath of the [absolute God] . . . God is not changed in the sense of being *made* merciful by the historical event. The event takes place because God is merciful and desires to be so concretely *for us*."[97] My concern here is that Rahner's transcendental Christology seems to allow for a view of Jesus as universal example of an abstract ideal, rather than concretely engaging the historical specificity of the cross and its concrete ramifications for sins actually being forgiven and the promise of mercy being actualized in history.

Secondly, while Christ's "incarnational solidarity" would presumably include Jesus' becoming sin for us, Rahner is curiously silent about this aspect of incarnational solidarity. Given his relative emphasis on other themes (importance of human freedom and Jesus' obedience unto death), as well as his previous statements about sin and suspicions regarding theories of vicarious satisfaction, it remains unclear and ambiguous whether, and to what extent, Jesus' becoming sin on the cross is relevant to Rahner's Christology. His transcendental Christology of predestined solidarity seems plausible without any significant affirmation or explication of *how* Jesus' becoming sin brings about divine forgiveness and reconciliation.

Thirdly, in stressing the importance of "acceptance," what requires acceptance: God's undifferentiated self-communication as revealing love, or rather God's word of law, judging our sin, guilt, and inability to fulfill the demands of the Law, in contrast to the promise of mercy? Is it acceptance of the truth of what it cost God to bear the consequences of our sin for us, to become sin for us on the cross? "Accept" sounds remarkably similar to "trust": what is the object of such trust? Is it sufficiently differentiated?

In terms of synthesizing grace prior to sin and the forgiveness of sins into a view of vicarious representation, Rahner lacks a robust enough understanding of Jesus' death as sacrifice. His view of forgiveness seems problematic in two ways. First, from a Lutheran perspective, it seems too abstract and sterile, not sufficiently emphasizing or delineating the cost, precisely to God, of forgiving human sin and guilt. While Rahner is concerned to strongly maintain human freedom throughout, a Lutheran emphasis on the bondage of the will asserts that such a concern with preserving free will misses what should be the main emphasis of a theology of the cross.[98] Second, Rahner's theology exhibits ambiguity about the very

97. Forde, "Reconciliation with God," 71–72.
98. Ibid., 68.

A Paradigm of Grace as Nature Fulfilled

possibility of forgiveness. While he certainly speaks about "God's free and forgiving self-communication," the dilemma of forgiveness highlights, from a Lutheran perspective, an unresolved ambiguity in his thought. As Highfield asks, "If sin in the strict sense is a transcendental "no" to God, a definitive refusal of God's gracious offer of self-communication, how can it be forgiven? . . . Original sin, concupiscence, and venial sin can be removed, but these are sin only in an analogous sense, as something we suffer. So, what is there to forgive?"[99]

Rahner's understanding of Jesus' mission as living the fully perfect human life, fully accepting God's self-communication (grace), this acceptance being "sealed in death" and affirmed in the resurrection, seems to run the danger of downplaying the essential in favor of what is true, yet secondary. Even if one grants that, due to sin, the priority of an incarnational motif adapts and morphs into a salvation motif, my concern still remains. In other words: whenever Jesus' death and resurrection, precisely because they accomplish what is needed for God's mercy to be actualized in the world, are subordinated in favor of another theological locus (such as incarnation), the theology and mystery of the cross loses its power, the cross and resurrection become merely instrumental rather than central, and the proper emphasis is misplaced. My concern here is deeply pastoral: that Jesus always be presented and proclaimed chiefly as the savior of sinners, and only secondarily as teacher and perfect example of humanity. Melanchthon's application question hits the nail on the head: are the benefits of Christ being properly used and utilized?[100] If these benefits are forgiveness of sin, the unconditional love and grace of God, and new life in and through Christ, then Jesus' death dealt primarily with our sin problem, and only secondarily helps us live a fully human life. While a Lutheran model emphasizes a theology of the cross without denying the significance of the incarnation, Rahner emphasizes the salvific significance of the incarnation without denying the significance of Jesus' passion, death, and resurrection.

A quote from Luther helps summarize the differences between Rahner and a Lutheran proposal on this point. While Luther has much to say about the "happy exchange" of human sin and divine righteousness, he also uses language reminiscent of *theosis*: "Therefore God becomes man in order that man may become God. Likewise strength becomes

---

99. Highfield, "The Freedom to Say 'No'?," 494, 496.
100. Kolb and Wengert, *Book of Concord*, 121.

weak in order that weakness may become strength. He put on our form and figure, image and likeness, in order to clothe us in his image, form, and likeness."[101] While both Rahner and confessional Lutherans can readily affirm this statement, the difference is a matter of emphasis: while Rahner emphasizes Jesus' incarnational solidarity with us, a Lutheran proposal insists that what must be assumed by God, precisely in order to redeem it, is human sin itself. Without such a strong emphasis on God becoming sin for us, the promised righteousness of God is not actualized.

The "Anonymous Christian"

My preceding argument now culminates in a practical critique of Rahner's category of the "anonymous Christian." While I agree with Rahner's inclusivist position that those who are saved are saved in and through Christ, I question his category of the "anonymous Christian" on several counts.

First, does such a category take sufficiently seriously the explicitly different, religious and doctrinal commitments of people of other faiths, if they would not define themselves as such? As Jeannine Hill-Fletcher notes, "In these self-referential constructions of otherness, the other is not allowed to be distinctive, but is named with reference to one's own categories and judged on the basis of one's own self-identity."[102] The term might just as easily be turned back on Christians in calling them anonymous Buddhists, Hindus, etc. Is it a patronizing view?

Second, does Rahner's approach undercut the importance and necessity of the Christian mission of proclamation? Rahner claims, "Even though anonymous Christianity is prior to explicit Christianity it does not render it superfluous. On the contrary, it itself demands this explicit Christianity." [103] He grounds this in the supernatural existential creating "the condition enabling the subject to act for his own salvation . . . [as] logically prior to the free act by which salvation is appropriated in the subject's own personal life."[104] While for Rahner "it is a perfectly logical process for the grace that creates salvation . . . to be logically and

---

101. Luther, quoted in Forde, "Atonement as Actual Event," 98.
102. Hill-Fletcher, "Rahner and Religious Diversity," 246.
103. Rahner, "Anonymous Christianity," 171.
104. Ibid., 170.

A Paradigm of Grace as Nature Fulfilled

temporally prior to the sacramental act which signifies it,"[105] this statement reveals a deeper difference between Rahner's sacramental theology and a Lutheran view of the performative Word of God. For Rahner, sacramental acts such as baptism or penance (two explicit examples Rahner cites) are, to a large degree, external signs or outward expressions of "the power of the habitual grace which is already present."[106] They reveal and confirm a pre-existing condition of grace, rather than creating it. In contrast, Luther's insight into the performative Word of God insists that this Word in its manifold forms (sacramental, written, and oral) creates in its recipient a new reality, namely saving grace. While Rahner does not outright exclude the Lutheran view,[107] he views it as insufficient and clearly emphasizes the prior necessity of habitual grace as a precondition for actual grace. Whether or not Rahner would view the proclaimed Word sacramentally (analogous to baptism, penance, etc.) remains unclear. While the limits of this study preclude an in-depth treatment of Rahner's theology of the symbol and sacraments, the differences between his view of grace as involving a unity of habitual and actual grace and a Lutheran emphasis on the performative Word of God actualizing grace in a person are rooted in more enduring differences regarding theological anthropology and the nature of grace itself. From my perspective, Rahner's approach does not sufficiently grapple with and express the radical disjuncture which the New Testament refers to as "the new birth" (John 3:5) and "the old and new creation" (2 Cor 5:16).

Since my next three points of critique center on Rahner's classic definition of what constitutes an "anonymous Christian," I will first share the quote and then elaborate my critique: "Therefore no matter what a man states in his conceptual, theoretical, and religious reflection, anyone who does not say in his *heart*, 'there is no God' . . . but testifies to him by the radical acceptance of his being, is a believer. But if in this way he believes in deed and in truth in the holy mystery of God . . . then the grace of this truth by which he allows himself to be led is always already the grace of

---

105. Ibid., 171.

106. Ibid., 170.

107. "[The pre-existing, habitual grace] presses forward towards this sacramental incarnation of itself, and thereby ensures that it is not impossible for this effective sacramental symbol of this same grace to be itself a cause of the grace and not merely an outward expression of it such as ultimately speaking would make no difference" (Rahner, "Anonymous Christianity," 171).

the Father in his Son. And anyone who has let himself be taken hold of by this grace can be called with every right an 'anonymous Christian.'"[108]

Far from being a condescendingly arrogant assertion, Rahner views this category, to the contrary, as epitomizing the deepest of humility. In his own words:

> Non-Christians may think it presumption for the Christian to judge everything that is sound or restored (by being sanctified) to be the fruit in every man of the grace of his Christ, and to interpret it as anonymous Christianity; they may think it presumption for the Christian to regard the non-Christian as a Christian who has yet to come to himself reflectively. But the Christian cannot renounce this "presumption," which is really the source of the greatest humility for both himself and for the Church. For it is a profound admission of the fact that God is greater than man and the Church. The Church will go out to meet the non-Christian of tomorrow with the attitude expressed by St. Paul when he said: What therefore you do not know and yet worship (and yet *worship*!) that I proclaim to you (Acts 17:23). On such a basis one can be tolerant, humble, and yet firm toward all non-Christian religions.[109]

These quotes raise immensely important questions regarding the nature of God, of faith, and of grace. We begin with the question of God before proceeding to the nature of faith and grace.

Third, does Rahner's view take seriously enough the radically different doctrines of God in the different religions? Is his assumption of the Christian, theistic God as the one whom people 'do not deny' an unwarranted assumption? How does this square with pantheist, non-personal, or atheistic visions of God and religion, such as Buddhism or Hinduism?

Fourth, is his approach too minimalist, diluting not only the nature and significant commitments of other religions but those of Christianity as well? Does he risk losing sight of the particularly distinctive shape and content of *Christian* revelation in his notion of the anonymous Christian (Hans Urs von Balthasar), particularly those of law and Gospel, cross and resurrection? For example, does he reduce Christian theology to anthropology (Barth's charge), or to a system of ethics (in his notion of the unity of the love of God and love of neighbor)?

---

108. Rahner, "Anonymous Christians," 395.
109. Rahner, "Christianity and the Non-Christian Religions," 134.

A Paradigm of Grace as Nature Fulfilled

Fifth, in terms of the question of the nature of faith, how does the claim for anonymous Christian faith square with the New Testament view of saving faith as *fides ex auditu*, "faith comes by hearing"? It is hard to see how the scriptural emphasis on saving faith as an explicit response to the proclaimed Gospel can be maintained within the framework of the anonymous Christian and implicit, saving faith.[110] How does Rahner's view relate to the externally proclaimed and preached word of the Gospel? While Rahner affirms Vatican II's view that saving faith is possible for those who have not yet heard the external proclamation of the Gospel,[111] how does such a view square with Paul's puzzled wonderment in Rom 10:14, "How shall they call on [or deny] Him in whom they have not believed? How can they believe on Him of whom they have not heard? How can they hear without preaching?"

Furthermore, in addressing the crucial question of the nature of grace, Rahner seems to assume a single, revelatory Word from God, that of God's grace in Jesus Christ. He seems to downplay, almost to the point of ignoring, God's other revelatory word of law as judgment of sin. What role does a doctrine of sin play in his view and evaluation of "anonymous Christianity" and, more broadly, in his theology of grace? As previously quoted, Rahner understands salvation as the experience of God's superabundant mystery, "not as consuming judgment, but as fulfilling nearness."[112] Why not also consuming judgment? Surely this superabundant mystery, according to Scripture, includes the mystery of both judgment and the promise of mercy fulfilled? While I agree that salvation is not the experience of God's consuming judgment, this quote pinpoints one of my chief criticisms of Rahner's theology: while acknowledging the reality of sin and divine judgment on some level, a sufficiently robust incorporation of sin and divine judgment into his theology of grace is missing. As argued in chapter 1, since the reality of law and judgment, articulated by the law/Gospel distinction, is a centrally enduring theme permeating Scripture, I am perplexed by its light treatment in Rahner's theological system. A crucial point of contention for my confessional Lutheran assessment of Rahner is this: viewing God's self-presence and self-communication as constituting grace, by definition, while philosophically appealing and compelling, is scripturally inaccu-

---

110. Lindbeck, "*Fides ex auditu*," 104.

111. Second Vatican Council, *Decree on the Church's Missionary Activity (Ad Gentes Divinitus)*, no. 7. Quoted in Flannery, ed., *Vatican Council II*, 821.

112. Rahner, "New Image of the Church," 7.

rate, at best, and misleading at worst. Such a definition of God's presence and revelation leaves out the significant, scriptural witness to the divine presence and revelation, not merely of loving grace, but precisely of consuming judgment and wrath! Rahner's system, especially his theology of grace, fails to sufficiently grapple with and incorporate this scripturally and theologically important category of divine judgment.

Finally, George Lindbeck summarizes my main concerns regarding Rahner's categories of the "anonymous Christian" and "implicit faith":

> The reasons which remain for using the concepts of anonymous grace and implicit faith are philosophical rather than properly theological. If one supposes that what is most fundamentally human in man is preconceptual and prelinguistic and that this can be arrived at by means of transcendental deductions or existential analyses, then it makes sense to follow Rahner in using these ideas to account for the salvation of non-Christians. It is doubtful, however, that his theory is persuasive apart from the German philosophical tradition of romanticism, idealism, and existentialism . . . [and] a highly reinterpreted Thomism.[113]

To conclude this section of critically engaging Rahner and begin to turn our attention to the further development and practical application of his theology in Dupuis' theology of mission, the question of what interreligious dialogue could or should consist of is important to raise. While I affirm the uniqueness of Christ, God's universal salvific will, the law/promise hermeneutic, and a theology of the cross as fundamental guideposts in approaching the question of a Christian encounter with religious pluralism, I believe the two-part question, "What is wrong with humanity and the world, and how can it be fixed?" to be the best diagnostic tool for getting to the heart of the religions' salvation agendas. I would argue that, while the notion of divine hiddenness produces a measure of interreligious convergence, the Christian notion of grace as promise of loving mercy fulfilled is a distinctive contribution to interreligious dialogue. While recognizing affirmations of God's loving presence and mercy in other religions, a Christian emphasis on loving mercy as "broken power," exhibiting divine vulnerability and self-condescension in the suffering, death, and resurrection of Jesus Christ, offers a distinctive interpretation of and solution to the world's brokenness. Intersecting such a distinctive view of grace as loving mercy with how divine hiddenness

---

113. Lindbeck, *"Fides ex auditu,"* 119.

A Paradigm of Grace as Nature Fulfilled

is understood and managed can lead interreligious dialogue to fruitful, perhaps previously underappreciated ground. Introducing such a move within the framework of interreligious dialogue constitutes one of the desired, practical outcomes of this project.

RAHNER'S CHALLENGE FOR CONFESSIONAL LUTHERAN THEOLOGY

Before concluding this chapter, Rahner challenges confessional Lutheran theology in several ways. What issues or problems does he find my approach insufficiently addressing? While claiming to speak for another is always a risky, I endeavor to raise questions that I believe he would raise for my proposal. First, must the "nature/grace" and "law/promise" paradigms be mutually exclusive, or might, for example, the category of "promise" be understood broadly enough to encompass both?[114] Secondly, in terms of the Christian doctrine of grace, does the law/Gospel distinction exaggerate the importance and role of sin within Christian theology?[115] In terms of the nature of faith, does the Lutheran emphasis on "faith comes by hearing" unnecessarily restrict God's freedom to be radically, universally gracious and loving? Fourthly, is the Lutheran view of grace as the promise of loving mercy too extrinsic, relying solely upon the external proclaimed Word? Fifthly, do the Lutheran categories of the law/Gospel distinction, sin, and grace sufficiently respect the depths of God's mystery and freedom? If Jesus is truly "the one for *all* others," surely God can and does find ways of conveying saving grace beyond the external means of the church's ministry of Word and sacrament, by means more internal to the human condition? Finally, might the "strangeness" of divine grace structure Christian (Lutheran) grammar in ways that might be more open to the surprising wonder of discovering God's loving mystery in unexpected ways? In other words: a Lutheran emphasis on the

---

114. Robert Jenson, in his contemporary thinking, strongly prefers the "nature/grace" paradigm while intentionally distancing himself from his former Lutheran position as insufficiently comprehensive or ecumenical. I respectfully disagree with Jenson's approach. While a complete negation of the "nature/grace" paradigm is not historically tenable, my claim is that which paradigm one emphasizes makes a real, significant difference in one's approach to other religions. I will further this claim in the final chapter.

115. Rahner explicitly raises this concern in his essay, "Reconciliation and Vicarious Redemption," 255.

"grammar" of law/Gospel, sin, and grace as mercy need not be construed as opposed to openness toward God's infinite, loving mystery. The more one immerses oneself in the grammar and lived practices of the Christian faith, the more deeply we are propelled into the mystery, not only of God's loving revelation of being "for us" in Jesus Christ, but also of God's hiddenness. Might confessional Lutherans view such Christian grammar, not merely as definitive "rules of Christian discourse," but as avenues propelling them to further explore the mysterious depths of God's being?[116]

CONCLUSION

The contrast between the "nature/grace" and "law/promise" paradigms can be brought into sharper focus and summarized by comparing their differing answers to the three, fundamental questions posed at the beginning of chapter 2, highlighting enduring differences. First, what is the nature of sin? According to Rahner's nature/grace model, the essence of sin is exercising the fundamental option of freedom to say a radical "no" to God himself, a rejection of God's offer of self-communication. However, since God is the transcendental horizon of our very being, such an act is by definition self-defeating and self-contradictory.[117] According to the law/promise model, sin is fundamentally a matter of misplaced trust and unbelief: not trusting the God whose promise of mercy in Christ is trustworthy and certain, while trusting that which is not trustworthy for one's ultimate meaning and fulfillment ("idols"). While the nature/grace model is optimistic about the human ability to exercise freedom properly, the law/promise model views human nature as chronically trusting in false gods and promises.

Secondly, how is sin related to grace? According to the nature/grace model, grace, as God's very self-communication and presence, perfects human nature by bringing it to its intended goal: union with God in the beatific vision. Such an experience and state of being, far from being the rare possession of select saints, is a common, everyday offer and reality for most people. As Rahner puts it: "grace can also sanctify everyday and reasonable activities and can transform them into a step towards God

---

116. This point is part of R. R. Reno's interpretation of Rahner's theological achievement, and I find it compelling. His argument is elaborated in *The Ordinary Transformed: Karl Rahner and the Christian Vision of Transcendence*.

117. Rahner, *Foundations*, 102.

A Paradigm of Grace as Nature Fulfilled

. . . once we experience the spirit in this way, we . . . have also already *in fact* experienced the *supernatural*."[118] Although sin nullified the intended purpose of human nature and history as a means for communicating grace, and while sin tempts humans to say a categorical "no" to the offer of divine grace, such grace, working through the supernatural existential, nevertheless woos human nature to its intended fulfillment as the "key" which fits its proper "keyhole."

According to the law/promise model, because sin is fundamentally a matter of misplaced trust, the grace conveyed by the Gospel is likewise an invitation to trust and accept the trustworthy promise of mercy and reconciliation in Christ. Grace (mercy), rather than merely fulfilling human nature, is the promise of mercy enacted in the person and work of Christ, offered in the Gospel, and actualized in reception through faith.

Thirdly, what is the nature of faith, what role does it play in relating sin and grace? In the nature/grace model, faith is human nature's proper orientation toward and acceptance of God, not only as the horizon and proper goal of all our knowing, willing, and doing, but also as absolute mystery. By contrast, in the law/promise model, faith involves trusting the promise of mercy in Christ so that Christ's merits and offer of grace aren't "wasted," but rather properly received, thus appropriating all the benefits of the Gospel and actualizing the reconciliation which has already occurred in God's self between God's wrath and mercy.

In contrast to the nature/grace paradigm which begins with and operates from the assumption of God being gracious *de facto*, a distinctively Lutheran theology of mercy, one which insists upon the "law/promise" paradigm as more scripturally accurate than the "nature/grace" paradigm, identifies the resolution within God's self of the tension between God's wrath and God's mercy as the key question and springboard for developing a theology of grace. When one starts there, rather than with transcendental anthropology, the depth dimensions of the Biblical notion of sin, God's longing to honestly love a world which resolutely resists God's love, the resolution of this tension in the cross of Christ, and the missional implications of such a theology of reconciliation centered on the cross are more adequately and comprehensively accounted for.

Such a Lutheran theology of loving mercy leads to and is intrinsically connected to God's law, which a confessional Lutheran approach proposes is universally and variously experienced by people, including

118. Rahner, "Reflections on the Experience of Grace," 88.

as the hiddenness of God (*deus absconditus*). This concept will serve as a fruitful bridge for connecting mission and interreligious dialogue (as further delineated in chapters 5 and 6).

4

A Missional Paradigm of Grace as Nature Fulfilled

Jacques Dupuis

JACQUES DUPUIS WILL SERVE as my conversation partner in this chapter, not only because his inclusive pluralism represents a paradigmatic example of *missio Dei*, especially in its Trinitarian framework and theology of revelation, but also because he explicitly embraces Rahner's nature/grace paradigm and elaborates the missiological implications of Rahner's system. In my judgment, Dupuis represents the most carefully nuanced and consistent example of how Rahner's theology of grace as nature fulfilled applies itself as a distinctive theology of religious pluralism. In his own words:

> While gratefully acknowledging my dependence on Rahner, I also claim to go beyond his open inclusivism. Rahner affirms a "transitory" saving efficacy of the religious traditions in individual cases of persons who have not yet been confronted with the mystery of Christ and received the grace of faith in him. I put no such restrictions in time or extension to the efficacy of the traditions in the order of salvation for their followers, and I base my position not only on the universal presence and efficacy of the risen Christ, but also on the universal presence and action of the Word of God as such before and after the incarnation.[1]

---

1. Dupuis, "Christianity and the Religions' Revisited," 370–71.

Mission Shaped by Promise

This quote captures, for Dupuis, where missiological energy should focus: in articulating, as clearly as possible, how "the universal and operative presence of the Word of God [Logos] and the unique salvific meaning of the historical event of Jesus Christ"[2] are to be properly related. While firmly advocating the importance of a Christocentric approach, Dupuis also wishes to affirm the importance of pneumatology. He therefore concedes and elaborates the permissibility, value, and intelligibility of speaking of Spirit Christology in relation to Trinitarian Christology, but never at the expense of pneumatology.

Certain fundamental convictions serve as guiding principles in Dupuis' argument for his theology of religious pluralism. These fall under six broad headings: a distinctive theological method, the Christ-event as the central point of salvation history, interpretation of Christian Scripture and tradition, the paradigm of inclusive pluralism and the saving value of the religions, the reign of God and the church, and a mutual, asymmetrical complementarity between Christianity and other religions.[3] This chapter will elaborate each of these six convictions, starting with theological method.

Before delving into the details of those principles, however, let us take a step back to glimpse the overall framework within which Dupuis argues for his inclusive pluralism, lest we lose sight of the forest for the trees. In my best judgment, two theological pillars form the overall framework for his argument in terms of an adequately robust economy of salvation. On the one hand, a proper interrelationship between Trinitarian Christology and pneumatology is essential in giving his inclusive pluralism the proper impetus and direction in moving outward, from the Trinity, to better appreciate "the way the Spirit of Christ is active, in all religions, in revealing the mystery of Christ- the mystery of what Christ is doing in the world."[4] In seeking to balance Trinitarian Christology and pneumatology, Christian theology must give proper attention to "the universal significance and constitutive role which Christianity attributes to Jesus Christ."[5] Such Trinitarian Christology and robust pneumatology, albeit nuanced and intricately related, are never ends in themselves.

---

2. Dupuis, *Christianity and the Religions*, 156.
3. Dupuis, "'Christianity and the Religions' Revisited," 363–83.
4. Dupuis, *Christianity and the Religions*, 94.
5. Ibid., 87.

Rather, they are guided and motivated by a broader vision of an "eschatological recapitulation" of all things under the headship of Christ.

For Dupuis, perhaps the clearest scriptural expression of the ultimate goal of an economy of salvation which takes seriously both the universal Word and the incarnate Word, within a Trinitarian framework, is Ephesians 1:10, which describes God's "plan for the fullness of time, to unite (gather up) all things in him [Christ], things in heaven and things on earth." Dupuis elaborates his vision of the eschatological recapitulation:

> The convergence between the religious traditions will reach its goal in the eschaton with the "recapitulation" (*anakephalaiosis*: Eph 1:10) of all things in Christ. This . . . will coincide with the final "perfection" (*teleiosis*) of the Son of God as "source of eternal salvation" (Heb 5:9), whose influence remains subject, up to this final fulfillment, to an "eschatological remainder." When the Reign of God is achieved, then will come the end when . . . God will be "all in all" (1 Cor. 15: 24–28). [This] is the common final fulfillment of Christianity and the religions.[6]

These twin poles, the vision of eschatological recapitulation and the relating of Trinitarian Christology to pneumatology, form the axis within which Dupuis elaborates the specific details of his proposal. One could even say that the former provides the "what" (the final goal), while the latter provides the "how" (the intermediate steps), of his inclusively pluralist proposal.

THEOLOGICAL METHOD: ONE GOD—ONE CHRIST— CONVERGENT PATHS

Dupuis' position and theological method has admittedly developed and matured over his career, deeply influenced by his thirty-six years spent in India. He describes his own, earlier theological stance as "theocentric Christocentrism," whose aim was to "open up a theological perspective which, while holding fast to faith in Jesus Christ as traditionally understood by mainstream Christianity and church tradition, would at the same time integrate, in their differences, the religious experiences of the living religious traditions and assign to those traditions a positive role

---

6. Ibid., 194.

and significance in the overall plan of God for humankind, as it unfolds through salvation history."[7]

While not rejecting his earlier stance, Dupuis sought to broaden the comprehensiveness of its scope, and his change in terminology from "theology of religions" to a "theology of religious pluralism" signifies a subtle, yet decisive, change in theological perspective:

> The new perspective is no longer limited to the problem of 'salvation' for members of the other religious traditions or even to the role of those traditions in the salvation of their members. It searches more deeply, in the light of Christian faith, for the meaning of God's design for humankind of the plurality of living faiths and religious traditions with which we are surrounded. Are all religious traditions of the world destined, in God's plan, to converge? Where, when, and how?[8]

In gaining a newfound appreciation for religious pluralism, not simply as a *de facto* reality to be tolerated but a *de jure* gift to be celebrated, Dupuis seeks to articulate an integrative approach, envisioning a theology of religious pluralism transcending the traditional, tripartite typologies of exclusivism/inclusivism/pluralism or theocentrism/Christocentrism/ecclesiocentrism.[9]

In seeking to describe the overarching framework of Dupuis' proposal, the twin categories of Trinitarian Christology and pneumatology, facilitating and aiming toward the eschatological fulfillment of all things in Christ, serve as the twin pillars of a hermeneutical key to his approach. Dupuis himself seems to agree. The challenge facing an adequate theology of religious pluralism, as he puts it, is "to combine and to hold in constructive tension the central character of the punctual historical event of Jesus Christ and the universal action and dynamic influence of the Spirit of God. It will thus be able to account for God's self-manifestation and self-gift in human cultures and religious traditions outside the orbit of influence of the Christian message without . . . construing Christology and pneumatology into two distinct economies of divine-human relationships. . . ."[10]

---

7. Dupuis, *Toward a Christian Theology of Religious Pluralism*, 1.
8. Ibid., 10.
9. Kärkkäinen, *Introduction to the Theology of Religions*, 207.
10. Dupuis, *Christianity and the Religions*, 94.

A Missional Paradigm of Grace as Nature Fulfilled

In explicitly addressing his theological methodology, Dupuis describes it as a combination of inductive and deductive methods.[11] Keenly aware of the need for what only comparative theology can provide—thorough comparative studies of Christianity and Buddhism, Hinduism, and Islam, etc.—Dupuis nonetheless asserts the urgent need for Christian theology to make some provisional judgments regarding "how Christianity relates in general to the other traditions in our present context."[12] Given this urgent concern and practical motivation, he freely concedes that his approach remains more deductive (proceeding from a priori judgments) than he might wish. However, Dupuis is quick to insist on the crucial role of the inductive element—engaging the lived reality of religious pluralism through interreligious dialogue—in interpreting and potentially modifying the revelatory material of one's tradition. As he states,

> I try to combine an inductive and a deductive method in theology. This means that a treatment of the theology of religions cannot proceed simply a priori in a deductive way, but must first be based on contact with the concrete reality of religious plurality through interreligious dialogue, and proceed then to interpret in the light of this reality the data of revelation and tradition. . . . My way of proceeding remains largely a priori. The task of the future would consist, before constructing a Christian theology of religions, engaging thoroughly in a comparative study of religions. . . . We cannot afford waiting till elaborate comparative studies of each religious tradition have brought conclusive results in order to ask how Christianity relates in general to the other traditions in our present context.[13]

Another way of clarifying Dupuis' theological method is by describing what it is not: the positions which his approach explicitly rejects, argues against, and seeks to correct. There are at least three approaches Dupuis finds problematic and seeks to offer a corrective to.[14] First, he judges a radical theocentrism (such as that of John Hick) which seeks to pit Christ and God against each other, emphasizing the universal scope of God the Father at the expense of the particularity of Christ, as insufficiently faithful to the Christian tradition. For a theology to remain dis-

---

11. Dupuis, "'Christianity and the Religions' Revisited," 364.
12. Ibid., 365.
13. Ibid., 364–5.
14. Kärkkäinen, *Trinity and Religious Pluralism*, 50–52.

tinctly Trinitarian and therefore Christian, it must affirm the distinction, yet integral and inseparable connection, between God the Father and God the Son. Christianity is theocentric precisely by being Christocentric, not despite it.

Next, Dupuis offers a nuanced corrective to both "regnocentrism" (the reign of God as central) and "soteriocentrism" (salvation as central) as the focal point and defining feature of a Christian approach to religious pluralism, to the exclusion or marginalization of Christology. Paul Knitter's advocacy of human and eco-liberation as the defining criterion for evaluating the religions is a prime example of this approach. While the reign of God certainly encompasses both human and cosmic "liberation" in the fullest sense of the word, a Christian understanding of both God's reign and salvation necessitates a central role for the person and work of Jesus Christ. As Dupuis notes, the role of Christ is central to a Christian notion of the reign of God: "the reign of God has broken through to history in Jesus Christ and the Christ-event . . . it is through the action of the risen Christ that the members of the various religious traditions share in the reign of God."[15] Positing the reign of God, salvation, or liberation as the central, unifying category in approaching religious pluralism inevitably begs the questions, "Which salvation? Whose liberation?" Whatever answer one gives to such questions inevitably betrays a very specific notion of salvation and liberation, one that is more indebted to one's own religious tradition and context and less universal than one readily admits.

Third, Dupuis deems any subordination of the role and work of Jesus Christ to that of the Spirit as insufficient. Whereas the first approach emphasized the universality of God at the expense of the particularity of Christ, here the Spirit's role and work is posited as more universal and fruitful than that of Christ for a theology of religious pluralism. While such a view, seeking to separate the universal Spirit from the historically particular Jesus, is almost irresistibly appealing for interreligious dialogue, Dupuis insists that the actions of the Spirit and Jesus, though distinct, must always be understood as inseparably complementary: "One needs to affirm clearly the universal action of the Spirit throughout human history, either before or after the historical event Jesus Christ. But Christian faith has it that the action of the Spirit and that of Jesus Christ, though distinct, are nevertheless complementary and inseparable.

---

15. Dupuis, *Toward a Christian Theology of Religious Pluralism*, 195.

A Missional Paradigm of Grace as Nature Fulfilled

Pneumatocentrism and Christocentrism cannot, therefore, be construed as two distinct economies of salvation, one parallel to the other."[16]

In other words: Trinitarian unity and coherence demands that, rather than parallel economies of salvation, the cosmic, universal work of *both* the Spirit *and* the ascended Christ, rather than separated, must be held together. Such complementarity, however, always serves to focus attention on the centrality of Christ. As Dupuis puts it, "The proper function of the Spirit is to center, by its immanent presence, the human being- and the church- on Christ ... The Spirit is not at the center."[17] Nevertheless, Dupuis unambiguously affirms the Spirit's universal dimension: "The Spirit of God has been universally present throughout human history and remains active today outside the boundaries of the Christian fold. He it is who 'inspires' in people belonging to other religious traditions the obedience of saving faith, and in the traditions themselves a word spoken by God to their adherents."[18]

Affirming Vatican II's *Gaudium et Spes* paragraph 22, he concurs that the Spirit's special function involves allowing and calling people to become sharers of the paschal mystery of Jesus' death and resurrection: "Thus, through the power of the Spirit, the Jesus Christ-event is being actuated through all times; it is present and active in every generation. In all cases the immediate influence of the Spirit gives expression to the operative presence of God's saving action which has come to a climax in Jesus Christ."[19]

In contrast and nuanced correction to each of these three alternative approaches—theocentrism, regnocentrism/soteriocentrism, and pneumatocentrism—Dupuis builds and argues for his proposal of inclusive pluralism which he describes in terms of "One God—One Christ—Convergent Paths."[20] What distinctive methodological emphases does such a title convey? Dupuis prioritizes and privileges the first two phrases as decisive for understanding the third. While his strong, Trinitarian framework (one God- one Christ) prevents him from lapsing into radical, theocentric pluralism (Hick, Knitter, etc.), his equally strong insistence on 'convergent paths' prevents a strict exclusivism. His third phrase reflects

---

16. Ibid., 197.
17. Dupuis, *Jesus Christ at the Encounter of World Religions*, 153.
18. Dupuis, *Toward a Christian Theology of Religious Pluralism*, 196.
19. Ibid., 197.
20. Ibid., 203ff.

his deep conviction regarding the revelationist framework of all religions: to a greater or lesser degree, God reveals Godself salvifically in all religions. I have already voiced some Lutheran concerns with this approach and will voice some further constructive correctives to Dupuis' model in chapter 5. In trying to balance and capture the significance of each phrase in his title, Dupuis notes: "[it] evokes at once the foundational character of the Christ-event as the guarantee of God's manifold way of self-manifestation, self-revelation, and self-gift to humankind in a multifaceted yet organically structured economy of salvation, through which the diverse paths tend toward a mutual convergence in the Absolute Divine Mystery which constitutes the common final end of them all."[21]

THE CHRIST EVENT AT THE CENTER OF SALVATION HISTORY

While Dupuis clearly affirms God's definitive revelation in and through Jesus Christ as universal Savior, he adamantly affirms an openness to God's presence and work, through both the Spirit and the pre- and post-incarnate Word of God (*Logos spermatikos*), in the history of religions. Since absoluteness is an attribute of ultimate reality in its divine immanence, Dupuis deems talk of Jesus Christ's "absoluteness" as inappropriate and unnecessary. Instead, he prefers naming the universal uniqueness of Jesus Christ as "constitutive" and "relational," rather than "absolute" or "relative." Such a constitutive Christology requires further elaboration.

By means of a high Christology, Dupuis insists on holding together the universal presence of Christ (via Spirit and Logos Christology) with the particularity of salvation through Christ (via Trinitarian Christology).[22] This salvific significance and particularity of Christ, far from being exclusive, must be understood in radically inclusive terms. How? On what basis? On the basis of the cumulative effect of the following five principles.

First, as the incarnate Son and Logos, Jesus Christ does not exhaust the mystery of God. If God (as the immanent Trinity) remains beyond the man Jesus as the ultimate source of both revelation and salvation, then God has more revelation to reveal than God can and does reveal in

---

21. Ibid., 209.
22. Dupuis, *Christianity and the Religions*, 89–95.

A Missional Paradigm of Grace as Nature Fulfilled

the historical Christ event.²³ Second, not only was the pre-incarnate Logos active throughout the world and in the history of religions, likewise the pre-incarnate Logos (*Logos asarkos*) continues its universal ministry in the world and among the religions even after the incarnation. Third, while Jesus alone is the Christ and Son of God, "other 'saving figures' may be . . . 'enlightened' by the Word or 'inspired' by the Spirit to become pointers to salvation for their followers, in accordance with God's overall design for humankind."²⁴ The role of these other saving figures, however, is inclusive in relation to Christ: ". . . their role does not consist in saving; it is limited to pointing to paths where salvation through the mystery of Christ may be encountered."²⁵ Fourth, the concrete mediation of divine grace happens through the other religious traditions in their historical, social forms.²⁶ Finally: the Spirit may be doing something truly different from what one finds in Jesus Christ as the incarnate Logos and Word of God, precisely in and through other religions as social structures, yet never contradictory to the revelation of Christ. As Dupuis puts it, "God may have—and indeed seems to have—more to say to humanity than what God has said in Jesus."²⁷ While that may be true, Jesus still serves as a check and safeguard on what the Spirit may say or do: "Christ, not the Spirit, is at the center as the way to God."²⁸ In other words: whatever God has to say, through the Spirit, in other religions must be understood and interpreted "in light of" Christ. Dupuis summarizes how his Trinitarian, constitutive Christology, Logos theology, and pneumatology integrate to support his theology of revelation and appreciation of the distinctive "truth and grace" other religions offer:

> The Trinitarian Christological model, the universal enlightenment of the Word of God, and the enlivening by his Spirit make it possible to discover, in other saving figures and traditions, truth and grace not brought out with the same vigor and clarity in God's revelation and manifestation in Jesus Christ. Truth and grace found elsewhere must not be reduced to "seeds" or "stepping stones" simply to be nurtured or used and then superseded

---

23. For a fuller discussion of this point, see Dupuis, *Toward a Christian Theology of Religious Pluralism*, 235–53, and Dupuis, *Christianity and the Religions*, 138–62.
24. Dupuis, *Toward a Christian Theology of Religious Pluralism*, 298.
25. Dupuis, "'Christianity and the Religions' Revisited," 374.
26. Dupuis, *Toward a Christian Theology of Religious Pluralism*, 218.
27. Ibid., 388.
28. Ibid., 197.

in Christian revelation. They represent additional and autonomous benefits. More divine truth and grace are found operative in the entire history of God's dealings with humankind than are available simply in the Christian tradition. As the "human face" or "icon" of God, Jesus Christ gives to Christianity its specific and singular character. But, while he is constitutive of salvation for all, he neither excludes nor includes other saving figures or traditions. If he brings salvation history to a climax, it is by way not of substitution or supersession but of confirmation and accomplishment.[29]

Dupuis concludes that, given the preceding argument, religious pluralism is not simply to be endured as a *de facto* reality, but rather should be celebrated and embraced in principle (*de jure*) as a divine gift. Why? If the Spirit is able to grant revelation which truly, substantially differs from that received in and through Jesus, then the other religions must have a "lasting role" and "specific meaning," both for Christians and for adherents of those religions.[30] This means that the religions cannot be mere stepping stones, leading inevitably to Christianity (the fulfillment theory), but rather can and indeed do play a crucial role as mediators of God's saving purposes, although incompletely and less clearly than the revelation through Christ.

INTERPRETATION OF SCRIPTURE AND TRADITION

Given the preceding delineation of Dupuis' methodological principles and overarching argument, we are now better positioned to consider his exegesis of Scripture and the Christian tradition. Dupuis holds to the organic unity of Scripture, meaning that, while various affirmations of Scripture may initially seem contradictory, they are "in reality complementary and must be combined and integrated."[31] In terms of exegeting both the Christian tradition and the Scriptures themselves, the central issue at stake can be summarized as how "the universal and operative presence of the Word of God [Logos] and the unique salvific meaning of the historical event of Jesus Christ"[32] are to be properly

29. Ibid., 388.
30. Ibid., 211.
31. Dupuis, "'Christianity and the Religions' Revisited," 367.
32. Dupuis, *Christianity and the Religions*, 156.

A Missional Paradigm of Grace as Nature Fulfilled

related. All other exegetical issues, like spokes on a wheel, relate to and emanate from this hub.

Drawing on the rich tradition of interpretation regarding both the *Logos* and the *spermatikoi logoi*, Dupuis argues that the universal Word and incarnate Word, far from being radically separated or uncritically identified, should be distinguished in a manner which nonetheless emphasizes their mutually complementary roles within the one, universal economy of salvation.[33] Dupuis vigorously opposes two, parallel economies of salvation (through Christ and the Spirit, respectively). In fact, he argues for the importance of distinguishing "the Word of God" in three distinct senses: 1) the universal Word, present and active throughout human history; 2) the incarnate Word (the historical event of Jesus Christ); and 3) the glorified and ascended Word.[34] Such a position is crucial for undergirding Dupuis' constitutive Christology.

We now turn to examine Dupuis' theology of covenants as a key link between the particularity of Christian revelation and the universal scope of divine revelation through other religions. While acknowledging that a "salvation-history perspective is deeply rooted in biblical revelation," Dupuis asserts that such a perspective "allows for a more positive appraisal of other religious traditions than has often been thought."[35] The key issue is this: can a salvation-history paradigm attribute to other religious traditions more than a temporary nature, going beyond mere replacement and fulfillment to grant them a permanent, salvific status and relevance within the economy of salvation?[36] Can such a perspective affirm *de jure* religious pluralism, anchoring it within a Trinitarian Christological model? Dupuis believes that "the interrelatedness between the distinct modalities of God's self-communication" to people throughout human history undergirds precisely such a view of religious pluralism *de jure*.

In his discussion of the universal extent of salvation history, Dupuis vehemently rejects any views that propose either to situate the beginning of salvation history in the call of Abraham, or a "'prehistory' of salvation based upon a natural knowledge which God gives through the order of creation."[37] Viewing any scheme which would distinguish between

---

33. Dupuis, *Christianity and the Religions*, 156–62.
34. Dupuis, "'Christianity and the Religions' Revisited," 370.
35. Dupuis, *Christianity and the Religions*, 96.
36. Ibid.
37. Dupuis, *Toward a Christian Theology of Religious Pluralism*, 215.

salvation history and revelation history as "unduly truncated," Dupuis instead asserts that, given the coinciding and coextensive relationship between world history and salvation history, all of world history must be viewed as located within a "'supernatural order' entailing God's offer of self-communication through grace. Such an order of world and history always brings with it . . . a divine self-manifestation and the offer of salvation."[38] In cautioning against a rigid distinction between a "general" and "special" salvation history, Dupuis wonders "whether the history of other peoples cannot play for them, in the order of salvation, a role 'analogous' to that played for the Hebrew peoples by the history of Israel, in the sense of comprising historical events whose divine salvific significance is guaranteed by a prophetic word."[39] In pursuing this line of thought, Dupuis posits that "the basis for such divine interventions in their history . . . consists in a 'covenant' relationship between God and the peoples."[40] Invoking and utilizing the category of covenant allows Dupuis to argue for divine covenants throughout the history of religions as being irrevocable, mutually interrelated, and progressive within a Trinitarian structure of history.

Viewing Christianity's relationship to other religions as parallel and analogous to the covenantal parallelism between Judaism and Christianity, Dupuis asserts that God's single, unified plan of salvation history, while "filtered" through the single, definitive "lens" of Jesus Christ, nevertheless is concretely mediated through a diverse plurality of covenants throughout history.[41] Rather than Biblical salvation history operating on a soteriological plane distinct from world history, Dupuis views world history as always already coextensive with God's universal covenant with Noah: "The covenant with Noah constitutes the lasting foundation for the salvation of every human person."[42] God's dealings with Israel, rather

---

38. Dupuis, *Christianity and the Religions*, 99–100.

39. Ibid., 101.

40. Ibid., 102.

41. A more extensive treatment of his argument on this topic can be found in chapter 8, "History of Covenants: One and Many," of his *Toward a Christian Theology of Religious Pluralism*.

42. Dupuis, *Toward a Christian Theology of Religious Pluralism*, 226. Dupuis construes the relationship between world history and Biblical, salvation history in the same way as Rahner does: world and salvation history are always coextensive. As Rahner puts it, "As God's real self-communication in grace, therefore, the history of salvation and revelation is coexistent and coextensive with the history of the world

A Missional Paradigm of Grace as Nature Fulfilled

than being a unique, isolated strand of salvation history, serve as the clearest paradigm of God's salvific dealings with all people. Dupuis argues for the continuing validity of God's covenant with the Jews, vis-à-vis God's new covenant in Christ, as analogous of Christianity's relationship to the other religions:

> What applies in the first instance [Judaism and Christianity] holds good, analogically, in the other [Christianity and other religions] . . . Even as the Mosaic covenant has not been suppressed by the coming to its fullness in Jesus Christ, neither has the cosmic covenant in Noah with the nations been obliterated by reaching in the Christ-event the goal for which it was ordained by God. The implication is that the distinction between the general and special history of salvation must not be taken too rigidly; extrabiblical traditions . . . cannot be excluded a priori from belonging to special salvation history. To include them in it would presuppose . . . events in the history of people which, in function of a prophetic charism, are interpreted as divine interventions.[43]

Affirming a Trinitarian structure to the universal history of salvation which largely rejects a distinction between "general" and "special" salvation history, Dupuis argues for an understanding of the diverse covenants, Biblical and extra-biblical, as irrevocable, complementary expressions of God's progressively unfolding history of salvation. Citing Irenaeus' famous description of the unfolding of salvation history in terms of four Biblical covenants (the Adamic, Noahic, Abrahamic-Mosaic, and Christic), Dupuis argues that the three Old Testament covenants lay the theological basis and framework for a new openness toward the work of the divine Logos and Spirit in other religious traditions, based on the irrevocable nature of these covenants. Not only does the Mosaic covenant retain its validity and salvific value in relation to the new covenant in Christ, but, analogously, "even the other religious traditions symbolized by the covenant with Noah retain, *mutatis mutandis*, a permanent value . . . [they] still have saving value for their followers, but not unrelated to the Christ event."[44]

---

and of the human spirit, and hence also with the history of religion" (*Foundations of Christian Faith*, 153).

43. Dupuis, *Toward a Christian Theology of Religious Pluralism*, 233.
44. Dupuis, *Christianity and the Religions*, 109.

Dupuis' covenant theology can be summarized as the enduring value of the one, cosmic covenant of Noah diversely expressed in "the Trinitarian rhythm of the divine covenants" throughout history.[45] In other words, "The Trinitarian structure informs the various stages [in the entire process] in which God's self-communication unfolds in salvation history."[46] Such a Trinitarian Christological model means the entire Trinity has been, and continues to be, actively engaged in salvation-revelation, in and throughout history: "The Trinitarian rhythm of God's self-revelation . . . informs the stages of the unfolding of God's self-communication in salvation history . . . This amounts to saying that every divine covenant with humankind necessarily involves the active presence of God, of his Word, and of his Spirit."[47] While Christocentric, this model avoids the error of "Christomonism." It does so by affirming the interrelationship and irrevocable nature of God's universal covenants throughout human religious history. The implication of such covenant theology for understanding the significance of the Christ event is clear: "The centrality of the Christ event does not obscure but rather supposes, calls forth, and enhances the universal operative presence of the 'Word of God' and of the 'Spirit of God' through salvation history and, specifically, in the religious traditions of humankind."[48]

Dupuis' view of covenant theology leads him, inevitably and logically, to affirm a revelationist framework for all religions. What I mean by 'revelationist framework' is this: While God does not reveal himself definitively and exhaustively in any one religion, and while some religions, particularly Christianity, embody divine revelation in unsurpassed depth and clarity, God nonetheless gives salvific revelation in all religions. This means that, notwithstanding possible limitations, errors, and distortions, all religions are affirmed as revelatory. Dupuis clearly espouses this, as evidenced by his use of the term "salvation-revelation" and the claim that "the religious experience of the sages and *rishis* (seers) of the nations is guided and directed by the Spirit. Their experience of God is an experience in God's Spirit."[49] However, the reality of such multiform,

---

45. Dupuis, *Toward a Christian Theology of Religious Pluralism*, 226–7.
46. Dupuis, *Christianity and the Religions*, 112.
47. Dupuis, *Toward a Christian Theology of Religious Pluralism*, 227.
48. Dupuis, *Christianity and the Religions*, 110.
49. Dupuis, *Toward a Christian Theology of Religious Pluralism*, 247.

continually unfolding divine revelation in no way negates or minimizes the "qualitative fullness" of God's self-revelation in Jesus.[50]

Before moving on to consider Dupuis' constitutive Christology, his definition of salvation history serves as a helpful overview of his covenant theology: "Salvation history is in its entirety the history of the origin of all things from God through His Word in the Spirit and of their return to God through the Word in the Spirit."[51] All things, including all peoples and their religious traditions, not only originate in God, but are destined to return to God through the Trinitarian, universal operations of Father, Word (Son), and Spirit throughout human history. Not only is God's covenant with and gifts to the people of Israel irrevocable (Rom 11:29), but the same holds true for the other religious traditions as well, since such confidence is grounded upon the cosmic, Noahic covenant enacted and sustained by the Trinity.

CONSTITUTIVE CHRISTOLOGY

We now turn to consider the claims and implications of Dupuis' constitutive Christology. While Dupuis adamantly affirms that "the total Jesus Christ event itself . . . constitutes the fullness of revelation. In him God has uttered to the world his decisive word," he equally clearly insists that "this fullness is not to be understood quantitatively . . . but qualitatively."[52] How are Christians to understand Jesus' uniqueness in such qualitative rather than quantitative terms, as constitutive rather than absolute? How is it possible that, while "Jesus speaks the word [of God] because he *is* the Word,"[53] nonetheless God continues to bestow authentic salvation-revelation through other religious traditions?

The key, for Dupuis, lies in recognizing that, because the human consciousness of Jesus was limited, it could not exhaustively contain the totality of God's revelation and mystery. The very act of transposing the divine mystery into the human condition imposes a further limitation on the divine revelation through Jesus. This means that, while God's revelation in Christ is "decisive, unsurpassed, and unsurpassable,"[54] be-

---

50. Ibid., 249–50.
51. Ibid., 228.
52. Dupuis, *Christianity and the Religions*, 129.
53. Ibid., 130.
54. Ibid., 130.

ing qualitatively unique, it does not and cannot exhaust the quantitative fullness of revelation: God has more to say than God has said in Jesus.

Dupuis' constitutive Christology is firmly grounded in Rahnerian transcendental Christology, which concentrates the revelation of God, not mainly in what Jesus taught or did, but in a "unique, unsurpassable human experience" of intense depth in relation to God.[55] What was revealed in Jesus was not particular doctrines about God, but rather the experience of the reign and love of God in singular, unsurpassed intensity. This experience is available to others as well, although not in its original intensity, given Jesus' identity as the incarnate Son of God. However, since God remains hidden, to a certain extent, even after the Christ event, divine revelation will "remain 'unfinished' until its complete manifestation in the eschaton."[56]

Dupuis does not explicitly subscribe to Rahner's formulation of transcendental Christology and is even critical of it in his book on Christology—"Rahner's transcendental Christology—and anthropological Christology in general—rests on a limited biblical foundation and tends to lose touch with the concrete life and story of Jesus in his historical cultural circumstances."[57] That being the case, and while Dupuis clearly emphasizes the importance of a Christology "from above" while never at the expense of a Christology "from below," my contention is this: to the extent that Dupuis' theology fails to incorporate the Biblical portrayal of the world's sinful, broken condition as well as the law/Gospel distinction, to that extent his Christology, as it is elaborated and extended by his robust pneumatology, *practically* ends up employing the "nature/grace" paradigm and *practically* relates to the religious others as "anonymous Christians" anonymously participating in the grace of Christ. To the extent this is accurate, to that extent my reservations with and critique of Rahner's Christology and category of "anonymous Christian" (see chapter 3) also apply to Dupuis.

---

55. Ibid., 129. Rahner's formulation of transcendental Christology is worth quoting: "[T]he categoriality of God's irreversible offer of himself to the world as a whole . . . can only be a man who on the one hand surrenders every inner-worldly future in death, and who on the other hand in this acceptance of death is shown to have been accepted by God finally and definitively . . . such an 'individual' destiny has 'exemplary' significance for the world as a whole. Such a man with this destiny is what is meant by an 'absolute savior'" (*Foundations*, 211).

56. Dupuis, *Christianity and the Religions*, 132.

57. Jacques Dupuis, *Who Do You Say I Am?*, 25.

A Missional Paradigm of Grace as Nature Fulfilled

In terms of answering his critics, Dupuis clarifies his exegesis of a range of important passages, including (but not limited to) John 1:9, John 14:6, Acts 4:12, Col 2:9, and various passages relating to God's covenant with Israel and Israel's idolatry in relation to the surrounding religions. His main point in critiquing unduly exclusivistic interpretations of such passages is that, given their inter-Jewish and intra-Jewish context, they do not automatically rule out an understanding of divine, salvific revelation and presence in other religions. My concerns and reservations regarding his exegesis will be articulated in chapter 5. The practical import of this position is that, while not explicitly advocating universalism, Dupuis would be very optimistic regarding the salvation of all peoples in and through their own religious traditions as "participated mediations" (a formula that will be explained shortly) within the one, universal economy of salvation centered in Christ.

INCLUSIVE PLURALISM AND THE SALVIFIC VALUE OF OTHER RELIGIONS

Based upon the preceding articulation of Dupuis' argument, it becomes clear how Dupuis' concern is to argue for and justify how his inclusive pluralism holds together two seemingly contradictory, but complementary, affirmations: "the universal constitutive character of the Christ event in the order of salvation and the saving significance of the religious traditions in a plurality of principle of the religious traditions within the one manifold plan of God for humankind."[58] How is it possible that other religious traditions, as such, can participate in and mediate the salvation of Christ? This claim forms, not only a crucial step in Dupuis' argument, but also a prime illustration of how Rahner's transcendental anthropology is essential to Dupuis' model. Dupuis uses transcendental anthropology to argue for the various traditions as valid, concrete mediations of the mystery of salvation in Christ, and against the "fulfillment theory" view that, while individuals within other traditions "may obtain salvation through the sincerity of their subjective religious life, their religion itself has no saving value for them."[59] How does he accomplish this?

According to Rahner's transcendental anthropology, both human nature and the various religious traditions have an inevitably historical,

---

58. Dupuis, *Christianity and the Religions*, 95.
59. Ibid., 187.

concrete, and social character to them. As stated in chapter 3, such an anthropology posits that, not only are humans transcendentally oriented toward God as their transcendent horizon, but that transcendental realities inevitably find categorical, historically concrete expression in the world. Just as a human person is an "incarnate spirit," in the same manner "what is true of the life of the human being in general is also true of his or her religious life."[60] Because the subjective religious life of members of other religions is inextricably bound up with, influenced by, and expressed in their communal tradition, the following argument can be made: 1) If members of other religions have genuine experiences of the Mystery of God, and 2) if these experiences occur, not despite, but precisely through the historical, social reality of their religious tradition, then 3) these traditions in their concrete, social form must, in some sense, contain "components due to a supernatural influence of grace"[61] and mediate such grace. Their status in relation to Christianity can then be viewed as "participated mediations" of the "one mediation" of salvation in Christ.[62]

While affirming that the founders, holy men and women, and leaders of other religions can and indeed do serve as "sign-posts pointing for their followers to ways along which they may encounter unknowingly the mystery of salvation in Jesus Christ"[63] and therefore can be considered "saving figures," Dupuis clearly defines what he means by such a controversial phrase: "their role does not consist in saving; it is limited to pointing to paths where salvation through the mystery of Christ may be encountered."[64]

THE REIGN OF GOD AND THE CHURCH

Building upon his covenant theology, constitutive Christology, and use of Rahnerian transcendental anthropology to view the religious traditions as valid, albeit "participated" mediations of the salvation and grace of Christ, we now reach the crowning pinnacle of Dupuis' argument: a distinctive understanding of the reign of God. The expression "reign of

---

60. Ibid., 186–7.
61. Rahner, "Christianity and the Non-Christian Religions," 121, 130.
62. Dupuis, *Christianity and the Religions*, 163–94.
63. Dupuis, "'Christianity and the Religions' Revisited," 374.
64. Ibid.

A Missional Paradigm of Grace as Nature Fulfilled

God" raises profound, thorny questions for Christian theology, which Dupuis aptly summarizes:

> Is it (the Reign of God) restricted to the hope of Israel and, in its historical realization in the world, to Christianity and the church? Are the "others" excluded from it? Or are they fully members of it, even while remaining outside the church? Or, otherwise, do they belong to it "in some manner" that could be qualified as implicit or invisible? In short, should Christianity and the church be identified with the Reign of God insofar as it is present in the world and history? Or is that Reign a universal reality that extends far beyond the confines of the church . . . ? In that case, what is the relationship of the church . . . and the religions . . . to the universal Reign of God? . . . Are Christians and the "others" equally members of the Reign of God?[65]

As Dupuis' proposal moves toward its missiological culmination, he seeks to explicate the relationship between the reign of God, the church, and the other religious traditions. Breaking down his discussion into two parts, the relationship between the reign of God and the church (part one), followed by the relationship of the church and the other religions to the universal reign of God (part two), Dupuis aims to show how the universal reign of God encompasses both the church and the other religions as "joint members and builders" of that reign. This penultimate piece of his argument sets the stage for claiming, not only a mutual, asymmetrical complementarity between Christianity and other religions, but also the nature of interreligious dialogue as a conversation between those who are already co-members of God's universal reign. For these reasons, this piece of his argument is especially important for the whole.

Having earlier rejected a purely regnocentric approach to the religions (associated with Paul Knitter), Dupuis now incorporates such an approach as a central, albeit nuanced, aspect of his Trinitarian theology of religious pluralism. His argument proceeds as follows. First, the reign of God has an "already, but not yet" character: while it is already a universal reality in history, it will not realize its fulfillment and eschatological fullness until the eschaton.[66] Second, while the reign "is present in a special way in the church . . . it extends beyond the limits of the church."[67] In other words: while the reign of God constitutes "the very reason for

65. Ibid., 195.
66. Ibid., 198.
67. Ibid., 199.

the being of the church,"⁶⁸ and thus the reign is truly present within the church, it nonetheless is a reality that exceeds the church's boundaries. Third, the late Pope John Paul II defined the reign of God as "the manifestation and the realization of God's plan of salvation in all its fullness."⁶⁹

The fourth point regarding gospel values and values of the kingdom is important enough to merit further elaboration. In light of *'spermatokoi logoi'* theology and comments such as the one by Yves Congar that "there have existed and exist gifts of light and grace working for salvation outside the visible boundaries of the Church. We do not even deem it necessary to hold . . . that these graces are received *through* the Church,"⁷⁰ contemporary Catholic theology has sought to establish how the reign of God can be identified outside the church. Dupuis affirms the growing consensus in Catholic theology that, based on Jesus' beatitudes and the sermon on the mount, wherever "Gospel values," "saving values," "evangelical values," or "values of the Kingdom" are lived, as evidence of being "open to the working of the Spirit," such values constitute evidence of the reign of God.⁷¹ These kingdom/gospel values include love, justice, peace, working for human rights and human dignity, promoting spiritual/religious values, and advocacy for the poor and the oppressed-everything Lutheran theology would view as social ethics. *Redemptoris Missio* explicitly states that the reign of God, although hidden like a seed, is present in all people "to the extent that they live 'gospel values' and are open to the working of the Spirit."⁷² As the Federation of Asian Bishops' Conferences put it, "Where God is accepted, where the Gospel values are lived, where the human being is respected . . . there is the Kingdom."⁷³ Jon Sobrino further reiterates this perspective: "this ultimate reality (the reign of God) . . . is at work and comes close to human beings wherever, following Jesus himself, they share the values of the Kingdom- love and justice."⁷⁴ This understanding of "gospel values" or "saving values" forms the crucial bridge needed to cross over from the traditional formula "outside the church no salvation" to a view of the reign of God as "a universal

---

68. Ibid., 200.
69. Pope John Paul II, *Redemption and Dialogue*, 12.
70. Dupuis, *Christianity and the Religions*, 211.
71. Pope John Paul II, *Redemption and Dialogue*, 15.
72. Ibid.
73. Dupuis, *Christianity and the Religions*, 200.
74. Ibid., 201.

A Missional Paradigm of Grace as Nature Fulfilled

reality, extending far beyond the boundaries of the Church."[75] To the extent such kingdom values are present, to that extent the reign, through the Spirit's work, is already present in those religions. This view of gospel/kingdom values has produced a seismic shift in how Catholic theology approaches other religions, which Dupuis' proposal exemplifies.

Fifth, Dupuis reiterates the dual distinction which needs to be made, "on the one hand, between the Reign in history and its eschatological dimension and, on the other hand, between the Reign and the church."[76] Sixth, Dupuis asserts that "the universality of the reign of God consists in the fact that Christians and the 'others' share the same mystery of salvation in Jesus Christ, even if the mystery reaches them in different ways."[77] Seventh, Dupuis seeks a Christocentric anchoring to his view of the reign of God by claiming, "one cannot separate the Reign of God in history from the Jesus of history . . . nor from Christ, whose present kingship is its expression."[78] Finally, as "participated mediations" of the mystery of salvation, the other religious traditions "contribute . . . to the building up of the Reign of God among their followers and in the world."[79] In this qualified sense, members of other religions are truly co-members and joint builders of the reign of God.[80]

As Dupuis transitions from articulating the church's relationship to the reign to a discussion of how both the church *and* the religions relate to the reign of God, how should the church's role now be properly understood? How ought the concrete reality of the church in the world and the universal reign of God in history be related?

Before delving into how Dupuis seeks to relate the church's role and function to the reign of God, it is crucial to note how he is building upon and seeking to give a clearer rationale for Rahner's category of "anonymous Christian" without using the term itself. Rahner's category intends to highlight the primary importance of a person's "relationship to Jesus Christ in the order of grace and salvation, not a relationship directly to the church."[81] Thus, those who are saved beyond the church are inevitably

---

75. Ibid., 200.
76. Ibid., 199.
77. Ibid., 201.
78. Ibid.
79. Ibid., 202.
80. Ibid., 201.
81. Ibid., 212.

"oriented" toward it as "the sign willed by God to signify what his grace in Jesus Christ has accomplished and continues to accomplish in the world."[82] This means that, for Dupuis, both individuals and their religious traditions are properly viewed as being "oriented" toward, not only the reign of God and the mystery of salvation, but also toward the church as the universal sacrament of that reign and salvation.

With this foundation in mind, Dupuis proceeds to correlate and synthesize seemingly incompatible statements and tenets of Roman Catholic magisterial teaching. I now seek to articulate the logical flow of his argument. First of all, Dupuis strongly affirms the church as the "universal sacrament of salvation (*Lumen Gentium* 48)," "sign and instrument of the reign of God," "necessary" for salvation (*Lumen Gentium* 14) and therefore possessing a "specific and necessary role (*Redemptoris Missio* 18)" within the economy of salvation. However, this need not and indeed does not imply a "universal mediation" for the church in terms of the salvation of all who are saved in Jesus Christ. Second, others are saved in and through Jesus Christ "in a way known to God" (*Ad Gentes* 7, *Gaudium et Spes* 22). Therefore, there is room for the "participated" and "substitutive" mediations of other religions.[83] Furthermore, the nature of the church's relationship to the "others" thus consists of final, rather than efficient and instrumental, causality. Why? Because only the risen humanity of Jesus Christ can save instrumentally and efficiently; the church can only point to and participate in that efficient causality through its orientation toward the final, eschatological consummation. Saving grace, in other words, is always "Christic."[84] Fifth, because the church possesses the "ordinary means" of salvation (*Evangelii Nuntiandi* 80) and the "fullness of the means of salvation" (*Redemptoris Missio* 55), therefore it remains the "ordinary way" for salvation (*Evangelii Nuntiandi* 80). Sixth, the church and reign of God have "a unique and special relationship which, while not excluding the action of Christ and the Spirit outside the church's visible boundaries, confers upon her a 'specific and necessary role'" (*Redemptoris Missio* 18). If that is true, and if those who are saved in Jesus Christ outside of the church possess a "mysterious relationship to the Church" (*Redemptoris Missio* 10), then how can these two affirmations be meaningfully related? The answer, according to Dupuis,

---

82. Ibid., 215.
83. Ibid., 164–94.
84. Ibid., 212.

A Missional Paradigm of Grace as Nature Fulfilled

lies in recognizing an "explicit, universal mediation" of the church, in the order of salvation, on behalf of others. Such a universal mediation or instrumentality of the church, in the order of salvation, should be understood "as expectation and hope, based on [the orientation of the others] to it" (*Lumen Gentium* 9, *Redemptoris Missio* 9). This means that "orientation" of others toward the church as the "sacrament of the reign of God" is a more accurate description of the status of the others, "regardless of where they find themselves in relation to the church," rather than the pre-Vatican II terminology of implicit "membership" in the church via desire or intent. In other words: "Divine grace is operative when the church is not present, but the church is the universal sacramental sign of the presence of divine grace in the world."[85] Dupuis further clarifies the relationship of the church to the reign:

> The presence of the church-as-sign of the Reign of God in the world bears witness, therefore, that God has established in this world his Reign in Jesus Christ. Furthermore, as efficacious sign, the church contains and effects the reality which it signifies, giving access to the Reign of God through word and sacrament. However, the necessity of the church is not of such a nature that access to the Reign of God would be possible only through being members of it; the "others" *can be part of the Reign of God and of Christ without being members of the church. The presence of the Reign of God in the church* is, nevertheless, *a privileged one*, for it has received from Christ "*the fullness of the benefits* and means of salvation" (*Redemptoris Missio* 18). [86]

Building upon the classical, sacramental distinction between 1) the sacramental sign, 2) the first, ecclesial, sacramental effect, and 3) the second effect of grace, Dupuis applies this framework analogously to the question of grace within and beyond the church. In doing so, he specifies three categories which must be distinguished: "the sign of the church, becoming members of the church, and being members of the Reign of God."[87] Two practical points emerge from such an application of the sacramental theory. First, people outside the church, while not (yet) members of it, are nonetheless "oriented" toward the church by being "oriented" toward the salvation the church proclaims, points to, and sacramentally embodies. Second, the church is "necessary for salvation" in

---

85. Ibid., 213.
86. Ibid., 214–5, italics added for emphasis.
87. Ibid., 213.

the qualified sense that the gifts of God, means of salvation, and benefits of that salvation are mediated, while not exclusively, yet fully through the church's ministry of Word and sacrament. Only in this qualified sense can the church be described as the "sacrament of salvation," having a privileged relationship to the Reign of God.[88]

COMPLEMENTARITY AND CONVERGENCE

In conclusion, Dupuis seeks to balance and hold in dialectical tension the uniqueness of Christ as "universal constitutive Savior" and an appreciation of religious pluralism in principle, affirming a saving value for the other religious traditions within the one economy of salvation. In his own words: "Jesus Christ is indeed the constitutive Savior of humankind, and the Christ event is the cause of the salvation of all human beings; but this does not prevent the other traditions from serving as 'mediations' of the mystery of salvation in Jesus Christ for their followers within God's design for humankind."[89] Dupuis views his Trinitarian framework, incorporating and correlating a Trinitarian, constitutive Christology and pneumatology, as overcoming the problematic pitfalls of the exclusivist and inclusivist paradigms without falling into the pluralist paradigm. He claims to successfully combine a robust, Christological inclusivism with an affirmation of religious pluralism in principle. Dupuis articulates how his proposal synthesizes constitutive Christology, Logos theology, and a robust pneumatology to accentuate saving grace and truth in other religious traditions: "The inclusive efficacy of the Christ event through the risen humanity of Jesus, the universal "illumination" by the Word of God, and the equally universal "enlivening" by the Spirit make it possible to discover in other saving figures and traditions, truth and grace not made explicit with the same force and clarity in the revelation and manifestation of God in Jesus Christ."[90]

This makes possible a mutual complementarity between the truth and grace of Christian revelation and that of other traditions, involving a truly reciprocal, dynamic interaction whereby "saving values" are reciprocally exchanged. Dupuis further clarifies what he means by such mutual, asymmetrical complementarity: "Thus, whereas other religious

---

88. Kärkkäinen, *Introduction to the Theology of Religions*, 215.
89. Dupuis, *Christianity and the Religions*, 253.
90. Ibid., 256.

A Missional Paradigm of Grace as Nature Fulfilled

traditions can find, and are destined to find, in the Christ event their fullness of meaning—but without being absorbed or dispossessed—the reverse is not true: God's self-manifestation and self-giving in Jesus Christ are not in need of a true completion by other traditions, even though they are interrelated with the other divine manifestations in the overall realm of God's self-revelation to humankind, and can be enriched by mutually interacting with other religious traditions."[91]

In conclusion: Dupuis submits that his theology of inclusive pluralism offers a constructive, "qualitative leap" forward in Christianity's attitude toward and relationship with other religions, one which, in avoiding unnecessarily exclusive and restrictive understandings of the faith, "will help [Christians] discover, to our surprise, new breadths and depths in the Christian message."[92] The breadth of his proposal, combining Christocentric faith with a heartfelt longing to incorporate the other religions within the one economy of salvation, is impressive and unparalleled. Even though I have some fundamental disagreements with his proposal, I am awed by the sophistication with which Dupuis seeks to unfold the eschatological vision of all things being reunited under Christ in terms of synthesizing a Trinitarian Christology with a robust pneumatology.

APPRECIATION OF DUPUIS

What positive contributions of Dupuis' can a confessional Lutheran missiology affirm? I wish to affirm Dupuis on six points.[93] First of all, the greatest strength of Dupuis' model is its insistence on taking both poles of the universality-particularity paradox (how God's universal will to love and save the world is to be balanced with the particularity of salvation through Christ) with utter seriousness, without compromising on either side. While I have some reservations about how he applies and extends

---

91. Ibid., 257. While Dupuis' asymmetrical complementarity is a logical implication of his constitutive Christology, aimed at safeguarding it, theologians of a pluralist orientation challenge such a stance as inevitably stifling genuine dialogue and rendering it impossible. For example, Paul Knitter notes, "The 'Spirit-centered' approach that Dupuis and others advocate does not, in the final analysis, seem to allow the Spirit to say anything *really* different from what was said in Jesus . . . This means, as we heard, that whatever Christians might learn from the Spirit in others will always be essentially only a clarification, a deepening of what they already know in Jesus" (Knitter, *Introducing Theologies of Religions*, 103–4).

92. Dupuis, *Christianity and the Religions*, 259.

93. Kärkkäinen, *Trinity and Religious Pluralism*, 61–62.

his constitutive Christology and robust pneumatology (to be articulated later), his strong insistence on maintaining the tension between both poles is virtually unparalleled. Second, Dupuis provides a strong, Trinitarian corrective to other approaches and models. Practically speaking, this entails avoiding the elevation of any one person of the Trinity above the others, as well as avoiding the subordination of Christ to some other category, whether it be God, the Spirit, the reign of God, etc. Third, not only does he seek to establish a dynamic balance within the Trinity, but he boldly brings the doctrine of the Trinity into a critical engagement and dialogue with alternative doctrines of God. Fourth, Dupuis provides a finely articulated, nuanced pneumatology which seeks to mutually relate the work of the Word and the Spirit. Fifth, in his insistence upon Christ's constitutive role for salvation, Dupuis avoids the pitfall of pluralism's downplaying and relativizing Christ's unique role in salvation. His proposal is truly an inclusivist one, charging pluralism with not sufficiently appreciating the central, constitutive role of Christology. Finally, the practical strength of Dupuis' model is that it takes dialogue with utter seriousness, affording it a central place in the church's understanding of its mission (further elaborated in chapter 6).

5

Missio Shaped by *Promissio*

Confessional Lutheran Engagement with Dupuis

HAVING ADVANCED A CONFESSIONAL Lutheran missiology centered on the promise of reconciliation (chapters 1 and 2), while affirming the strengths and contributions of Dupuis' proposal (chapter 4), we are now better positioned to engage it from a Lutheran perspective. This chapter will proceed in the following manner: a discussion of the *missio Dei* as single or dual, a critically constructive engagement with Dupuis on four aspects of his proposal (theological method, theology of grace, pneumatology, and relating the church and the reign of God), followed by an articulation of my theology of the cross utilizing the hiddenness of God, thus setting the stage for the practical outworking of my proposal in chapter 6.

MISSIO DEI: ONE MISSION OR TWO?

Does God have one or two missions in and to the world? This question directs our attention to my fundamental claim: that the nature of the Gospel, understood primarily as *promissio Dei*, gives Christian mission a distinctively dual shape. God's mission, while unified in a single economy of salvation, inevitably manifests itself in the dual form of law and Gospel, sin and grace, wrath and promised mercy. Luther describes these two divine missions in terms of God's "alien work" (*opus alienum*) in service of and directed toward God's "proper work" (*opus proprium*):

Mission Shaped by Promise

"Thus an action that is alien to God's nature results in a deed belonging to his very nature: he makes a person a sinner so that he may make him righteous."[1] The law/Gospel distinction, while articulating and safeguarding the Gospel as promise, ultimately serves as a hermeneutical key and roadmap in constructing a missiology arising from the Gospel as promise. In contrast, the majority of contemporary missiologies arising from the basis of *missio Dei* proceed from the conviction that, since the term *missio Dei* itself is singular, the *one*, triune God pursues *one* mission of speaking and bestowing *one* Word, a word of grace with astonishingly surprising reach, such that a graced horizon is critical for engaging the other religions today.

The difference between a confessional Lutheran, "*missio* shaped by *promissio*" proposal, and Dupuis' inclusive pluralist proposal, can be clearly discerned in the fundamental divergence which appears in analyzing the relevant, theological loci or building blocks for missiology. In each locus, the difference between a "univocal" *missio Dei* and my "duplex" *missio Dei* is clearly evidenced. I will now briefly survey and summarize these differences.

The critical, defining difference between my "*missio* shaped by *promissio*" proposal and Dupuis' inclusive pluralist proposal lies in advocating a "univocal" *missio Dei* versus a "duplex" *missio Dei*, one which recognizes and utilizes the law/Gospel distinction as an indispensable key for understanding and articulating the dual mission of God. For the sake of clarifying the flow of my overall argument, the topics treated will include one from chapter 2 (grace), five from chapter 4 and this chapter (the role and work of the Spirit, a theology of covenants, interpreting the mediation of Jesus Christ, the hiddenness of God, and the reign of God), and one from chapter 6 (church proclamation). This sketch will orient us to the remainder of my argument.

In terms of a theology of grace: is grace nature fulfilled, expressed as humanity's encounter with the God who reveals Himself as loving presence (Dupuis), or is grace the promise of mercy fulfilled on account of Christ, in contrast to the judgment of divine wrath against sin (confessional Lutheran)? In terms of pneumatology: is the Spirit's work conceived of primarily as discovering "traces of grace and truth" in other traditions (Dupuis), or is the Spirit's work more comprehensive, creating

---

1. Luther, *Luther's Works*, 31:51.

Missio Shaped by Promissio

both the conviction of sin and trust (faith) in the Gospel promise (confessional Lutheran)?

While Dupuis and other proponents of the "presence of Christ in the religions" approach would probably argue that such pneumatological emphases are compatible and not mutually exclusive, a Lutheran approach would argue for the primacy of the latter approach. The Lutheran concern is this: if the Spirit's work is conceived primarily as affirming and recovering "traces of grace and truth" in other religions, then there is a real risk of marginalizing, if not completely bypassing, the Spirit's testimony to the nature of the reconciling work of Christ as delineating how the power of God's loving grace overcomes the wrath of God. Lutheran theology cautions that, in concentrating on delineating *how* the salvific presence of Christ, through the Spirit, can be affirmed in the other religions, the Spirit's work of revealing and "convicting the world of guilt in regard to sin and righteousness and judgment" (John 16:8) and of necessitating Christ can easily become obscured and shortchanged. As a result, it maintains that it is precisely the depth reality of sin and brokenness, and the corresponding necessity of Christ overcoming divine wrath toward such brokenness, which constitutes a central aspect of the "all truth" which the "Spirit of truth will guide you into" (John 16:13).

Furthermore, in terms of covenant theology: do the various Biblical and extra-biblical covenants manifest the progressive unfolding of the one, universal covenant of grace (Dupuis), or is the distinction between covenants of law and covenants of promise central to fully appreciate the "new covenant" in Christ (confessional Lutheran)? In terms of the mediation of Jesus Christ: is it to be understood primarily in terms of an ontological mediation uniting human and divine natures (Dupuis' transcendental Christology), or is this mediation unique, differing from all other mediations in terms of reconciling humanity to God by actual sin being forgiven and redeemed through the cross of Christ (confessional Lutheran)?[2] In terms of the reign of God, is the reign "the dominion of God among human beings . . . reorienting human relations and organizing human society in accordance with God's intention"[3] (Dupuis), or is

---

2. As noted in chapter 4, Dupuis does not explicitly subscribe to Rahner's formulation of transcendental Christology. However, to the extent his theology fails to incorporate the biblical portrayal of the world's sinful, broken condition as well as the law/Gospel distinction, to that extent his Christology, as it is elaborated and extended by his robust pneumatology, is vulnerable to a confessional Lutheran critique.

3. Dupuis, *Christianity and the Religions*, 21.

it constituted by and centered on the forgiveness of sins and promise of mercy delivered by Christ, preserved by the two realms principle (confessional Lutheran)? In terms of the church's proclamation: does it announce the loving grace of God already present to all (Dupuis), or does it call and exhort people to be reconciled to God through Christ (confessional Lutheran)? As one can see from this overview of six key, missiological building blocks, the conviction of a dual mission of God, rooted in the Gospel as promise and expressed by the law/Gospel distinction, results in a radically different missiology, offering a distinctively contrasting alternative within the contemporary missiological landscape.

We have yet to explore the hiddenness of God as a missiological building block, which I will pursue later.[4] Given its importance for my "*missio* shaped by *promissio*" proposal, I wish to elaborate briefly on its significance, both within Dupuis' proposal and for my proposal. Whereas my confessional Lutheran claim, articulated in chapters 1 and 2, is that 1) the law accuses of sin and exerts pressure, 2) the gospel promises comfort and freedom from the law, and 3) God's hiddenness is mysterious, Dupuis, as we noted, has a very different approach to relating grace (as shorthand for the Gospel) and divine hiddenness, resulting in a different missiology.

A few examples of these contrasting approaches serve to illustrate my point. As a starting point for discerning divine hiddenness in creation:

---

4. Throughout this project, I use the phrase "hiddenness of God" in two ways: First, to indicate the divine inscrutability and "excess" within Christian revelation, specifically in a theology of the cross. While God is revealed in Christ, God is also, simultaneously, hidden in and beyond the cross. Second, the phrase refers to the ambiguity of divine activity in the world, beyond the Christian revelation of the Gospel of Christ. In this second sense, the phrase is not meant as a pejorative insult toward other religions, as if the sum total of their experience of God and their sacred texts is experiencing God as "hidden." Rather, my use of the phrase is meant to highlight the fact that, despite the revelation we receive through our diverse religious traditions, *nobody's* daily experience of God is one of only, or even primarily, divine goodness and benevolence. The Dupuis–Rahner–Aquinas tradition of a theology of grace, in my contention, does not sufficiently illumine this reality as a function of the depth reality of sin and brokenness in the world. While Rahner and his theological heritage certainly affirm the reality of God's hiddenness in the world (see, for example, Rahner's essays "The Hiddenness of God" and "An Investigation of the Incomprehensibility of God in St. Thomas Aquinas," in *Theological Investigations Vol. XVI*, 227–54), I will assert painful experiences of suffering and seeming divine absence or "hiddenness" as a fruitful basis for interreligious dialogue, primarily between the monotheistic religions, in contrast to Dupuis' approach of dialogue between those who are already considered co-members of the reign of God. I will expand on this further as my argument unfolds.

Missio Shaped by Promissio

is the emphasis placed on creation as inherently graced (Dupuis), or on the Christian conviction that creation has fallen *from* grace, *into* sin, and in need of divine reconciliation and restoration (confessional Lutheran)? What is the nature of the task of exploring divine hiddenness: to discover and identify "traces of grace and truth" throughout creation (Dupuis), or a clearer discernment of how God's law is operative throughout creation, caring for and preserving it (confessional Lutheran)? Finally, what is the goal of exploring divine hiddenness: to discern how the "grace of Christ" is already operative in other religions (Dupuis), or a deeper appreciation of how the grace (mercy) of Christ is *not* explicitly known and trusted and therefore all the more needed (confessional Lutheran)? How does the nature of the Gospel of grace as truly "good" and "new" news shape what we look for and expect to find in exploring divine hiddenness?

In chapter 4, I described how Dupuis treated the hiddenness of God outside of Christian revelation. By synthesizing a Rahnerian theology of grace, a universal history of covenants, a theology of the *logos spermatikos* and universally present Word of God, a constitutive Christology, a robust pneumatology, and a Spirit Christology, Dupuis was able to assert that, what remains to be more fully discerned and affirmed by Christian theology, what remains "hidden" requiring further elaboration, is that we live within a radically graced horizon. God's mission in the world, within the unified economy of salvation, involves discovering how grace is universal, and how other religions concretely embody such saving grace. God's mission truly is one: to unveil the one, hidden, salvific grace of God (Christ) throughout the world.

The differences in how Dupuis' proposal and a confessional Lutheran proposal interrelate grace (Gospel) and the hiddenness of God, without going into greater detail regarding the divine hiddenness at this time, find their ultimate, practical expression as starkly contrasting definitions of the mission of God. In the final analysis, how does Christianity understand the *missio Dei* and the church's role in relation to that mission? While I did not find Dupuis offering an explicit definition of the *missio Dei*, his description of the Gospel highlights the key features of his implicit view of that mission: the Gospel is "the breaking into history of the 'lordship' of God, the fulfillment of the divine promises, and the renewal of the relationship between God and human beings and among human beings themselves."[5] This reign and lordship of God and the renewal of

---

5. Dupuis, *Christianity and the Religions*, 196.

the divine-human relationship, while constituted by the Christ event, is actualized throughout the world religions as these serve as "participated mediations" of the salvation of Christ, enacting a mutual, asymmetrical complementarity within the single, universal economy of salvation. This leads to a view of the church's role, in relation to *missio Dei*, as one of dialogue and proclamation: dialogue between those who already jointly belong to the universal reign of God, and proclamation of how that reality is centered upon the Christ event. In other words: dialogue between those already in possession of salvation, and proclaiming how the others already have the saving grace of Christ.

In contrast to such a "univocal" understanding of *missio Dei* (God speaks and enacts only or primarily grace), a confessional Lutheran missiology views the *missio Dei* as "duplex," enacting a dual mission of law and Gospel, a dual revelation of wrath and promise of mercy, the former always in service of and leading to the latter. Klaus D. Schulz describes its Trinitarian origin: "The *missio Dei* is the Trinitarian redemptive and reconciling activity in history, motivated by God the Father's loving will for the entire world, grounded in the atoning work of Jesus Christ, and carried out by the Holy Spirit of Christ through the means of grace. God justifies man through the means of grace; delivers him from rebellion, sin, and death; subjects him under His kindly reign; and leads him and the redeemed community toward the final goal in history."[6] The significant implications of these differing views of the *missio Dei* for Christian missiology in terms of the church's mission will be explored in the remainder of this project.

We now return to a central question, initially raised and articulated in chapter 3, which now requires exploration in greater detail in this chapter. How can the relationship between divine grace and human nature be articulated in terms of the relationship between "salvation history" and human history? How one navigates this important move is fundamentally an articulation of one's theology of grace, theology of revelation, and, ultimately, one's understanding of the *missio Dei*. As explored in chapter 3, Karl Rahner grounds this move in his transcendental anthropology, using the notion of the supernatural existential to unite the transcendental and categorical dimensions of reality. On this basis, one can readily see how Dupuis, to the extent he builds on Rahner, would

---

6. Schulz, *Mission from the Cross*, 97.

Missio Shaped by Promissio

claim, "The history of salvation and revelation is one."[7] Dupuis explicitly endorses Rahner's view of the coexistent and coextensive relation between the histories of salvation and revelation:

> The universally present history of salvation must therefore be concretely embodied in the history of people. This happens in the history of religion in general and in particular in the historical religions of humankind. These may serve as historical mediations for the supernatural experience of God as divine revelation and thus "stir up" salvation in a positive manner. They may, therefore, be considered as willed by God insofar as they give concrete shape to the divine offer of grace universally present and operative throughout human history. In the religious traditions of the world, God's offer to people in revelation-salvation takes on an initial concrete shape.[8]

In contrast, a confessional Lutheran model navigates this move by proposing an "economy of salvation" consisting of a two-fold revelation informed by the law/Gospel dialectic: the revelation of law correlates divine wrath and human sinfulness within a broader history of divine judgment, while the revelation of Gospel correlates divine mercy and human faith within a broader history of the promise of salvation. While chapters 2 and 3 articulated the differing visions of the relationship between divine grace and human nature, this chapter will now tackle the second half of that crucial question: how God's salvific will as "salvation history" and human history should properly be related within a single economy of salvation. I believe this question ultimately boils down to differing, competing visions of what constitutes the *missio Dei*, and what that practically means for the church's mission.

CRITICAL ENGAGEMENT WITH DUPUIS

In engaging Dupuis' articulation of how God's loving grace is mediated through the diversity of religions, Lutheran theology contends that the reality of divine wrath is insufficiently attended to: "Love is not served by attempting to erase wrath from the system."[9] While Dupuis certainly does not intentionally erase or minimize God's wrath, his insufficient at-

---

7. Dupuis, *Christianity and the Religions*, 134.
8. Ibid., 100.
9. Forde, *Law-Gospel Debate*, 197.

tention to the reality and relevance of sin within his proposal leaves him vulnerable to this critique. This basic concern can be delineated through four broad categories.

First, Dupuis' theological method is a prime example of revelationism, a particular way of relating the categories of revelation and salvation based on the Rahnerian, "nature/grace" paradigm elucidated in chapter 3. Such an approach marginalizes the revelation of sin and law, rejects the nuanced distinction between revelation and salvation, insisting that "revelation is universal, even as is the offer of salvation."[10]

Second, from a Lutheran perspective, Dupuis' theology of grace is insufficiently nuanced.[11] To the extent that his theology of grace is built upon and an application of Rahner's theology of grace, this comes as no surprise. In terms of these first two concerns, my critique is mainly exegetical: Dupuis insufficiently incorporates the accusatory function of the law (*lex semper accusat*) and the promissory nature of the gospel.

Third, his robust pneumatology and references to Spirit Christology, as an elaboration of his constitutive Christology, raise several questions from a Lutheran perspective. How can Jesus Christ be both "constitutive" for salvation and "relative" at the same time? While Dupuis claims to subordinate the Spirit to the Christ event, does he in reality end up subordinating Christ to the Spirit in his desire to extend the scope of the Spirit's ministry? How does Dupuis' depiction of the Spirit's work square with the role and function of the Spirit as depicted in the New Testament? How does God's presence in the world, through the Spirit, relate to what Jesus' crucifixion and resurrection brought about?

Fourth, and finally, in terms of ecclesiology, does Dupuis' understanding of the relationship between the reign of God and the church undermine the church's role of Gospel proclamation? If other religions and their adherents are already co-heirs of the reign of God, is explicit conversion to Christianity still a valid goal and activity of the church's mission? If so, why, and on what grounds? In articulating this relationship, Dupuis seemingly downplaying the role of the church. As Kärkkäinen notes,

10. Dupuis, *Christianity and the Religions*, 115.

11. Implied in this critique is an implicit critique of Dupuis' theology of sin. Whereas I found only four explicit references to sin in Dupuis' work, his treatment and theology of grace, as well as his explicit admission that he is indebted to Rahner's theology while aiming to extend its missional implications (see chapter 4, opening paragraph), lead me to conclude that his doctrine of sin is similar to Rahner's. To the extent that is the case, my critique of Rahner's theology of sin in chapter 3 also applies to Dupuis.

"Dupuis [seems to believe] that linking salvation and the role of Christ too closely to the church would make the church take the place of Christ. This is an unnecessary and theologically less than convincing fear. . . . If the church is made the instrument of salvation only for Christians, then the biblically based view of the church as the sign of the unity of humankind and the coming of the new creation (Rev 21) is compromised."[12] To the extent Dupuis' understanding of the relationship between the reign of God and the Church is an extension of Rahner's "anonymous Christianity," to that extent my critique of Rahner's category in chapter 3 pertains to Dupuis as well. Due to the limited scope of this project, I am unable to treat each of these critiques in the detailed depth which they deserve. The issues involved in each are vast and complex. Therefore, the following discussion will elaborate my critique in terms of the first two points more fully, while providing an abbreviated sketch of the issues involved in pneumatology and relating the church and reign of God.

I begin my critical evaluation of Dupuis' proposal by noting a basic, unresolved tension in Dupuis' thought, namely: how is Jesus Christ the center and source of universal salvation without Christianity replacing other religious traditions? This bears directly upon the church's self-understanding of its mission. If the other religions already potentially have a positive, salvific role within the one economy of salvation, as Dupuis argues, does the church's mission still entail an explicit call to conversion? If so, on what grounds? If others experience the mystery of salvation "more fully" through the sacrament of the church, does this not entail, at the very least, an implicit call to conversion and thereby nullify the principle of religious pluralism *de jure*? If not, why not? A seemingly irreconcilable tension exists between his view of "asymmetrical complementarity" between Christianity and the religions and the claim that divine revelation through Jesus Christ is "not in need of a true completion by other traditions," on the one hand, and the claim that the influence of Jesus Christ as the source of salvation "remains subject, up to this final fulfillment, to an 'eschatological remainder'" to which the other religions contribute as "participated mediations" of salvation, on the other.[13] While Dupuis' entire project is an elaboration of his proposed answer to this set of concerns, I find his proposed answer unconvincing in terms of fidelity to the Lutheran interpretation of how the broad Christian tradition has viewed

---

12. Kärkkäinen, *Trinity and Religious Pluralism*, 65.
13. Dupuis, *Christianity and the Religions*, 257, 194ff.

the nature of the gospel and of grace, and the implications those have for God's "duplex" mission to the world.

Meta-Questions and Overall Theological Framework

Before delving into specific differences between the two proposals, I wish to sketch, in broad contours, the main differences between Dupuis' proposal and a Lutheran one. My hope is that, with this difference of overall theological framework in mind, my evaluation and critique of more specific aspects of his proposal will be sufficiently intelligible.

A crucial axiom which helps explain the underlying differences between these proposals, one which confessional Lutheran theology readily affirms, is that "Biblical hermeneutics is at no point separable from Biblical soteriology."[14] In other words: one's understanding of what constitutes salvation is intimately related to, and definitively shapes, how one interprets Scripture. I will elaborate on the significance of this axiom and apply it shortly.

Two sets of diagnostic questions, each with two parts, and the differing answers Dupuis and a Lutheran approach give to these questions, will serve as an overall guide for grasping, not only the animating concern for each proposal, but also why they construct their argument the way they do. My first set of questions has two parts, "what" and "how": 1) *What* is being communicated in and through divine revelation, and 2) *how* is that being communicated? My second set of questions places the differences between these two proposals into stark contrast: 1) What is the "material content" of Christian salvation and grace? 2) How, by what means, is that salvific grace mediated beyond the Christian tradition? This second question is a matter of Christology in relation to pneumatology and Spirit Christology, of relating the Word and the Spirit, which will be addressed later on.

For Dupuis' proposal, as we've noted, the "what" of divine revelation consists of God's self-communication and self-manifestation as grace. God's self-communication is everywhere, by definition, gracious and salvific. In terms of "how," this gracious self-communication is intelligible through a transcendental anthropology which facilitates and undergirds, not only the uniting of Trinitarian and Spirit Christologies, but also the

---

14. Bertram, "Hermeneutical Significance," 2.

subsequent elaboration of how other traditions serve as "participated mediations" of the "one mediation" of salvation in Christ.

For Rahner and Dupuis, experiences of God are, by and large, gracious. If one were to substitute "God" for every use of "grace" in Dupuis, his argument would retain its force and would not change significantly. This goes to show that, for the nature/grace paradigm, God's self-communication and experiences of God's presence are, to a large extent, defined as gracious.

In contrast, the "what" of divine revelation in a Lutheran proposal consists of the distinction between law and Gospel promise. Simply put: God speaks and reveals two words which are so diametrically opposed and contradictory that their reconciliation requires God to sacrifice, not only Jesus Christ as reconciliation for human sin, but seemingly God's logical coherence as well. The gospel is the promise of God's grace as reconciling the intractable problem created by the law's demands and human sinfulness, with grace specified as that promise of reconciling mercy realized for Christ's sake. How is this law/Gospel distinction, and its understanding of grace, conveyed? Through the performative Word of God, transmitted in its various forms (written, oral, sacramental) and active through the power of the risen, glorified Christ and his Spirit. It is received through faith as trust in the divine promises. God's Spirit freely binds itself to this Word, not only convicting people of sin but also driving them to the comfort of the Gospel's promise. In concluding this section, I believe these sets of questions helpfully illuminate fundamental differences in theological framework and emphasis, differences which undergird and illuminate subsequent differences.

My second set of diagnostic questions and their answers are set within the horizon of emphasizing different theological loci as normatively crucial. While mindful that the fullness of Christian salvation encompasses both the incarnational and cruciform dimensions of Christ's life, as well as his active ministry, which dimension of the Christ event one emphasizes as central for properly understanding Christian salvation (incarnation or cross) makes a significant difference in the practical contours of one's missiology. The following quote by Dupuis helps set the stage for better understanding his approach to these sets of questions:

> I have pointed to the practice of charity (*agape*) being, according to the Christian tradition, a sure criterion of the presence of grace and salvation in human beings.... This does not mean that charity is the only content of the "categorial" reality of

> salvation. It is well understood that, for the Christian tradition, salvation implies redemption from sins, or rather overcoming of sin. But this is only the negative aspect of Christian salvation which positively consists in the invitation extended by God to human beings of sharing in his own life here and in the hereafter. The question was whether salvation thus understood can apply to other religions and whether it comes to them through a certain mediation of their tradition.[15]

Two significant factors, determinative for shaping Dupuis' understanding of salvation and grace, are worth noting from this quote. First, his Rahnerian understanding of reality as composed of transcendental and categorical dimensions is clear. Secondly, this Rahnerian framework shapes his view of salvation as consisting primarily, but not only, of union with God, prompted by the divine self-communication and invitation. What is the significance of this?

"Biblical hermeneutics is at no point separable from Biblical soteriology."[16] What Dupuis fundamentally believes about the nature of salvation definitively shapes his understanding of the nature of the gospel, of grace, of Biblical covenants, of the reign of God—in other words, his view of salvation determines, not just his Biblical hermeneutic, but also how he extends that hermeneutic to interpret and "read" the world of religious pluralism as he constructs his missiology of inclusive pluralism. I will now elaborate how this works for Dupuis.

For theologians like Rahner and Dupuis, the framework of transcendental anthropology is central, the incarnational motif is primary, and therefore salvation consists of God's loving, self-communication to people. For Dupuis, what is the "material content" of Christian salvation and grace? The fact that, through transcendental Christology, "Jesus Christ, the Mediator . . . is at once God turning to us, in his Word, in self-communication and self-gift, and humankind . . . turned to God in grateful response."[17] The essence of grace, as noted in chapter 3, is God's universal, self-communication to people. If that is how salvation and grace is understood, how might we expect Dupuis to interpret Scripture? It becomes possible to view the issue of sin, as Dupuis does, as a relatively minor bump in the road on the way to what Christian salvation is mainly about: union with God. Once sin is under-diagnosed and marginalized

---

15. Dupuis, "Christianity and the Religions' Revisited," 376.
16. Bertram, "Hermeneutical Significance," 2.
17. Dupuis, *Who Do You Say I Am?*, 125.

(from a Lutheran perspective), the law/Gospel distinction becomes largely irrelevant, and it becomes plausible to look for "traces of grace and truth" in other religions as signs of divine, salvific presence. God is universally present, bestowing universal salvation, and the evidence of this is "signs of grace and truth." What Dupuis believes about the nature of salvation, within his Rahnerian framework, inevitably shapes how he approaches Scripture and, by extension, religious pluralism. We live in a graced horizon. In terms of the second question, Dupuis would view other religious traditions as potentially "participated mediations" of the "one mediation" of salvation in Christ (chapter 4).

In contrast to Dupuis' understanding of what constitutes the primary theological locus (incarnation) and salvation (grace as facilitating God's self-communication and communion with people), a confessional Lutheran approach prioritizes robust theologies of sin and the cross as indispensable for understanding salvation. The ramifications for constructing a missiology are momentous. First, the overcoming of sin, rather than a marginal aspect of salvation, becomes its central dilemma, in terms of how to reconcile sinful humanity to God in a manner that honors both divine love and justice, mercy and holiness. Secondly, the law/Gospel distinction, in addressing the depth dimension of sin, becomes central in articulating the nature of salvation and grace. Thirdly, while divine truth permeates creation, including the world religions, such traces of truth would not necessarily be identified as "traces of grace," since the reconciling grace of Christ is not yet explicitly present and not yet being trusted as good news. Again, Lutheran soteriology is integral to Lutheran hermeneutics: salvation as the promise of mercy and reconciliation, fulfilled in the work of Christ on the cross (see chapter 2), is elaborated by the law/Gospel distinction as a distinctive approach to religious pluralism, centered on God's hiddenness both in the cross and in the world. The realities of law, Gospel, and divine hiddenness, understood in terms of and filtered through the cross, shape what can and cannot be affirmed in terms of God's gracious activity in the world.

In terms of the second question, unlike Dupuis, a Lutheran model intentionally refrains from elaborating how this action reaches people beyond the bounds of the performative Word, leaving that within the realm of unrevealed, divine mystery. In balancing the poles of God's universal, salvific will (John 3:16, 1 Tim 2:4) and salvation through Christ alone, it vigorously asserts both truths, while insisting that the mechanics of how the former is enacted remains a hidden mystery. Lutheran missiology boldly affirms that salvation is *sola gratia, solus Christus,* and that *fides ex auditu,* while being unwilling to engage in unwarranted speculation regarding how the grace of Christ may be operative beyond the performative Word of God. While Dupuis and Rahner also affirm *sola gratia* and *solus Christus,* "the *fides ex auditu* is missing from [their] position."[18]

Revelation of Law and Gospel

Building on the preceding introductory comments, a Lutheran model contests and critiques Dupuis' approach as advocating an overly restrictive view of divine revelation, collapsing the central law/Gospel distinction into grace. While Rahner addressed the reality of sin within his theological system,[19] one is hard pressed to find references to sin in Dupuis' work.[20] A discussion of sin and the divine law seems incompatible with and irrelevant to Dupuis' discussion of saving values, gospel values, and traces of grace and truth in other traditions. Such an approach inadequately addresses the scriptural witness to the centrality of the law/Gospel distinction and the role of the divine law in God's mission to the world.

I now pose for Dupuis the most fundamentally basic question this project addresses: What is the nature of the gospel? How does Dupuis define the gospel? While he has much to say about "gospel (or saving) values" and "traces of truth and grace" in other religions, I found only one

---

18. D'Costa, *Christianity and World Religions,* 19.

19. See my critique of Rahner's theology of sin in chapter 3.

20. I was only able to find four explicit references to sin in Dupuis' work, three in his *Who Do You Say I Am? Introduction to Christology:* 93, 120, 129, and one in "'Christianity and the Religions' Revisited," 376. What is of great significance and supports my point is the first three references to sin are in the context of Dupuis explicating issues in classic Christological formulations, rather than explicating and delineating the legitimate place and significance of a sufficiently robust theology of sin in one's theologies of grace, revelation, and mission. Dupuis' treatment of sin gives the impression of being limited to how to properly understand the affirmation of Jesus' sinlessness in light of his human psychology and incarnation, rather than the problem actual sin in humans poses for a God who insists on being both a God of love and holy justice. As Dupuis puts it: "The human psychology of the Word incarnate in kenosis thus appears as a deep mystery. How do we reconcile and combine in it elements that seem to contradict and cancel each other, such as the absence of sin with true temptation? the vision of God with the sense of being abandoned on the cross? the obedience to God's will in death and a free offering of self?" (*Who Do You Say I Am?,* 120).

place where Dupuis gives a direct, explicit definition of the gospel. As he puts it, "The 'gospel' (*euanggelion*) that is, the 'good news,' is the breaking into history of the 'lordship' of God, the fulfillment of the divine promises, and the renewal of the relationship between God and human beings and among human beings themselves."[21] From a Lutheran perspective, I eagerly awaited to hear his elaboration of the *content* of such divine promises and his understanding of *how* they are fulfilled, *how* specifically the relationship between God and humanity is renewed. Unfortunately, the gospel as "fulfillment of the divine promises" remained a passing reference, while Dupuis focused on elaborating the universal reign of God as extending beyond the church to include others. His stated position seems to imply that members of other traditions are "co-members" of that reign.[22] The conclusion I draw from such sparse treatment of the content and nature of the gospel is that, for Dupuis, since humanity operates within a "graced horizon," the promissory nature of the gospel is largely subsumed under the Rahnerian category of grace as God's self-communication. For Dupuis, articulating *how* "God's saving grace can reach humankind in different ways which must be combined and brought together"[23] is a more centrally important question than, "What is the gospel?" This is intelligible only to the extent that consensus on the nature of the gospel as God's self-communication of grace is already assumed.

My critique that Dupuis fails to appreciate and utilize the law/Gospel distinction can also be made by means of Irenaeus' metaphor of God's two hands. Dupuis' proposal can be understood as an elaborate answer to the question of how "God's two hands, the Word and the Spirit . . . are paired hands," a pairing which "produces a single work, namely, the one economy of salvation."[24] The undifferentiated Word and the Spirit are largely assumed to bestow salvific grace and defined, by their very nature, to be gracious. Starting from a Rahnerian framework whereby the gospel and grace are defined as God's self-communication, the relevantly significant questions revolve around the dynamics of how, within

---

21. Dupuis, *Christianity and the Religions*, 196.

22. As Dupuis states, "[T]he 'others' can attain the reality of the Kingdom of God present without belonging to the body of the church. They can be members of the Reign of God without becoming part of the church as its members" (*Christianity and the Religions*, 214).

23. Dupuis, *Christianity and the Religions*, 186.

24. Ibid., 179.

a Trinitarian framework, a Trinitarian Christology (the Word) and Spirit pneumatology (the Spirit) are to be related.

A confessional Lutheran proposal for relating the Word and the Spirit, utilizing the law/Gospel distinction, seeks to express a Trinitarian framework and motivation for mission. As Paul R. Hinlicky states, referencing St. Paul's letter/Spirit distinction in 2 Cor 3:

> [T]he economic distinction between the Word of God as letter that kills and as Spirit who gives life, or rhetorically, between the Word of God as a demand that exposes human incapacity and the Word of God as promise that gives what God commands, is a function of the procession/missions from the Father of the divine Word and the Spirit into the world . . . The law-gospel dialectic as interpretation of Scripture then subsists within the Trinitarian dialectic of the external Word which points to the Spirit in order to be understood, and of the Spirit which points to the Word in order to be received.[25]

While God's Word and Spirit, speech and actions, certainly require coordination, Lutheran theology claims that how one "parses" God's speech to humanity is decisive for one's approach toward other religions. It posits the law/Gospel distinction, expressing the conflicting words of God's demand and promise, as a fundamental dialectic undergirding and directing how Word and Spirit should properly be related. To the extent that God's speech to humanity is understood as largely grace, to that extent the relationship between Word and Spirit is open to distortion.

The distinction between law and Gospel is centrally illuminative and crucial in order to properly relate the actions of God's two hands, Word and Spirit, within the one economy of salvation. While Dupuis affirms the promissory nature of the gospel as renewal of the divine-human relationship, when he overlooks the accusatory function of the divine law and judgment of sin, this inevitably results in the central importance of the cross of Christ and its mediation of mercy being insufficiently illuminated. Without a clear, sufficiently robust theology of the law, which is the correlative of a theology of sin, a theology of the gospel as promise of God loses its sharp focus. This problematic highlights the importance of maintaining *both* terms of key, scriptural dialectics and pairings (such as law and gospel, sin and grace, flesh and spirit, bondage and freedom, old creation and new creation, etc.). To the extent that one term in such

---

25. Hinlicky, *Luther and the Beloved Community*, 115.

dialectical pairings is marginalized or lost, to that extent the term which is retained loses the clarity of its core meaning. This is precisely what happens when Dupuis discusses the gospel, gospel values, and traces of grace without a solid anchoring in the Biblical treatment of sin's depth and brokenness. Simply put: without a deep appreciation of the role of sin and the divine law, the nature of the gospel as promise of mercy becomes inevitably obscured.

As noted earlier, Lutheran pneumatology views the Spirit's work as sharpening one's awareness of sin and the law, in order to drive people to the gospel as loving mercy. By largely ignoring the law's function in judging sin, what the Spirit reveals in Dupuis' pneumatology is inevitably interpreted as "gospel values," "traces of truth and grace," and "the Christian spirit" manifested as love, rather than a recognition of human brokenness and sin.[26] In this way, what constitutes gospel shifts decisively from a solid anchoring in the scriptural promise of loving mercy and forgiveness to something else.

My critique of Dupuis' proposal, at its most basic level, boils down to this: one cannot sufficiently understand the *gospel* without a sufficiently robust understanding of the *law*, just as one cannot sufficiently understand divine *grace* without a sufficiently robust understanding of *sin*. One cannot adequately understand the gospel without the law, and one cannot sufficiently understand divine grace without sin. In terms of both the law/Gospel and sin/grace dialectic, by largely overlooking the categories of "law" and "sin," Dupuis operates with restrictive meanings of "gospel" and "grace." While this is understandable, operating within the Rahnerian framework of a "nature/grace" paradigm, it nonetheless skews the trajectory of his entire proposal, resulting in the "center of gravity" of his model shifting from the gospel as *promissio Dei* and grace as the promise of mercy, to a basis in Rahnerian, transcendental anthropology and assumptions.

In terms of relating revelation and salvation, not only as histories (of salvation and revelation), but as fundamental theological categories, how do the two proposals compare? For Dupuis, while he emphasizes the nature and process of divine revelation as progressive, differentiated, and complementary,[27] it is the universal scope of that revelation which leads him to conflate the histories of salvation and revelation: "the history of

---

26. Dupuis, *Christianity and the Religions*, 190ff.
27. Ibid., 132–6.

salvation and revelation is one."[28] Wherever and in whatever way God has chosen to reveal Godself, there, by definition, divine salvation is present as well. As Dupuis puts it, "Religious pluralism in principle is then based on the immensity of a God who is Love and communication."[29]

In contrast, a Lutheran proposal views the histories of salvation and revelation as overlapping, rather than concentric, circles: related, yet distinct. The fact that God is love, contrary to Dupuis, does not legitimate religious pluralism in principle or the religions as the means by which God will save everyone. As Rahner has noted, God's universal will for salvation does not mean that God is compelled to save all nor that all are, in fact, saved. While this remains a possibility, it can never be a divine necessity. As Wingren reminds us, "That everyone should be saved is not an assertion of fact that has any biblical support. But it is something one can certainly pray for. . . . No one has arrived. So, while we are in the process of moving toward the goal, we can pray what we cannot assert."[30] Carl Braaten captures the eschatological vision of a Lutheran, "inclusive exclusivity" proposal: "The presence of the eschatological kingdom in Jesus and in the apostolic mission is the anticipation of the future of all religions as well as the entire religious life of humanity. These other religions are not striving after nothingness or false gods. They are looking toward union with the Divine Mystery that the Christian Gospel announces is ultimately the same divine reality as that revealed in the person of Jesus."[31]

A Lutheran critique of Dupuis asserts that, if divine revelation is dual in its content (law and Gospel), then, while some divine revelation is indeed salvific, there is also revelation of divine judgment of sin. To the extent that this is the case, the central concern and thrust of revelation becomes how to resolve and reconcile these opposing words (revelations) of God. While Dupuis affirms the importance of affirming universal revelation as progressively differentiated and complementary,[32] his view of revelation is, ironically and contrary to his claim, insufficiently progressive and unduly restrictive. A Lutheran view would deem it insufficiently differentiated. In his fervent desire to affirm and elaborate the complementary nature of universal revelation, he fails to sufficiently incorporate

28. Ibid., 134.
29. Ibid., 255.
30. Wingren, *Credo*, 183.
31. Braaten, *No Other Gospel!*, 47.
32. Dupuis, *Toward a Christian Theology of Religious Pluralism*, 250–53 and *Christianity and the Religions*, 135–7.

the radical disjuncture between the revelation of divine judgment and mercy, or wrath and promise. Precisely to the extent that his complementary view of revelation fails to make this critical distinction, to that extent Dupuis is led away from, rather than toward, recognizing the nature of the gospel as promise of mercy.

Building further upon this very point: while Dupuis, with confidence in the power of God's grace, may expect Christians "to discover with surprise amazing convergences between the words of God [in other religions] and his Word in Jesus Christ," in his writings Dupuis does not substantiate this expectation by specific examples.[33] From a Lutheran perspective, such a claim is at best a theological hope, based on a transcendental framework of grace, rather than a substantial claim supported by specific, empirical evidence.

Having said that, I recognize Dupuis' perspective and seek to affirm the positive motivation behind his intention. Standing within the Roman Catholic dogmatic tradition and affirming Jesus Christ as the *norma normans non normata*, Dupuis, in numerous conversations with Bede Griffiths and Henri le Saux (Abhishiktananda), seeks to theologically articulate the experience and evidence of the power of grace he saw operative in other traditions, especially the Hindu tradition he lived and dialogued among for thirty years. While witnessing the power of that tradition to produce lives that Dupuis could only describe as exhibiting the "fruit of the Spirit" (Gal 5:22ff.), it is still important to remember that the spirit of Christ remains the criterion for discerning authentic manifestations of the Spirit.[34]

From a Lutheran perspective, Dupuis displays unsubstantiated confidence in viewing and expecting lines of convergence between Christian revelation and revelation in other traditions. To the extent this happens, it becomes possible to view "elements of truth and grace" as salvific in other religions. Given his personal experience of affirming positive elements in other traditions, combined with his eschatological emphasis on all things being united under Christ (Eph 1:10), this is both understandable and to be expected. In contrast, to the extent that the gospel is understood as the promise of mercy realized in Christ, and the law/Gospel distinction is affirmed as hermeneutically significant, to that extent it becomes much

---

33. Dupuis, *Christianity and the Religions*, 137.

34. The apostle Paul makes precisely this point in his exhortation to "discern the spirits."

harder to affirm a mutual complementarity between Christian revelation and revelation in other traditions.

Theology of Grace

Secondly, Dupuis' definition of grace and his theology of grace merits closer scrutiny. Dupuis claims, "God's saving grace can reach humankind in different ways which must be combined and brought together."[35] He further elaborates how he understands the mystery of Christic salvation being genuinely, albeit incompletely and implicitly, present in other religions:

> The mediation of the mystery of Christ takes place in a variety of ways. While God's grace is certainly one, it is visibly mediated in different ways—differing from one another not only in degree but in nature. This means that the religious practices and sacramental rites of other religions are not on the same level as the Christian sacraments deriving from Jesus Christ; but it does also mean that we must attribute to them a certain mediation of grace. There is only one mystery of salvation in Christ. But this mystery is present to human beings outside the bounds of Christianity . . . In the other religious traditions, it is present hiddenly and implicitly, through a modality of incomplete, but no less real, mediation, constituted by such traditions.[36]

We have now arrived at an important point of simultaneous convergence and divergence with respect to Dupuis' proposal. While Lutheran theology readily admits that people everywhere do indeed experience God as the transcendental horizon of their lives, that there is true experience of God's reality and divine revelation, its critique of Rahner and Dupuis lies in their interpretation of that experience and revelation as *de facto* gracious. In nuanced affirmation of such a "graced horizon," confessional Lutheran theology adds that the "storm clouds" of divine judgment upon human sin constitute at least as significant a feature of that transcendental horizon as does divine grace, according to the Biblical witness. It is precisely this balance of experiencing God as both graciously loving and fearfully awe-inspiring that seems missing in Dupuis' theology.

---

35. Dupuis, *Christianity and the Religions*, 186.
36. Ibid., 188–9.

Missio Shaped by Promissio

Are the "traces of grace and truth" in the religions to be identified with cruciform loving mercy, the "grace of our Lord Jesus Christ"? Dupuis insists they are; Lutheran theology says no. Why not? A Lutheran reading of Dupuis critiques his theology of grace by insisting that the nature of the Gospel, as the promise of loving mercy in Christ, is not reducible to or deducible from "traces of grace and truth" in other religions. While Dupuis himself does not make this specific claim, his theological orientation and attitude results in such a practical outcome.

This concern over Dupuis' insufficient treatment of sin is elaborated in greater detail in terms of a discussion of covenant theology and the unique mediation of Jesus Christ, which must be included in a proper evaluation of Dupuis' theology of grace. On what grounds? Because Dupuis himself treats these two as integral pieces in the development of his argument (see chapter 4). Having evaluated and critiqued a Rahnerian theology of grace as nature fulfilled in chapter 3, we now return to the centrality of grace for constructing a missiology, this time through the twin lenses of covenant theology and the unique mediation of Jesus Christ, respectively. In doing so, I hope to demonstrate how a Lutheran critique of Dupuis is primarily directed toward his theologies of grace and of revelation, inasmuch as the latter articulates and applies the former.

Theology of Covenants

Dupuis begins his discussion of covenants in Scripture with a healthy note of caution:

> Quite apart from the use of covenant terminology, interpreters are not agreed regarding the number of covenants that need to be distinguished in the biblical account and on the relationship existing between them. Are there distinct covenants, or do all those mentioned in the Bible refer to a unique cosmic covenant, established by God with humankind in creation?[37]

While a Lutheran approach recognizes the reality of distinct covenants with their differing elements of law and promise, Dupuis emphasizes the foundational nature of the Noahic covenant as "a unique cosmic covenant established by God with humankind in creation." While being critical of single covenant theories which construe "the process of salvation history [as] reduced to the restoration of an original state, thereby

37. Dupuis, *Toward a Christian Theology of Religious Pluralism*, 224.

being deprived of any dynamic movement,"[38] he nonetheless affirms the "enduring value of the cosmic covenant" with Noah as unfolded by "the Trinitarian rhythm of divine covenants" throughout history.[39] This pattern of "one and many" reflects his theology of revelation as "differentiated and complementary."[40] In other words, Dupuis' theologies of covenants and revelation are both rooted in and expressions of his theology of grace, his fundamental conviction that the Word of God, as an ultimate word of grace, is "single and universal."[41] In contrast, a Lutheran approach insists on the importance of recognizing a diversity of covenants in the Hebrew Scriptures "centered about two opposite, almost contradictory notions" of law and promise.[42] I will now elaborate this critique of Dupuis.

A helpful starting point is to affirm what Dupuis and a confessional Lutheran approach share in common. First of all, both affirm the reality of a salvation history (economy of salvation) consisting of human history "as a 'dialogue of salvation' freely initiated by God with humankind from creation itself and pursued through the centuries until the fulfillment of God's Reign in the eschaton."[43] Secondly, the event and person of Jesus Christ is the radically inclusive center of that salvation history. Thirdly, both affirm God's unwavering commitment of faithfulness toward humanity: whether it is called "economy of salvation" (my preferred term) or one cosmic covenant diversely manifested (Dupuis), Dupuis and confessional Lutherans both view the promissory faithfulness of God to be at stake.

How, then, do the two approaches differ in terms of a theology of covenants grounded in a broader theology of grace? For Dupuis, the cosmic covenant with Noah, understood as a universal covenant of grace, serves as the basis for the potential of universal salvation and a positive appraisal of the salvific potential of the world religions and their covenants. Dupuis agrees with B. Stoeckle's conclusions: "The covenant with Noah constitutes the lasting foundation for the salvation of every human person . . . The particular characteristics recorded in the Scripture concerning the Noah covenant make it clear that there is question here of a

---

38. Ibid., 224.
39. Ibid., 227–33.
40. Ibid., 250–53.
41. Ibid., 235–53.
42. Hillers, *Covenant*, 6.
43. Dupuis, *Toward a Christian Theology of Religious Pluralism*, 217.

Missio Shaped by Promissio

true event of salvation, marked by grace . . . Israel and the nations have thus a common base: they are in a state of covenantship with the true God and under the same salvific will of that one God."[44]

Utilizing Rahner's notion of the supernatural existential and conviction that "the 'transcendental' history of salvation, universally present, needs to take concrete form in the history of people," Dupuis asserts that "the history of salvation and revelation is one. In its various stages-cosmic, Israelite, and Christian-it bears, in different ways, the seal of the influence of the Holy Spirit."[45] Viewing the Noahic covenant in this manner is congruent with his overarching claim that there is one God, one Christ, but convergent paths to the salvation inclusively centered on Christ.[46]

While an in-depth study of Biblical covenant theology is beyond the scope of this study, some salient remarks are in order.[47] In stark contrast to Dupuis' view of an original, cosmic covenant of grace manifested in subsequent covenants, Reformation theology in general, and confessional Lutheran theology in particular, "recognizes the crucial differences between different types of covenants that we find in Scripture—specifically, law—covenants (suzerainty treaties) and promise-covenants (royal grants)."[48] Michael Horton outlines this distinction:

> *The deepest distinction in Scripture is not between the Old and New Testaments, but between the covenants of law and the covenants of promise that run through both.* The two covenant traditions are distinguished both in form and content. There is a covenant of law . . . according to which each and every person swears to fulfill the stipulations. There is also a covenant of promise . . . according to which God swears to bring redemption through the promised heir (seed). These two covenant traditions are united . . . yet always remain distinguished.[49]

Supported by the work of ancient Near Eastern scholarship, a Lutheran approach affirms the validity and importance of recognizing how

---

44. Ibid., 217ff.
45. Ibid., 218, 251.
46. Ibid., 211, 203.
47. For excellent overviews of the pertinent issues, see Hillers, *Covenant*; Mendenhall, *Law and Covenant in Israel*; McCarthy, *Treaty and Covenant*; McKenzie, *Covenant*; and Moshe Weinfeld, "The Covenant of Grant in the Old Testament and the Ancient Near East," in Greenspahn, ed., *Essential Papers*, 69–102.
48. Horton, *Covenant and Salvation*, 12.
49. Ibid., 17–18.

ancient near Eastern diplomacy has affected the distinctly dual shape of Biblical covenants. Horton, quoting Moshe Weinfeld and Delbert Hillers, describes the salient features relevant to a proper understanding of Biblical covenants:

> Israel's history is determined by a covenantal tradition in the form of "royal grant" on the one hand and the "suzerainty treaty" on the other, both well-attested in Ancient Near Eastern diplomacy. The suzerainty treaty is akin to a contract between a greater and lesser ruler, or suzerain and vassal. Included in such ancient Hittite formularies were the following features: 1) preamble (identifying the suzerain who imposes the treaty), 2) a historical prologue (justifying the suzerain's claims over the vassal's realm), 3) stipulations (commands), and 4) sanctions (curses for violation, blessings for obedience) . . . However, the royal grant was a gift bestowed by the suzerain upon a vassal . . . Royal grants were "an outright gift by a king to a subject."[50]

Building upon this distinction between suzerainty treaties (with their attendant stipulations and sanctions) and royal grant treaties (of a gracious, unconditional nature), confessional Lutheran theology recognizes such contrasting elements of demand and promise, sanctions and gracious gift, as concrete instances of God's dual speech of law and gospel present throughout the various Biblical covenants. Rather than identifying the covenant with Noah as the original, cosmic covenant of grace, Lutheran theology views this law/Gospel dynamic already operative prior to Noah in the creation/fall narrative as the earliest instance of "covenant": explicit stipulations and sanctions are spelled out in Gen 2:17 ("You must not eat from the tree of the knowledge of good and evil, for when you eat of it you will surely die."), followed by the promise of the "proto-Gospel" in Gen 3:15.[51] A Lutheran perspective views the narrative of the fall as the original expression of command and promise, law and Gospel, the contours of which subsequent, Biblical covenants elaborate. In terms of the promise of mercy, grace, and eschatological victory over evil through the work of the promised Messiah (Gen 3:15),

---

50. Ibid., 12–13.

51. Reformation theology in general and Lutheran theology specifically has interpreted this passage, "I will put enmity between you and the woman, between your offspring and hers; he will crush your head, and you will strike his heel," as referring to the spiritual battle between Satan and Jesus Christ. While Satan "struck" Jesus' heel (metaphorically speaking) as he died on the cross, Jesus "crushed" his head in and through the resurrection.

Missio Shaped by Promissio

the promissory motif becomes concretized in the covenant with Abraham (Gen 15 and 17) as a prime example of the "royal grant" treaty: in a radically unconditional promise of grace, God takes upon himself all the consequences, including death, of violating this covenant. The covenants with Noah, David, and, ultimately, the Christic covenant, increasingly concentrate and intensify this original promise.

Having elaborated key features of a Lutheran hermeneutic of Biblical covenants, what are enduring differences between a Lutheran approach and Dupuis? First, what is at stake for both is God's faithfulness to God's promise. But which promise, what is the content of that promise? For Dupuis, divine grace consists of God's promise never again to destroy life through a flood (Gen 9:15).[52] From a confessional Lutheran perspective, the promise consists of God's pledge to defeat evil through a coming Messiah (Gen 3:15), the promise of universal mercy and grace extending through Abraham, the patriarchs, and Jesus Christ to the ends of the earth. The promise of physical preservation is not equivalent to or an adequate representation of "grace" as the promise of mercy in Christ. Secondly, if and to the extent Dupuis shares Rahner's view of sin, particularly sin as analogous rather than pertaining directly to human subjectivity, to that extent he is unable to sufficiently appreciate and incorporate the severity of the punishments for covenant violation. Dupuis largely overlooks the reality of concrete sanctions and consequences for covenant violation in the various covenants. My claim is this: regardless of how many covenants one recognizes and how one configures their relationship, the dynamic of contrasting elements of stipulations and sanctions, command and promise, law and Gospel in many Biblical covenants (such as the Sinai covenant and Josh 24) simply cannot be overlooked or uncritically incorporated into a preconceived framework of cosmic grace. This is precisely what I see Dupuis doing. Due to his prior commitment to Rahnerian understandings of the supernatural existential and grace, Dupuis seeks to affirm God's grace and salvific presence as accessible through and a universal reality in all religious covenants.[53] This apriori commitment leaves little room for appreciating how sin and covenant unfaithfulness results in the real possibility of forfeiting the grace of God.

---

52. Dupuis, *Toward a Christian Theology of Religious Pluralism*, 224–6.

53. Early in his discussion of covenants, Dupuis explicitly utilizes the supernatural existential as a central component of properly relating general salvation history and special salvation history. See Dupuis, *Toward a Christian Theology of Religious Pluralism*, 217–9.

Thirdly, from a Lutheran perspective, the promise of mercy on account of Christ is a central truth other scriptural categories, including covenant, serve to illuminate. In contrast, Dupuis makes his view of the cosmic covenant a cornerstone of his overall system.

While the prologue to John's Gospel maintains, "The law came through Moses, grace and truth came through Jesus Christ"[54] the issue of how the "new covenant" in Jesus Christ relates to the earlier covenants in the Hebrew Scriptures is a complex one.[55] The issue of whether and how the "new covenant" in Christ is superior to the first covenant should be distinguished from traditional supercessionist theologies that deny the enduring validity of the covenant with Israel. In contrast to both an ultimate disjuncture (as if the Gospel promise were unrelated to earlier covenants) and a universal view of covenants which insufficiently recognizes the distinctiveness of the Christ event/covenant, I wish to affirm the nature of this "new covenant" as an intensification, clarification, and ultimate fulfillment of the original promise of gracious mercy extended through Abraham to Israel. While the various New Testament writers emphasize different aspects of this relationship, with Paul articulating the

---

54. John 1:17.

55. In terms of New Testament theology, the book of Hebrews and Pauline theology have much to say about the relationship of the new covenant to the covenants of the Hebrew Scriptures. The writer of Hebrews clearly views the new covenant in Christ as superior to, even superceding, the old covenant (8:13). The repeated use of the adjective "better" drives the point home: Jesus enacts a "better" covenant, one enacted on "better" promises. As the "mediator of the new covenant," Jesus is the greater Moses. Delbert Hillers aptly describes the overlapping, yet distinct, approaches of the writer of Hebrews and the apostle Paul, as well as the Lutheran conviction that covenant is one means of clarifying the distinction between law and Gospel promise: "Paul follows the same path as the writer to the Hebrews, yet his emphasis is different. In Hebrews the stress is on the new as foreshadowed in the old. The new covenant is better than the Sinai covenant, but it does not contradict it; it fulfills it and reveals its deepest meaning. In Paul, on the other hand, the two are contrasted so sharply that there is no apparent continuity left between the Sinai covenant and the new covenant in Christ, and the apostle has to reach back to the covenant with Abraham as an anticipation for his gospel and has to elaborate the view that the Sinai covenant is only an episode, an interruption in the history of faith. This polarizing tendency in Paul's use of 'covenant' appears in very characteristic form in II Corinthians 3 . . . Another highly characteristic passage in which Paul uses 'covenant' is Galatians 3, which is especially interesting because Paul takes up here the question involved in his radical distinction between the promise to Abraham and the 'law' given at Sinai: Is the law then against the promises of God? . . . Paul is not really talking about covenant but is presenting a new drama of ideas: faith and works, law and gospel, are the main actors, and covenant comes in only to swell a scene or two" (Hillers, *Covenant*, 182–4).

radical distinction between the promise given to Abraham and the law given at Sinai, the main point I wish to make is this: the New Testament uses various terms, categories, and images in its attempt to convey the richness and depth of the promise of God *par excellence*—the promise of mercy, reconciliation, and new life—offered in Jesus Christ. In their attempts to describe the conviction that "All the promises of God are 'yes' in Christ Jesus,"[56] the New Testament writers employ whatever tools they have at their disposal to convey the essence of this promise fulfilled. As Hillers states, "High priest, tent, blood, sacrifice, covenant: every term here is old, yet each is transmuted. Each has become a way of asserting what happened through Christ . . . For Christians, the coming of the substance [Christ] made shadows out of a rich array of Old Testament events, persons, and ideas, among them covenant."[57]

While recognizing the complex issues involved in covenant theology, the question of the ongoing validity of the Mosaic covenant for salvation, and issues raised by the so-called "new perspective" on Paul regarding Second Temple Judaism, confessional Lutheran theology insists upon the vital importance of contrasting elements in Biblical covenants which defy easy harmonization: conditional vs. unconditional, legal vs. promissory, those evoking punitive measures for disobedience vs. ones depending solely upon God's unconditional faithfulness. In terms of covenants clearly discernible in Scripture, the Mosaic/Sinai covenant (Exod 20) and covenant in Josh 24 are conditional, suzerainty-treaty covenants of law, whereas the covenants to Adam (Gen 3:15), Noah (Gen 9), Abraham (Gen 15 and 17), David (2 Sam 7), and the new covenant in Jesus Christ are unconditional in form and content.[58]

Dupuis' vehement opposition to situating the beginning of salvation history in the call of Abraham,[59] likewise, exhibits a failure to appreci-

---

56. 1 Cor 1:20.

57. Hillers, *Covenant*, 180, 188.

58. One could add Jer 31:31, where God promises to internalize the law upon human hearts.

59. Dupuis, *Toward a Christian Theology of Religious Pluralism*, 215. As he puts it, "Every attempt to situate the beginning of salvation history in the vocation of Abraham, and thereby to reduce its extension to 'sacred history' (*histoire sainte*) initiated there, must be firmly resisted." "Against all reduction of the history of salvation-revelation to the Hebrew-Christian tradition it must be affirmed that salvation history coincides and is coextensive with the history of the world" (*Toward a Christian Theology of Religious Pluralism*, 217). For Dupuis' fuller discussion of this point, see *Toward a Christian Theology of Religious Pluralism*, 31–45, 215–23. For a succinct summary of

ate this distinction between legal and promissory covenantal elements. Given his Rahnerian convictions regarding transcendental anthropology and the universality of grace, Dupuis insists "that salvation history is co-extensive with the history of the world."[60] However, a proper recognition of the reality of divine law, divine judgment, the reality of human sin thwarting the divine, salvific will, and the nature of grace as enacting the promise of mercy prevents one from conflating revelation and salvation, but rather supports their nuanced distinction.

The Unique Mediation of Jesus Christ

We begin our discussion of Jesus Christ's unique mediation by affirming a Lutheran point of agreement with Dupuis: "Christ is not just a revelatory transmitter of grace from God to us-ward, much less the first in a series of such mediations. Rather, he is the only Mediator between God and humanity in 'both' directions, also God-ward."[61] This sounds remarkably similar to Dupuis who, echoing *Gaudium et Spes* no. 22, views this mediation ontologically as grounded in transcendental Christology: "Jesus Christ is 'mediator' between God and humankind inasmuch as he unites divinity and humanity in his person in such a way that in him the Divinity and humankind have become united in a permanent bond."[62] While confessional Lutheran theology does not deny this, it insists that such a view of mediation offers an unnecessarily restrictive meaning of the "mediation" of grace by Jesus Christ in the New Testament.

What is of primary importance in understanding the revelation and mediation of God's love, from a Lutheran perspective, is that "first of all there must be a divine love worth revealing, one which so loves sinners out of their sin as to vindicate God's love as just."[63] I argued this point in chapter 2. While both Dupuis and a Lutheran model affirm Jesus' mediation as the "human face of God," Lutheran missiology insists that what is crucially important to properly understand the Gospel, and what is prior to mere mediation (in the sense of conveying or communicating) of this

---

the opposing view of the Gospel as the fulfillment of the promise to Abraham, see Schreiner, *Paul*, 73–85.

60. Dupuis, *Toward a Christian Theology of Religious Pluralism*, 215.
61. Bertram, "Luther on the Unique Mediatorship of Christ," 249.
62. Dupuis, *Christianity and the Religions*, 168.
63. Bertram, "Luther on the Unique Mediatorship of Christ," 250.

Missio Shaped by Promissio

Gospel, is a prior mediation different in kind: "Christ as Mediator in the sense of a medium of exchange, a [generous] exchange. Christ is the point of transference, the crossover at which God replaces sinful people with righteous ones, thus doing justice . . . precisely by doing mercy . . . No one else but Christ provides that kind of mediation . . ."[64] Only such "cruciform mediation," centered on the cross as reconciliation and redemption from sin, achieves the peace, justice, and mercy (grace) which alone can serve as the basis of any and all "traces of grace and truth" in other religions. When it is explicitly offered through the proclaimed Gospel and trusted (received) in faith, the mediation of Christ is realized; when it is not, it stretches the imagination to conceive how "traces" of such mediation of peace and mercy with God (*coram Deo*) can be discovered in other religions. The "mediation" of the revelation of God's universal love, through transcendental anthropology, transcendental Christology, and grace as nature fulfilled, is not equivalent to the revelation of Jesus Christ as "mediator" of the loving merciful forgiveness of God. "Revelationist mediation," to the extent it marginalizes or overlooks the significance of "cruciform mediation," insufficiently recognizes the Gospel promise centered precisely on such "cruciform mediation."

In other words: while the uniqueness of Jesus as mediator is certainly grounded in his personal identity as the Son of God,[65] what is central to his work of mediation is not simply his transcendental identity (the fact of the incarnation), but rather his sacrificial death on the cross achieving reconciliation and redemption ("cruciform mediation"). While Dupuis acknowledges the many New Testament references to Jesus as mediator (1 Tim 2:5, Heb 8:6, 9:15, 12:24) of the "new covenant" and reconciler between God and humanity (2 Cor 5:19), even acknowledging "the necessary relationship between faith and salvation in the New Testament,"[66] his treatment of Jesus as mediator curiously falls short of directly addressing and utilizing the nature of that mediation for his proposal. Instead, utilizing transcendental anthropology and a robust pneumatology, he proceeds to articulate a constitutive Christology which views other religious traditions as "participated mediations" of Christ's unique mediation.

To summarize: Dupuis' treatment of the "one mediator" Jesus Christ seemingly ends up, inadvertently, doing precisely what he rejects elsewhere: subsuming Christ to the Spirit. In his earnest desire to include

---

64. Ibid.
65. Dupuis, *Christianity and the Religions*, 175.
66. Ibid., 167.

other religions as "participated mediations" in the "one mediation" of Christ, Dupuis sacrifices what is central, marginalizes what is most important, and downplays what is definitive. Confessional Lutheran theology insists that, to the extent that the substantive content of Christ's mediation as reconciliation of sinners to God is marginalized in favor of elaborating a robust pneumatology and Spirit Christology (i.e. *how* the ontological mediation of Christ as uniting God and humanity is extended to and effective within other religious traditions), to that extent the mediatory work of Christ appears to be subsumed under the Spirit. While Dupuis would argue that, in his proposal, the mediatory work of Christ is extended within the religions by means of the Spirit, I agree with Kärkkäinen's assessment: "Dupuis is so enthusiastic in stretching the boundaries of the ministry of the Spirit that he almost ends up going with those he otherwise criticizes for divorcing the Spirit from the Christ."[67] In conclusion: when the Spirit is used to extend the mediatory work of Christ within the world religions, viewing them as potentially participated mediations in that one mediation, it becomes difficult to ascertain how such grace can be identified as the New Testament promise of mercy for Christ's sake and how the lived faith of adherents of those religions can be viewed in any sense as trust in that promise. Such a Lutheran critique reiterates deep, abiding differences regarding the nature of grace and faith (see chapters 2 and 3), whether, and on what grounds, such grace and faith operating beyond the bounds of the explicit Gospel can be identified as "anonymously" relating to and oriented toward Christ and his church.

Dupuis' Pneumatology: the role and work of the Spirit

Thirdly, in terms of Dupuis' robust pneumatology, Lutheran concerns center around how, despite claiming to subordinate the Spirit to Christ, he *seemingly* ends up subordinating Christ to the Spirit. I articulated this concern in the previous section in terms of Dupuis' approach to Christ's unique mediation. Lutheran theology insists that the pressing question which any pneumatology must answer is this: How does God's presence in the world, through the Spirit, relate to what Jesus' crucifixion and resurrection brought about? When the Spirit is connected to Jesus being "lifted up" on the cross (John 7:39, John 12) and uniquely poured out at

---

67. Kärkkäinen, *Trinity and Religious Pluralism*, 63.

Pentecost, how does one square the work of this Spirit with the cross and resurrection?

This concern becomes even more pressing when viewed in light of a Lutheran concern to affirm the importance of the *filioque* clause ("the Spirit proceeds from both the Father and the Son"). In affirming an explicit connection between the Holy Spirit and Jesus Christ, Lutheran theology affirms that the Spirit is the Spirit of Christ whose primary task is to extend the benefits and salvation of Christ into the world. Klaus Detlev Schulz summarizes Lutheran concerns:

> If the Holy Spirit were to be divorced from the person of Christ, the Spirit's role and His outward salvific economy would change from making Christ present to some different role. Moreover, there is the very real danger that if the Holy Spirit is given pivotal attention apart from His connection to Christ, the role and relevancy of Christ Himself is changed . . . We should not delve into investigations . . . by seeking out evidence or testimonies of the presence of the Holy Spirit in other religions apart from the presence of Christ and the Word [of the gospel] as His vehicle.[68]

In other words: to the extent the Spirit's work is understood as discovering "traces of grace and truth" in other religions, to the extent these traces are viewed as evidence of salvific grace, to that extent the Spirit's work of convicting people of sin and of illuminating and conveying the work of Christ ("He [the Spirit] will take from what is mine and make it known to you"[69]) is diminished and marginalized.[70] To the extent such concerns accurately describe Dupuis' proposal, to that extent the constitutive mediation and work of Christ is seemingly subordinated to the Spirit. Such is the confessional Lutheran concern.

In terms of the claim that "traces of grace and truth" constitute "saving values" in other religions, I concur with Kärkkäinen's assessment: "If the Spirit of God is the Spirit of Christ (Rom 8:9) and if the task of the Spirit, the Spirit of truth, is to take from what is Christ's and make it

---

68. Schulz, *Mission from the Cross*, 95.

69. John 16:14.

70. The *Formula of Concord, Solid Declaration Article V* makes this very point: "Therefore, the Spirit must not only comfort but through the function of the law must also 'convict the world of sin' [John 16:8]. Thus, in the New Testament the Holy Spirit must perform . . . an *opus alienum, ut faciat opus proprium* (that is, he must perform an alien work—which is to convict—until he comes to his proper work—which is to comfort and to proclaim grace). For this reason Christ obtained the Spirit for us and sent him to us" (Kolb and Wengert, *Book of Concord*, 583).

known to us (John 16:15) . . . , then whatever truth will be found in other religions or outside religions, it still belongs to Christ . . . I see [this] as a more satisfying way to approach the 'extra' revelation found among religions."[71]

Dupuis ponders how to properly understand the controlling function of the Christ event upon the nature and extent of the Spirit's work in the world: "Nevertheless, it is not apparent why, whereas before the Christ event the Spirit was at work in the world and in history, without being communicated through the risen humanity [of Christ]—which did not yet exist—its activity after the Christ event would have to be so tied to such communication as to be limited to it."[72] A Lutheran response to Dupuis is that he is very close to answering his own question. While affirming the one, unified economy of salvation, and that "the gift of the Spirit before the incarnation takes place 'in view' of the Christological event,"[73] I am puzzled why Dupuis does not conceive of the Spirit's action after the Christ event as similar to its action before the Christ event: being oriented toward the Christ event by pointing people toward it. This occurred typologically in the Hebrew Scriptures and explicitly in the New Testament.[74] A Lutheran conviction does not deny that "after that [Christ] event no action of the Spirit as such . . . may be conceived,"[75] but rather insists that, due to the assurance that God's Spirit is present with the performative Word in its oral, written, and sacramental forms, we can speak with a measure of confidence about the Spirit's work of conveying law and Gospel, while a measure of caution is warranted in trying to assess what the Spirit may be saying or doing independently of or unconditioned by that Word.

A central tenet of confessional Lutheran pneumatology affirms that "the reconciliation of God with fallen mankind through Christ is made present through the activity of the Spirit in Word and Sacrament."[76] Mar-

71. Kärkkäinen, *Trinity and Religious Pluralism*, 63.

72. Dupuis, *Christianity and the Religions*, 181.

73. Ibid.

74. Some examples of such a typological approach to interpreting the Hebrew Scriptures in light of the New Testament include, for example, viewing the lives of Abraham, Joseph, Moses, David, and Elijah as conveying a theological "excess" of meaning which is more fully grasped and appreciated in view of the life, ministry, death, and resurrection of Jesus Christ.

75. Dupuis, *Christianity and the Religions*, 181.

76. Schulz, *Mission from the Cross*, 96.

Missio Shaped by Promissio

tin Luther, in his explanation to the third article of the Apostles' Creed, emphasizes the Spirit's work of offering the Gospel's promised benefits through the concrete, external Word:

> Neither you nor I could ever know anything about Christ, or believe in him and receive him as Lord, *unless these were offered to us and bestowed on our hearts through the preaching of the Gospel by the Holy Spirit.* The work is finished and completed . . . But if the work remained hidden so that no one knew of it, it would have been all in vain, all lost. In order that this treasure might not remain buried but be put to use and enjoyed, God has caused the Word to be published and proclaimed, in which he has given *the Holy Spirit to offer and apply to us this treasure.*[77]

Luther articulates how the Spirit carries out the dual work of convicting of sin, in order to deliver the gifts of the gospel: "In the first place . . . one hears the Word of God, in which the Spirit punishes the world on account of sin, John 16[:8]. If sin is recognized, then one hears of the grace of Christ. The Spirit comes [once again] in the same Word and gives faith, where and to whom he will."[78]

Oswald Bayer further clarifies how the law-Gospel distinction is centrally illuminative for such a Lutheran pneumatology: "If the Holy Spirit calls only 'through the gospel,' but the gospel is gospel only as it is distinguished from the law, then the distinction between law and gospel is decisive with respect to . . . pneumatology, as well. Thus the work of the Spirit is, first of all, to sharpen the law and to bring about God's judgment against sin; only then does the Spirit work through the second and final Word of God, the gospel, in that he forgives sin and creates faith . . ."[79]

Within a broader Trinitarian framework, Luther argues for the Holy Spirit's work as the one who unveils and delivers the hidden gifts of God, namely Christ and the benefits of the gospel, through the oral and sacramental forms of the gospel:

> But since this grace [the works, suffering, wisdom, and righteousness of Christ] would not be useful to anyone if it were to remain hidden, and could not come to us, the Holy Spirit comes; he also gives himself to us utterly and completely. He teaches us how to recognize this wonderful deed of Christ . . . helps us to receive and maintain it, how to use it and share it . . . This he

77. Kolb and Wengert, *Book of Concord*, 436, italics added for emphasis.
78. Luther, *Luther's Works*, 40:149.
79. Bayer, *Martin Luther's Theology*, 247.

does internally as well as externally: internally through faith and other spiritual gifts, but externally by means of the gospel, by means of baptism and the Sacrament of the Altar.[80]

The Reign of God and the Church

Building upon the preceding treatment of covenant theology, mediation, and pneumatology, Lutheran theology has reservations about how Dupuis employs and applies his reign of God theology, specifically in terms of viewing adherents of other religions as joint members and joint builders of that reign. To the extent Dupuis overlooks the distinction between the "opposing, almost contradictory" elements of stipulations/sanctions and promises in Biblical covenants, to the extent he fails to appreciate the nature of Christ's mediation as centering on achieving reconciliation, to the extent he fails to appreciate the Gospel as a distinctive promise of God and the hiddenness of God as a distinctive contribution to interreligious dialogue, to that extent I find his proposal problematic. Lutherans employ a distinctive resource—the "two realms" principle—to critique Dupuis.

For Lutheran theology, justification and reconciliation through loving mercy constitute the core of the reign of God. As Martin Luther put it: "You should learn that Christian justification . . . is nothing but the forgiveness of sins, which means that God's kingdom is such a kingdom or sovereignty which *deals only with sins and with such overflowing grace as takes away all wrath* . . ."[81] Luther further spells out the Trinitarian dimensions of his view of the reign of God, centered on the redeeming work of Christ, in his explanation of the second petition of the Lord's Prayer, "May your kingdom come": "God [the Father] sent his Son, Christ our Lord, into the world to redeem and deliver us from the power of the devil, to bring us to himself, and to rule us as a king of righteousness, life, and salvation against sin, death, and an evil conscience. To this end he also gave his Holy Spirit to deliver this [kingdom] to us through his holy Word and to enlighten and strengthen us in faith by his power."[82]

---

80. Luther, *Luther's Works*, 37:366.

81. Martin Luther, quoted in *Day By Day We Magnify Thee*, 255, italics added for emphasis.

82. Kolb and Wengert, *Book of Concord*, 446.

Missio Shaped by Promissio

In a nutshell: the two-realms principle emphasizes the proper distinction between and proper realm for ethics and salvation. God interacts with the world "ambidextrously," with two different, although related, agendas carried out in two different realms. On the one hand, God's "left-hand" rule and agenda entails caring for His creation, including this-worldly blessings of peace, justice, and everything Luther includes under the fourth petition of the Lord's Prayer for daily bread, as spelled out in his *Large Catechism*. On the other hand, God's "right-hand" rule and agenda entails redeeming creation into a 'new creation,' forgiving mercy, and all other spiritual blessings through Christ. "One cares for creation, the other redeems it . . . One is ethics *coram hominibus* (before people), the other salvation *coram deo* (before God)."[83] Only the costly love of God, demonstrated on and mediated through the cross, can mediate (offer) the *peace* with God which undergirds our human work for peace, the *mercy* of God which motivates our human work for mercy, the *justice* of God which alone can justify and energize our human work for justice.

In other words: Luther locates matters of peace, justice, and creation care, matters often viewed as "values of the kingdom" and indicative of God's reign, in his explanation of the fourth petition of the Lord's Prayer (pertaining to daily bread), rather than in the second petition, "your kingdom come."[84] In contrast, the second petition focuses solely on the spiritual petition that God would "rule us as a king of righteousness, life, and salvation against sin, death, [the devil], and an evil conscience."[85] As one can see, the two-realms principle aims to safeguard the uniquely 'good' and 'new' aspects of Christ's work. In summary: what Dupuis deems "traces of grace," Lutheran theology views as civil righteousness: the capacity for goodness inherent in all people, exercised to a greater or lesser extent, but not as evidence of salvific grace at work.

In seeking to articulate a confessional Lutheran missional ecclesiology, Luther's reformational discovery of the Word of God as a means of grace, a powerful speech-act which creates the new reality it offers, serves as a guiding conviction. As Luther put it: "Where the Word is, there is the church."[86] Oswald Bayer captures the centrality of the Word for Luther's ecclesiology: "Everything that makes the church the church

---

83. Schroeder, "Second Look at the Gospel of Mark," 294.
84. Kolb and Wengert, *Book of Concord*, 450–51.
85. Ibid., 446.
86. Luther, quoted in Bayer, *Martin Luther's Theology*, 257.

is contained in the "Word": the *preaching* of the gospel, its visible and tangible form in the *sacrament*, and the *Holy Spirit* by the gospel, whose office is to sanctify. The Holy Spirit who is given in the Word is the one who makes a human being into a Christian and makes a gathering of Christians into the church. For this reason, where the Word of God is, there the church is."[87]

Given its articulation of the divine promise attached to God's Word as assisting that Word to accomplish its purposes, Isaiah 55:10-11 plays a central role in both Luther's and the Lutheran Confessions' ecclesiology: "For as the rain and snow come down from heaven, and do not return there until they have watered the earth, making it bring forth and sprout . . . , so is my Word that goes out from my mouth: it will not return to me empty, but will accomplish what I desire and achieve the purpose for which I sent it."[88] Such is the confessional Lutheran confidence in the power of God's creative, performative Word.

While Luther describes identifying characteristics of the church in several of his writings,[89] the tantalizing question for the purposes of engaging Dupuis is Luther's assertion that, not only is God's revelation hidden in the cross of Christ (his theology of the cross), but furthermore that "the church is hidden, the holy ones are kept out of sight."[90] The church, ultimately, is not an objectively verifiable reality, despite the visible signs of the Word and sacraments.[91] Oswald Bayer puts it well: "[While] the Word and the other identifying characteristics show *that* there is on earth, at all times, a holy Christian church and that this also remains . . . *where* its borders are to be found and *who* belongs to her in individual cases cannot be described perfectly . . ."[92] Belief in the "one, holy, catholic, apostolic" church is ultimately an article of faith due to many factors: human sinfulness, institutional sinfulness within the church, the

---

87. Bayer, *Martin Luther's Theology*, 257.

88. Isa 55:10-11.

89. These "marks of the Church" (*notae ecclesiae*) are are especially elaborated in two places: "On the Councils and the Churches" (1539) and "Against Hans Wurst" (1541), in *Luther's Works* 41:185-256. These marks include, but are not limited to, the following: preaching of the Gospel, the sacraments of baptism and the Lord's Supper, confession and absolution, the office of the ministry (to support the divine service of Word and sacrament), prayer and praise of God, Christian catechesis in teaching the Creed, etc., and Christian suffering and persecution on account of the gospel.

90. Luther, *Luther's Works*, 33:89.

91. Bayer, *Martin Luther's Theology*, 278.

92. Ibid.

oppositional work of Satan, and the nature of Christian life as simultaneously saint and sinner (*simul iustus et peccatur*), among others. The final victory of Christ, in and through the church, is an eschatological reality which "will be seen by all eyes only at the end of days. Only then will the church be hidden no longer."[93]

While Dupuis' Roman Catholic, inclusive pluralism elaborates a way to interpret "traces of grace and truth" in other religions as one of the hidden signs of Christ's saving presence in the world, among other signs, a confessional Lutheran model cannot go so far in specifying the grace of Christ. The reasons for this, as articulated in chapters 1 and 2, center on an understanding of the nature of the Gospel as a performative, external promise of God connected to visible means of grace, grace as the promise of mercy fulfilled in Christ, the nature of revelation as law and Gospel, and viewing the Spirit's work as illuminating and offering the benefits of Christ. Dupuis poses the issue clearly: regarding the saving power of Christ reaching other religions, "Does this take place solely through an invisible action of the glorified humanity which through his resurrection/glorification has become "transhistoric" . . . ? Or does [it] reach [them] through a certain 'mediation' of their own traditions?"[94] Confessional Lutheran convictions, while being unable to affirm the latter, qualify the former with an important proviso: "Yes, but not merely transhistoric; the power and mercy of Christ reaches them as the promise and benefits of Christ are offered through the Word in its various, concrete forms." In further addressing Dupuis' question, Robert Kolb, recalling Jesus' words from Luke 13, offers a valuable exhortation: "All your guesses and attempts at mastering the Holy Spirit's *modus operandi* will do you no good. Just turn to Jesus and listen to him, to his commission that sends you to preach, not to solve the mysteries of his way of gathering his chosen. Focus on the Lord of the church, not upon its ragged edges."[95] While Dupuis would not be satisfied with such self-imposed theological limits, confessional Lutherans would respond by reminding Dupuis of his own exhortation to theological humility which chapter 4 began with: not "to claim to describe or define the "how" and "in which way" of the essential relationship between the universal action of the Word—and

---

93. Ibid., 281.
94. Dupuis, *Christianity and the Religions*, 186.
95. Kolb, "The Church and Her Mission."

Mission Shaped by Promise

the Spirit—and the historical event of Jesus Christ."[96] A Lutheran model takes such humility with utter seriousness, and respectfully urges Dupuis to do likewise.

What does all this (the two realms principle, the church's hidden nature, and its centeredness upon the Word of God) imply for the church's ministry and mission, specifically in relating to the church's mission of proclamation and dialogue? While this question will be pursued more in-depth in chapter 6, the church's mission, filtered through the lens of the two-realms principle and grounded in the Gospel as promise, centers on the apostolic "ministry of reconciliation" (2 Cor 5:18). While the ministry of reconciling sinners to God is truly *missio Dei*, originating in and propelled by the Spirit, nevertheless it is "God [who] is making his appeal through us" (2 Cor 5:20). The God of mission makes this appeal for reconciliation precisely through such a humanly frail "ambassador of reconciliation" as the church (2 Cor 5:20). The church's authority, purpose, and role in mission comes, not from anything inherent in itself, but rather from the Gospel as "the power of God for the salvation of all who believe" (Rom 1:16). It is the "message of reconciliation" (2 Cor. 5:18, 19), the Gospel promise itself, which authorizes and impels the church to humbly, yet boldly, implore, invite, and urge others to "be reconciled to God" (2 Cor 5:20).[97] Such an apostolic ministry of reconciliation is truly "the ministry of the Spirit" (2 Cor 4:1), "the ministry of justification" (2 Cor 3:7–9), and, at its core, a proclamation of the *promissio Dei* centered on Christ crucified and risen. We now turn to a Lutheran theology of the cross, emphasizing the promise of divine faithfulness and mercy hidden in the apparent opposite of divine abandonment, wrath, and judgment. Martin Luther described encountering this God as an experience of the *deus absconditus*, the "hidden God," hidden precisely because his loving mercy is obscured.[98] Such a theology of the cross will serve as a critical bridge to religious pluralism as engaged through interreligious dialogue.

---

96. Dupuis, *Christianity and the Religions*, 162.
97. Bertram, *Time for Confessing*, 170.
98. Luther drew this term from Isa 45:5, "Truly you are a God who hides himself."

A THEOLOGY OF THE CROSS: GOD HIDDEN AND REVEALED

While Luther's theology is known as a theology of the Word of God and this project argues for its fruitfulness as such, specifically as a paradoxical tension between law and gospel, Luther is perhaps best known for his articulation and recovery of a theology of the cross. His classic expression of God's hiddenness in the cross, expressed in the Heidelberg Disputation of 1518, is worth quoting:

> *He deserves to be called a theologian . . . who comprehends the visible and manifest things of God, seen through suffering and the cross . . .* The "visible things of God" are placed in opposition to the invisible, namely, his human nature, weakness, and foolishness . . . Nor is it sufficient for anyone, and it does him no good, to recognize God in his glory and majesty, unless he recognizes him in the humility and shame of the cross . . . For this reason true theology and recognition of God are in the crucified Christ . . . He who does not know Christ does not know God hidden in suffering . . . God can be found only in suffering and the cross.[99]

Gerhard Ebeling echoes the centrality of a theology of the cross for Lutheran theology: "The knowledge of God which is given in Jesus Christ does not therefore constitute a particular item of doctrine which supplements a general knowledge of God, but is the beginning of all true knowledge of God and man . . . [It] points us towards God who came in the flesh and was therefore clothed in promises . . . and was thereby revealed."[100]

Four important theses concerning Luther's theology of the cross orient us to the relevance of this topic for my project.[101] First, a theology of the cross as a distinctive theology of revelation is indirect and concealed, discernible only by faith. Second, such knowledge of God is centered on and recognized in Jesus' cross and sufferings. Third, such revelation is a matter of faith, since faith alone recognizes and receives it

---

99. Luther, *Luther's Works*, 31:52–3. I would nuance Luther's assertion by affirming that, while, for Christians, God's loving mercy is most clearly manifested or concentrated in the cross, this certainly does not mean that God's gracious, merciful presence is exclusively limited to the cross. God may be found uniquely, but not solely, in the cross and in suffering.

100. Ebeling, *Luther*, 234.

101. McGrath, *Luther's Theology of the Cross*. I am indebted to McGrath, especially chapters 5 and 6, for his articulation of these insights.

as divine revelation. Lastly, God's "alien work" of judging human sin in the event of the cross (the Law) serves God's "proper work" of justifying and reconciling sinners (the Gospel). Such a theology of the cross is thoroughly paradoxical: "In Christ, God works in a paradoxical mode *sub contrariis*. His wisdom is hidden under folly, his strength under abject weakness. He gives life through death, righteousness to the unrighteous; he saves by judging and damning. The Hidden God is God incarnate, crucified, hidden in suffering."[102]

Having argued how a Lutheran theology of mercy as promise realized, utilizing the law-gospel distinction, preserves and articulates an economy of salvation, the notion of God's hiddenness (*deus absconditus*) articulated here will serve as a bridge between this theology of mercy and the broader context of religious pluralism. In other words: as a theology of promise and the performative Word of God, a confessional Lutheran proposal for mission is best able to establish a point of contact and dialogue with other religions when it seriously engages them through the category of God's hiddenness.[103] In doing so, such a Lutheran missiological proposal makes a distinctive contribution to interreligious dialogue, raises important questions for others and itself to consider, and opens itself up for genuine dialogue with and questioning from other religious traditions.

The hiddenness of God is a helpful category for navigating the ambiguity of natural human experience. It is a useful tool for Lutheran missiology in at least three ways: 1) it facilitates an intra-Christian approach toward religious pluralism, 2) connects Lutheran missiological discourse with the wider, theological/philosophical discourse, as well as 3) offers, in the Gospel, a hopeful word in the midst of ongoing distress and angst.

While all religions have hopeful words to say, they also wrestle with whether such words of "grace" will indeed be the final word. I wish to contend that the most important similarities and overlaps concerning human religious experience are best described, not by categories of being

---

102. Gerrish, "To the Unknown God," 268.

103. Given that divine hiddenness is most readily understood in monotheistic traditions such as Judaism and Islam, my project is most directly applicable to dialogue with these fellow "religions of the book." However, while non-theistic religions like Buddhism, Taoism, and Confucianism do not recognize a personal God whose hiddenness can be intelligibly discussed, I contend that this category may potentially be translated into the framework of these religions in a meaningful, intelligible manner. The theoretical and theological justification for such a claim, however, remains beyond the scope of this study.

Missio Shaped by Promissio

or existence (ontology or anthropology), but rather in nuanced, cultural-linguistic terms as the paradoxical relationship between divine wrath and promise, sin and grace, law and Gospel, human brokenness and divine healing. Because human religious experience *is* ambiguous, left to our own devices, we don't really quite know how to "read" or interpret nature. The "hidden God" whom nature ambiguously reveals requires unveiling, in and through the revelation in Christ, if humanity is to have a gracious relationship of trust with this God. As Edward Schroeder comments on the formulation, "There is grace, and there is grace," by Melanchthon, "the 'grace' we encounter in our daily experience of God's creation is something other than the 'grace' that comes in Jesus the Christ."[104]

While much remains hidden about God despite the revelation of the cross, and while adherents of other religions may be reluctant to consider a Christian theology of the cross as having any relevance to their experiences, a Christian stance toward dialogue on the topic of divine hiddenness and experiences of suffering seemingly cannot help but commend a theology of the cross as a relevant, even illuminating, resource to such a dialogue. Luther's emphatic claim, "The cross alone is our theology,"[105] directs us to focus our attention on God's paradoxical absence and presence, hiddenness and revelation, wrath and loving mercy, as those realities are conveyed in and through a theology of the cross.[106] To the extent that a theology of the cross is helpful in interpreting and applying the Gospel as promise, to that extent it is missiologically fruitful. While other religions and philosophical systems have their own strategies for dealing with questions of divine hiddenness and human suffering, Lutheran missiology would caution all such attempts to beware of the potential overstepping of their limitations.

104. Schroeder, "Encountering the Hidden God," 2.

105. Luther, *Luther's Works*, 25:287.

106. I am acutely aware of the immensely complex nature of issues related to the hiddenness and unknowability of God, apophatic and negative theologies, theology of the cross, and theodicy. While the limits of this study do not allow for more in-depth treatment of divine hiddenness and unknowability as they have been classically articulated by early Christian theologians as Gregory of Nyssa, Maximus the Confessor, Pseudo-Dionysius, and Meister Eckhardt, nor theologies of the cross of contemporary theologians such as Jürgen Moltmann, Eberhard Jüngel, John Stuart Hall, and others, my aim is very modest: simply to suggest how the hiddenness of God, interpreted within the framework of a theology of the cross, can serve as a missiologically fruitful topic for interreligious dialogue. Such a focus on the missiological implications of a theology of the cross in no way minimizes or negates an emphasis on a theology of the resurrection.

Christian theology has always affirmed, not only that certain things can and must be said about God's being, but also that, ultimately, the mystery of God's inner being is hidden, transcending human speech and categories: there is an "excess" to God's being and nature which no human language can fully capture. Reflecting on Luther's treatment of one prominent expression of the "hidden" or "unknown" God (Acts 17: 16–34) and other instances of God's hiddenness in Scripture, "Luther scholarship has gathered under the general rubric of 'the Hidden God' several different theological ideas."[107] The theme of God's incomprehensible hiddenness emerges very early in Luther's thought, as is evidenced in *Lectures on the Psalms* (1513–1516). Commenting on the notion of God's "hiding place" (Ps 18:11), Luther speaks of at least five places or modes whereby God is hidden: in the darkness of faith, in light inaccessible, in the mystery of incarnation, in the church and Mary, and in the Eucharist.[108] Robert Jenson further suggests three ways in which Luther's theology of God's hiddenness is relevant today: when God is viewed as hidden in creation (natural disasters, the harsh realities of the natural world, the sufferings and horrors of history, etc), in the cross of Jesus, and in faith.[109] While the differing strands in Luther's thought concerning the *deus absconditus* are expressed in such diverse terms as the revealed God (*deus revelatus*), God clothed in his Word (*deus indutus*), the "naked" God as God's terrifying inapproachability (*deus nudus*), the absolute God as God's unknowable immanence (*deus absolutus*), and the truly unknown and unknowable God (*deus ignotus*),[110] the broader, more important issue for the purposes of this project is to suggest how Jenson's threefold hiddenness of God (in creation, in the cross, and in Christian faith) correlates with Bayer's threefold distinction (of the law as accusing and pressuring, the Gospel as promising, and divine hiddenness as mystifying), and how both offer a promising, distinctively Lutheran approach to interreligious dialogue and religious pluralism. Having addressed the law/Gospel distinction in chapter 1 and divine hiddenness earlier in this project, we now turn to delineate significant, missiologically relevant aspects of the divine hiddenness in the cross.

---

107. Gerrish, "To the Unknown God," 265.
108. Luther, *Luther's Works*, 10:119–20.
109. Jenson, "Luther's Contemporary Theological Significance," 279–80.
110. Gerrish, "To the Unknown God," 267.

Missio Shaped by Promissio

Not only does the 'hiddenness of God' in the cross underscore the distinction between God's law and God's promise, I submit it also provides a better theological basis and springboard for interreligious dialogue than inclusive pluralism offers. Martin Luther, employing the hiddenness of God, commented in his explanation to the third article of the Apostles' Creed: "These articles of the Creed, therefore, divide and distinguish us Christians from all other people on earth. All who are outside the Christian church, whether heathen, Turks, Jews, or false Christians and hypocrites, even though they *believe in and worship only the one, true God,* nevertheless do not know what his attitude is toward them. They cannot be confident of his love and blessing . . . *for they do not have the Lord Christ,* and, besides, they are not illuminated or blessed by the gifts of the Holy Spirit."[111]

Emphasizing the possessive verb "have" throughout his explanation of the Creed, Luther makes the crucial distinction between having a natural, "first article" relationship with God, grounded in creation, versus having a saving, "second article" relationship with God through Jesus Christ. All people have the former relationship, by virtue of creation; only Christians can be confident of having the latter, by virtue of the proclaimed Gospel. As Melanchthon so eloquently expressed it: "To know [have] Christ is to know His benefits." Luther saw the gospel, defined specifically as God's revelation of mercy fulfilled in Jesus Christ, as adding something significantly "good" and "new" to what sinners otherwise, by nature, do not have.[112]

Therefore: a confessional Lutheran approach affirms that, while all people may worship the one true God, albeit anonymously, their worship, apart from Christ, lacks many important benefits, such as a consciousness of and confidence in God's benevolent attitude toward them, as well as the practical comfort arising from trusting the offer of divine, loving mercy in the cross. This distinction is meant to highlight and emphasize the crucial connection between the God one explicitly "has" and the benefits that God bestows. That is why Luther, commenting on the sailors in Jonah 1:5 ("All the sailors were afraid and each cried out to his own god."), asserts, "These men in the ship all know of God, but they have no sure God."[113] Oswald Bayer expresses the same insight in these

---

111. Kolb and Wengert, *Book of Concord*, 440, italics added for emphasis.
112. Schroeder, "Luther's Commentary on the Third Article," 7.
113. Bayer, *Theology the Lutheran Way*, 75.

terms: "The office of Christ is to make us certain of God."[114] This section introduces the potential fruitfulness of such a view of the "hiddenness of God" for approaching religious pluralism; chapter 6 will then further articulate how I utilize the hiddenness of God as a fruitful category for interreligious dialogue.

While Luther speaks both of God's hiddenness within the revelation in Scripture and Christ and of divine hiddenness outside of that revelation, his clear preference is to focus on the former. Christian theology as a whole has been uncomfortable or reluctant to delve into the hidden God behind/outside Christian revelation for at least three reasons: it seems to contradict the hiddenness of God revealed in Scripture and the cross, it implies knowledge of God outside of Christ, and it converges upon the problematic doctrine of divine election or predestination.[115]

A classic place to turn for understanding Luther's treatment of the theme of God's hiddenness is his *On the Bondage of the Will*, in which both kinds of divine hiddenness (within Christian revelation and outside or beyond it) are found. Luther's main concern throughout this treatise is to affirm and protect God's sole, gracious agency in the matter of salvation. He adamantly affirms God's predestinating will as the sole source of salvation; if it were otherwise, the assurance of our salvation would be lost; only the knowledge that God has taken salvation out of our hands and placed it in his hands alone preserves such assurance.

In addition to the concern for preserving God's gracious prevenience, Luther emphasizes a double relation of God to the world: *outside of* Christ, God is absolutely free, majestic, and awesomely mysterious; *in* Christ, God has freely chosen to bind himself to the promise of the Gospel. Brian Gerrish aptly summarizes the theological dilemma Luther's approach leads to:

> Luther's argument ends up by jeopardizing his own theological starting point. He insisted at the outset that he proclaimed nothing but Christ crucified. But one of the doctrines that "Christ crucified brings with him" finally forces us to acknowledge an inscrutable will of God behind and beyond the figure of Christ. We began from God's revelation in Christ as the only secure basis for a knowledge of God's gracious will; we end up discovering that, after all, God wills many things which he does not show us in his Word. And the problem is not merely that there

---

114. Ibid.
115. Gerrish, "To the Unknown God," 268.

is a hidden will *alongside* of the revealed will of God, but that the two are found to be in apparent *contradiction*.[116]

Gerrish pinpoints the fundamental tension which a confessional Lutheran missiology insists must be at the center of any missiological proposal, often missing in contemporary missiology, and which, I submit, identifies the problematic which a "duplex" *missio Dei* seeks to address: the hidden will of God (the wrath of God, manifested in God's law and divine hiddenness in creation) seems to contradict and defeat God's revealed, gracious will to save. A Christian missiology must address this crucial dilemma: how can it be resolved? While the Rahner-Dupuis approach seemingly dissolves the paradox by largely ignoring the hidden will of wrath (God's law), my proposal directs us to search for resolution in the homiletical distinction between "God proclaimed" and "God not proclaimed," to which we now turn.

I wish to illustrate a confessional Lutheran resolution of the enduring tension between God's revealed will and hidden will by means of a concrete example, one which featured prominently in Luther's debate with Erasmus, namely how to interpret Ezek 18:23. In this passage, God says, "I desire not the death of the sinner, but rather that he should turn and live." Few passages provide a clearer example of God's hidden will seemingly contradicting God's revealed will. This text provides an excellent case study for illustrating Luther's strategy to approaching the question of God's hiddenness, namely that of applying the distinction between law and Gospel, of moving from abstract theology to proclamation, and ultimately of employing the distinction between "God not proclaimed" and "God proclaimed."

We begin with analyzing Erasmus' interpretation of this passage, followed by Luther's critique of that interpretation and his alternative analysis and interpretation. In doing so, I believe the distinctive emphases of Luther's approach to God's hiddenness will emerge.

Forde suggests Erasmus understood Ezek 18:23 as a statement of general, universal, theological truth about God. If God, in fact, does not desire the death of any sinner, then the only way to account for the reality of such deaths is that human free will thwarts God's loving will. How would such an interpretation impact the preaching of this text? It would

---

116. Ibid., 273.

shape the proclamation to be something like this: if you are a sinner and do not wish to die, use your free will properly, repent, and turn to God.[117]

Luther's critique of Erasmus' interpretation charged the latter with fundamentally misunderstanding the genre of the text, viewing it as abstract theology rather than a prophetic word of proclamation. That initial mistake led to further mistakes of turning a comforting word of Gospel promise ("God does not desire the death of a sinner.") into a burdensome word of law ("If you want to avoid death, stop sinning and turn to God."), of confusing the "God not preached" with the "God preached." If the text were about God not desiring the death of any individual, then it could not be a general statement about God (because God permits deaths of all kind), but rather must be homiletical instruction for the prophet on what to preach to a people in distress.[118]

While Luther argued that Erasmus' mistake was confusing the proper distinction between law and Gospel (by taking the statement to be abstract theology), the further, inevitable question would be about that very distinction. Even if you grant Luther that this text is a Gospel word of comfort rather than an exhortation of law and prescription for avoiding death, the crucial question still remains: Why are some converted to faith by hearing the Gospel, while others are not? Why some and not others? This brings us back to the question of election/predestination and the hidden, divine will as the flip side of that question.[119] The problem is *not* the hiddenness of the fact of predestination; that assertion has clear, scriptural warrant. What remains hidden, what *is* unknown, is the reason *why* God would work that way.

Luther's answer is that in this question, and in the hidden will of God it presumes, all theology reaches a dead end and is reduced to utter, reverent silence. As Forde notes, "*This God wills not to be known . . . and so will not be known*"[120] Luther's classic description of this hidden, frustratingly elusive God is worth quoting:

> God must therefore be left to himself in his own majesty, for in this regard we have nothing to do with him, nor has he willed that we should have anything to do with him. But we have something to do with him insofar as he is clothed and set forth in

117. Forde, *Preached God*, 50.
118. Ibid..
119. Gerrish, "To the Unknown God," 272.
120. Forde, *Preached God*, 51.

his Word, through which he offers himself to us and which is the beauty and glory with which the psalmist celebrates him as being clothed (the clothed God!). In this regard we say, the good God does not deplore the death of his people which he works in them, but he deplores the death which he finds in his people and desires to remove from them. For it is this that God as he is preached is concerned with, namely, that sin and death should be taken away and we should be saved. For "he sent his word and healed them" [Ps 107:20]. But God hidden in his majesty neither deplores nor takes away death, but works life, death, and all in all. For there he has not bound himself by his word, but has kept himself free over all things.[121]

The implication of this last sentence is disturbingly unsettling for any theological system which seeks to marginalize the consequences of sin and manage God: the hidden God is one who, not only will not be managed, but inexplicably allows the death of his creatures. Faced with the tension between this hidden God and the revealed God of loving mercy in Jesus Christ, Luther urged people to flee from the former to the latter.

What might be some of the implications of such a view of the hiddenness of God for Christian theology? At least four implications emerge. First, the triune God is truly, but never fully or comprehensively, to be identified with the crucified Christ. There is much about God which we do not know and which will remain hidden, despite the revelation of God in Christ. In other words: "The image of God does not, after all, *fully* coincide with the picture of Jesus."[122] Second, to counterbalance the tendency of emphasizing God's power and presence as gracious by definition, God's hiddenness accentuates the destructive and awe-inspiring dimensions of God's power. Creative and powerful? Yes. Benevolent and gracious? Not necessarily. Third, the hidden God drives us *to* the revealed Word of God in Scripture and Christ because the hidden will offers scant guidance or comfort. Fourth, Christian theology requires further, nuanced sophistication, realizing that it always lives and breathes on a continuum, between the paradoxical tensions of the mysterious, unknown God (God hidden in and beyond revelation) and God revealed in the crucified Christ.[123] What Christian theology might learn from dialogue

---

121. Luther, *Luther's Works*, 33:140.
122. Gerrish, "To the Unknown God," 276.
123. Ibid., 278.

with other religions concerning God's hiddenness and presence might inductively add to such nuanced appreciation.

CONCLUSION

Having offered a constructive, critical evaluation of Dupuis' proposal from a Lutheran perspective, how might Dupuis counteract my concerns? In what ways does his inclusive pluralism challenge a Lutheran "inclusive exclusivity" to go further than it does? While it is always hazardous to venture to speak for another, I believe Dupuis poses several challenges for an emergent, confessionally Lutheran missiology. First, having articulated a robust pneumatology and Spirit Christology, Dupuis' model challenges a Lutheran one to develop a more robust pneumatology and Spirit Christology, one which seeks to articulate how the Spirit works universally, beyond the performative Word of God. As Pope John Paul II states, "The Gospel contains both Christological and pneumatological aspects."[124] How might Lutheran missiology express the Gospel's pneumatological aspect more rigorously? How might Lutheran missiology articulate, more robustly, the relationship between the Word and the Spirit? Is the law/Gospel distinction the only valid way of conceiving that relationship? What more might the Spirit be doing besides bearing witness to Christ?

Second, Dupuis' model challenges my model to identify more clearly and elaborate more fully how God's loving grace, and not simply hiddenness or pressure applied through law, is operative in other religions. In other words: how might confessional Lutheran missiology assess more positively what God is doing in and through the other religions? How can those other traditions enrich Lutheran theology's understanding of God? How might the "traces of grace and truth" in other religions be understood more positively? This would be the hoped for result of complementing my largely deductive approach with the inductive method of actual encounter and dialogue with the religiously other.

Third, what resources could Lutheran missiology employ in constructing a theology of religions beyond the sources of Scripture, the Lutheran Confessions, and Luther's theology? How might Lutheran missiology be open to true, positive revelation of God's being and nature beyond the bounds of Christian revelation, specifically through the sacred

---

124. Pope John Paul II, *Dominum et Vivificantem*, no. 53.

texts, traditions, and experiences of other religions? All these points challenge confessional Lutheran missiology to press further than it has or is willing to articulate *how* God's universal, salvific will might be at work beyond the bounds of the proclaimed Word of God. We now turn to identify how a Lutheran proposal utilizes the hiddenness of the triune God to dialectically relate proclamation and dialogue.

6

Proclamation and Interreligious Dialogue

A Dialectical Relationship

"No peace among the nations without peace among the religions. And no peace among the religions without dialogue between the religions."[1] In such stark terms, Hans Küng portrays the urgency of interreligious dialogue: what is at stake is world peace and the very survival of our planet. In our increasingly interconnected world and age of global terrorism, "the possibility for understanding across religious difference is held up as an admirable goal."[2] While interreligious dialogue may indeed be necessary for fostering world peace and thwarting the growth of religiously inspired violence and terrorism, and while it is an increasingly popular and theologically fruitful field, what is a methodologically responsible framework for engaging in dialogue? What presuppositions and conditions are necessary for proceeding? In terms of my nuanced appropriation of the cultural-linguistic model, I will be cautioning us to mostly expect abiding differences between religions as well as modest goals for and results from dialogue.

We have now arrived at the culmination of this project: how might a confessional Lutheran missiology engage the contemporary scene of religious pluralism? What principles and convictions shape its approach to the religious other? What practical implications does my "*missio* shaped by *promissio*" proposal have for approaching other faiths? What unsettled

1. Küng, Speech given at the University of San Diego, undetermined date.
2. Hill-Fletcher, "As Long as We Wonder," 531.

questions and issues merit further investigation and research? This chapter will unfold in the following sections: definition of key terms, models for relating proclamation and dialogue, a methodological framework for engaging in genuine dialogue, a confessional Lutheran approach to proclamation and dialogue, Dupuis on proclamation and dialogue, and concluding reflections.

DEFINITION OF TERMS

It is necessary, for the sake of precision, to define key terms: what is meant by evangelizing mission, dialogue, and proclamation? As in previous chapters, Jacques Dupuis will continue to serve as my specific conversation partner, and his definitions of these terms will serve as a basis for discussion. For Dupuis, the Church's evangelizing mission, broadly construed, is a single, complex reality embracing five aspects: 1) the witness of individual Christians to their faith, 2) social development aimed at promoting human justice and dignity, 3) liturgical life and practice, 4) interreligious dialogue aiming at a mutual growth toward divine truth, and 5) Gospel proclamation of salvation in and through Jesus Christ.[3]

The second key term, dialogue, Dupuis understands to include "all positive and constructive interreligious relations with individuals and communities of other faiths which are directed at mutual understanding and enrichment . . . in obedience to truth and respect for freedom."[4] As Dupuis summarizes documents of the Pontifical Council for Interreligious Dialogue, the term "dialogue" is itself a complex reality, including at least the following four dimensions: 1) a dialogue of shared life experiences, 2) dialogue centered on common work toward promoting human dignity and social justice, 3) an intellectual dialogue focusing on theological and doctrinal concepts, and 4) a spiritual dialogue of joint prayer, contemplation, and worship.[5]

Finally, the term proclamation denotes "the communication of the gospel message, the mystery of salvation realized by God for all in Jesus Christ by the power of the Spirit. It is an invitation to a commitment of faith in Jesus Christ and to entry through baptism into the community

---

3. Dupuis, *Christianity and the Religions*, 220.

4. Pontifical Council for Interreligious Dialogue and the Congregation for the Evangelization of Peoples, *Redemption and Dialogue*, 96.

5. Dupuis, *Christianity and the Religions*, 220.

of believers which is the Church . . . [It] is the foundation, center, and summit of evangelization."[6]

MODELS FOR RELATING PROCLAMATION AND DIALOGUE

In addressing the possibilities of relating proclamation and interreligious dialogue, Volker Küster identifies four possible models.[7] The two positions at the ends of the spectrum involve either dialogue substituting for proclamation, on the one hand, or proclamation instrumentally using dialogue as a means of conversion, on the other hand. A third, mediating approach involves the conscious attempt to keep proclamation and dialogue structurally separate. This approach is exemplified by the World Council of Churches (WCC) and the Vatican, with their separate units for mission and evangelization (WCC)/the Congregation for the Evangelization of Peoples (Vatican), and the subunit for interreligious dialogue (WCC)/the Pontifical Council for Interreligious Dialogue (Vatican), respectively.

A fourth alternative, overcoming the deficiencies of the previous three models, explores the possibility of relating proclamation and dialogue dialectically. Within this model, Küster describes the "double command" of interreligious dialogue: "1) to try to understand the religious other in a way that the other can recognize himself or herself in my perception; 2) to give witness and to share the best of one's own faith with each other."[8] Küster further articulates a key component of genuine interreligious dialogue, one which my confessional Lutheran approach readily affirms: "As a matter of fact, there can be no real dialogue without witness. Only someone who has a religious conviction and is willing to share it not only by questioning the other but also by allowing himself to be questioned gives due respect to the religious conviction of the other and can be taken seriously."[9] While my approach, due to its largely deductive nature, will emphasize the second command mentioned above, this does not diminish its sincere desire to understand the religious other on its own terms (the first command). My positing of the hiddenness of God

6. Burrows, *Redemption and Dialogue*, 97.
7. Küster, "Toward an Intercultural Theology," 171–84.
8. Ibid., 179.
9. Ibid.

as a means for interreligiously accessing a broad range of shared experience is certainly open to being corrected, nuanced, and even challenged through the inductive practice of actual dialogue.

This chapter will articulate a dialectical relationship between Gospel proclamation and interreligious dialogue, one which commends the category of "divine hiddenness" as a promising avenue for dialogue while remaining open to accurately hearing the deepest witness of the religious other. Such an approach will also simultaneously draw from and engage current, prevailing insights from the Roman Catholic tradition on this topic.[10] I will analyze and draw upon Dupuis' approach of relating proclamation and interreligious dialogue as it is explicated in two places: Dupuis' commentary on the document *Dialogue and Proclamation* and chapter 9 of his *Christianity and the Religions*, entitled "Interreligious Dialogue in a Pluralistic Society".[11]

A METHODOLOGICAL FRAMEWORK FOR ENGAGING IN DIALOGUE

What are possible features of a responsible, defensible, and theologically fruitful framework for engaging in dialogue? Before describing such features, I will highlight several contemporary challenges to dialogue.

As Catherine Cornille observes, "If dialogue presupposes some degree of interconnection or commonality, it has become far from evident that such common ground exists, or that religions agree on a common ground or goal for dialogue."[12] Whereas the ultimate, common unity of all religions has been argued on the basis of mystical unity (by Sarvepalli Radhakrishnan, William James, etc.) and on philosophical grounds (by John Hick, Paul Knitter, etc.), George Lindbeck's cultural-linguistic model, viewing the religions as "incommensurable" and "untranslatable" systems, questions the validity and very possibility of a common foundation

---

10. The Roman Catholic debate and discussion is laid out in *Redemption and Dialogue: Reading Redemptoris Missio and Dialogue and Proclamation*.

11. As an official publication of the Pontifical Council for Interreligious Dialogue and the Congregation for the Evangelization of Peoples articulating current Roman Catholic teaching on the subject, the document *Dialogue and Proclamation* will serve as a helpful context for Dupuis' commentary. Given Dupuis' role as a theological advisor in the process which produced *Dialogue and Proclamation*, it is all the more relevant to include it in this discussion.

12. Cornille, *Im-possibility of Interreligious Dialogue*, 212.

for dialogue. As Lindbeck states: "The gravest objection to the approach we are adopting is that it makes interreligious dialogue more difficult. Conversation between religions is pluralized or balkanized when they are seen as mutually untranslatable. Not only do they no longer share a common theme, such as salvation, but the shared universe of discourse forged to discuss that theme disintegrates . . . Those for whom conversation is key to solving interreligious problems are likely to be disappointed."[13] As I indicated in my earlier section on methodology (see introduction), I believe there are ways to address Lindbeck's concern that allow for a dialogue centered on the broad, shared experience of "divine hiddenness."

Besides a lack of consensus on a common basis for dialogue, other contemporary challenges to dialogue include disagreements regarding the necessary conditions for dialogue (see below), appropriate topics and partners for dialogue, proper goals of dialogue, as well as attitudinal challenges.[14] In terms of the latter, viewing dialogue with suspicion, as a monologue (as a vehicle for proselytizing), or as unnecessary are common obstacles. Not only are popular attitudes of suspicion grounded in fear of the unknown or fear of how one might be changed by dialogue, but philosophical arguments for replacing dialogue with "mutual suspicion" have also been made.[15] Viewing dialogue as an unnecessary luxury entails practicing it "as a form of mutual edification or as an expression of sympathy and solidarity, but without any essential effect on the inner reality of religions."[16]

In light of these and other challenges, is the task of dialogue a fruitless, impossible endeavor doomed to failure and frustration? Whereas for much of Christian history interreligious dialogue was viewed as unnecessary and subsumed under the primary task of Gospel proclamation, in our postmodern context is the very possibility of dialogue and interreligious understanding threatened by radical difference and epistemological limitations? While Jeannine Hill-Fletcher convincingly offers the category of "wonder" as ethically and theologically fruitful in breaking

---

13. Lindbeck, "Gospel's Uniqueness," 427.

14. In terms of topics or people who might be excluded from the dialogue process, Martin Forward wonders in *Interreligious Dialogue*, 83: "Should such dialogue avoid contentious theological issues and concentrate instead on matters of social justice, ethical endeavor, and the like? Are there people with whom one ought not to dialogue?"

15. See, for example, Milbank, "End of Dialogue," in D'Costa, ed., *Christian Uniqueness Reconsidered*, 174–91.

16. Cornille, *Im-possibility of Interreligious Dialogue*, 213.

the impasse created by the "impossibility of dialogue," are we limited to inductively appreciating and incorporating the concerns of others, or does Christian faith have something compelling to offer at the dialogue table which might elicit similar wonder from its dialogue partners?[17] In the remainder of this chapter, I will delineate my argument for just such a proposal, utilizing the hiddenness of God within the context of a theology of the cross.

I believe the path toward, rather than away from, genuine dialogue is constituted by a stance which exhibits and delicately navigates openness in commitment, normativity and difference, empathy and alterity, similarity and difference, a sense of interconnection and respect for distinctive difference, and doctrinal or epistemic humility combined with commitment to a particular tradition.[18] Various theological responses have attempted to address this balance. For example, Dupuis and Gavin D'Costa navigate these factors by means of a robust pneumatology, while Mark Heim does so by appealing to the inner dynamics of the Trinity.

A confessional Lutheran approach, on the other hand, seeks to navigate this balance by nuanced appropriation of Lindbeck's cultural-linguistic model. Five implications follow from doing so. First, expect deep, abiding, irresolvable differences between the religions. Second, modest expectations and goals will be set for dialogue. Third, centering dialogue on the common experience of "divine hiddenness" should bear promising fruit. Fourth, commitment to the confessional Lutheran tradition will serve as both a point of departure and a place of return. Finally, the intelligibility and plausibility of "confessional ultimate reality" is affirmed with critical awareness.[19] Practically speaking this means that the fact "that all individuals engaged in dialogue between religions judge the truth of the other . . . on the basis of their own particular worldview

---

17. Hill-Fletcher, "As Long as We Wonder," 549–54.

18. For a nuanced treatment of these complex issues, see Cornille, *Im-possibility of Interreligious Dialogue*.

19. Catherine Cornille further explains what is meant by "confessional ultimate reality": "The natural tendency of any religious tradition is to situate the origin or basis for interconnection between religions in their own particular conception of ultimate reality. Religions indeed presuppose that the fullness of truth is concentrated in their own conception of ultimate reality and that whatever form or degree of truth is found elsewhere will be derived from or oriented toward this truth . . . From the point of view of the believer—and this is the point of view that matters in dialogue—there is no ultimate reality higher than the one addressed within one's own religious tradition . . ." (*Im-possibility of Interreligious Dialogue*, 127–8).

and norms . . . becomes a matter of hermeneutical necessity rather than theological triumph."[20]

A pluralist emphasis on the equality of all religions as a basis for dialogue sounds appealing and is a sober reminder of how attitudes of religious superiority have sometimes led to disastrous consequences. John Hick and Paul Knitter, for example, in their desire to establish a level playing field for dialogue, "have come to either downplay or reinterpret Christian claims to uniqueness and superiority."[21] Despite its role in raising our consciousness of how various forms of prejudice and illegitimate uses of power have distorted interreligious dialogue in the past, the critical question remains "whether such respect and recognition necessarily requires affirmation of the religious equivalence or equal truth of all religions, and whether such notion of equality is even coherent or possible in the context of a dialogue between religions."[22] In contrast to the pluralism of Hick, Knitter, and others, I agree with Paul Griffiths on the necessity of letting the religious traditions voice their own strong, normative truth claims. Cornille states it well: while the nature of religious commitment seems to "logically preclude affirmation of the equal truth of alternate religious worldviews . . . [S]uch claims to uniqueness and truth form the very content of the dialogue . . . It is in the meeting between strong convictions that dialogue takes place."[23] Wolfhart Pannenberg, among others, has forcefully argued this point.[24] While both Dupuis and Langdon Gilkey seek to recognize the nature of religious commitment (in terms of internal logic and inner coherence) with their categories of "asymmetrical complementarity" and "relative absoluteness," respectively, I do not find their claims compelling.

Building on what has come before, I agree with Cornille in rejecting two conditions which are neither necessary nor foundational to genuine dialogue. First, I affirm "the impossibility of reconciling religious commitment with a recognition of the radical equality of religions." Second, "to require openness to the possibility of conversion as a condition for dialogue may be both unrealistic and unnecessarily limiting."[25]

20. Cornille, *Im-possibility of Interreligious Dialogue*, 79.
21. Ibid., 85.
22. Ibid., 86.
23. Ibid., 87.
24. Pannenberg, "Religious Pluralism and Conflicting Truth Claims," 96–106.
25. Cornille, *Im-possibility of Interreligious Dialogue*, 88–90.

Before further delineating how I utilize my Lutheran tradition, we turn to address one more plank in my methodological framework, namely necessary conditions for genuine dialogue. Cornille has identified five conditions as foundational for dialogue: doctrinal or epistemic humility, commitment to a particular tradition, interconnection, empathy, and hospitality. While recognizing the broad scope of these conditions as practical habits and stances, for the purposes of this study, I will show how doctrinal/epistemic humility can indeed be combined with a commitment to the confessional Lutheran tradition. I will first offer four conditions I believe are foundational for dialogue, followed by a discussion of how commitment to a particular tradition facilitates such dialogue.

Necessary Conditions for Genuine Dialogue

Which conditions are truly indispensable and necessary for a genuine dialogue to take place? I propose four conditions as absolutely necessary. First, a genuine dialogue requires "a recognition of the presence of elements of genuine truth and value in the other religion and of the equal dignity and religious integrity of the partner in dialogue."[26] As John Cobb puts it, "The issue is not whether one holds some truth as absolute, but whether one considers oneself to be in possession of all truth worth having."[27] Next, an "openness to change, while preserving the integrity and truth of one's own fundamental religious convictions," is indispensible.[28] Third, genuine dialogue is undergirded and motivated by a sincere desire and attempt to understand the plausibility and internal coherence of the religious other. Finally, a solid anchoring within a particular tradition serves as an asset to facilitate dialogue.[29] Cumulatively, these four conditions lead to a dialectical relating of proclamation and dialogue in a stance of bold humility. Cornille captures this dialectical nature of genuine dialogue well: "[A]ll authentic dialogue necessarily contains a missionary and apologetic dimension. The fullness of dialogue may be regarded as a form of mutual proclamation in which participants alternately adopt the roles of missionary and seeker. While seemingly

---

26. Ibid., 88.
27. Cobb, "Dialogue," 82.
28. Cornille, *Im-possibility of Interreligious Dialogue*, 92.
29. Ibid., 94.

contradictory, these roles may coexist in a religious attitude capable of balancing humility and conviction."[30]

Tradition as a Point of Departure and Point of Return

As I have argued in this project, I am convinced that certain core treasures of Luther's theology and the confessional Lutheran tradition are relevant to and helpful in facilitating genuine dialogue. These include understanding the Gospel as promise of God, the law/Gospel distinction, and a theology of the cross utilizing God's hiddenness. Since I have repeatedly emphasized the confessionally Lutheran nature of these claims and their origin in the confessional Lutheran tradition (in terms of Luther's writings and the Lutheran Confessions), on what basis can these gifts of the Lutheran tradition be offered, not only as ecumenical gifts, but also as gifts to the interreligious discussion? William E. Lesher expresses this intra-Lutheran struggle articulately, "What does our faith community believe about people of other faiths? What gifts do we have to contribute? What gifts might we receive? What obstacles prevent us from participation in interreligious engagements? What compels us to reach out?"[31] In other words: how might the confessional Lutheran tradition serve simultaneously as a point of departure and point of return in the process of interreligious dialogue?

A CONFESSIONAL LUTHERAN APPROACH TO RELATING PROCLAMATION AND DIALOGUE

In considering the Church's mission broadly construed, how might a confessional Lutheran missiology dialectically relate proclamation and dialogue? The underlying logic of this project has been the following: if the Gospel itself should be understood as a promise of God, and if the nature of the Gospel should direct and guide the nature of Christian mission, then mission should also be illumined by promise. Thus, "*promissio* is the secret of *missio*."[32]

Building especially on chapters 1, 2, and 5, a confessional Lutheran missiology offers the categories of "promise" and "hiddenness God"

30. Ibid., 71–72.
31. Lesher, "Intra-Lutheran Perspective on the Interreligious Movement," 208.
32. Bertram, "Doing Theology in Relation to Mission," 41.

(*deus absconditus*) as fruitful contributions to and promising avenues for exploration within interreligious dialogue. Bayer's contention that the law/Gospel distinction undergirds and propels Lutheran missiology to engage religious pluralism specifically through the category of divine hiddenness will now be further explicated. The hiddenness of God, as I will argue momentarily, serves as a bridge between the confessional Lutheran tradition and the reality of religious pluralism, as a touchstone interrelating various themes of this project thus far: law, Gospel, grace, faith, and *missio Dei*.

The following correlation clarifies the contours of a confessional Lutheran strategy: while "promise" should be the central content of Gospel proclamation, "divine hiddenness" is a valuable resource illuminating interreligious dialogue. Let me be crystal clear about what I am and am not saying. I *am* claiming that the categories of "promise" and "divine hiddenness," for reasons I have already elaborated, are uniquely Lutheran contributions to the missiological and interreligious discussion. This is *not* to say that "promise" cannot be utilized in interreligious dialogue, nor that the Christian stance to such dialogue is triumphalistically one of bringing the light of Christ to an otherwise "darkened" conversation, nor that such dialogue is actually, at the end of the day, subsumed under Christian proclamation or in service of conversion to Christianity. Instead, as Dupuis notes, dialogue is an important and essential aspect of Christian mission *on its own terms*, gifting its participants with a simultaneous enrichment of and challenge to their own faith.[33]

As noted in chapters 4 and 5, Dupuis' model is univocal in its treatment of grace and approach to Christian mission. While implicitly, sometimes even unreflectively, building upon the nature/grace paradigm, it "sees God's mission to be all the good things God is doing in and for the world, with Jesus the Christ as God's grand finale in that mission. Christians are thus called to 'join in God's mission' with its accents on peace, justice, wholeness of human life, and care for the environment—along with salvation for sinners."[34] Such an approach, while not completely ignoring the necessity of Gospel proclamation or explicit faith in Jesus Christ, relegates such proclamation and faith to one item among many others. This leads to a strategy of seeking out and identifying "traces of grace and truth" already present in a given context before the Christian

---

33. Dupuis, *Christianity and the Religions*, 232–5.
34. Schroeder, "Using Luther's Concept of *Deus absconditus*," 2.

Gospel is explicitly proclaimed or introduced. The nature of Christian mission then becomes connecting and correlating the explicitly Christian revelation of God's grace in Christ to the divine "grace" already present in that context. Such mission does indeed bring something new: a new awareness and appreciation of what people already possess, to a greater or lesser extent, but not something qualitatively new.

In sharp contrast, a confessional Lutheran model, employing the law/Gospel distinction for interpreting Scripture and the two realms principle for discerning divine action in the world (see chapter 5), insists that such an approach is insufficiently nuanced. While readily affirming God's universal presence and action, it offers the question, "Which God is already at work in a given context: God hidden or God revealed?" as a more helpful diagnostic tool for what God may be doing in a given context.

This distinction between the hidden God (*deus absconditus*) and revealed God (*deus revelatus*), for Luther, is firmly grounded in his distinction between two realms: God's care for and preservation of creation, on the one hand, and God's mercy and forgiveness in and through Jesus Christ, on the other hand. Luther saw God's various gifts and blessings in creation as distinctly different in quality from God's gifts and blessings in Christ. The first and second articles of the Creed are distinct and offer different connections to God. Before proceeding further, it is helpful to let Luther describe the difference between these divine gifts, blessings, and works in his own words. Luther views the gifts and blessings of creation in these terms: "[God] has given me and constantly sustains my body, soul, and life, my members great and small, all my senses, my reason and understanding, and the like; my food and drink, clothing, nourishment . . . he makes all creation help provide the benefits and necessities of life . . . Moreover, he gives all physical and temporal blessings—good government, peace, security . . . [I]t inevitably follows that we are in duty bound to love, praise, and thank him without ceasing."[35]

In sharp contrast to such gifts and blessings of creation, Luther describes the divine gifts offered in and through Jesus Christ: "Here . . . we see what we have from God over and above the temporal goods mentioned above . . . It means that he [Jesus Christ] has redeemed and released me from sin, from the devil, from death, and from all misfortune . . . [H]e who has brought us back from the devil to God, from death to

---

35. Kolb and Wengert, *Book of Concord*, 432-3.

Proclamation and Interreligious Dialogue

life, from sin to righteousness, and keeps us there."[36] The created world, fallen through sin, is a qualitatively different realm from God's "new creation" in Christ, and God has two related, but distinct, strategies for managing each: creation care and preservation versus forgiving, reconciling mercy in Christ. Whereas Rahner and Dupuis blur and do not recognize this distinction, viewing saving grace as present in both realms, it is a crucial one for a Lutheran approach to other religions.

While Luther used the term "hiddenness of God" to express various dimensions of divine illusiveness,[37] two meanings of *deus absconditus* are particularly relevant for my argument here. First, what is "hidden" beyond and indiscernible among God's manifold blessings within creation is God's mercy and favor toward sinners. What gets revealed in and through Christ is not general divine benevolence or goodwill, but rather something very specific: God as merciful on account of the crucified and risen Christ. Second, not only does God's mercy in Christ require revealing, but this mercy is further hidden or "'covered' under what looks like the opposite." God's mercy is hidden in the paradox, shame, and defeat of Christ crucified, in the God who is "incarnate, crucified, hidden in suffering."[38] I will thus be using "hiddenness of God" as a technical, not pejorative, term referring to God's work and activity in the world apart from Christ.

In order to clarify the remainder of my argument, I reintroduce a key quote from Luther employing the hiddenness of God, namely his explanation to the third article of the Apostles' Creed. Luther's understanding of God's two realms, reflected in the first and second articles, and differing operations in each qualify and shape his view of the religious others anonymously, inclusively worshipping the one true God:

> These articles of the Creed, therefore, divide and distinguish us Christians from all other people on earth. All who are outside the Christian Church, whether heathen, Turks, Jews, or false Christians and hypocrites, even though they *believe in and worship only the one, true God*, nevertheless do not know what his attitude is toward them. They cannot be confident of his love and blessing . . . *for they do not have the Lord Christ*, and,

---

36. Ibid., 434.
37. Gerrish, "To the Unknown God," 267.
38. Ibid., 268.

besides, they are not illuminated or blessed by the gifts of the Holy Spirit.[39]

Unpacking the theological implications of this statement and based on what has already been said, we are now better positioned to formulate some confessional Lutheran principles for engaging adherents of other religions. First, all religious people of goodwill potentially believe in and worship the one, true God. Second, God is actively, universally present in the lived experience of people, "since what may be known about God is plain to them, because God has made it plain to them."[40] Genuine, natural knowledge of God is available through the created order. Third, such people have encountered *deus absconditus*, God at work in the world apart from Christ, rather than *deus revelatus*, God revealed in Christ.[41] Fourth, as previously argued, the experience of God's blessings and gifts in creation, while described as "the hiddenness of God," is positive yet incomplete:

> Our common human experience of *deus absconditus* is not all gloom and doom. It includes all the gifts of creation that make human life possible and even enjoyable . . . But there always comes a "but." "But" none of those good gifts suffice to get sinners forgiven, to remedy the . . . [for all of which I am already in debt to God] . . . God's gifts of creation are gifts that obligate us receivers to "thank and to praise, to serve and obey him. This is most certainly true." And where is there one human who is "paid up" in fulfilling these obligations?[42]

Fifth, God's gift of mercy in Christ is distinctly different from the divine gifts through creation: the "Good News of God's mercy in Christ is not 'common experience' in the God-encounters of daily life, even those that do indeed bring blessings."[43] Sixth, encounters with God's hiddenness in creation entail, not only blessings (as Luther articulated them), but also experiences of deep ambiguity, elusiveness, pain, disappointment, distress, and chaos. Seventh, the Christian and her dialogue partner share

---

39. Kolb and Wengert, *Book of Concord*, 440, italics added for emphasis.

40. Rom 1:19.

41. From a Lutheran perspective and usage, these are technical terms. They are not meant as a pejorative assessment of the presence or absence of elements of divine truth or revelation in other religions.

42. Schroeder, "Using Luther's Concept of *Deus absconditus*," 5.

43. Ibid.

a broad basis of common experience of the "hidden God." Finally, this leads to a practical strategy of centering interreligious dialogue and conversation on the question, "How do you cope in your encounters with the hidden God? You tell me how you cope, and I'll tell you how I do," rather than, "What do you believe about God? You tell me and I'll tell you."[44]

The methodological strength of this approach is its expansive nature. In terms of the definition of dialogue offered earlier, a dialogue centering on "divine hiddenness" incorporates and can be extended into experiential, theological/doctrinal, and spiritual/liturgical dimensions. It potentially addresses such wide-ranging experiences as theological interpretation of natural disasters and devastations, issues of suffering and theodicy, and experiences of "the dark night of the soul" in prayer/contemplation, to name but a few.

Based on the distinction between the hidden and revealed God just elaborated, a confessional Lutheran missiology offers several hunches about the lived, faith experiences of adherents of other religions.[45] These hunches remain to be confirmed, modified, or rejected in actual, lived dialogical encounters. First, nobody's daily religious experience is one of only or primarily grace. Second, to ground a theology of religions or interreligious dialogue on how various religions articulate their experiences of grace (e.g. Raimon Panikkar's Christophanies) leaves vast areas of religious experience untouched, assuring that Christian grace, as the promise of mercy realized in the crucified and risen Christ, will become blurred or marginalized. Third, the grace of God in Christ is not simply an unexpected, undeserved experience of diffuse 'goodness;' rather, it is a surprising word of mercy from our Creator whom we chronically mistrust, and to whom we owe an unending debt. Fourth, should not the fact of Christian sinfulness—lack of faith, etc.—serve a central role in dialogue? Christians admit to being "simultaneously saints and sinners," and echo the Markan father's desperate cry, "Lord, I believe, help my unbelief " (9:24)! Fifth, Christians are no better in their moral virtue or performance than others; their claim is not about themselves, but rather about a gracious Word of promise they have heard and received, giving them hope against all evidence to the contrary. Sixth, to the extent that Christian theology is not enriched by listening to the experiences

---

44. Ibid., 3.

45. I am indebted to Edward Schroeder's articulation of these in "Encountering the Hidden God," 4–5.

of God's hiddenness in other religions, to that extent Christian theology remains impoverished.

While suggesting that interreligious dialogue include and elaborate humanity's common experience of divine hiddenness may sound overly pessimistic or a seeming diversion from more important topics such as the nature of God, peace, or justice, such an approach has four distinct advantages. First, it is a radically inclusive approach, allowing and inviting the input of all regardless of education or theological sophistication.[46] Second, this approach centers on lived experience rather than theological belief, on praxis rather than only doctrine. Third, obstacles in traditional forms of academic, interreligious dialogue—Christian doctrines of Jesus Christ's divinity, the Trinity, etc.—are moved from the center to the periphery. Fourth, this approach facilitates a narrative approach to proclamation and dialogue by offering the story of Jesus, especially the narrative of his paradoxical experience of God's presence and absence, as a contribution and letting it speak for itself.

JACQUES DUPUIS ON RELATING PROCLAMATION AND DIALOGUE

Dupuis anchors his treatment of dialogue and proclamation within the Church's mission in the practical question of what attitudes toward the "others" Christian faith lived within the context of an acute, intensified awareness of religious pluralism requires.[47] Drawing from and interpreting the document *Dialogue and Proclamation*, Dupuis articulates a framework of ten theological convictions for properly interpreting and dialectically interrelating dialogue and proclamation.

To begin with, Dupuis views dialogue as being "established on a double foundation: the community which has its origin in God through creation, and its destiny in him through salvation in Jesus Christ."[48] This conviction about humanity's common origin and destiny in God is articulated in various places in the Church's magisterial teaching.[49] Second,

---

46. One of the criticisms of interreligious dialogue as it has often been practiced is that it has been elitist, engaged by theologians, academics, and intellectuals.

47. Dupuis, *Christianity and the Religions*, 218.

48. Ibid., 222.

49. See Vatican Council II, "*Nostra Aetate*: Declaration on the Relations of the Church to Non-Christian Religions." In Flannery, *Vatican Council II, Volume I: The Conciliar and Post-Conciliar Documents*, no. 1.

Dupuis' robust pneumatology leads him to affirm "that the Spirit of God is universally present and operative in the religious life of the 'others' and in the religious traditions to which they belong."[50] Third, as elaborated in chapter 4, the reign of God forms a critical foundation and motivational impetus for Dupuis' model. The universally present and interreligiously shared reign of God has important implications for his approach to dialogue:

> This dialogue takes place between persons who are already bound to each other in the Reign of God inaugurated in history in Jesus Christ . . . That explains the deep communion in the Spirit that interreligious dialogue is able to establish, if it is sincere and authentic, between Christians and other believers . . . Dialogue makes explicit this communion preexisting in the reality of salvation . . . Probably nothing provides interreligious dialogue with so deep a theological basis and a motivation so true as the conviction that despite the differences that set them apart, those who belong to the different religious traditions are walking together—joint members of the Reign of God in history—toward the fullness of the Reign . . .[51]

We will return to analyze the significance of this point in the next section. Fourth, a constitutive, inclusive Christology which builds upon and augments Dupuis' reign of God theology is central to his approach. In his own words, "Everything hangs together and must be taken in its entirety: all the rest stands or falls with Christology--considered as constitutive or not."[52] Such a constitutive Christology means that "The universal saving impact of Jesus Christ . . . leaves space . . . for other 'saving figures' and other religious traditions, where God is present and at work through God's Word and Spirit."[53] Fifth, while the motivation for dialogue is based on the mysterious unity of a shared reign of God, Christian motivation for Gospel proclamation is firmly rooted in a deep love for Jesus Christ:

---

50. Dupuis, *Christianity and the Religions*, 222. As Dupuis notes, this emphasis on the Spirit's universal presence and action was one of Pope John Paul II's enduring contributions. As the pope notes, the firm belief of the followers of other religions is "an effect of the Spirit of truth operating outside the visible confines of the Mystical Body." See Pope John Paul II, *Redemptor Hominis*, no. 6.

51. Dupuis, *Christianity and the Religions*, 225.

52. Ibid., 227.

53. Ibid.

> [How] could [Christians] not hope and desire to share with others their joy of knowing and following Jesus Christ, Lord and Savior? We are here at the heart of the mystery of love. Insofar as the Church and Christians have a deep love for the Lord Jesus, the desire to share him with others is motivated not merely by obedience to the Lord's command, but by this love itself. It should not be surprising, but quite normal, that followers of other religions should also desire sincerely to share their faith. All dialogue implies reciprocity . . .[54]

Sixth, "dialogue is an integral part of the evangelizing mission to which proclamation belongs."[55] Seventh, dialogue can never replace mission, nor can mission simply be reduced to dialogue (contra Knitter). *Dialogue and Proclamation* states this point clearly: "Dialogue . . . does not constitute the whole mission of the Church . . . [I]t cannot simply replace proclamation, but remains oriented towards proclamation, in so far as the dynamic process of the Church's evangelizing mission reaches in [proclamation] its climax and fullness."[56]

As Dupuis notes, "The 'orientation' of dialogue toward proclamation in fact corresponds to the 'orientation' (*ordinantur*) of the members of other religious traditions toward the church, spoken of in *Lumen Gentium* 16."[57] Furthermore, not only are dialogue and proclamation grounded in the differing motivations articulated above, they also have distinctly different goals: while dialogue aims at "the convergence of both dialogue partners to a deeper shared conversion to God and to others," proclamation "invites others to become disciples of Christ in the Christian community."[58] As Dupuis states, "there remains space—where God so wills—for inviting the others to become disciples of Jesus in the church."[59] Ninth, since dialogue has inherent value, it cannot be reduced to an instrument of proclamation.[60] Finally, dialogue and proclamation are dialectically interrelated, both properly belonging to the Church's

---

54. Pontifical Council for Inter-Religious Dialogue and the Congregation for the Evangelization of Peoples, "Dialogue and Proclamation," 116.

55. Dupuis, *Christianity and the Religions*, 219.

56. Pontifical Council for Inter-Religious Dialogue and the Congregation for the Evangelization of Peoples, "Dialogue and Proclamation," 116.

57. Dupuis, *Christianity and the Religions*, 221.

58. Ibid., 219.

59. Ibid., 227.

60. Ibid., 220, 222, 234.

mission: "Interreligious dialogue and proclamation, though not on the same level, are both authentic elements of the Church's evangelizing mission. Both are legitimate and necessary. They are intimately related, but not interchangeable . . . The two activities remain distinct, but . . . one and the same local Church, one and the same person, can be diversely engaged in both."[61]

Dupuis seeks to navigate this dialectical tension between dialogue and proclamation by utilizing his reign of God theology within an eschatological perspective:

> The tension between the "already" and the "not yet" is reflected in the Church's evangelizing mission and, markedly so, in the relationship within it between interreligious dialogue and proclamation: Insofar as the Church remains on her pilgrimage, together with the "others," towards the fullness of the Kingdom, she engages with them in dialogue; insofar as she is the sacrament of the reality of the Kingdom already present and operative in history, she proclaims to them Jesus Christ in whom the Kingdom of God has been established by God.[62]

While Dupuis recognizes that "a certain tension remains and must remain, in the reality of the Church's evangelizing mission, between dialogue and proclamation," he is deeply convinced that a "Kingdom of God perspective is able to overcome the dichotomy and to relax the tension between dialogue and proclamation" as the reign of God grows toward its eschatological fullness.[63] While the "not yet" aspect of that reign necessitates ongoing dialogue, its "already" aspect in Jesus Christ equally necessitates Gospel proclamation. Dupuis would affirm the conclusion of *Dialogue and Proclamation*: "Dialogue and proclamation are difficult tasks, yet absolutely necessary . . . Yet more than tasks to be accomplished, [they] are graces to be sought in prayer."[64]

Finally, Dupuis identifies four Christian positions for relating dialogue and proclamation:

---

61. Pontifical Council for Inter-Religious Dialogue and the Congregation for the Evangelization of Peoples, "Dialogue and Proclamation," 114.

62. Dupuis, "Theological Commentary," 155.

63. Ibid.

64. Pontifical Council for Inter-Religious Dialogue and the Congregation for the Evangelization of Peoples, "Dialogue and Proclamation," 117–8.

> 1. Dialogue is but a "means" for proclamation, not in itself an "authentic form" of evangelization; 2. Dialogue is part of evangelization but needs at all times and in any circumstances to be accompanied by proclamation, without which "there is no true evangelization"; 3. Dialogue is in itself an authentic form of evangelization, yet remains "oriented" toward proclamation without which evangelization remains incomplete and in which its dynamic process reaches its "climax and fullness"; 4. Dialogue and proclamation are "interchangeable" and therefore simply objects of free choice on the part of the evangelizers.[65]

While *Dialogue and Proclamation* clearly excludes the first and fourth positions, "ambiguity remained as to the way in which to conceive that dialogue and proclamation are 'not on the same level.'"[66] One commentator of *Dialogue and Proclamation* highlights this ambiguous tension between dialogue and proclamation: "If one is really subsidiary to the other, can they *both be absolutely* necessary? Or to put it another way: if both are really taken to be absolutely necessary, can one of them be considered to be subsidiary to the other?"[67]

In my assessment, this ambiguous tension between how dialogue and proclamation can both be absolutely necessary while the former is "oriented" toward the latter remains unresolved in Dupuis' thought. Dupuis aptly captures a Lutheran approach to dialectically relating dialogue and proclamation in his second option above: while dialogue has inherent value, Lutheran theology would not define it as "an authentic form of evangelization." Instead, it defines "mission" or "evangelization" more narrowly and specifically than Roman Catholic theology as Gospel proclamation, without which there is "no true evangelization."

In utilizing the category of divine hiddenness, have I succeeded in my goal of dialectically relating proclamation and dialogue? One's assessment of the relative merits of a Lutheran approach will largely hinge upon one's own theological convictions. While pluralists will likely be unconvinced, viewing my use of *deus absconditus* as a Christian imposition upon dialogue partners and as a failure to let the religious other speak in his own voice, I would beg to differ. While the religious other will inevitably voice her deepest convictions and concerns in dialogue, my approach remains open to hearing those concerns and being challenged by them.

---

65. Dupuis, "Theological Commentary," 147.
66. Ibid.
67. Ibid., 154.

While cognizant of divine hiddenness as a Christian theological category and nuanced by a Lutheran understanding of the two realms principle, I would invite my dialogue partner to evaluate it on the basis of its experiential validity and potential for dialogue, rather than prematurely dismissing it for a priori reasons. Divine hiddenness, I submit, can indeed be understood as a universal human experience which, while variously experienced and articulated in different religious and cultural contexts, nonetheless constitutes, not only a promisingly fruitful locus for interreligious dialogue, but also a robust bridge between my confessionally Lutheran Christian tradition and the reality of religious pluralism.

CONCLUSION

"*Promissio* is the secret of *missio*."[68] For Lutheran theology, because the Gospel is fundamentally a promise from God, and since the nature of the Gospel should shape the nature of Christian mission, therefore the promise of God is the secret of mission. In beginning my project with this assertion, I claimed to offer four resources—the Gospel as promise, the law/Gospel distinction, a theology of mercy, and the hiddenness of God—not only for internally renewing Lutheran theology of mission, but also as gifts to the wider Christian Church and its theology of mission. I have delineated my proposal as an alternative to and constructive critique of prevailing models of *Missio Dei*, specifically Jacques' Dupuis theology of religious pluralism. Dupuis' theology represents a mature, missiologically creative version of classic Roman Catholic theology, building upon while extending beyond the theologies of Thomas Aquinas and Karl Rahner, specifically. We are now in a position to evaluate to what extent I have succeeded in achieving my stated goal. Can a confessional Lutheran model and Dupuis' model interact in such a way as to constructively critique, challenge, and mutually enrich each other? What might the fruit of such an interaction look like? In this conclusion, I seek to identify the relative merits and strengths of each approach, as well as remaining issues, points of tension, and unresolved questions meriting further investigation.

Paul Knitter describes how vastly differently the nature/grace and law/promise paradigms view salvation, "The difference between these two views of how Jesus saves—as bridging what is divided or revealing

---

68. Bertram, "Doing Theology in Relation to Mission," 41.

what is present—makes for major differences in a theology of religions. To understand and experience Jesus as he who reveals, symbolizes, and represents the already-given love of God would seem to allow, or even call for, other sacraments."[69]

Stephen Duffy further specifies the foundational issues our respective models build upon: "Differences concerning grace reflect differences concerning sin, which in turn are traceable to different images of the divine/human relationship."[70] In other words: both models address and delineate missiologically significant aspects of one's doctrine of God and theological anthropology, namely what is wrong/deficient in human nature, what constitutes sin, what constitutes grace, and therefore what constitutes salvation. In what follows, I will analyze the answers each model gives to key questions in constructing its distinctive vision of the divine/human relationship and, specifically, how Jesus saves.

We begin with two key features of theological anthropology. First, what is the foundational paradigm for constructing divine/human relations? For Rahner and Dupuis, the paradigm of "grace fulfilling nature" is foundational, setting the course of their theological trajectories. My confessional Lutheran model builds upon the foundational paradigm of law/promise. As noted in chapter 5, the dual revelation of law and Gospel promise correlates to an analogous dual revelation with respect to God and anthropology: while wrath and mercy become revealed in God, sin and faith are revealed in humanity.[71] The law/Gospel dynamic, therefore, lies at the very heart of both the doctrine of God and theological anthropology.

Second, "is there any such thing as universal human experience?"[72] While "it has become far from evident that such common ground [of shared, ontological structures of experience] exists, or that religions agree on a common ground or goal for dialogue," Dupuis and I concur that such universal human experience indeed exists and is crucial for constructing the divine/human relationship.[73] However, we disagree on what that universal experience is. While Rahner and Dupuis would identify this experience as grace, God's self-manifestation and presence

---

69. Knitter, *Introducing Theologies of Religion*, 105–6.
70. Duffy, *Dynamics of Grace*, 390.
71. Elert, *Christian Faith*, 87.
72. Duffy, *Dynamics of Grace*, 392.
73. Cornille, *Im-possibility of Interreligious Dialogue*, 212.

through the supernatural existential, I have argued that the hiddenness of God serves as such a universal experience, albeit nuanced by specific, religio-cultural variations.

My confessional Lutheran model integrates the categories of Gospel, promise, sin, and faith into the following missiological vision. Within an overarching "economy of salvation," God is on a mission to reconstitute the divine/human relation tarnished by human sin. God promises to do so through God's performative, dual Word of law and Gospel promise. This duplex *missio Dei* unfolds as follows: while the law's theological use convicts of sin and its civil use orders and preserves creation, its' overall thrust and aim is to necessitate Christ and the Gospel promise. The Gospel promises and offers mercy and, in doing so, always aims at eliciting a response of faith. Therefore, both the Gospel itself and God's mission have a promissory core which aims at faith (trust). While this divine mission of law and Gospel promise are often hidden and indiscernible in daily experience, Lutheran missiology views such "hiddenness of God," not as an obstacle or barrier to dialogue, but rather as a shared, fruitful, promising avenue for dialogue. While respectfully hearing its dialogue partner, it would nonetheless proclaim the ministry, death, and resurrection of Jesus as grounds for trusting the promise of the eschatological resolution of such hiddenness, claiming that "the crucified and hidden God" will one day be revealed as the loving, gracious, and faithful God of all.

As this summary indicates, Christology is a linchpin, not only for uniting one's doctrine of God and theological anthropology, but also for extending its missiological implications. I agree with Dupuis' claim: "all the rest stands or falls with Christology—considered as constitutive or not."[74] While the Christian tradition has always recognized Christology as integral to constructing a properly Christian doctrine of God and theological anthropology, what is the specific nature of that role? What constitutes a "constitutive Christology," and how is Jesus Christ necessary for mediating the divine/human interface?

The differences between Dupuis' constitutive Christology as "incarnational mediation" and a Lutheran view of Christology as "cruciform mediation" are firmly rooted in Dupuis' transcendental anthropology, on the one hand, and Lutheran theologies of sin and mercy, on the other. What constitutes "constitutive Christology?" For Dupuis, "Jesus Christ

---

74. Dupuis, *Christianity and the Religions*, 227.

is 'mediator' between God and humankind inasmuch as he unites divinity and humanity in his person in such a way that in him the Divinity and humankind have become united in a permanent bond."[75] It is precisely this configuration of the divine/human relationship, reflecting a theology of grace as nature fulfilled, that defines Christology for Dupuis and propels him to extend this configuration as a universal possibility for all through the Spirit. In contrast, a Lutheran approach insists that, while the uniqueness of Jesus as mediator is certainly grounded in his personal identity as the Son of God,[76] what "constitutes" Christology and his work of mediation is not simply his transcendental identity, but rather his sacrificial death on the cross accomplishing reconciliation and actual atonement for sin ("cruciform mediation"). To the extent that the substantive content of Christ's mediation as reconciling atonement of sin is marginalized in favor of elaborating a robust pneumatology and Spirit Christology, to that extent the mediatory work of Christ appears to be subsumed under the Spirit.

"The Christian, while knowing where Christ is, can never be certain where he is not."[77] This insight introduces further issues extending and applying the foundational themes of doctrine of God and theological anthropology treated above, issues which extend the trajectories of the two models into areas of disagreement and potential enrichment. While Rahner's inclusivism, Dupuis' inclusive pluralism, and my inclusive exclusivity all share the dual conviction of Jesus Christ being uniquely Savior, "the one for all others," and God's universal will of salvation, they differ in terms of navigating this tension between the particularity of grace in Christ and the universality of God's gracious will. The central issue is how the ministry, salvation, and saving grace of Jesus Christ can be viewed as extending beyond the bounds of the visible Church. This issue manifests itself in abiding differences concerning anonymous faith, pneumatology, and the relationship between the Church and the reign of God, respectively.

Given their theology of grace and convictions regarding the histories of revelation and salvation always being coextensive, Rahner views "the anonymous Christian" and Dupuis views "other saving figures" as helpful categories for extending and discerning the saving grace of Christ

---

75. Ibid., 168.
76. Ibid., 175.
77. Oleksa, "Orthodox Missiological Education," 86.

beyond the bounds of the visible Church. In contrast, given a Lutheran theology of grace as loving mercy and emphasis upon faith resulting from hearing and trusting the external offer of grace (*fides ex auditu*), Lutheran theology is concerned that any articulation of grace and faith as implicit or anonymous ends up unwittingly undermining the necessity and benefits of Christ, as well as the promissory character of the Gospel itself. This abiding difference concerning the possibility of grace and faith as implicit or anonymous remains.

Second, the nature and logic of a cosmic, robust pneumatology highlights enduring differences. While Dupuis utilizes a robust pneumatology to argue for a constitutive Christology operating salvifically through the saving figures of other religions, a Lutheran approach is more cautious and reserved. In affirming that a cosmic pneumatology is necessary, Lutheran theology also recognizes it as potentially "perilous, for it must be the particular Spirit of Jesus and of the Church to whom we attribute cosmic efficacy."[78] While freely admitting the critique of an underdeveloped pneumatology, Lutheran pneumatology is guided by several foundational convictions. First, the Spirit is always the Spirit of Christ who "takes from what is [Christ's] and makes it known to you."[79] God's presence in the world, through the Spirit, must always be related to what Jesus' crucifixion and resurrection brought about. Second, the varying insights of the Christian tradition on the cosmic Spirit (the Spirit as the Wisdom of God, the freedom of universal history, the spontaneity of natural process, and the beauty of creation, etc.) must never lose "the offensive claim that it is *Jesus'* individual spirit of whom the insights are true."[80] Third, as argued earlier, the law/Gospel distinction is an intrinsic feature of Lutheran pneumatology.[81] What the Spirit reveals and unveils as "rays of truth" includes not only "traces of grace," but also the pervasive reality and brokenness of sin. Furthermore, when the perspective of the two realms is added to the function of distinguishing law and Gospel, "traces of grace and truth" in other religions can be affirmed as evidence of God's presence, enabling and sustaining civil righteousness, even contributing to our knowledge of the good and true, without interpreting them as signals of the Spirit's salvific presence and work.

78. Jenson, "Cosmic Spirit," 165.
79. John 16:14.
80. Jenson, "Cosmic Spirit," 166.
81. Bayer, *Martin Luther's Theology*, 247.

Finally, the relationship between the Church and the reign of God remains an enduring area of disagreement. While both models agree that the Church and the reign of God are distinguishable, but never separable, the reign being "an inchoate reality which needs to find completion through being related to the Kingdom of Christ already present in the Church," they differ in terms of treating the question of to what degree, and in what manner, the Church and the reign of God are hidden.[82] If others experience the mystery of salvation "more fully" through the universal sacrament of the Church as the "ordinary" means of salvation, does this not entail, at the very least, an implicit call to conversion and thereby nullify the principle of religious pluralism *de jure*? While Dupuis wishes to affirm both religious pluralism *de jure* and the legitimacy of Gospel proclamation aiming at conversion, I deem his navigation of this tension through his constitutive Christology overly optimistic. My concern is that, to the extent it foregoes the revelation of sin, to that extent it distorts the nature of the Gospel as promise. In contrast to delineating criteria for identifying the reign of God at work in the religions (traces of love, grace, and truth), a Lutheran model deems such a strategy unhelpful, emphasizing instead the hidden nature of the true Church.

Roman Catholic magisterial teaching asserts: "God can accomplish this salvation in whomsoever he wishes by ways which he knows. And yet, if his Son came, it was precisely in order to reveal to us, by his word and his life, the ordinary paths of salvation," and "[the mystery of salvation] holds true not for Christians only but for all men of good will in whose hearts grace is actively invisible . . . [W]e must hold that the Holy Spirit offers to all the possibility of being made partners, in a way known to God, in the paschal mystery."[83] While Lutheran theology views the Church as "transparent and accountable to" the reign of God, and Dupuis views the Church as the sign, instrument, and universal sacrament of that reign, they differ in terms of their attitude toward these two key magisterial statements.[84] While Dupuis' theology of inclusive pluralism elaborately spells out how such invisible grace relates the others to the

---

82. Pontifical Council for Inter-Religious Dialogue and the Congregation for the Evangelization of Peoples, "Dialogue and Proclamation," 103.

83. Pope Paul VI, *Evangelii Nuntiandi: On Evangelization in the Modern World*, no. 80; Vatican Council II, "*Gaudium et Spes:* Pastoral Constitution on the Church in the Modern World," no. 22.

84. Hefner, "Church and the Kingdom of God," 246–7; Dupuis, *Toward a Christian Theology of Religious Pluralism*, 349–53.

paschal mystery, a Lutheran model would affirm the first statement while insisting that the mechanics of *how* the Spirit may offer salvation to all, "the 'how' and 'in which way' of the essential relationship between the universal action of the Word- and the Spirit- and the historical event of Jesus Christ," remains a mystery.[85]

The models of inclusive pluralism and inclusive exclusivity share significant, common affirmations. First, both models are inclusive: all saving grace is truly the grace of Christ, wherever it may be found. Second, both affirm God's loving, universal will of salvation as intended for all people. Third, both affirm the importance of a Trinitarian framework and impetus for constructing their missiology. Fourth, both employ a dialectical relationship between dialogue and proclamation.

The enduring mystery of God provides a fruitful avenue for mutually enriching interaction between the two models. As Karl Rahner notes, "'Mystery' is not merely another word for that which for the time being has not yet been comprehended and perceived; it is both possible and meaningful explicitly to come to terms with mystery as such and in itself . . ."[86]

In considering the paradox of how the universality of God's saving will relates to the particularity of saving grace in Jesus Christ, Dupuis challenges a Lutheran model to consider the possibility of grace being more radical in nature and more surprisingly comprehensive than Lutheran theology currently construes it. While my model emphasizes where Christ is present in his saving power—in the Gospel in its oral, written, and sacramental forms—one can never be certain where He is not present. This is a reminder which Lutheran theology should take to heart as it wrestles to articulate a more robust pneumatology, how grace might be operative beyond the bounds of the external Word of God, and how resources other than the Christian Scriptures and Lutheran Confessions might contribute to its missiology. How might the nature/grace paradigm challenge confessional Lutheran theology to consider dimensions of grace internal to the structure of human subjectivity?

On the other hand, a Lutheran model challenges Dupuis to refine its understanding of grace in light of a more robust doctrine of sin. While Dupuis is generous in asserting the presence of Christ's saving grace in other religions, it is important to recognize that where Christ is present,

---

85. Dupuis, *Christianity and the Religions*, 162.
86. Rahner, "Position of Christology," 185.

his presence is characterized, not only by saving grace, but also by judgment of sin, as evidenced by Jesus' life and ministry in the Gospels. A Lutheran model would challenge Dupuis on three points: beware of marginalizing or overlooking the promissory nature of the Gospel, recognize and incorporate more deeply the reality of sin, and consider whether your constitutive Christology adequately incorporates the "cruciform" mediation of reconciliation and atonement centered on the cross.

A missiologically adequate engagement of the mystery of God, Lutheran theology insists, entails recognizing, not only the mystery of divine love and grace, but also incorporating the paradoxes of divine wrath and mercy, law and Gospel, the mystery of God's hiddenness and revelation, and the promise of reconciling mercy *in* Christ (2 Cor 5:19) with the eschatological promise of uniting all things *under* Christ (Eph 1:10). While the last pair reflects the differing emphases between Dupuis and I, both models have further work to do in more deeply grasping that, "The 'grammar' of Christianity is structured by the strangeness of grace."[87] As Joseph DiNoia notes, the final, inclusive victory of the cross entails an "eschatological promise whose fulfillment will come only as a stunning and undeserved gift."[88]

While recognizing the polyvalence of grace in the Christian Scriptures, and ever mindful of the complex nature and pitfalls of relating Christian doctrine and human experience, my nuanced appropriation of the cultural-linguistic model offers certain words—promise and mercy in particular—as centrally illuminative for understanding the nature of the Gospel and Christian mission today. The Gospel as promise, safeguarded by the law/Gospel distinction and grounded in theologies of mercy and of the cross, is offered to the Church catholic as an illuminating resource for engaging in mission. As such mission is carried out in the context of religious pluralism and practice of interreligious dialogue, the hiddenness of God serves as both a fruitful bridge between Christianity and the other religions, as well as a humble invitation to consider the promise of God's eschatological victory over sin, grounded in the cross and resurrection of Jesus.

By recovering these resources from its confessional heritage and creatively offering them to the Church at large, Lutheran missiology can

---

87. Reno, *Ordinary Transformed*, 222.
88. Dinoia, *Diversity of Religions*, 170.

Proclamation and Interreligious Dialogue

take an initial step from "reactive reform" toward "innovative initiative."[89] Robert Bertram captures the Trinitarian accents of my proposal for mission shaped by promise:

> *Promissio* is the secret of *missio*. For the mission's Sender was Himself the keeping of that promise. And the mission's gaps, across which we move with our theological doings, are ultimately spanned by that same promise—of Himself by the Spirit through His Word.[90]

---

89. Bliese, "Lutheran Missiology," 13.
90. Bertram, "Doing Theology in Relation to Mission," 41.

Bibliography

Aagaard, Johannes. "The Lutheran Tradition and Mission Theology." *Ekumenisk Orientering* 38 (1984) 3–10.
Ahonen, Risto. *Lähetys uudella vuosituhannella*. Helsinki: Saarijärven Offset OY, 2000.
———. *Maailmanlähetys tienhaarassa*. Helsinki: Suomen Lähetysseura, 2012.
Althaus, Paul. *The Theology of Martin Luther*. Translated by Robert Schultz. Philadelphia: Fortress, 1972.
Aquinas, St. Thomas. *The Summa Theologica of St. Thomas Aquinas, 5 Volumes*. Translated by the Fathers of the English Dominican Province. New York: Glencoe, 1981.
Arand, Charles. *Testing the Boundaries: Windows to Lutheran Identity*. St. Louis: Concordia, 1995.
Arand, Charles, and Robert Kolb. *The Genius of Luther's Theology: A Wittenberg Way of Thinking for the Contemporary Church*. Grand Rapids: Baker Academic, 2008.
Augustiny, Waldemar. *Gehet hin in alle Welt. Zwei Jahrtausende christliche Mission*. Gütersloh, 1962.
Aulen, Gustaf. *The Faith of the Christian Church*. Translated by Eric H. Wahlstrom. Eugene, OR: Wipf and Stock, 2002.
Austin, John L. *How to Do Things with Words*. Cambridge, MA: Harvard University Press, 1962.
———. "Performative-Constative." In *The Philosophy of Language*, edited by John R. Searle, 13–22. Oxford: Oxford University Press, 1971.
Barth, Karl. *Church Dogmatics, Volume II/1, The Doctrine of God*. Edinburgh: T. & T. Clark, 1957.
———. *Church Dogmatics IV/1, The Doctrine of Reconciliation*. Edinburgh: T. & T. Clark, 1961.
———. *Community, State, and Church*. Garden City, NY: Doubleday, 1960.
Bayer, Oswald. "The Being of Christ in Faith." Translated by Christine Helmer. *Lutheran Quarterly* 10 (1996) 135–50.
———. "The Doctrine of Justification and Ontology." Translated by Christine Helmer. *Neue Zeitschrift für systematische Theologie und Religionsphilosophie* 43 (2001) 44–53.
———. "God as Author of My Life-History." *Lutheran Quarterly* 2 (1988) 437–56.
———. "Hermeneutical Theology." Translated by Gwen Griffith-Dickson. *Scottish Journal of Theology* 56 (2003) 131–47.
———. "Justification as the Basis and Boundary of Theology." Translated by Christine Helmer. *Lutheran Quarterly* 15 (2001) 273–92.
———. *Living By Faith: Justification and Sanctification*. Grand Rapids: Eerdmans, 2003.

Bibliography

———. "Martin Luther as an Interpreter of Holy Scripture." In *The Cambridge Companion to Martin Luther*, translated by Mark Mattes, edited by Donald K. McKim, 73-85. Cambridge: Cambridge University Press, 2003.

———. *Martin Luther's Theology: A Contemporary Interpretation*. Translated by Thomas Trapp. Grand Rapids: Eerdmans, 2008.

———. "Nature and Institution: Luther's Doctrine of the Three Orders." Translated by Luis Dreher. *Lutheran Quarterly* 12 (1998) 125-59.

———. "Notae Ecclesiae." In *Lutheran Contributions to the Missio Dei*, 69-82. Geneva: Department of Church Cooperation of the Lutheran World Federation, 1984.

———. "Preaching the Word." Translated by Jeffrey Silcock. *Lutheran Quarterly* 23 (2009) 249-69.

———. *Promissio: Geschichte der reformatorischen Wende in Luthers Theologie*. Göttingen: Vandenhoeck and Ruprecht, 1971.

———. "Rupture of Times: Luther's Relevance for Today." Translated by Christine Helmer. *Lutheran Quarterly* 13 (1999) 34-50.

———. "Self-Creation? On the Dignity of Human Beings." *Modern Theology* 20 (2004) 275-90.

———. "Theology in the Conflict of Interpretations—Before the Text." Translated by Gwen Griffith Dickson. *Modern Theology* 16 (2000) 495-502.

———. *Theology the Lutheran Way*. Grand Rapids: Eerdmans, 2007.

———. "The Word of the Cross." Translated by John Betz. *Lutheran Quarterly* 9 (1995) 47-55.

Bertram, Robert. "Doing Theology in Relation to Mission." In *The Promising Tradition: A Reader in Law-Gospel Reconstructionist Theology*, 41A-41F. St. Louis: Concordia Seminary in Exile, 1974.

———. "Luther on the Unique Mediatorship of Christ." In *The One Mediator, the Saints, and Mary: Lutherans and Catholics in Dialogue VIII*, edited by H. George Anderson et al., 249-61. Minneapolis: Augsburg Fortress, 2009.

———. "The Hermeneutical Significance of Apology IV." In *The Promising Tradition: A Reader in Law-Gospel Reconstructionist Theology*, 2-4. St. Louis: Concordia Seminary in Exile, 1974.

———. "'Scripture and Tradition' in the Lutheran Confession." *Pro Ecclesia* 10/2 (2001) 179-94.

———. *A Time for Confessing*. Grand Rapids: Eerdmans, 2008.

Bevans, Stephen B. "Missiology After Bosch: Reverencing a Classic by Moving Beyond." *International Bulletin of Missionary Research* 29/2 (2005) 69-84.

———. *Mission for the 21st Century*. Chicago: CCGM, 2001.

Bevans, Stephen B., et al., eds. *Dictionary of Mission: Theology, History, Perspectives*. Maryknoll: Orbis, 1997.

Bevans, Stephen B., and James A. Scherer, eds. *New Directions in Mission and Evangelization 1: Basic Statements 1974-1991*. Maryknoll: Orbis, 1992.

———, eds. *New Directions in Mission and Evangelization 2: Theological Foundations*. Maryknoll: Orbis, 1994.

———, eds. *New Directions in Mission and Evangelization 3: Faith and Culture*. Maryknoll: Orbis, 1999.

Bevans, Stephen B. and Roger Schroeder. *Constants in Context: A Theology of Mission for Today*. Maryknoll: Orbis, 2004.

Bibliography

Bielfeldt, Dennis, et al. *The Substance of the Faith: Luther's Doctrinal Theology for Today.* Minneapolis: Fortress, 2008.

Bliese, Richard. "Lutheran Missiology: Struggling to Move from Reactive Reform to Innovative Initiative." In *The Role of Mission in the Future of Lutheran Theology*, edited by Viggo Mortensen, 11–30. Aarhus: University of Aarhus, 2003.

Bosch, David. *Transforming Mission.* Maryknoll: Orbis, 1996.

Braaten, Carl. *The Apostolic Imperative: Nature and Aim of the Church's Mission and Ministry.* Minneapolis: Augsburg, 1985.

———. *Because of Christ: Memoirs of a Lutheran Theologian.* Grand Rapids: Eerdmans, 2010.

———. "Confessional Lutheranism in an Ecumenical World." *Concordia Theological Quarterly* 71 (2007) 219–31.

———. *The Flaming Center: A Theology of the Christian Mission.* Philadelphia: Fortress, 2007.

———. *History and Hermeneutics.* Philadelphia: Westminster, 1966.

———. *Justification: The Article by Which the Church Stands or Falls.* Minneapolis: Augsburg Fortress, 1990.

———. *No Other Name! Christianity Among the World's Religions.* Eugene, OR: Wipf & Stock, 2001.

———. *That All May Believe: A Theology of the Gospel and the Mission of the Church.* Grand Rapids: Eerdmans, 2008.

Braaten, Carl, and Robert Jenson, eds. *Union with Christ: The New Finnish Interpretation of Luther.* Grand Rapids: Eerdmans, 1998.

Brondos, David. *Fortress Introduction to Salvation and the Cross.* Minneapolis: Fortress, 2007.

Bunkowske, Eugene. "Was Luther a Missionary?" *Concordia Theological Quarterly* 49/2 (1985) 161–79.

Burrows, William R., ed. *Redemption and Dialogue: Reading Redemptoris Missio and Dialogue and Proclamation.* Maryknoll: Orbis, 1994.

———. "Participation in and Transformation by the Promise." Address given for the Third International Crossings Conference, Belleville, IL, January 27, 2010.

———. "Reconciling All in Christ: An Old New Paradigm for Mission." *Mission Studies* 15/29 (1998) 79–98.

Busch, Eberhard. *The Great Passion: An Introduction to Karl Barth's Theology.* Translated by Geoffrey Bromiley. Grand Rapids: Eerdmans, 2004.

Camps, A., et al, eds. *Missiology: An Ecumenical Introduction: Texts and Contexts of Global Christianity.* Grand Rapids: Eerdmans, 1995.

Caton, Charles E., ed. *Philosophy and Ordinary Language.* Urbana: University of Illinois Press, 1963.

Clooney, Francis X. *Hindu God, Christian God: How Reason Helps to Break Down the Boundaries between Religions.* New York: Oxford University Press, 2001.

Commission on Theology and Church Relations of the Lutheran Church—Missouri Synod. *A Theological Statement of Mission.* St. Louis: Concordia, 1991.

Cornille, Catherine. *The Im-possibility of Interreligious Dialogue.* New York: Crossroad, 2008.

———. *Many Mansions? Multiple Religious Belonging and Christian Identity.* Maryknoll: Orbis, 2002.

D'Costa, Gavin, ed. *Christian Uniqueness Reconsidered: The Myth of a Pluralistic Theology of Religions.* Maryknoll: Orbis, 1990.

Bibliography

———. *Christianity and World Religions: Disputed Questions in the Theology of Religions*. West Sussex: Wiley-Blackwell, 2009.
———. "Karl Rahner's Anonymous Christian—A Reappraisal." *Modern Theology* 1/2 (1985) 131–48.
———. *The Meeting of Religions and the Trinity*. Maryknoll: Orbis, 2000.
———. "Whose Objectivity? Which Neutrality? The Doomed Quest for a Neutral Vantage Point to Judge Religions." *Religious Studies* 29 (1993) 79–96.
Demut, Andre. *Evangelium und Gesetz. Eine systematisch-theologische Reflexion zu Karl Barths Predigtwerk*. Berlin: De Gruyter, 2008.
Dillenberger, John. *God Hidden and Revealed: The Interpretation of Luther's Deus Absconditus and Its Significance for Religious Thought*. Philadelphia: Muhlenberg, 1953.
———, ed. *Martin Luther: Selections From His Writings*. New York: Anchor, 1957.
DiNoia, Joseph A. *The Diversity of Religions: A Christian Perspective*. Washington D.C.: Catholic University of America Press, 1992.
Duffy, Stephen J. *The Dynamics of Grace: Perspectives in Theological Anthropology*. Collegeville: The Liturgical Press, 1993.
———. *The Graced Horizon: Nature and Grace in Modern Catholic Thought*. Collegeville: The Liturgical Press, 1992.
Dulles, Avery. *Models of Revelation*. Maryknoll: Orbis, 1992.
Dupuis, Jacques. *Christianity and the Religions: From Confrontation to Dialogue*. Maryknoll: Orbis, 2002.
———. "'Christianity and the Religions' Revisited." *Louvain Studies* 28/4 (Winter 2003) 363–83.
———. "The Church's Evangelizing Mission in the Context of Religious Pluralism." *Pastoral Review* 1/1 (Jan–Feb 2005) 20–31.
———. "From Religious Confrontation to Encounter." *Theology Digest* 49/2 (Summer 2002) 103–8.
———. "Interreligious Dialogue, A Challenge to Christian Identity." *Svensk missionstidskrift* 92/1 (2004) 21–40.
———. *Jesus Christ at the Encounter of World Religions*. Maryknoll: Orbis, 1991.
———. "Renewal of Christianity Through Interreligious Dialogue." *Bijdragen* 65/2 (2004) 131–43.
———. *Toward a Christian Theology of Religious Pluralism*. Maryknoll: Orbis, 1997.
———. "'The Truth Will Make You Free': The Theology of Religious Pluralism Revisited." *Louvain Studies* 24 (1999) 211–63.
———. *Who Do You Say I Am? Introduction to Christology*. Maryknoll: Orbis, 1994.
Ebeling, Gerhard. "Die Anfänge von Luthers Hermeneutik." *Zeitschrift fur Theologie und Kirche* 48 (1951) 172–230.
———. *Luther: An Introduction to His Thought*. Philadelphia: Fortress, 1970.
———. *Lutherstudien*, vol. 3. Tübingen: Mohr, 1985.
———. *Word and Faith*. Philadelphia: Fortress, 1964.
Elert, Werner. *The Christian Ethos*. Translated by Carl J. Schindler. Philadelphia: Fortress, 1957.
———. *The Christian Faith: An Outline of Lutheran Dogmatics*. Translated by Martin H. Bertram and Walter R. Bouman. Columbus, OH: Lutheran Theological Seminary, 1974.

———. *Law and Gospel*. Translated by Edward H. Schroeder. Philadelphia: Fortress, 1967.

———. *The Structure of Lutheranism: The Theology and Philosophy of Life of Lutheranism Especially in the Sixteenth and Seventeenth Centuries*. St. Louis: Concordia, 1962.

Engelsviken, Tormod. "*Missio Dei*: The Understanding and Misunderstanding of a Theological Concept in European Churches and Missiology." *International Review of Mission* 42/367 (2003) 481–97.

Flannery, Austin, ed. *Vatican Council II, Volume I: The Conciliar and Post-Conciliar Documents*. Northport: Costello, 1998.

Flett, John G. *The Witness of God: The Trinity, Missio Dei, Karl Barth, and the Nature of Christian Community*. Grand Rapids: Eerdmans, 2010.

Forde, Gerhard. "Atonement as Actual Event." In *Christian Dogmatics: Volume 2*, edited by Carl Braaten and Robert Jenson, 79–99. Philadelphia: Fortress, 1984.

———. *The Law-Gospel Debate: An Interpretation of Its Historical Development*. Minneapolis: Fortress, 2007.

———. "Luther's Theology of the Cross." In *Christian Dogmatics, Volume 2*, edited by Carl Braaten and Robert Jenson, 47–63. Philadelphia: Fortress, 1984.

———. *On Being a Theologian of the Cross: Reflections on Luther's Heidelberg Disputation, 1518*. Grand Rapids: Eerdmans, 1997.

———. *The Preached God: Proclamation in Word and Sacrament*, edited by Mark Mattes and Stephen Paulson. Grand Rapids: Eerdmans, 2007.

———. "Reconciliation with God." In *Christian Dogmatics, Volume 2*, edited by Carl Braaten and Robert Jenson, 65–77. Philadelphia: Fortress, 1984.

———. *Theology is for Proclamation*. Minneapolis: Augsburg Fortress, 1990.

Forsberg, Juhani. *Abraham als Paradigma der Mission in der Theologie Luthers: Lutherische Beiträge zur Missio Dei*. Veröffentlichungen der Luther-Akademie e.V. Ratzeburg. Band 3. Erlangen: Martin Luther, 1982.

Forward, Martin. *Inter-religious Dialogue: A Short Introduction*. Oxford: Oneworld, 2001.

Francisco, Adam. *Martin Luther and Islam: A Study in Sixteenth-Century Polemics and Apologetics*. Leiden: Brill, 2007.

Gassman, Günther, and Scott Hendrix. *Fortress Introduction to the Lutheran Confessions*. Minneapolis: Fortress, 1999.

Gensichen, Hans Werner. "Akzente und Problemstellungen in der gegenwärtigen Missionstheologie." *Zeitschrift für Missionswissenschaft* 70 (1986) 112–27.

———. *Das Taufproblem in der Mission*. Gutersloh: Bertelsmann, 1971.

———. *Glaube für die Welt. Theologische Aspekte der Mission*. Gutersloh: Bertelsmann, 1971.

Gerrish, Brian. *Grace and Reason: A Study in the Theology of Luther*. Oxford: Clarendon, 1962.

———. *The Old Protestantism and the New: Essays on the Reformation Heritage*. Chicago: University of Chicago, 1982.

———. "To the Unknown God: Luther and Calvin on the Hiddenness of God." *Journal of Religion* 53 (1973) 263–93.

Gilkey, Langdon. *Reaping the Whirlwind: A Christian Interpretation of History*. New York: Seabury, 1976.

Greenspahn, Frederick E., ed. *Essential Papers on Israel and the Ancient Near East*. New York: NYU Press, 2000.

Bibliography

Grenz, Stanley. *Reason for Hope: The Systematic Theology of Wolfhart Pannenberg.* Grand Rapids: Eerdmans, 2005.
Griffiths, Paul. *An Apology for Apologetics: A Study in the Logic of Interreligious Dialogue.* Maryknoll: Orbis, 1991.
Gritsch, Eric W., and Robert W. Jenson. *Lutheranism: The Theological Movement and Its Confessional Writings.* Philadelphia: Fortress, 1976.
Guder, Darell L. *Missional Church: A Vision for the Sending of the Church in North America.* Grand Rapids: Eerdmans, 1998.
Harnack, Theodosius. *Luthers Theologie.* 2 vols. München: Christian Kaiser, 1927.
Hefner, Philip. "The Church and the Kingdom of God." In *Christian Dogmatics: Volume 2*, edited by Carl E. Braaten and Robert W. Jenson, 243–47. Philadelphia: Fortress, 1984.
Heim, S. Mark. *The Depth of the Riches: A Trinitarian Theology of Religious Ends.* Grand Rapids: Eerdmans, 2001.
———. *Salvations: Truth and Difference in Religion.* Maryknoll: Orbis, 1995.
Helmer, Christine, ed. *The Global Luther: A Theologian for Modern Times.* Minneapolis: Fortress, 2009.
Hendrix, Scott. *Recultivating the Vineyard: The Reformation Agendas of Christianization.* Louisville: Westminster John Knox, 2004.
Hengel, Martin. "Salvation History." In *Reading Texts, Seeking Wisdom: Scripture and Theology,* edited by David F. Ford et al., 229–44. Grand Rapids: Eerdmans, 2003.
Highfield, Ron. "The Freedom to Say 'No'? Karl Rahner's Doctrine of Sin." *Theological Studies* 56 (1995) 485–505.
Hinze, Bradford. *Practices of Dialogue in the Roman Catholic Church: Aims and Obstacles, Lessons and Laments.* New York: Continuum, 2006.
———. "The End of Salvation History." *Horizons* 18 (1991) 227–45.
Hillers, Delbert R. *Covenant: The History of a Biblical Idea.* Baltimore: Johns Hopkins, 1969.
Hill-Fletcher, Jeannine. "As Long as We Wonder: Possibilities in the Impossibility of Interreligious Dialogue." *Theological Studies* 68 (2007) 532–54.
———. "Rahner and Religious Diversity." In *The Cambridge Companion to Karl Rahner,* edited by Mary Hines et al., 235–47. New York: Cambridge, 2005.
Hinlicky, Paul R. *Luther and the Beloved Community: A Path for Christian Theology After Christendom.* Grand Rapids: Eerdmans, 2010.
Hodgson, Peter. *God in History: Shapes of Freedom.* Minneapolis: Fortress, 2007.
Horton, Michael S. *Covenant and Salvation: Union with Christ.* Louisville: Westminster John Knox, 2007.
———. *The Gospel-Driven Life.* Baker: Grand Rapids, 2009.
———. "Theologies of Scripture in the Reformation and Counter-Reformation." In *Christian Theologies of Scripture: A Comparative Introduction,* edited by Justin Holcomb, 83–93. New York: NYU Press, 2006.
Jenson, Robert. "Cosmic Spirit." In *Christian Dogmatics: Volume 2,* edited by Carl E. Braaten and Robert W. Jenson, 165–78. Philadelphia: Fortress, 1984.
———. "How the World Lost Its Story." *First Things* 36 (October 1993) 19–24.
———. "Luther's Contemporary Theological Significance." In *The Cambridge Companion to Martin Luther,* edited by Donald K. McKim, 272–88. Cambridge: Cambridge University Press, 2003.

———. *Story and Promise: A Brief Theology of the Gospel About Jesus*. Philadelphia: Fortress, 1973.
———. *Systematic Theology*. 2 vols. New York: Oxford, 2001.
———. *The Triune Identity: God According to the Gospel*. Eugene, OR: Wipf and Stock, 2002.
Jüngel, Eberhard. *God as the Mystery of the World*. Grand Rapids: Eerdmans, 1986.
Kähler, Martin. *Schriften zur Christologie und Mission*. Munich: Christian Kaiser, 1971.
Kärkkäinen, Veli-Matti. *An Introduction to the Theology of Religions*. Downers Grove: InterVarsity, 2003.
———. *Trinity and Religious Pluralism: The Doctrine of the Trinity in Christian Theology of Religions*. Burlington: Ashgate, 2004.
Kelsey, David H. *Proving Doctrine: The Uses of Scripture in Modern Theology*. New York: Continuum, 1999.
King, J. Norman. *The God of Forgiveness and Healing in the Theology of Karl Rahner*. Washington, D.C.: University Press of America, 1982.
Kirk, J. Andrew. *Mission Under Scrutiny: Confronting Contemporary Challenges*. Philadelphia: Fortress, 2006.
Knitter, Paul. *Introducing Theologies of Religion*. Maryknoll: Orbis, 2002.
———. *Jesus and the Other Names: Christian Mission and Global Responsibility*. Maryknoll: Orbis, 1996.
———. "Towards a Protestant Theology of Religions: A Case Study of Paul Althaus and Contemporary Attitudes." Phd. diss., University of Marburg, 1974.
Koenig, Richard. "The Future of Justification—A Response to N. T. Wright." N.p. Online: http://www.crossings.org/thursday/2010/thuro40110.shtml.
Kolb, Robert. "The Church and Her Mission: Toward a Missional Ecclesiology." Address given at the Lutheran Ecclesiology for the Third Millenium symposium, St. Louis, MO, September 23, 2008.
———. *Martin Luther: Confessor of the Faith*. New York: Oxford University Press, 2009.
———. *Sources and Contexts of the Book of Concord*. Philadelphia: Fortress, 2001.
Kolb, Robert, and Timothy J. Wengert, eds. *The Book of Concord: The Confessions of the Evangelical Lutheran Church*. Minneapolis: Fortress, 2000.
Köstenberger, Andreas J. "The Place of Mission in New Testament Theology." *Missiology* 27 (1999) 347–62.
Küng, Hans. Speech given at the University of San Diego, undetermined date.
Küng, Hans, et al. *Christianity and World Religions: Paths of Dialogue With Islam, Hinduism, and Buddhism*. Maryknoll: Orbis, 1993.
Küster, Volker. "Toward an Intercultural Theology: Paradigm Shifts in Missiology, Ecumenics, and Comparative Religion." In *Theology and the Religions: A Dialogue*, edited by Viggo Mortensen, 171–84. Grand Rapids: Eerdmans, 2003.
Langmead, Ross. *The Word Made Flesh: Towards An Incarnational Missiology*. Lanham: University Press of America, 2004.
Lazareth, William, and Peri Rasolondraibe. *Lutheran Identity and Mission: Evangelical and Evangelistic?* Philadelphia: Fortress, 1994.
Legrand, Lucien. *Unity and Plurality: Mission in the Bible*. Maryknoll: Orbis, 1990.
Lescher, William E. "An Intra-Lutheran Perspective on the Interreligious Movement." *Currents in Theology and Mission* 33/3 (June 2006) 208–15.
Lindbeck, George. *The Church in a Postliberal Age*. Grand Rapids: Eerdmans, 2003.

Bibliography

———. "Ecumenical Directions and Confessional Construals." *Dialog* 30 (1991) 118–23.

———. "*Fides ex auditu* and the Salvation of Non-Christians." In *The Gospel and the Ambiguity of the Church*, edited by Vilmos Vatja, 92–123. Philadelphia: Fortress, 1974.

———. "The Gospel's Uniqueness: Election and Untranslatability." *Modern Theology* 13 (1997) 423–50.

———. *The Nature of Doctrine: Religion and Theology in a Postliberal Age*. Philadelphia: Westminster, 1984.

Lohse, Bernard. *Martin Luther's Theology: Its Historical and Systematic Development*. Translated by Roy Harrisville. Minneapolis: Fortress, 1999.

Loughlin, Gerard. "Postmodern Scripture." In *Christian Theologies of Scripture: A Comparative Introduction*, edited by Justin Holcomb, 300–22. New York: NYU Press, 2006.

Loewenich, Walther von. *Luther's Theology of the Cross*. Minneapolis: Augsburg, 1976.

Lubac, Henri de. *The Mystery of the Supernatural*. Translated by R. Sheed. New York: Herder and Herder, 1967.

Lull, Timothy, and William R. Russell, eds. *Martin Luther's Basic Theological Writings*. Minneapolis: Augsburg Fortress, 2005.

Luther, Martin D. *Martin Luthers Werke. Kritische Gesamtausgabe. Schriften*. 68 vols. Weimar: Herman Böhlaus Nachfolger, 1883–1999.

———. *Day By Day We Magnify Thee: Daily Readings for the Church Year Selected from the Writings of Martin Luther*. Translated and edited by Percy Scott and Margarete Steiner. Philadelphia: Fortress, 1982.

———. *The Large Catechism of Martin Luther*. Minneapolis: Augsburg Fortress, 1981.

———. *Luther's Works*. American edition, vols. 1–30. Edited by Jaroslav Pelikan. St. Louis: Concordia, 1955–1967.

———. *Luther's Works*. American edition, vols. 31–55. Edited by Helmut T. Lehmann. Philadelphia: Fortress, 1955–1986.

———. *The Table Talk of Martin Luther*. Charleston, SC: Nabu, 2010.

Lutheran World Federation. *Mission in Context: Transformation, Reconciliation, Empowerment: An LWF Contribution to the Understanding and Practice of Mission*. Geneva: LWF, 2004.

———. *Together in God's Mission: An LWF Contribution on Mission and Evangelism*. Geneva: LWF, 1983.

Lutheran World Federation and the Roman Catholic Church. *Joint Declaration on the Doctrine of Justification*. Grand Rapids: Eerdmans, 2000.

Luzbetak, Louis J. *The Church and Cultures: New Perspectives in Missiological Anthropology*. Maryknoll: Orbis, 1989.

Mannermaa, Tuomo. *Christ Present in Faith: Luther's View of Justification*. Translated by Kirsi Stjerna. Minneapolis: Augsburg Fortress, 2005.

Mansi, J. D. *Sacrorum Conciliorum Nova et Amplissima Collection*. Venice, 1759ff.

Marshall, Bruce. *Trinity and Truth*. Cambridge: Cambridge University Press, 2000.

Martinson, Paul Varo. "Justification—Learning Its Meaning Amidst the Religions." In *The Gospel of Justification in Christ: Where Does the Church Stand Today?*, edited by Wayne C. Stumme, 141–59. Grand Rapids: Eerdmans, 2006.

———, ed. *Mission at the Dawn of the 21st Century: A Vision for the Church*. Minneapolis: Kirk, 1999.

Marty, Martin E. *Martin Luther*. New York: Penguin, 2004.
Mattes, Mark. *The Role of Justification in Contemporary Theology*. Grand Rapids: Eerdmans, 2004.
———. "Review Essay: A Future for Lutheran Theology?" *Lutheran Quarterly* 19/4 (Winter 2005) 439–57.
———. Review of *Justification and Participation in Christ: The Development of the Lutheran Doctrine of Justification from Luther to the Formula of Concord* by Olli-Pekka Vainio. *Lutheran Quarterly* 23/1 (Spring 2009) 114–17.
Mattox, Mickey. "Martin Luther." In *Christian Theologies of Scripture: A Comparative Introduction*, edited by Justin Holcomb, 94–113. New York: NYU Press, 2006.
McGrath, Alister E. *Christian Theology: An Introduction*. 4th edition. Oxford: Blackwell, 2007.
———. *The Genesis of Doctrine: A Study in the Foundation of Doctrinal Criticism*. Grand Rapids: Eerdmans, 1997.
———. *Luther's Theology of the Cross: Martin Luther's Theological Breakthrough*. Oxford: Blackwell, 1985.
McKim, Donald, ed. *The Cambridge Companion to Martin Luther*. Cambridge Companion to Religion. Cambridge: Cambridge University Press, 2003.
Moltmann, Jürgen. *The Crucified God*. New York: Harper & Row, 1974.
Mortensen, Viggo, ed. *The Role of Mission in the Future of Lutheran Theology*. Aarhus: University of Aarhus, 2003.
———, ed. *Theology and the Religions: A Dialogue*. Grand Rapids: Eerdmans, 2003.
Müller, Karl, and Werner Ustorf. *Einleitung in die Missionsgeschichte: Tradition, Situation, und Dynamik des Christentums*. Stuttgart: Kolhammer, 1995.
Neill, Stephen. *Creative Tension*. London: Edinburgh House, 1959.
Netland, Harold, and Craig Ott, eds. *Globalizing Theology: Belief and Practice in an Era of World Christianity*. Grand Rapids: Baker Academic, 2006.
Newbigin, Lesslie. *The Gospel in a Pluralistic Society*. Grand Rapids: Eerdmans, 1989.
———. *The Open Secret*. Rev. ed. Grand Rapids: Eerdmans, 1995.
Nygren, Anders. *Meaning and Method: Prolegomena to a Scientific Philosophy of Religion and a Scientific Theology*. Eugene, OR: Wipf & Stock 2009.
Öberg, Ingemar. *Luther and World Mission: A Historical and Systematic Study with Special Reference to Luther's Bible Exposition*. St. Louis: Concordia, 2007.
Oberman, Heiko. *Luther: Man Between God and the Devil*. New Haven: Yale, 1990.
Oborji, Francis. *Concepts of Mission: the Evolution of Contemporary Missiology*. Maryknoll: Orbis, 2006.
O'Donovan, Leo, ed. *A World of Grace: An Introduction to the Themes and Foundations of Karl Rahner's Theology*. New York: Seabury, 1980.
Oeming, Manfred. *Contemporary Biblical Hermeneutics: An Introduction*. Burlington: Ashgate, 2006.
Oleksa, Michael. "Orthodox Missiological Education for the Twenty-first Century." In *Missiological Education for the Twenty-First Century: The Book, the Circle, and the Sandals*, edited by Edgar J. Elliston et al., 83–90. Maryknoll: Orbis, 1996.
Olsson, Herbert. *Schöpfung, Vernunft und Gesetz in Luthers Theologie*. Uppsala: Acta Universitatis Upsaliensis, 1971.
Panikkar, Raimundo. *The Intra-religious Dialogue*. New York: Paulist, 1978.

Bibliography

Pannenberg, Wolfhart. "Religious Pluralism and Conflicting Truth Claims." In *Christian Uniqueness Reconsidered: The Myth of a Pluralistic Theology of Religions*, edited by Gavin D'Costa, 96–106. Maryknoll: Orbis, 1990.

———. *Systematic Theology*. 3 vols. Grand Rapids: Eerdmans, 1991–1997.

Paulson, Steven P. *Lutheran Theology*. New York: Continuum, 2011.

Phan, Peter. *Being Religious Interreligiously: Asian Perspectives on Interfaith Dialogue*. Maryknoll: Orbis, 2004.

———. *Eternity in Time: A Study of Karl Rahner's Eschatology*. Cranbury: Associated University, 1988.

———. *Grace and the Human*. n.p.: Michael Glazier, 1988.

———. *In Our Own Tongues: Perspectives from Asia on Mission and Inculturation*. Maryknoll: Orbis, 2003.

Pieris, Aloysius. "Interreligious Dialogue and Theology of Religions: An Asian Paradigm." *Horizons* 20 (1993) 106–14.

Pinomaa, Lennart. *Faith Victorious: An Introduction to Luther's Theology*. Philadelphia: Fortress, 1963.

Pontifical Council for Interreligious Dialogue and the Congregation for the Evangelization of Peoples. "Dialogue and Proclamation: Reflections and Orientations on Interreligious Dialogue and the Proclamation of the Gospel of Jesus Christ." In *Redemption and Dialogue: Reading Redemptoris Missio and Dialogue and Proclamation*, edited by William R. Burrows, 93–118. Maryknoll: Orbis, 1993.

Pope John Paul II. *Dominum et Vivificantem*. London: Catholic Truth Society, 1986.

———. *Redemptor Hominis: First Encyclical Letter of Pope John Paul II*. Washington, D.C.: United States Catholic Conference of Bishops, 1980.

———. "*Redemptoris Missio*: An Encyclical Letter on the Permanent Validity of the Church's Missionary Mandate." In *Redemption and Dialogue: Reading Redemptoris Missio and Dialogue and Proclamation*, edited by William R. Burrows, 3–55. Maryknoll: Orbis, 1994.

———. *That They May Be One: Ut Unum Sint*. Washington, D.C.: United States Conference of Catholic Bishops, 1995.

Pope Paul VI. *Evangelii Nuntiandi: On Evangelization in the Modern World*. Edison: Pauline, 1976.

Rae, Murray A. *History and Hermeneutics*. London: T & T Clark, 2005.

Rahner, Karl. "Anonymous and Explicit Faith." In *Theological Investigations Vol. XVI*. Translated by David Morland, 52–59. New York: Seabury, 1979.

———. "Anonymous Christianity and the Missionary Task of the Church." In *Theological Investigations Vol XII*. Translated by David Bourke, 161–78. New York: Seabury, 1974.

———. "Anonymous Christians." In *Theological Investigations Vol VI*. Translated by Karl-H Kruger and Boniface Kruger, 390–98. Baltimore: Helicon, 1969.

———. "The Christian Understanding of Redemption." In *Theological Investigations Vol. XXI*. Translated by Hugh M. Riley, 239–54. New York: Crossroad, 1988.

———. "Christianity and the Non-Christian Religions." In *Theological Investigations Vol. V*. Translated by Karl-H. Kruger, 115–34. Baltimore: Helicon, 1966.

———. "Concerning the Relationship between Nature and Grace." In *Theological Investigations Vol. I*. Translated by Cornelius Ernst, 297–317. Baltimore: Helicon, 1961.

---. "Experiences of a Catholic Theologian." In *The Cambridge Companion to Karl Rahner*, translated by Declan Marion and Gesa Thiessen, edited by Mary Hines and Declan Marmion, 297–310. New York: Cambridge University Press, 2005.

---. *Foundations of Christian Faith: An Introduction to the Idea of Christianity*. Translated William V. Dych. New York: Seabury, 1978.

---. "Guilt and Its Remission: The Borderland between Theology and Psychotherapy." In *Theological Investigations Vol. II*. Translated by Karl-H. Kruger, 265–81. Baltimore: Helicon, 1963.

---. "Guilt, Responsibility, and Punishment within the View of Catholic Theology." In *Theological Investigations Vol. VI*. Translated by Karl-H. Kruger and Boniface Kruger, 197–217. Baltimore: Helicon, 1969.

---. *Hearer of the Word*. Translated by Joseph Donceel. New York: Continuum, 1994.

---. "The Hiddenness of God." In *Theological Investigations Vol. XVI*. Translated by David Morland, 227–43. New York: Seabury, 1979.

---. "History of the World and Salvation History." In *Theological Investigations Vol. V*, 97–114. London: Darton, Longman, and Todd, 1966.

---. "An Investigation of the Incomprehensibility of God in St. Thomas Aquinas." In *Theological Investigations Vol. XVI*. Translated by David Morland, 244–54. New York: Seabury, 1979.

---. "Jesus Christ in the Non-Christian Religions." In *Theological Investigations Vol. XVII*. Translated by Margaret Kohl, 39–50. New York: Crossroad, 1981.

---. "Justified and Sinner at the Same Time." In *Theological Investigations Vol. VI*. Translated by Karl-H. Kruger and Boniface Kruger, 218–30. Baltimore: Helicon, 1969.

---. "Nature and Grace." In *Theological Investigations Vol. IV*. Translated by Kevin Smyth, 165–88. Baltimore: Helicon, 1966.

---. "The New Image of the Church." In *Theological Investigations Vol. V*. Translated by David Bourke, 3–29. New York: Seabury, 1977.

---. "Observations on the Problem of the 'Anonymous Christian.'" In *Theological Investigations Vol. XIV*. Translated by David Bourke, 280–94. New York: Seabury, 1976.

---. "On the Importance of the Non-Christian Religions for Salvation." In *Theological Investigations Vol. XVIII*. Translated by Edward Quinn, 288–95. New York: Crossroad, 1983.

---. "The One Christ and the Universality of Salvation." In *Theological Investigations Vol. XVI*. Translated by David Morland, 199–224. New York: Seabury, 1979.

---. "The Position of Christology in the Church Between Exegesis and Dogmatics." In *Theological Investigations Vol. XI*. Translated by David Bourke, 185–214. New York: Seabury, 1974.

---. "Reconciliation and Vicarious Representation." In *Theological Investigations Vol. XXI*. Translated by Hugh M. Riley, 255–69. New York: Crossroad, 1988.

---. "Reflections on the Experience of Grace." In *Theological Investigations Vol. III*. Translated by Karl-H. Kruger and Boniface Kruger, 86–90. London: Darton, Longman, Todd, 1967.

---. "The Sin of Adam." In *Theological Investigations Vol. XI*. Translated by David Bourke, 247–62. New York: Seabury, 1974.

Bibliography

———. "The Theological Concept of *Concupiscentia*." In *Theological Investigations Vol. I*. Translated by Cornelius Ernst, 347–82. Baltimore: Helicon, 1961.

———. "Theology and Anthropology." In *Theological Investigations Vol. IX*. Translated by Graham Harrison, 28–45. New York: Herder and Herder, 1972.

———. "Theology of Freedom." In *Theological Investigations Vol. VI*. Translated by Karl-H. Kruger and Boniface Kruger, 178–96. Baltimore: Helicon, 1969.

Ramachandra, Vinoth. *Faiths in Conflict? Christian Integrity in a Multicultural World*. Downers Grove: InterVarsity, 1999.

———. *The Recovery of Mission: Beyond the Pluralist Paradigm*. Grand Rapids: Eerdmans, 1996.

Reno, R. R. *The Ordinary Transformed*. Grand Rapids: Eerdmans, 1995.

Rescher, Nicolas. *Pluralism: Against the Demand for Consensus*. Oxford: Clarendon, 1993.

Richebacher, Wilhelm. "*Missio Dei*: The Basis of Mission Theology or a Wrong Path?" *International Review of Mission* 42/367 (2003) 588–605.

Röper, Anita. *The Anonymous Christian*. Translated by Joseph Donceel. New York: Sheed and Ward, 1966.

Ruokanen, Miikka. *The Catholic Doctrine of Non-Christian Religions According to the Second Vatican Council*. Leiden: Brill, 1992.

Saarinen, Risto. "The Word of God in Luther's Theology." *Lutheran Quarterly* 4 (1990) 31–44.

Sanneh, Lamin. *Whose Religion is Christianity? The Gospel Beyond the West*. Grand Rapids: Eerdmans, 2003.

Sauter, Gerhard. *The Question of Meaning: a Theological and Philosophical Orientation*. Grand Rapids: Eerdmans, 1996.

Scherer, James. *Gospel, Church, and Kingdom: Comparative Studies in World Mission Theology*. Minneapolis: Augsburg Fortress, 1987.

Schmidlin, Josef. *Katholische Missionsgeschichte*. Kaldenkirchen: Steyl, 1924.

Schreiner, Thomas R. *Paul: Apostle of God's Glory in Christ*. Downers Grove: Intervarsity, 2001.

Schreiter, Robert. "The Anonymous Christian and Christology." *Missiology: An International Review* 6/1 (January 1978) 29–52.

———. *The New Catholicity: Theology between the Global and the Local*. Maryknoll: Orbis, 1997.

Schroeder, Edward. "Encountering the Hidden God." In *Areopagus—A Living Encounter with Today's Religious World*, 2–5. Hong Kong: Tao Fong Shan Christian Centre, 1993.

———. "Is There a Lutheran Hermeneutic?" In *The Promising Tradition: A Reader in Law-Gospel Reconstructionist Theology*, 111–19. St. Louis: Concordia Seminary in Exile, 1974.

———. "The Kingdom of God in Today's Mission Theology—A Controversy. Part One." N.p. Online: http://www.crossings.org/thursday/Thuro70705.htm.

———. "Luther's Commentary on the Third Article as a Clue to His Theology of Other Religions." *Missio Apostolica: Journal of the Lutheran Society for Missiology* 7/1 (May 1999) 4–10.

———. "Luther's Missiology: A Conference Paper." N.p. Online: http://www.crossings.org/thursday/Thuro62608.htm.

———. "Pluralism's Question to Christian Missions: Why Jesus at All?" *Currents in Theology and Mission* 26/3 (June 1999) 164–70.

———. "A Second Look at the Gospel of Mark—Midway in the Year of Mark." *Currents in Theology and Mission* 33/4 (August 2006) 291–9.

———. "Using Luther's Concept of *Deus absconditus* for Christian Mission to Muslims." Address given at the Luther Research Congress, Copenhagen, Denmark, August 4–9, 2002.

Schulz, Klaus Detlev. *Mission from the Cross: the Lutheran Theology of Mission*. St. Louis: Concordia, 2009.

Schumacher, William. *Who Do I Say That You Are? Anthropology and the Theology of Theosis in the Finnish School of Tuomo Mannermaa*. Eugene, OR: Wipf and Stock, 2010.

Schüssler Fiorenza, Francis. "Method in Theology." In *The Cambridge Companion to Karl Rahner*, edited by Mary Hines et al., 65–82. New York: Cambridge, 2005.

———. "Systematic Theology: Task and Methods." In *Systematic Theology: Roman Catholic Perspectives, Volume I*, edited by John Galvin and Francis Schüssler Fiorenza, 3–87. Minneapolis: Fortress, 1991.

Searle, John R. *Speech Acts: An Essay in the Philosophy of Language*. Cambridge: Cambridge, 1970.

Senior, Donald, and Carol Stuhlmueller. *The Biblical Foundations for Mission*. Maryknoll: Orbis, 1983.

Stolle, Volker. *The Church Comes From All Nations: Luther Texts in Mission*. St. Louis: Concordia, 2003.

Strieter, Thomas W. *Contemporary Two-Kingdoms and Governances Thinking for Today's World*. Ann Arbor: University Microfilms International, 1986.

Sumner, George R. *The First and the Last: The Claim of Jesus Christ and the Claims of Other Religious Traditions*. Grand Rapids: Eerdmans, 2004.

Swidler, Leonard, et. al, eds. *Death or Dialogue? From the Age of Monologue to the Age of Dialogue*. Philadelphia: Trinity, 1990.

Tennet, Timothy. *Invitation to World Missions: A Trinitarian Missiology for the Twenty-First Century*. Grand Rapids: Kregel Academic, 2010.

Tennett, Timothy, et al., eds. *Encountering Theology of Mission: Biblical Foundations, Historical Developments, and Contemporary Issues*. Grand Rapids: Baker Academic, 2010.

Thiemann, Ronald. *Revelation and Theology: The Gospel as Narrated Promise*. Notre Dame: University of Notre Dame Press, 1985.

Thomsen, Mark. *Christ Crucified: A 21st Century Missiology of the Cross*. Minneapolis: Lutheran University Press, 2004.

Tracy, David. *The Analogical Imagination: Christian Theology and the Culture of Pluralism*. New York: Crossroads, 1998.

———. *Blessed Rage for Order: The New Pluralism in Theology*. Chicago: University of Chicago Press, 1996.

Troelstch, Ernst. *Die Absolutheit des Christentums und die Religionsgeschichte*. Tübingen: Mohr, 1912.

Truemper, David. "The Lutheran Confessional Writings and the Future of Lutheran Theology." In *The Gift of Grace: The Future of Lutheran Theology*, edited by Niels H. Gregersen et al., 131–46. Minneapolis: Augsburg Fortress, 2005.

Bibliography

U. S. Roman Catholic Church. *Catechism of the Catholic Church: Second Edition.* New York: Doubleday, 2003.

Vainio, Olli-Pekka, ed. *Engaging Luther: A (New) Theological Assessment.* Eugene, OR: Cascade, 2010.

———. *Justification and Participation in Christ: The Development of the Lutheran Doctrine of Justification from Luther to the Formula of Concord (1580).* Leiden: Brill, 2008.

Vandervelde, George. *Original Sin: Two Major Trends in Contemporary Roman Catholic Reinterpretation.* Washington: University Press of America, 1981.

Van Engen, Charles, et al., eds. *The Good News of the Kingdom: Mission Theology for the Third Millenium.* Maryknoll: Orbis, 1993.

Vatican Council II. "*Gaudium et Spes*: Pastoral Constitution on the Church in the Modern World." In *Vatican Council II, Volume I: The Conciliar and Post-Conciliar Documents*, edited by Austin Flannery, 903–1001. Northport: Costello, 1998.

Vicedom, George F. *The Mission of God: An Introduction to a Theology of Mission.* St. Louis: Concordia, 1965.

Voelz, James. *What Does This Mean? Principles of Interpretation in the Post-Modern World.* St. Louis: Concordia, 1995.

Walther, C. F. W. *Law and Gospel.* St. Louis: Concordia, 1981.

Wannenwetsch, Bernd. "Luther's Moral Theology." In *The Cambridge Companion to Martin Luther*, edited by Donald K. McKim, 120–35. Cambridge: Cambridge University Press, 2003.

Warneck, Gustav. *Abriss einer Geschichte der protestantischen Missionen: Von der Reformation bis auf die Gegenwart.* 9th ed. Berlin: M. Warneck, 1910.

———. *Evangelische Missionslehre,* 5 vols. Gotha: Perthes, 1892–1903.

Westerholm, Stephen. *Perspectives Old and New on Paul: The "Lutheran" Paul and His Critics.* Grand Rapids: Eerdmans, 2004.

Wingren, Gustaf. *Theology in Conflict.* Philadelphia: Muhlenberg, 1958.

Wittgenstein, Ludwig. *Philosophical Investigations I.* Oxford: Blackwell, 1958.

Wright, Christopher J. H. *The Mission of God: Unlocking the Bible's Grand Narrative.* Downers Grove: InterVarsity, 2006.

Index

Abraham, 5, 21, 43, 161, 201–4, 208
Ad Gentes, 145, 172
anonymous Christian, 118, 133–134, 142–46, 166, 171, 248
anonymous Christianity, 133, 142–45, 185
anthropology, 21, 44, 60, 75, 78, 93, 97, 111, 115–16, 121–23, 132–34, 136, 143, 149, 167–68, 182, 186, 188, 204–5, 217, 246–48
    Aristotelian, 115–16
    foundational, 122–23, 133–34
    Lutheran, 44
    patristic, 116
    transcendental, 44, 90, 93, 97, 121–22, 132, 136, 149, 167–68, 182, 186, 188, 193, 204–5, 247
Ap. II. *See* Apology II, 85–86
Ap. IV. *See* Apology IV, 47
Apology IV. *See* Ap. IV, 43, 46–49, 57, 59, 81
Apology to the Augsburg Confession, Article II: Original Sin, 85
Aquinas, Thomas, 12, 66, 79, 87, 114–17, 180, 245
Arand, Charles, 32–33
Article V. *See* FCSD Article V, "Concerning Law and Gospel," 48, 207

atonement, 88–89, 94, 98–99, 102–4, 128–29, 134, 137–39, 142, 248, 252
    confessional Lutheran view of, 98–111, 138–42
Augsburg Confession, 23–24, 38, 40, 85
Augustine, 39, 66, 93, 112–14, 116

Balthasar, Hans Urs von, 11, 133–34, 144
Barth, Karl, 3–4, 12, 51, 69–74, 77, 92, 97, 139, 144
Bayer, Oswald, 6, 12, 27–28, 31, 33–36, 39–41, 44, 47, 50, 53, 59–61, 64, 76–77, 84–85, 89, 209, 211–12, 218–19, 235, 249
Benjamin, Walter, 20
Bertram, Robert, 4, 6, 10, 56–58, 91, 94–97, 105, 108–9, 111, 186, 188, 204, 214, 234, 245, 253
Bliese, Richard, 2, 7, 23, 253
Book of Concord, 1, 24, 38, 43, 45–47, 49, 54, 57–59, 61, 83, 85–88, 141, 207, 209–11, 219, 236, 238
Bosch, David, 1–2, 29
Braaten, Carl, 7, 17, 23, 51, 90–92, 94, 111, 194
Burrows, William, 5, 228

Christology, 60, 118, 121, 127, 131, 134–35, 140, 152–54, 156,

269

Index

Christology (*cont.*)
  158–59, 161, 165–66, 168, 174–76, 179, 181, 184, 186, 188, 190, 192, 204–6, 224, 241, 247–52
  constitutive, 158–59, 161, 165–66, 168, 174–76, 181, 184, 205, 241, 247, 249–50, 252
  Spirit, 152, 181, 184, 186, 206, 224, 248
  transcendental, 131, 134–35, 140, 166, 179, 188, 204–5
  Trinitarian, 152–54, 158, 175, 192
Cobb, John, 233
concupiscence, 87, 126, 141
Cornille, Catherine, 53, 229–33, 246
covenant theology, 76, 164–65, 168, 179, 197, 199, 203, 210
cultural-linguistic model, 16, 19, 226, 229, 252

D'Costa, Gavin, 190, 230–31
de Lubac, Henri, 11, 115–19
deus absconditus. See hiddenness of God, 21, 63, 150, 214, 216, 218, 235–38, 244
deus revelatus, 218, 236, 238
dialectical theology, 93
Dialogue and Proclamation, 182, 229, 240, 242–44, 250–51
Dinoia, Joseph, 252
Dominum et Vivificantem, 224
Duffy, Stephen, 77, 79, 112–119, 124, 246
Dupuis, Jacques, 6, 11, 26, 68, 73, 82, 90, 146, 151–99, 201–8, 210–14, 221, 224, 227, 229, 231–32, 235, 237, 240–52
Ebeling, Gerhard, 16–17, 72–73, 215

economy of salvation, 6, 9, 20–21, 23, 50, 73–74, 81, 152–53, 158, 161, 167, 172, 174–75, 177, 181–83, 185, 191–92, 198, 207–8, 216, 247
Elert, Werner, 1–2, 4, 6, 46, 52–55, 72, 89, 92–93, 95–96, 106–7, 246
Evangelii Nuntiandi, 172, 250

faith, 8, 11, 17, 20, 22, 26–27, 31–33, 35–36, 38–47, 51–52, 55–63, 65, 68–69, 72–73, 76, 80–84, 92, 95, 98–99, 105–6, 110–11, 120–21, 123, 125–27, 129, 131, 134, 144–49, 151, 153–54, 156–57, 163, 175, 179, 183, 187, 202, 205–6, 209–10, 212, 215, 218, 222, 227–28, 231, 234–35, 239–40, 242, 246–49
  as trust, 32, 44, 46, 56, 59, 76, 110, 134, 187
  implicit, 146
  saving, 106, 145, 157
FCSD Article I, "Concerning Original Sin," 85, 87
FCSD Article II, "Concerning the Free Will or Human Powers," 61
FCSD Article V, "Concerning Law and Gospel," 207
FCSD Article VI, "Concerning the Third Use of the Law," 53
Federation of Asian Bishops' Conference, 170
fides ex auditu, 145–46
Finnish school of Luther studies, 37, 64, 66–67
Freytag, Walter, 110

Gaudium et Spes, 157, 172, 204, 250

Gerrish, Brian, 216, 218, 220–23, 237
Gilkey, Langdon, 10, 232
gospel, 1–6, 8–12, 14–15, 18–21, 23–53, 55–82, 88–89, 91–96, 99–102, 104, 106–11, 113, 134, 139, 144–45, 147–49, 166, 170–71, 177–84, 186–95, 197, 200–202, 204–22, 224, 227, 229–30, 234–36, 241, 243–47, 249–52
  as promise, 1, 3, 5–6, 8–9, 18, 20, 23–24, 26–29, 31–49, 51, 53, 55–63, 65–67, 69, 71, 73, 75–77, 80–81, 113, 178, 180, 192–93, 195, 214, 217, 234, 245, 250, 252
  values, 170, 190, 193
grace, 3–4, 6, 9–12, 18, 21, 24–27, 29, 31, 38, 42–43, 45–46, 51–53, 59–60, 65–67, 69–74, 77–83, 85–97, 99–103, 105, 107, 109–49, 151, 153, 155, 157, 159–63, 165–75, 177–84, 186–93, 195–202, 204–7, 209–11, 213, 216–17, 224, 235–37, 239, 245–46, 248–52
  and truth, 51, 174, 178–79, 181, 189–90, 197, 202, 205, 207, 213, 224, 235, 249
  as anonymous, 146
  as favor of God, 81
  as God's self-communication, 79, 94, 113, 120, 124–25, 130, 133, 135–36, 140–41, 145, 148, 162, 186, 188–89, 191
  as promise of mercy, 3, 6, 9, 41, 45, 55, 59, 64, 67, 76–77, 79, 81–83, 85, 87, 89, 91, 93–95, 98–100, 113, 137, 140, 145, 148–49, 178, 180, 182, 189, 193, 195, 200–204, 206, 213, 239
  Augustine on, 93, 112–14
  confessional Lutheran theology of, 79–111
  created, 116–17, 124, 133
  Dupuis on, 196–206
  historical overview of the doctrine in the western tradition, 112–19
  medieval synthesis of, 114–16
  neoscholastic corruption of, 112, 117–18
  polyvalence of the term, 80, 113–15, 252
  Rahner on, 120–132
  Roman Catholic view of grace as fulfilling and perfecting human nature, 112–32, 147–49
  uncreated, 116, 124, 127
Griffiths, Paul, 232
Gritsch, Eric, 18, 36–37, 42, 50, 62, 75

Harnack, Adolph von, 89
Heim, Mark, 231
hermeneutical, 7–9, 12–17, 19, 21–22, 38, 42, 49–50, 53, 57–58, 76, 154, 178, 186, 188, 232
Hick, John, 108, 155, 157, 229, 232
hiddenness of God. *See deus absconditus*, 3, 6, 9, 18, 21, 26–28, 77, 150, 177–78, 180–81, 210, 216–20, 223, 228, 231, 235, 237–38, 245, 247, 252
  as a resource for interreligious dialogue, 231, 234–40
Highfield, Ron, 125–26, 136, 141
Hill-Fletcher, Jeannine, 142, 226, 230–31
Hillers, Delbert, 198–200, 202–3

Index

Hinlicky, Paul, 74, 192
Hinze, Bradford, 6
Horton, Michael, 18, 43, 199–200

inclusive exclusivity, 12, 108–9, 111, 194, 224, 248, 251
inclusive pluralism, 82, 151–52, 157, 167, 175, 188, 213, 219, 224, 248, 250–51
interreligious dialogue, 3, 6, 10, 19, 24, 26–28, 53, 64, 146–47, 150, 155–56, 169, 180, 210, 214, 216–20, 226–35, 237, 239–41, 243, 245–47, 249, 251–53
Islam, 7, 25–26, 155, 216
   God as gracious and merciful in, 25–26
   Martin Luther and, 7

Jenson, Robert, 18, 36–37, 42, 50, 62, 67, 75–76, 112, 114, 116–18, 147, 218, 249
Jesus Christ, 5–7, 11–18, 21–22, 25–28, 32, 35–38, 40–43, 45–49, 51, 53, 56–69, 71, 73, 75–78, 80–83, 86–92, 94–96, 98, 100–102, 105–9, 111, 113, 120–21, 123–24, 127–31, 134–35, 137–42, 144–46, 148–49, 151–68, 171–76, 178–82, 184–85, 187–90, 192, 195–217, 219–20, 223–24, 227, 235–43, 247–52
   as absolute savior, 120, 123, 158, 166
   confessional Lutheran theology on the sacrifice of, 102–4
   cruciform mediation of, 187, 197, 205–6, 247–48, 252
   incarnational, ontological mediation of, 167, 179, 187–88, 204, 206, 247–48

   inclusive exclusivity of, 12, 108–9, 111, 194, 224, 248, 251
   mercy in, 6, 28, 47, 148–49, 197, 201, 213, 237–38, 252
justification, 55, 62–68
   as indwelling presence of Christ, 64–65
   effective, 64–68
   forensic, 55, 64–68

Kärkkäinen, Veli-Matti, 154–55, 174–75, 184–85, 206–8
Knitter, Paul, 12–13, 24–25, 79, 108, 156–57, 169, 175, 229, 232, 242, 245–46
Kolb, Robert, 6, 12, 32–33, 43, 45–47, 49, 54, 57–59, 61, 67, 83, 85–88, 141, 207, 209–11, 213, 219, 236, 238
Küng, Hans, 226
Küster, Volker, 228

law, confessional Lutheran view of, 52–56
law/gospel distinction, 3, 6, 9, 12, 14–15, 24, 26–28, 32, 36–38, 45–46, 48–52, 56–62, 64–65, 69, 72, 74, 76–77, 91, 94–96, 145, 147, 166, 178–80, 187, 189–92, 195, 218, 224, 234–36, 245, 249, 252
   critical appraisal of, 62–75
   in Luther and the Lutheran Confessions, 59–62
   missiological implications of, 18, 59, 89, 235–40, 249, 252
   revelation of, 111, 190–95
   serving the gospel as promise, 58–59, 178, 186, 235
law/promise paradigm, 95
Lesher, William, 234
Lindbeck, George, 13, 16, 19, 23–24, 133, 145–46, 229–31

Logos spermatikos, 158, 181
Loughlin, Gerard, 21–22
Lumen Gentium, 172–73, 242
Luther, Martin, 1–2, 7–12, 14–15, 18–24, 28, 30–42, 44–48, 50, 54, 56, 59–68, 74–77, 81–88, 98, 135, 137–39, 141–43, 177–78, 192, 204, 209–12, 214–15, 217–24, 234–38, 249
Lutheran confessional writings. *See* Lutheran Confessions, 1, 23–24, 28, 65, 80
Lutheran Confessions. *See* Lutheran confessional writings, 9–10, 23–24, 30–31, 38–40, 42, 44–47, 50, 59, 61, 66, 82–83, 85–86, 88, 212, 224, 234, 251
Lutheran missiology, 1–2, 10, 23–24, 28, 31, 36, 64, 77, 80, 90, 175, 177, 182, 189, 204, 216–17, 221, 224–26, 234–35, 239, 247, 252–53
Lutheran World Federation, 92

Mannermaa, Tuomo, 36–37, 64–66
Martinson, Paul V., 25
Mattes, Mark, 62–63, 65–68
McGrath, Alister, 14, 18–20, 22, 113, 115, 215
Melanchthon, Philip, 12, 48, 56–59, 81, 86–87, 141, 217, 219
missio Dei, 2–4, 6, 23, 27, 29, 151, 177–78, 181–83, 214, 221, 235, 245, 247
missio shaped by *promissio*, 4, 177–179, 226, 234

nature/grace framework, 3–4, 11, 26–27, 66, 79–82, 88, 93–95, 111, 118, 124, 127, 129, 131, 147–49, 151, 166, 184, 187, 193, 235, 245, 251

Neill, Stephen, 29

Oeming, Manfred, 16–17
Oleksa, Michael, 11, 27, 248

Pannenberg, Wolfhart, 36, 51, 62–64, 67, 232
Pauline theology, 81, 202
pneumatology, 152–54, 159, 166, 174–79, 181, 184–86, 192–93, 205–6, 208–10, 224, 231, 241, 248–249, 251
  Dupuis on, 206–8
  Lutheran, 193, 208–9, 249
  robust, 152, 166, 174–76, 179, 181, 184, 205–6, 224, 231, 241, 248–49, 251
Pontifical Council for Interreligious Dialogue, 227–29, 243
Pope John Paul II, 170, 224, 241
proclamation and dialogue, 5, 214, 225, 227–28, 233–34, 240, 244
promise of God, 4–5, 29–31, 33, 35, 37, 39–43, 45–47, 49, 51, 53, 55, 57, 59, 61, 63, 65, 67, 69, 71, 73, 75–77, 81, 84, 100, 106, 187, 192, 203, 210, 213, 234, 240, 245, 252
promissio Dei, 4, 30–31, 40–42, 46, 75, 137, 177, 193, 214
promissio is the secret of *missio*, 10, 234, 245, 253

Rahner, Karl, 11, 13, 23, 44, 73, 77, 82, 88–90, 93–94, 96–97, 111–12, 114, 118–49, 151, 162, 166–68, 171, 179–80, 182–85, 187–88, 190, 194, 196, 199, 201, 221, 237, 245–46, 248, 251
reconciliation, 21, 29, 73, 80–81, 88–92, 98–102, 104–6, 108, 111, 127–31, 134, 136–37,

Index

reconciliation (*cont.*)
    139–40, 147, 149, 177, 181, 187, 189, 203, 205–6, 208, 210, 214, 248, 252
  confessional Lutheran theology on, 99–101, 104–11
  Rahner's theology of, 127–31, 134, 137–42
redemption, 21, 127–31, 138, 147, 170, 188, 199, 205, 227–29
  confessional Lutheran theology on, 99–101, 104–11
  Rahner's theology of, 127–31, 134, 137–42
Redemptoris Missio, 170, 172–73, 229
reign of God, 6, 152–53, 156, 168–74, 176–80, 182, 184–85, 188, 191, 210, 241, 243, 248, 250
  and the Church, 168–74, 210–14
  Dupuis on, 168–74
  Lutheran theology on, 210–14
Reno, R. R., 112, 132, 148, 252
revelation, 5, 12–13, 21, 23, 42–44, 51–52, 55, 70–71, 73, 77, 81–82, 88–96, 99, 105–6, 108, 116, 120–23, 127, 132–33, 139, 144, 146, 148, 151, 155, 158–62, 164–67, 174–75, 180–87, 190, 193–99, 203–5, 208, 212–13, 215–17, 219–20, 223–24, 236, 238, 246, 248, 250, 252
  as categorical and transcendental, 120–23, 168, 182, 188
  inflation of the concept of, 90–93
  of law and gospel, 111, 190–95
  twofold concept of, 52, 91, 94
Ritschl, Albrecht, 89, 95

salvation history, 6, 10–11, 17, 20–21, 50, 62–63, 89, 93–94, 120, 124, 133, 152, 154, 156–65, 171, 181–83, 191, 193, 198–99, 201, 203–4, 208
saving values, 170, 174, 190, 207
Schreiter, Robert, 118
Schroeder, Edward, 4, 6–7, 46–48, 51, 57, 59, 79, 81, 89, 91, 95, 211, 217, 219, 235, 238–39
Schulz, Klaus Detlev, 182, 207–8
Schüssler Fiorenza, Francis, 8–9, 13–14, 19, 121, 133
sin, 3–4, 10, 13, 21, 25–27, 29, 33, 50, 52, 55–56, 58, 66, 69, 71, 73–74, 76–77, 80–94, 96–98, 101, 103–5, 109, 111, 113–14, 116, 118, 123–28, 130–31, 133–42, 145, 147–49, 177–82, 184, 187–90, 192–94, 196–97, 201, 204–5, 207, 209–11, 216–17, 223, 236–37, 246–52
  Dupuis on, 190
  Luther and the Lutheran Confessions on, 83–89
  Rahner on, 134–38
Smalcald Articles, 85, 88
St. Paul, 5, 7, 12, 24–25, 43, 46, 51, 62–63, 68–69, 72, 74, 79, 83, 96–97, 99–101, 104–5, 108, 110, 135, 144–45, 156, 169–70, 175, 192, 195, 202–4, 224, 229, 232, 241, 245, 250
supernatural existential, 124–27, 133–36, 142, 149, 182, 199, 201, 247

theological method, 9, 111, 133, 152–53, 155, 177, 184
  confessional Lutheran, 9–28
  cultural-linguistic, 13, 16, 19, 21, 226, 229, 252

theological method (*cont.*)
  deductive, 24–26, 155, 224
  inductive, 24–26, 155, 224, 229, 231
  of Jacques Dupuis, 151–58
  of Karl Rahner, 120–27, 134–38
theology of the cross, 3, 6, 9, 18, 21, 27–28, 31, 88, 94, 127, 140–41, 146, 177, 180, 212, 214–17, 231, 234
theory of speech acts, 33–34
theosis, 37, 76, 141
Thiemann, Ronald, 42–44
Tracy, David, 9, 13–14, 79
two realms principle, 180, 211, 214, 236, 245

Vainio, Olli-Pekka, 64
Voelz, James, 16–17

Warneck, Gustav, 1–2
Westerholm, Stephen, 69
Wingren, Gustaf, 72, 89, 92, 194

Word of God, 9, 15, 19, 30–33, 35, 45–46, 50, 65, 67, 69–70, 106, 143, 151–52, 158–61, 164, 174, 181, 187, 190, 192, 198, 209, 211–12, 214–16, 223–25, 251
  as creative, 32–33, 55, 67, 76, 212
  as performative, 15, 32–35, 63, 67, 76, 139, 143, 187, 189–90, 208, 212–13, 216, 224, 247
wrath, 4–5, 10, 12, 21, 25, 52, 56, 58, 63, 65, 73–74, 76, 88–94, 96–99, 105–6, 110, 113, 134–35, 137–38, 140, 146, 149, 177–79, 182–83, 195, 210, 214, 217, 221, 246, 252
  and mercy, 73, 93, 96–97, 105–6, 149, 246, 252
  and promise, 5, 21, 76, 93, 182, 195, 217
  of God, 56, 74, 88–89, 96, 99, 134, 179, 221
Wright, N. T., 68, 100

www.ingramcontent.com/pod-product-compliance
Lightning Source LLC
Chambersburg PA
CBHW070237230426
43664CB00014B/2329